T0387117

COMPARATIVE REGIONALISM

This book comprises key essays on comparative regionalism and, more broadly, on regional conflict and cooperation by Professor Etel Solingen.

The study of regionalism, a subject pioneered by Solingen in the 1990s, is now an established field of inquiry, with a large community of scholars and practitioners around the world. This book provides a window into an evolving conceptual framework for comparing regional arrangements, with a special emphasis on non-European regions. Framed by a comprehensive, previously unpublished introduction, the chapters provide a broad spectrum of analysis on domestic political economy, democracy, regional institutions, and global forces as they shape different regional outcomes and trajectories in economics and security. Themes as different as the regional effects of democratization in the Middle East and East Asia, the rise of China, Euro-Mediterranean relations, and regional nuclear trajectories are traced back to a common conceptual core. The nature of domestic ruling coalitions serves as the pivotal analytical anchor explaining the effects of globalization and economic reform on different regional arrangements.

This collection provides a focal point that brings this work together in a new light and will be of much interest to students of regionalism, international relations theory, international and comparative political economy, international history and grand strategy.

Etel Solingen is Thomas T. and Elizabeth C. Tierney Chair in Peace and Conflict Studies at the University of California Irvine, USA, and former Chancellor's Professor. She served as president of the International Studies Association.

'Etel Solingen is one of the leading scholars in the world who helped recreate the field of comparative regional analysis. Put conveniently between two covers, the chapters in this book summarize her trenchant and highly original views. A standard reference work for all serious scholars for years to come.'

Peter J. Katzenstein, Cornell University, USA

'Etel Solingen's work has provided unique contributions to our understanding of regionalism. Her detailed knowledge of three major regions – East Asia, Latin America, and the Middle East – is the underpinning for insights into the forces shaping regional orders around the world. This superb volume will be required reading for all who are interested in the relationship between globalization, regionalism and domestic political coalitions'.

John Ravenhill, Balsillie School of International Affairs, Canada

'Etel Solingen is one the most distinguished and thoughtful scholars of regionalism. Comparative Regionalism: Economics and Security includes some of her most important and influential work on this topic. Skillfully blending novel theoretical insights with a broad empirical sweep, Solingen's study will be of interest to scholars of comparative politics and international relations alike.'

Edward Mansfield, University of Pennsylvania, USA

COMPARATIVE REGIONALISM

Economics and security

Etel Solingen

LONDON AND NEW YORK

First published 2015
by Routledge
2 Park Square, Milton Park, Abingdon, Oxon OX14 4RN

and by Routledge
711 Third Avenue, New York, NY 10017

Routledge is an imprint of the Taylor & Francis Group, an informa business

© 2015 Etel Solingen

The right of Etel Solingen to be identified as author of this work has been asserted by him/her in accordance with sections 77 and 78 of the Copyright, Designs and Patents Act 1988.

All rights reserved. No part of this book may be reprinted or reproduced or utilised in any form or by any electronic, mechanical, or other means, now known or hereafter invented, including photocopying and recording, or in any information storage or retrieval system, without permission in writing from the publishers.

Trademark notice: Product or corporate names may be trademarks or registered trademarks, and are used only for identification and explanation without intent to infringe.

British Library Cataloguing-in-Publication Data
A catalogue record for this book is available from the British Library

Library of Congress Cataloging-in-Publication Data
Solingen, Etel, 1952-
Comparative regionalism : economics and security / Etel Solingen.
pages cm
Includes bibliographical references and index.
1. Regionalism. 2. Regional economics. 3. Security, International.
4. International relations. I. Title.
JZ5330.S65 2014
337--dc23
2014007453

ISBN: 978-0-415-62278-3 (hbk)
ISBN: 978-0-415-62279-0 (pbk)
ISBN: 978-1-315-75865-7 (ebk)

Typeset in Stone Sans and Bembo
by Fish Books

For Fanny

CONTENTS

List of illustrations ix
Acknowledgments x
Preface xii

1 Introduction and overview 1

PART I
Globalization, economic reform, and regional relations 33

2 Internationalization and domestic coalitions 35

3 Coalitions, strategic interaction, and regional outcomes 66

4 Mapping internationalization: Domestic and regional impacts 91

PART II
Regional effects of democratic institutions 117

5 Pax Asiatica versus Bella Levantina: The foundations of war and peace in East Asia and the Middle East 119

6 Democratization in the Middle East: Quandaries of the peace process (1996) 152

7 Economic and political liberalization in China: Implications for
   US–China relations   162

PART III
Regional institutions: Sources, design and effects   **171**

8 The genesis, design and effects of regional institutions:
  Lessons from East Asia and the Middle East   173

9 The triple logic of the European–Mediterranean partnership:
  Hindsight and foresight   205

PART IV
Regional security trajectories   **213**

10 Nuclear logics: Contrasting paths in East Asia and the Middle East   215

Appendices   262
References   272
Index   288

ILLUSTRATIONS

Figures

1.1	Domestic-international linkages	4
2.1	The global political economy, coalitional effects, and grand strategy	37
3.1	Coalitional combinations and regional orders	68
4.1	Positions regarding international economic and security regimes	93
4.2	Causal logic	101
5.1	Causal sequence	125
5.2	Permissive and catalytic conditions	135
5.3	Domestic institutions and regional effects	139
7.1	Regime type and domestic coalitions	166
10.1	Models of political survival and nuclear outcomes: Four scenarios	247

Table

2.1	Selected characteristics of competing grand strategies	53
5.1	Differences in the incidence of militarized conflict: East Asia and the Middle East (1965–2006)	121
5.2	East Asia and the Middle East compared	127
8.1	Approaches to the study of institutions: Basic assumptions and hypotheses	175

Appendices

I	Internationalizing coalitions	263
II	Inward-looking coalitions	264
III	Hybrid coalitions	265
IV	Coalitions by country	266
V	Test of significance	269

ACKNOWLEDGMENTS

The author and publishers would like to thank the following for granting permission to reprint segments or adapted versions of the originals:

Chapter 1: Figure 1 originally appeared in Etel Solingen, "The global context of comparative politics," in *Comparative Politics: Rationality, Culture, and Structure*, 2nd Edition, edited by Mark Irving Lichbach and Alan S. Zuckerman, Copyright © 2009 Cambridge University Press. Reprinted with permission.

Chapters 2 and 3: Adapted from Etel Solingen, *Regional Orders at Century's Dawn: Global and Domestic Influences on Grand Strategy*. Princeton University Press, 1998: 18–89.

Chapter 4: Adapted from Etel Solingen, "Mapping Internationalization: Domestic and Regional impacts." *International Studies Quarterly*, 45, 4 (2001): 517–556.

Chapter 5: Adapted from Etel Solingen "Pax Asiatica versus Bella Levantina: The Foundations of War and Peace in East Asia and the Middle East." *American Political Science Review*, 101, No. 4 (November 2007): 757–780.

Chapter 6: Adapted from Etel Solingen, "Democratization in the Middle East: Quandaries of the Peace Process." This article first appeared in the *Journal of Democracy*, Vol. 7, No.3 (July 1996): 139–153. Copyright © 1996 National Endowment for Democracy and the Johns Hopkins University Press. Reprinted with permission by The Johns Hopkins University Press

Chapter 7: Adapted from Etel Solingen, "Economic and Political Liberalization in China: Implications for US-China Relations." In Richard Rosecrance and Gu Guoliang, eds., *Power and Restraint: A Shared Vision for the U.S.-China Relationship* (Public Affairs, 2009): 67–78.

Chapter 8: Adapted from Etel Solingen, "The Genesis, Design and Effects of Regional Institutions: Lessons from East Asia and the Middle East," *International Studies Quarterly*, 52, 1 (June 2008): 261–294.

Chapter 9: Adapted from Etel Solingen, "The Triple Logic of the European-Mediterranean Partnership: Hindsight and Foresight." *International Politics*, Vol. 40, No. 2 (June 2003): 179–194.

Chapter 10: Reprinted from Etel Solingen, *Nuclear Logics: Contrasting Paths in East Asia and the Middle East* (Princeton University Press, 2007): 249-299.

PREFACE

This collection of essays builds on a core argument first developed in the early 1990s in articles not reproduced in this volume for reasons of space (see references, particularly Solingen 1994a, 1994b). Europe represented the lion share of studies related to regionalism at the time, when research comparing other regions in the post-Cold War era was embryonic. Indeed much of the study of regionalism back then was cast in the language of regional integration that typified scholarship on Europe. My own interest, however, lied in exploring the deep and complex connections between global, regional, and domestic orders in what is now labelled the "emerging" world. I found the nature of domestic coalitions forming in response to globalization a convenient analytical anchor at the vortex of those connections. *Regional Orders at Century's Dawn* (Solingen, 1998, Princeton University Press) provided a more comprehensive theoretical formulation than earlier iterations. I include two of its four conceptual chapters here as a theoretical core providing the leitmotiv for the rest of the volume. The intention was to lean on a conceptual framework of broad applicability inspired by cases that offered greater comparative value, and hence seemed better suited to explain broad patterns of regional conflict and cooperation than European integration theories. Initial applications to East Asia, the Middle East, and Latin America informed subsequent comparisons with other regions.

In the intervening 16 years since the publication of *Regional Orders* further analytical and empirical extensions appeared in diverse venues, often addressing audiences with different substantive and methodological interests. This volume provides an opportunity for bringing them together to contribute to contemporary debates on the comparative study of regionalism broadly defined. The study of regions, regionalism, regional orders and cognate concepts are now established fields of inquiry worldwide and increasingly taught in specialized courses. This volume was not conceived as a synthetic literature review and does not fully cover the field's enormous conceptual and methodological diversity. It rather takes on the opportunity extended to reflect on the topic, for which I thank Routledge's editor and anonymous reviewers. Andrew Humphrys saw the completion of the manuscript through during a very demanding stretch of professional commitments, with great understanding. Preparing new material for incorporation into an extended introductory chapter allowed me to return to themes of enduring relevance for regionalism from the impact of globalization to regional institutions, democratization, the resource curse, the 2011 Arab upheavals, political Islam, the re-emergence of China, the East Asian peace, Euro-Med relations, and nuclear trajectories in different regions. Most chapters are slightly abridged from the originals and edited for clarity but not updated. Citations have been reduced to enhance flow and minimize interruptions but the originals contain far more comprehensive bibliographies on wide-ranging work on regionalism.

I incurred many debts in efforts to deepen my understanding of regions, benefitting greatly from a John D. and Catherine T. MacArthur Foundation Fellowship on Peace and International Cooperation, a Social Science Research Council-MacArthur Foundation Fellowship, awards by the Center for Global Partnership, United States Institute of Peace, University of California's Pacific Rim Research Program, and Social Science Research Council-Abe Fellowship among others. Extensive participation in invited conferences and "Track Two" meetings on regional conflict and cooperation provided an invaluable learning experience. I am profoundly grateful to so many institutions and colleagues nationally and overseas for enriching my understanding of dozens of countries and their region. Chapter 1 of this volume, previously unpublished, benefitted from exchanges at successive meetings sponsored by Harvard University's John F. Kennedy School and the Chinese Academy of Social Sciences, and from a Celia Moh Professorship at Singapore Management University sponsored by Dean James Tang. I would also like to acknowledge support over the years from the University of California's system-wide Institute on Global Conflict and Cooperation Directors Susan Shirk and Peter Cowhey, University of California Irvine's Dean of Social Sciences Barbara Dosher, Center for the Scientific Study of Ethics Director Kristen Monroe, and Global Peace and Conflict Studies Director Cecelia Lynch. My colleague Dave Easton's infallible critical eye and encouragement has been crucial all along.

In addition to the many institutions and individuals acknowledged in the original publications, I am especially grateful for comments from organizers and participants in special panels on my work on regionalism at meetings of the International Studies Association (2012 and 2013), including Audie Klotz, Anja Jetschke, John Ravenhill, Leslie Armijo, Kathleen Hancock, and William Potter, and for helpful suggestions from T.J. Pempel, Miles Kahler, Diana Tussie, Peter Katzenstein, Tanja Börzel, Thomas Risse, Mark Lichbach, Galia Press-Barnathan, Ed Mansfield, Richard Rosecrance, Arthur Stein, Lourdes Sola, Nicola Phillips, Steven Brams, Leonard Binder, Steph Haggard, Saori Katada, Jack Snyder, Ajin Choi, Kim Sung-Chull, Richard Stubbs, Saadia M. Pekkanen, Martonio Mont'Alverne Barreto Lima, Mehran Kamrava, Tang Shiping, Henrik Stålhane Hiim, Stein Tønnesson, and Hans Blix. For superb research and bibliographic assistance I especially thank Wilfred Wan, Helen Klein, Celia Reynolds, Joshua Malnight, Timma Medovoy, Grant Speckert, and Tom Le. I am very grateful to the three anonymous referees for Routledge for excellent advice that guided me through revisions, to Mark Fisher for careful copy-editing, and to Karl Harrington for helping to steer the manuscript through the final stages of production.

My family has the most special of places in my voyage through regions, the literal and figurative ones, as they accompanied me in both. I dedicate this book to my mother Fanny, a source of inspiration as a woman and scholar, but it is also a tribute to Fito's inquisitive intellect and love of geography, as well as to Simon, Gabrielle, Aaron, Quito, Dina, Chelo, Ana María, Norah, Iris, and last but not least Ruby and Ben. I am grateful for their love and encouragement which makes anything possible and everything worthwhile.

1
INTRODUCTION AND OVERVIEW

The literature on comparative regionalism has exploded since the end of the Cold War. *Regional Orders at Century's Dawn* was part of an early salvo published in the 1990s amidst growing interest in globalization and regionalization.[1] It thus sought to understand the impact of globalization on the nature of regional orders along the conflict and cooperation spectrum, a theme much broader than regional institutions. Institutions, embedded as they are in regional orders, can hardly be understood except against that wider background. Indeed, regional orders are political constructs that may or may not be codified in regional institutions; and there is great variance in the latter's influence on regional orders. Yet much work on regions in the 16 years since publication has been circumscribed to formalization and institutional design. Several reasons account for this more restricted focus on institutions rather than on broader features of regional conflict and cooperation. First, the European Union – a much legalized institution – casts a large shadow as an unprecedented case but can also set up an analytical trap that turns Europe into the key empirical referent for understanding regionalism as a universal category.[2] As an anomaly rather than the norm, the EU provided a distorted lens through which to examine other experiences.[3] Comparing Europe with other regions is a perfectly legitimate exercise but turning the EU into the benchmark for comparative regionalism helped confine the latter analytically to the study of institutions with an emphasis on degrees of formalization. Second, the explosion of theoretical work on international institutions in international relations more generally reinforced the focus on regional institutions. Whether in their rationalistic renditions emphasizing institutional design or constructivist ones focused on norms, the study of regionalism became – to a significant extent – largely identified with the study of institutional forms.[4]

This volume returns to the broader focus in *Regional Orders* and to the deeper forces driving regions in more conflictive or cooperative directions, over and above formal institutions, but also transcends that earlier focus, inviting attention to five main features worthy of consideration in the study of comparative regionalism.

First, as argued, the volume approaches regionalism as a broader phenomenon than that captured by institutional expressions of regional relations. Regional institutions are embedded in a wider context characterized by different degrees of conflict and cooperation, a context that may be logically prior to the nature of those institutions. This revision is not designed to replace an important concern with institutions and their causal effects, a core concern of Parts II and III in this volume. It is rather an effort to broaden the analytical scope to include more spacious understandings of regional relations. Regions can be more or less cooperative, more or less "regionalized" (often meaning economically interdependent), more or less cohesive in terms of identity, more or less stable, and so on. Yet these outcomes are not necessarily a function of their institutions, let alone their degree of formalization or legalization. Those relationships can be explored empirically rather than assumed a priori. Even some of the early work included in this volume anticipated that regional institutions were only one dimension in the evolution of world regions (or regionalism in a broader sense); and that institutions were neither entirely epiphenomenal nor encoded a region's complete DNA.

Second, the bulk of this volume shifts attention away from the widely studied European irregularity and unto other regions that are all too often more subjected to comparisons with Europe than with each other. The puzzles and questions that animate the different chapters stem from broader theoretical themes in international relations and a more expansive set of empirical cases. This set includes what are sometimes labelled "emerging regions;" regions that join both advanced and industrializing states (East Asia); regions that include primarily industrializing states (the Middle East, Latin America and others); regions that join together contrasting models of regionalism (the Euro-Mediterranean construct); and sub-regions within all of the above. Third, as with *Regional Orders,* this volume retains an emphasis on the relationship between globalization and regionalism. The two intercept as globalization influences domestic competition between two ideal-typical models of political survival, each advanced by internationalizing or inward-looking coalitions respectively. These coalitions of state and private actors – rather than monolithic states – are the deeper driving agents of regional outcomes and are themselves influenced by the region's *coalitional* context. Fourth, the volume goes beyond *Regional Orders* by exploring more systematically the antecedent and catalytic conditions – domestic, regional, and international – that underlie the emergence of some coalitions in certain contexts but not others. Finally, the volume focuses on regions and regionalism as an important analytical category in international relations but is agnostic on the extent to which either one may or may not be *the* central feature of international relations today or even a more central one today than ever before. The work included here does not address that debate.

The remainder of this introductory chapter provides an overview of conceptual, thematic and empirical applications of the generic argument, previewing some of the themes developed in the rest of the book. Part I, Globalization, Economic Reform and Regional Relations, lays out in greater detail the foundations of the core analytical framework that informs the rest of the volume. Part II extends the framework to examine the Regional Effects of Democratic Institutions. Part III analyses the framework's implications for understanding the Sources, Design and

Effects of Regional Institutions on regional orders. Part IV assesses the framework's applicability to comparisons across Regional Security Trajectories, with special reference to nuclear weapons. The conclusions explore the general argument's continued relevance, glancing back to the outbreak of World War I exactly 100 years ago and forward to evolving regional orders in the second decade of the twenty-first century, with suggestions for further research.

The framework in Part I draws from various world regions including East Asia, the Middle East, Latin America, the Euro-Mediterranean region, South and Southeast Asia, and others. An ascendant East Asia and an effervescent Middle East attract special attention in some comparative empirical chapters in Parts II–IV. The two are often considered regions of greatest interest in world politics yet surveys reveal that very few articles on these regions appeared in major international relations journals and that only a small fraction of international relations scholars considered them to be their own core research interests.[5] This under-representation was even more dramatic when *Regional Orders* appeared in the 1990s but remains until today. The study of international relations of East Asia fared somewhat better as a subject of research but all too often as a putative "puzzle" not fitting theoretical expectations drawn from the EU experience. Furthermore, there was only a dearth of studies in the tradition of international and comparative political economy of the Middle East region in recent decades, a trend that 2011 Arab upheavals may have helped overturn. Dedicated comparisons between the two regions remain rare despite clear methodological advantages outlined in Chapters 5 and 10.

Globalization, economic reform and regional orders

Chapter 2, adapted from *Regional Orders*, provides an expanded discussion of the micro-foundations proposed for the study of comparative regionalism. In brief, the analytical point of departure is the domestic distributional consequences of internationalization.[6] Increased openness to international markets, capital, investments, and technology affects individuals and groups through changes in employment, incomes, prices, public services, as well as through their evolving commitments to international regimes and institutions in security, the global environment, and other domains (Keohane and Milner 1996; Mansfield and Milner 1997). These second-image-reversed (Gourevitch 1986) or outside-in effects lead to the constitution of two ideal-typical coalitions – internationalizing and inward-looking – vying for power and control of their states.[7] Domestic politics and institutions, in turn, convert those effects into competing grand strategies of local, regional, and global reach – inside-out effects that are synergistic across all three levels. Figure 1.1 summarizes these linkages between the domestic and international realms.

Politicians rely on available rules and structures to fashion coalitions that maximize their own relative power and control over resources, leading constituencies to logroll across material economic and ideational interests of both state and private actors. Internationalizing coalitions attract beneficiaries (or potential beneficiaries) of economic openness such as export-intensive sectors and firms, highly skilled labor employed in competitive industries or firms, analysts oriented towards an open global economic and knowledge (technology) system, competitive agricultural

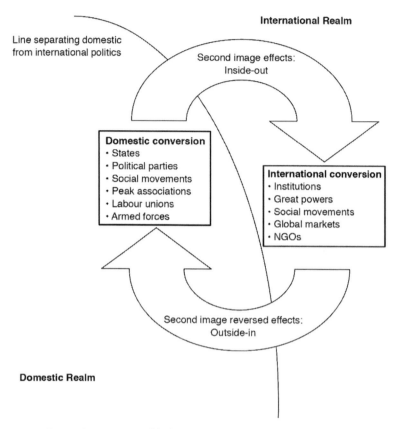

Figure 1.1 Domestic-international linkages

Adapted from Solingen, E. (2009). 'The Global Context of Comparative Politics,' In M. I. Lichbach and A. S. Zuckerman (eds), *Comparative Politics: Rationality, Culture, and Structure*. Cambridge: Cambridge University Press

sectors, consumers of imported products, and bureaucracies central to economic reform (independent central banks, finance ministries, managers of export-processing zones). Inward-looking coalitions attract import-competing firms and banks closely tied to the state, state-owned enterprises and banks, urban unskilled blue-collar and white-collar sectors, state bureaucracies rendered obsolete by reform, considerable segments of the military and its industrial complex, and civic-nationalist, ethnic, and religious movements threatened by internationalization. High uncertainty about the impact of internationalization leaves many behind the "veil of ignorance," unable to figure out where and how they will come out at the end of the process. When crafting coalitions, politicians portray the benefits and pitfalls of internationalization on the basis of actual or putative impacts.

At times the two competing coalitions carve out different parts of a state cleaved by this coalitional competition. At other times either coalition succeeds in controlling the state and is thus able to implement its preferred model (grand strategy) of political survival in power. Internationalizing models rely on economic performance and growth via integration into the global economy whereas inward-looking models rely on autonomous "self-sufficiency." The two ideal-types also differ in the extent to which states (including military-industrial complexes) replace or enhance markets. Where internationalizing coalitions successfully realize their favored model of political survival, they capture opportunities offered by the global political economy and institutions. Their grand strategy emphasizes regional cooperation and stability and access to global markets, capital, investments, and technology; they accord primacy to macroeconomic stability and international competitiveness because both are expected to reduce uncertainty, encourage savings, and enhance the rate of investment (including foreign). Why are these coalitions more prone to cooperate with their neighbors? Because conflict-prone postures require mobilization of resources for potential military conflict which, in turn, contributes many of the ailments afflicting the domestic political economy from the standpoint of internationalizers. Such ailments include unproductive and inflation-inducing military investments and the protection of state enterprises under a mantle of "national security." Mobilization of resources for conflict often emasculate macroeconomic objectives via expansive military budgets, government and payments deficits, rising cost of capital, inhibited savings and productive investment, depleted foreign exchange coffers, overvalued exchange rates, currency instability and unpredictability, and foiled foreign investment. Many East Asian ruling coalitions steered their states in an internationalizing direction.

Where inward-looking coalitions realize their favored model, they challenge the reach of markets, international institutions, and powerful states, asserting complete sovereignty and control across issue-areas. Their grand strategy, in its purest form, hinges wholly on the interests of state industry and ancillary inward-looking military-industrial sectors, as well as of ethnic, religious, and nationalist groups threatened by internationalization. Regional insecurity and competition helps sustain these coalitions in power whereas rising regional cooperation has the potential of eroding their resources and undermining their objectives. Inward-looking state and private actors are generally unconcerned with the prospects that regional instability might undercut foreign investment. Classically these coalitions rely on populism, active states controlling prices, increasing nominal wages, overvaluing the currency to raise wages and profits in non-traded goods sectors, and dispensing rents to private firms by discriminating against competing imports through tariffs, controls, and multiple exchange rates. Inward-looking coalitions flout an array of international economic, political, and security regimes that they depict as anathema to the economic, national, ethnic, or religious objectives they safeguard. Many Middle Eastern ruling coalitions steered their states in an inward-looking direction.

Models of political survival don't envelop states overnight or in linear fashion. They evolve through coalitional competition and causal mechanisms linking comparative and international politics.[8] The relative strength of coalitions – at home and throughout the region – accounts for the degree to which grand strategies are more pristine or diluted versions of the ideal-type. What are the effects of strategic interaction among different coalitional combinations in a given region? Chapter 3 explains the logic underlying these regional configurations, hinging on the relative incidence of coalitions of one type or another (rather than on the nature of regional institutions). A state's regional environment can be defined as an aggregate measure of the relative strength of internationalizing or inward-looking coalitions. An internationalizing regional environment is one dominated by a more or less homogeneous cluster of internationalizing coalitions. The reverse is true for an inward-looking regional environment dominated by a more or less homogeneous cluster of inward-looking coalitions. *The incidence of each coalitional type, and the different regional coalitional clusters they constitute in the aggregate, define a region's propensity for conflict and cooperation.*

Different coalitional mixes throughout a region create and reproduce typical regional orders and, conversely, are affected by them. Strong internationalizing coalitions in a region are expected to create more cooperative and peaceful regional orders ("zones of peace") than those typical of clusters dominated by strong inward-looking coalitions ("zones of war"). Regions dominated by mixed or hybrid coalitional forms exhibit "zones of contained conflict" that elude extensive cooperation or war. Converging internationalizing grand strategies in a given region are collectively stable, creating an environment least propitious for inward-looking strategies. The more internationalizing the region's center of gravity, the higher its reliance on cooperative (though not necessarily formal) arrangements that enable implementation of all pillars of internationalizing grand strategies. Converging inward-looking strategies are also collectively stable, feeding on each other's existence, resulting in war zones more immune to internationalizing strategies. Internationalizing "zones of peace" challenge lingering inward-looking coalitions in their region undermining their grand strategy, from the merits of economic closure to the advantages of militarization. In time these regional orders can overturn coalitional balances within outstanding inward-looking states, easing their eventual inclusion into their regional framework. ASEAN (Association of Southeast Asian Nations) has operated in that fashion to integrate erstwhile inward-looking coalitions in Vietnam and Burma. Where inward-looking coalitions dominate a region, "zones of war" trigger pressures that loom large on the survival of internationalizers, weakening them and forcing them to dilute their preferred strategy. Regions dominated by inward-looking coalitions like the Middle East threatened the viability of would-be internationalizers in Jordan, Lebanon and elsewhere for many decades.

The empirical chapters in *Regional Orders*, not reproduced here, provide detailed qualitative evidence for patterns consistent with this coalitional framework. They document why competing models of political survival offer compelling explanations for decades of Middle East wars and enduring rivalries in the inter-Arab, Arab–Israeli, and Arab–Iranian arenas; for cooperative Arab–Israeli breakthroughs in the early 1990s and reactive responses to them; for why regional economic barriers among Arab states never receded and regional institutions such as the Arab Common Market existed largely on paper, much as their Latin American counterparts; and for the evolving texture of regional relations in Latin America's Southern Cone, where the virtual absence of war between Argentina and Brazil for well over a century should have produced deeper cooperation. They also explain why Argentina's entrenched inward-looking strategies spearheaded an ambiguous nuclear program, military crises and mobilizations vis-à-vis Chile and a war with the United Kingdom; and why there were effective steps toward economic integration through Mercosur with the ascent of internationalizers in the 1990s but much less so since.⁹ A coalitional analysis also sheds light on the outbreak of the Korean War; subsequent shifts away from war and cooperative overtures by the South; evolving North–South Korean relations; divergent nuclear postures in the North and South since the 1970s; North Korea's internal cleavages as drivers of foreign policy shifts and its trespassing of the nuclear brink; and the taming of conflicts among East Asian states via internationalizing strategies. The framework also explains why inward-looking models account for greater proneness to use chemical weapons and spearhead more wars than internationalizing ones, and why the Cold War era provided a more supportive global structure for inward-looking coalitions – economic protection, militarization and regional conflict – than the post-1989 era. Despite significant differences among them, the modal East Asian ruling coalition remains closer to an export-oriented internationalizing model than most other industrializing regions. The progressive integration of East Asian coalitions into the global economy and piecemeal steps toward regional cooperation and stability, particularly the absence of war, conformed to the hypothesized synergies in their coalitional grand strategies. The prospects of future war may not be nil in East Asia, as I discuss below, yet the region has largely avoided war for several decades despite serious disputes.

Neorealist approaches that focus on structural balance of power and anarchy cannot explain many of these outcomes, including prolonged peace, denuclearization, or grand strategic shifts toward deeper cooperation in the Southern Cone or shifts away from war in the Korean peninsula since the 1950s, the north-south modus vivendi of the 1970s, different responses by the North and South to comparable strategic predicaments or evolutionary changes in such responses, and many other regional outcomes elsewhere, analyzed in the empirical chapters. Yet it would be naive to ignore contextual variations across regions regarding the depths and longevity of security dilemmas. Coalitions filter such dilemmas in their design of grand strategies. The shadow of past trajectories in the Middle East, the Korean peninsula, and South Asia raise higher barriers for internationalizers, affecting the speed and shape of cooperation. Internationalizers thus differ across regions regarding their starting points for the construction of cooperative regional orders; the distance that must be travelled towards Pareto frontiers that make everybody better off is consequential. Initial security conditions matter but do not tell us enough: different coalitions can embrace radically different grand strategies under virtually identical structural conditions.

World systems frameworks ignore that while the global political economy imposes constraints on "peripheral" states, but it also provides them with opportunities. China and many others moved from the periphery to the center in one generation, riding those opportunities. As "peripheral" states became more globally integrated, many also became less involved in regional conflict. The major East Asian wars unfolded prior to the rise of internationalized states that have managed to avoid wars since. Deeper cooperation between Brazil and Argentina followed their most unprecedented turn towards the global economy. The Middle East and South Asia resisted global markets for decades, contributing many entries to war statistics. Notably, many villains of dependency theory seeking integration in the global economy have become heroes of regional cooperation. Conversely, some heroes of import-substituting nationalism have unleashed massive wars and hindered regional economic cooperation. Dependency theory has overlooked several missing links that are consequential for regional conflict and cooperation: global economic access and investments require domestic economic and regional stability, not war; inward-looking statism and military-industrial complexes are synergistic, often perpetuating wasteful military allocations and autocratic rule; internationalization, macroeconomic stability and fiscal conservatism have some undesirable consequences but have also dramatically weakened military-industrial complexes and their basis for domestic political control.

Coalitional analysis is amenable to constructivist work that captures dimensions of coalition formation such as ideational, cultural and identity-based proclivities vis-à-vis the global economy and related institutions. Persuasion, socialization, shaming, and other mechanisms used by international institutions or transnational networks can enhance or diminish the appeal of competing coalitions, internationalizing or inward-looking. Constructivist analysis also forces greater attention to the contextual character of cooperation and conflict: dialogue between adversaries may be taken for granted in some contexts (Southern Cone) but constitute gargantuan cooperative strides in others (North and South Korea, Middle East). Interpretive methods also help identify the boundaries of regions and the mechanisms by which coalitions mobilize support for or against reliance on the global economy, for or against nationalism and the military, for or against regional cooperation.

Chapter 4 (Mapping Internationalization: Domestic and Regional Impacts) extends *Regional Orders* in a number of ways. First, it provides further conceptual elaboration of patterns of logrolling and the political landscapes out of which competing coalitions emerge. Second, it provides a schematic design for mapping the domestic impact of internationalization across the industrializing world. Third, it amplifies discussion of hybrid coalitional types as a straddling category between internationalizing and inward-looking ideal-types that can strain a strategy's internal coherence. Fourth, it includes a quantitative analysis of ninety-eight successive coalitions in nineteen states across five regions: the Middle East, East and Southeast Asia, South Asia, and the Southern Cone of Latin America. These regions account for a significant portion of the industrializing world, much of which shared similarly high levels of anarchic, self-help historical contexts, and much of which was poorly endowed with effective regional institutional infrastructures that might facilitate cooperation. These similarities help control for the effect of variables that cannot easily account for observed outcomes related to regional conflict and cooperation.

Aggregate data on the five regions for the period between 1948 and 1993 provides support for the relationship between the three coalitional types and international behavior. Internationalizing coalitions are found to be more prone to deepen trade openness, expand exports, attract foreign investments, tame profligate military-industrial complexes, initiate fewer international crises, eschew weapons of mass destruction, defer to international economic and security regimes, and strive for regional cooperative orders that reinforce those objectives. Pristine and coherent grand strategies of any sort are rare but the links between a commitment to internationalization and regional cooperation and stability are evident. In contrast, inward-looking coalitions are found to be more prone than internationalizing ones to restrict and reduce trade openness and reliance on exports, curb foreign investment, build expansive military-industrial complexes, develop weapons of mass destruction, initiate international crises, challenge international regimes, and exacerbate civic-nationalist, religious, or ethnic differentiation by emphasizing territoriality, sovereignty, militarization, and self-reliance. These policies' risks and externalities make wars more likely even when they are not the most favored option. Hybrids straddle the grand strategies of their purer types, intermittently striving for economic openness, contracting the military complex, initiating international crises, and cooperating regionally and internationally but neither forcefully nor coherently.

Regional effects of democratic institutions

Part II focuses attention on the relationship between democratic and autocratic institutions (regime-type), models of political survival (inward-looking/internationalizing), and their regional effects (conflictive/cooperative orders). Regime-type and models of political survival are analytically distinctive categories.[10] Democracy and autocracy provide politicians and coalitions with different opportunities and constraints. Both coalitional types can thrive in non-democratic and cartelized systems; both types can also benefit from democratization, particularly when they are in the opposition. The coalitional perspective predicts a generally positive relationship between strong internationalizers and incentives to cooperate regionally – particularly with similarly oriented neighbors – and a reverse relationship for inward-looking coalitions, regardless of whether or not they are democratic. Neither democracy nor internationalizers may be necessary for cooperation (other things can produce cooperation as well); yet both seem to create near-sufficient conditions for avoiding war. The Southern Cone and South Asia do not provide strong support for democratic dyads invariably enhancing cooperation. The absence of war in the Southern Cone endured throughout successive democratic and autocratic regimes. Furthermore, democratic dyads in the 1980s did not create a radically different regional order than their autocratic predecessors; internationalizers did. The Middle East and much of East and Southeast Asia over the latter part of the twentieth century were bereft of democratic dyads, pointing to the essential insignificance of democratic peace theory for explaining dramatic reversals from conflict to cooperation in East Asia over that period.

Both democratic and autocratic (including democratizing) regime-types have relied on internationalizing and inward-looking strategies. Regime-type does not appear to determine success in implementing internationalizing strategies. Yet political closure and repression, as in much of the Middle East, can be a major barrier to internationalization, and consequently to regional peace. Democracy is not a precondition for implementing internationalizing grand strategies yet the affinity between inward-looking statist-nationalism and transitional democracy poses significant barriers for internationalization. There is also some evidence that the confluence of democracy and internationalization makes cooperative behavior with like-minded counterparts (homophily) more robust. Democracy can invest internationalizing strategies – and regional cooperation – with greater legitimacy. Successful internationalizers can afford to reinvent themselves through the democratic process, as in Taiwan, South Korea, and Chile upon departure of repressive autocrats that incepted internationalizing models. It is, however, important to consider that stable democratic dyads have been rare for most of the twentieth century in the industrializing world, making the democratic peace hypothesis far less applicable to many cases relevant to comparative regionalism beyond Europe. Despite remarkable strides in East Asia, for instance, internationalizing leaders from Singapore to China, Vietnam, and others still grope with whether internationalizing contexts can resist democratization.

Chapter 5 clarifies the relationship between models of political survival and regime type further by delving on the puzzle of an evolving Pax Asiatica in East Asia and continuous wars in the Middle East. Adapted from the *American Political Science Review*'s "Pax Asiatica versus Bella Levantina," the chapter begins by exploring the antecedent and immediate conditions explaining why different coalitional types entrench themselves in different regions. Why has East Asia evolved toward dominance of internationalizing ruling coalitions? Why have inward-looking ruling coalitions endured in the Middle East for many decades? The analysis then turns to the first-order implications of coalitional trajectories for three institutions: democracy, the military and the nature of states. It follows with second order effects of models on the incidence of regional conflict or cooperation. The contrasts are particularly puzzling because states across both regions shared relatively similar initial domestic conditions in the 1950s and early 1960s, including harsh autocratic rule, ethnic diversity, state-building challenges, and involvement in militarized conflicts. Since 1965, however, the incidence of interstate wars and militarized conflicts has been nearly five times higher in the Middle East as has been their severity, including use of ballistic missiles and chemical weapons. By contrast, declining wars and militarized conflict and rising intra-regional cooperation have replaced earlier patterns in East Asia. The two regions looked dramatically different in the early twenty-first century as East Asia became the engine of the global economy.

Why, then, these divergent paths out of common initial conditions? Leading theories of international relations do not provide satisfactory answers. First, for neorealism the very premise of a Pax Asiatica is erroneous; the universal logic of power distribution reigns, leading to cyclical war or pauses in war-making at best. But what explains the pause? A standard hypothesis – robust, bipolar, and symmetric distribution of nuclear weapons – does not apply here. Other neorealist variables – dramatic changes in power distribution with China's rise, Japan's normalization, North Korea's nuclearization – should have led to war, as some have predicted for decades, but they have not. Fluctuations between US hegemonic assertion and defection have not altered the no-war outcome either. One crucial difficulty with power-based explanations is stipulating whether East Asia has been multipolar, bipolar, or under US hegemony but there are many others. Second, neoliberal-institutionalist approaches trace absence of war to institutions presumed to reduce transaction costs and enhance cooperation. However the decades-long Pax Asiatica has unfolded in the absence of legalized institutions. Regional institutions emerged after remarkable expansion in markets, investment, and cooperation but remained minimalist, informal, and consensus-based. Third, cultural interpretations like "Asian values" and "ASEAN way" have been properly debunked;[11] the same cultural construct could not explain both earlier periods of militarized conflict and a subsequent Pax Asiatica. Nor did the ancient "Oriental wisdom's" penchant for consensus, harmony, unity, and community produce peace in earlier times. Indeed East Asia is not at all culturally homogeneous – it is perhaps less so than the Middle East – yet extremely diverse cultures have not precluded cooperation. Traumatic memories of Japan's World War II cruelty or of repeated aggressions against Vietnam have not precluded extensive economic, political, and diplomatic rapprochements including informal institutions. Finally, democratic-peace theory is inapplicable because Pax Asiatica preceded the emergence of a cluster of democratic states and continues to operate in a region hosting several autocracies. And a fairly autocratic but internationalizing cluster spearheaded more peaceful conditions in Southeast Asia.

Competing models of political survival have less difficulty explaining the puzzle raised in Chapter 5. East Asian leaders pivoted their political control on economic performance and integration in the global economy whereas Middle East leaders relied on inward-looking self-sufficiency, state and military entrepreneurship, and a related brand of nationalism. The question that chapter seeks to answer is: why? What remote sources and causal mechanisms explain why two competing models took root in each region? The permissive and catalytic conditions explaining the respective models' emergence can be briefly summarized as follows: early and effective land reform, a relatively brief period of import-substitution, and natural resource scarcity weakened domestic political opposition to export-led growth in East Asia. By contrast, late, inefficient or nonexistent land reform; longer exposure to import-substitution through extensive state and military entrepreneurship; and abundant oil resources or second-order rentierism (in neighboring non-oil economies) empowered opponents of export-led growth throughout much of the Middle East. Put differently, politically stronger beneficiaries of relative closure, import-substitution, state entrepreneurship, and natural resource monopolies – mostly within the state itself – constituted powerful veto points against alternative models for decades.

Chapter 5 also clarifies the implications of each model for three crucial domestic institutions: states, militaries, and authoritarian institutions.[12] Despite broad divergence, competing models in the two regions shared three important features. First, both relied on state institutions; yet differences in the character of that reliance would have differing effects on the respective evolution of states. The two models differed in the extent to which states replaced or enhanced private capital. East Asian states were active lenders and regulators but significantly less active entrepreneurs than their Middle East counterparts. East Asian leaders watchfully steered states to macroeconomic stability and proper conditions for sustained export-led growth. States thus evolved into relatively adaptable institutions linking across the domestic, regional, and global economies. Middle East models shared rigid, exhausted, and depleted state institutions presiding over current account and budget deficits; high inflation and unemployment; and scarce foreign exchange. These states became too weak to exert control over society except through force, as remains widely the case today. Despite significant differences among them (and outliers like North Korea), East Asian states approximated ideal-typical developmental states, Weberian-style meritocratic bureaucracies able to extract resources from society and convert them into public goods (Evans 1995). Despite extensive variation across the Middle East, predatory states undercutting development even in the narrow sense of capital accumulation remained largely dominant, relying on patronage-based bureaucracies primarily supplying private goods to rapacious ruling coalitions (Arab Human Development Report 2002).

Second, military institutions played important roles initially in both models, particularly as repressive mechanisms of political control. Yet the military itself evolved along different lines, in tandem with prevailing political-economy models. The requirements of each model imposed different constraints on: (1) the relative size and missions of military-industrial complexes; and (2) the extent to which these complexes replaced private enterprise over and beyond arms production. In the Middle East, dismal economies notwithstanding, arms races typical of inward-looking models consistently attracted the highest levels of military expenditures relative to GNP worldwide, about twice East Asian averages. Internationalizing East Asian states could not accommodate the kind of militarized economies (i.e. percentages of military ownership of the economy) typical of Middle East states. This Middle East pattern replaced and often decimated the private sector whereas East Asian growth models nurtured it. The former entrenched *mukhabarat* repressive states; the latter professionalized militaries and curtailed their political control over the economy and polity.

Third, both models relied on authoritarian institutions; yet each would foreshadow differential paths regarding democratization, stemming from variations in the nature and role of military institutions and private entrepreneurship just described. Export-led models incepted by authoritarian leaders and ruling coalitions in East Asia were not precisely designed to advance democracy but unintendedly encouraged democratic institutions via several causal mechanisms: fostering economic growth, stronger private sectors and civil societies, and more professionalized militaries attuned to outward-oriented growth. Over time, several authoritarian regimes in East Asia evolved into full-fledged democracies. By contrast, Middle East models engendered higher barriers to the development of democratic institutions, weaker private sectors and weakened civil societies less able to demand political reform, and entrenched military industrial complexes better able to resist those demands.

Finally, Chapter 5 outlines the implications of each model for regional conflict and cooperation. Their inability to deliver resources and services to constituencies previously mobilized through revolutionary or nationalist fervor, and their efforts to divert attention from failed, economically depleted, entropic, crisis-prone, militarized and de-legitimized models led Middle East regimes to: (a) emphasize nationalism and military prowess; (b) externalize conflict; (c) exacerbate arms races; and (d) engage in competitive outbidding at the regional level. Each of these vectors individually enhanced the prospects for intended or unintended war, militarized incidents, and militarized or political intrusions in the domestic affairs of neighboring states. Collectively they made those even more likely, creating a structural tendency toward conflict even though war itself might not have been the preferred outcome. Mobilizations, overt subversions, and cross-border invasions were certainly intended but not always controllable. Lacking institutional power and legitimacy domestically and regionally, Middle East leaders deployed violence at home and abroad, evoking Tilly's arguments regarding the use of force.[13] Domestic fragility hidden behind pan-Arab or pan Islamic rhetoric fueled mutual assaults on sovereignty among Arab-states (Halliday 2005). By contrast, East Asia's developmental states required: (a) contained military-industrial complexes and limited military competition; (b) regional stability; (c) domestic stability, predictability, and attractiveness to foreign investors; and (d) tamed arms races that might adversely affect (a) through (c). Each of those requirements individually dampened the prospects for war and militarized conflict. Collectively they made them even less likely despite lingering hostility and nationalist resentment. Inter-state militarized conflict declined in East Asia since the 1980s and intra- regional trade and investment expanded dramatically.

Within-region variation challenges essentialist penchants for war or peace in any region. Most states in each region conformed to a general pattern but there were also anomalies such as North Korea and Burma in East Asia, which provide further support for the relationship between inward-looking models of political survival and external conflict. Middle East outliers strove to adopt alternative models to those prevailing in their region. Outliers in each region thus question the scope of micro-phenomenological theories emphasizing local cultural origins and regional uniqueness. Above all, the incidence of outliers counters deterministic views about inevitable outcomes in any region. Southeast Asia, once the "Balkans of the East" under inward-looking stewardship, eventually superseded old models and established cooperative foundations that have largely withstood the test of time.

Chapter 6 (Democratization in the Middle East: Quandaries of the Peace Process) probes deeper into the possibility of democratization in that region and its implications for regional conflict and cooperation. *The notion that democracies rarely wage wars against each other has gained remarkable acceptance in scholarly and policy circles. At the same time, various observers have expressed concern that incipient democratization in some Arab countries may pose a threat to the nascent peace between Israel and its neighbors. Are democratization and peace mutually exclusive or mutually supportive in this region? What are the dilemmas each process poses for the other?* The preceding paragraph was published not after the 2011 Arab uprisings but in 1996, as an abstract for the original publication in the *Journal of Democracy* (Solingen 1996b). Given the historical context, at a time when most scholarship focused on enduring authoritarianism with little possibility of change in the Middle East, this was a rather countercyclical effort to explore the possibility of democratization in the 1990s. Its themes have become even more relevant over the last three years.

The chapter examines the connections among political liberalization, economic reform, and incipient changes in regional cooperation reflected in the Oslo agreements, both the bilateral Palestinian-Israeli and the broader Arab–Israeli Multilateral Peace Process.[14] That brittle peace process, it argued, could hardly be traced to the region's fragile, stagnant or slow-paced democratization at that time.

Yet it also noted that some ruling coalitions in the Arab world, aware of the advantages of democratization for economic reform, also advanced limited democratization, economic liberalization, and regional cooperation. The synergies among these three processes evoke arguments discussed in Parts I and II of this volume. A core hypothesis held that progressive liberalization-from-above had facilitated civic inclusion of Islamist movements without completely dissipating concerns with potential Islamist reversals of democracy. Democratic inclusion (as in Jordan) had neither emasculated democratization for the most part nor shelved peace overtures at that time. Democratization throughout the region was piecemeal and geographically limited yet developments in the Palestinian camp and around the Oslo process compelled stock-taking on the relationship between incipient democratization and regional cooperation.

There has been remarkable continuity in the trends identified over the intervening 18 years since publication, but also some sharp discontinuities. Foremost among the latter were the Arab uprisings, a watershed expected to unleash dramatic changes with implications for war and peace. The uprisings may not have yet led to consolidated democracies but certainly have widened the variance in transitional regimes relative to 1996. The fact that Tunisia has made the most impressive strides as of late 2013 may well be related to some of the conditions described earlier, absent thus far in Egypt, including a more pragmatic Islamist party as well as a military that has kept out of politics and business. The article also summoned the so-called "balloon theory" of radical Islamism that predicts volatile, unsteady allegiance to such movements. Initial post-2011 elections in Egypt and Tunisia brought Islamist parties to power. Within a year, however, support for the Muslim Brotherhood (Ikhwan) had waned with President Mohammed Morsi's decree placing his decisions above the law, his violent response to protests, and his inability to stem economic breakdown. Many secularists and others who had voted for Morsi became disillusioned, interpreting his performance as evidence that Islamist electoral victories indeed lead to the emasculation of democracy in the cradle. Disenchantment with the Ikhwan was evident even within its own ranks, rendering some support for the 1996 article's claim that political inclusion may lead to diminishing returns for Islamist movements, sharpening their internal divisions and reducing their appeal to voters. The ousting of President Morsi by the military and civilian allies has not yet restored democracy as of late 2013 and the possibility of more violence remains. Volatile support for Islamist movements suggests that the "balloon theory" could be applicable to contemporary dynamics but there may not be enough cases yet that enable more systematic testing of that theory.

Another theme raised by the 1996 article and made even timelier by the 2011 uprisings relates to the Mansfield and Snyder (1995) hypothesis stipulating that former authoritarian states with increasing democratic participation are more likely to engage in wars than stable democracies or autocracies. Concerns with the "sudden transition–increased bellicosity" hypothesis resurfaced with a vengeance after 2011 although here again the limited time frame allows only for preliminary, tentative assessments of its applicability. Egypt's transition did not lead to the unraveling of treaty commitments with Israel, let alone war, even under President Morsi who accompanied his rhetoric of strong support for Hamas and his recall of

Egypt's ambassador to Israel with a truce with Israel. The constraints imposed by fear of economic collapse operated under Morsi at least as much as under Mubarak if not more, given greater demands for accountability by a mobilized electorate. Defective democratization in Iraq and elsewhere in the region forced attention to internal ethnic and economic cleavages as well. The Syrian regime's heightened aggressiveness toward neighboring countries is not a product of democratization but an extension of its ghastly aggression against its own citizens.

Beyond fueling internal and external conflict there was no evidence in 1996, and there is no evidence today, that more radical Islamist variants brought about any of the promised improvements in the lives of their citizens from Sudan to Iran. None have yielded more just, more equal, or more productive societies. Radical Islamist groups continue to fuel internal conflict from Iraq to Syria, Iran, and the Gulf and throughout North Africa. They also remain at the vanguard of fratricidal of Sunni–Shi'a wars and the opposition to Arab–Israeli reconciliation. Sudan's regime resumed genocidal wars at home and aggressive regional policies. Following Israel's 2005 withdrawal from Gaza, Hamas violently ejected Fatah competitors and launched persistent missile attacks on Israeli civilians that led, in turn, to Israeli military offensives in Gaza. Western hesitance to support Syria's uprising against Bashar Assad's brutal dictatorship stemmed in part from concerns that Al-Qaida affiliates may replace Assad, though some considered this a self-fulfilling policy. An ever more radical regime in the Islamic Republic of Iran exacerbated conflict in Syria, Lebanon, Gaza, and the Gulf; engaged in terrorism within the region and beyond; developed conventional and unconventional weapons in violation of its international legal obligations; and threatened to obliterate Israel, unleashing reactive Israeli counter-threats to eliminate Iran's nuclear weapons. The 2009 Iranian elections brought greater repression and elimination of thousands of regime opponents. The 2013 elections revealed popular exhaustion with the regime's dismal economic performance, autocratic nature, and aggressive international defiance. President Hassan Rouhani unleashed a diplomatic turnaround leading to an unprecedented interim agreement with the P5+1 on the nuclear file. It remains unclear whether recalcitrant inward-looking opponents will allow a shift in Iran's domestic and foreign policies (Solingen 2012a, 2012b), including changes toward democratization.

The original article also reflected on Netanyahu's triumph in the 1996 Israeli elections following terrorist campaigns by radical Islamist groups. Replacing the internationalizing Labor–Meretz coalition that produced the Oslo accords, Netanyahu's went on to dismantle them with enduring negative effects on Israeli politics and the peace process. The claim that "Benjamin Netanyahu's coalition is likely to burden the Palestinian Authority with new challenges" was as true in 1996 as it is today. The strategically interactive dynamic that mutually buttressed the extremes in both Israel and Palestine have become ever more dominant, narrowing down the window for the two-state solution envisaged in the Oslo accords, albeit not shutting it down completely. As noted in the 1996 piece, Israeli coalitions under the stranglehold of radical religious and secular nationalist parties also tightened the spheres of civil rights for women, minorities, and reformist strands of Judaism. Bastions of civil liberties and accommodation with Israel's neighbors – from the Supreme Court to selected media – have endured relentless challenges. Despite efforts by extremists to drive Israel closer to the standards of a region known to suppress democratic rights, Israel remains a vibrant democracy within its 1967 borders, with constitutional protections for free political expression, sexual orientations, and religious freedom.

The quandary in the 1996 title remains valid for 2014: Will democratization lead to democracy or theocracy? The geographic scope and depth of the 2011 uprising has so far been limited, although it has leapt to a monumental struggle in Syria, which has now engulfed the region in a war by proxies. At least part of the answer hinges, as in 1996, on whether current regimes – democratizing or otherwise – can incept genuine internationalizing reforms of the kind they resisted for decades. The Mubarak era is sometimes conflated with "neoliberal reforms" but East-Asia style openness to the global economy and attentive to distributive issues has yet to reach most of the Middle East. Turkey, Tunisia, Jordan, Morocco, Iraq, Lebanon and some Gulf sheikhdoms have, to varying degrees, made important strides in the direction of economic openness and in some cases democratization as well. The conclusions in the 1996 piece remain apt:

> None of this is to say that regimes currently undergoing democratization are destined to regress toward authoritarian populism, Islamist or nationalist. The prospects of such regression increase when market-based reforms fail to transform the economies of the region. Economic restructuring is central to the connection between peace and democratization in the Middle East.
> (Solingen 1996: 150)

Chapter 2 (this volume) also noted that stabilization programs often led to recessions, reduced public subsidies and infrastructural investments, and that reductions in staple subsidies had led to food riots in Egypt and elsewhere creating conditions for an inward-looking turn. This sequence may have become reality in some of the cases leading to the 2011 uprisings.

The issue of sequences between political and economic reform resurfaces in Chapter 7 (Economic and Political Liberalization in China: Implications for US–China Relations) adapted from a collaborative volume sponsored by Harvard University's Belfer Center and the Chinese Academy of Social Sciences. The relationship between economic openness and regional cooperation, examined earlier for the Middle East, is also under scrutiny here. A major difference between the two regions, however, lies in the fact that China's leadership advanced internationalization for a sustained period of over three decades. Some neorealist scholarship has associated China's dramatic economic rise with predictions that a "power transition" will inevitably lead to defiance, regional and global hegemonic aspirations, and war. Yet choices between presumed atavistic tendencies toward war or peaceful alternatives exist and they largely hang on the domestic competition between internationalizing and inward-looking models vying for political dominance in various East Asian states. On the ashes of a Maoist autarchic model, Deng Xiaoping and his successors have moved China along an internationalizing path that benefited from a strategy of "peaceful rise," "peaceful development," and "charm offensives" launching a new matrix of relations with neighbors and openness to multilateral and regional institutional arrangements.[15] From the perspective of the architects of this model, regional and global instability were anathema to luring foreign investment, natural resources, and broad international acceptability, without which continued economic growth and domestic political stability would be threatened. An internationalizing China would pave the road to *xiaokang shehui*, a "well-off" society endowed with a majoritarian middle class (Shirk 2007). However, less charming offensives surfaced in recent years in China's relations with neighbors in the South and East China seas. As might be expected given this volume's general framework, the volatility in the charm index can be traced to protracted domestic competition between forces backing one model or the other.

When, whether, and how China might transition to a democratic system are known unknowns. Chapter 4 in *Regional Orders* (not reprinted in this volume) surveys different paths and temporal sequences followed by states regarding twin transitions to economic and political reform. For resilient inward-looking Middle East autocracies, as discussed earlier, the transition has been hard to attain on both axes. Democratic India continues its intermittent transition into an internationalizing model whereas autocratic Singapore has forged a paradigmatic internationalizing state. Internationalizing autocracies in Taiwan, South Korea, Turkey and Chile evolved into internationalizing democracies. And so on. China's internationalizing coalition has thus far prevailed over domestic forces favoring a return to closure yet concerns remain that democratization could empower farmers, local officials, and those segments of the military, state enterprises and Communist party that have been adversely affected by economic openness. An economic downturn could multiply the power of inward-looking forces as can economic inequality, corruption, environmental threats, inadequate social safety nets and the challenges of rural reform and urbanization, rising unemployment, an aging population, tensions between central and local interests and other bottlenecks on the road to sustainable development.

The assumption that there have been no losers, no demands for political change, and that nationalism can always deflate domestic criticism is questionable. Furthermore, the Mansfield and Snyder (2005) hypothesis predicts more aggressive foreign policies during democratization and urge the consolidation of democratic institutions – rule of law, independent courts, property rights, impartial and efficient administration, and an independent mass media – as barriers against reliance on nationalism for political survival. Mobilizing nationalist support as a rallying theme is invariably a double-edged sword – in democracies and autocracies alike. In line with this volume's overall findings, clusters of internationalizing democracies are better equipped to stay an internationalizing and cooperative course. By contrast, a potential overlap between pro-democracy, nationalist, and economic protectionist forces in democratizing states bodes less well for regional stability and cooperation.

Regional institutions: Sources, design and effects

Part III probes the relationship between domestic coalitions and regional institutions. Although *Regional Orders* was originally conceived to explain broader patterns of regional conflict and cooperation, subsequent work explored the argument's implications for regional institutions. In brief, internationalizing regions are generally cooperative but do not require regional economic or political integration à la EU. The underlying logic of internationalizing orders is global; the emergence of peaceful regional orders does not hinge on regional economic or institutionalized interdependence. At the heart of such orders are preferences for regional cooperation and stability that enable common objectives: foreign investment, global economic access, domestic economic reform and controlled military expenditures. Such orders may lead to increasing regional trade and investment and to institutions attuned to market-friendly "open regionalism" that lubricate ties to the global economy. Yet those institutions may be thin and informal. More formal and legalized ones may emerge but need not be side-products of prior economic regionalization.[16] Internationalizing regional clusters can indeed lock in preferences through more formal institutions but can also cooperate in their absence. By contrast, as Chapter 3 of this volume describes in greater detail, regional institutions in inward-looking clusters typically help perpetuate statist, protectionist, and militarized political economies and are hence unsuitable for preventing militarized conflicts, sometimes exacerbating them.

Chapter 8, adapted from *International Studies Quarterly* (2008), explores those connections in the context of a broader theoretical analysis of regional institutions. The chapter generates hypotheses on scope conditions under which different theories might be most useful for explaining the genesis, design and effects of such institutions, an approach to cross-paradigmatic research inspired by March and Olsen (1998). The first hypothesis holds that the nature and strength of dominant domestic coalitions best explains the *origins* of regional institutions under the following conditions: when the domestic distributional implications of creating those institutions are clear to relevant actors; when the consequences for regional power distribution are negligible or unclear; when state-level transaction costs are unclear or not easily measurable; and when there is little normative convergence around the demand for an institution. The second hypothesis stipulates that the nature and strength of domestic coalitions best explains regional institutional *design* when: the domestic distributional implications of design are clear to relevant actors; consequences for power distribution across states are negligible or unclear; variations in institutional design have little effect on transaction costs or such costs are not easily measurable; and when there is little normative convergence around a favored design. The third hypothesis specifies regional institutional *effects*, which are more likely to benefit the dominant domestic coalitions that created those institutions when: the domestic distributional effects of institutions are both sizeable and clear to dominant actors; institutional effects on power distribution across states are negligible or unclear; effects on reducing states' transaction costs are modest or not easily measurable; and effects on already weak normative convergence are marginal.

Following a discussion of the logic of case selection, Chapter 8 examines those hypotheses in four empirical contexts: ASEAN, the Asia-Pacific Economic Cooperation (APEC), the ASEAN Regional Forum (ARF), and the League of Arab States (League, henceforth). Findings suggest that domestic coalitions are crucial for explaining institutional genesis in these cases. ASEAN, APEC, and the League match the circumstances outlined by the first baseline hypothesis, privileging domestic coalitions as explanations under conditions of low normative convergence and negligible consequences for relative power and transaction costs. ASEAN's creation begins with incipient internationalizers seeking to grow their economies via the global economy. That strategy created incentives to nurture a stable and peaceful regional environment, minimize military expenditures that burden economic reform, and avoid policies inimical to macroeconomic instability. Internationalizing models invented ASEAN: the incentives to dampen conflict were logically prior to the institution itself. The same is true for ARF although one might also argue that its creation was congruent with normative and instrumental convergence around war avoidance and common security among big powers and smaller states (Johnston 2008). Neorealist versions of institutional origins that hinge on hegemony face difficulties in East Asia where middle powers and smaller states drove the process toward institutionalization. Weaker states were not mere institution-takers here. The League materialized under conditions of very low economic interdependence, and its consequences for power distribution across states were unclear at its inception. Ruling coalitions created it to protect themselves from competing pan-Arab nationalist agendas, regional or home-grown, as a means to reduce pressures for unification while foiling the latter at the same time.

Regarding the second hypothesis, only APEC's blueprint matches conditions where domestic coalitions do much of the explanatory work: internationalizing coalitions compromised over an informal APEC that accommodated diverse stages and forms of economic liberalization, export-led growth, and regime-type. Domestic coalitions, however, appear under-determining in explaining the design of ASEAN, ARF and the League. These institutions were compatible with the preferences of dominant coalitions to be sure but those preferences were in some cases also compatible with other designs. Furthermore, baseline conditions privileging domestic coalitions in explaining design were absent in these cases: the implications of design for relative power, transaction costs, and norms were not negligible. These three variables too were under-determining, i.e. compatible with alternative designs. Said differently, ASEAN's and the ARF's informal designs were well-suited to growth-oriented domestic coalitions, low normative convergence, and preventing hegemonic dominance. The League's informal design was over-determined by ruling coalitions' preferences and efforts to stem hegemonic aspirations and pan-Arab norms of formal unity. The informal, sovereignty-sensitive nature of all four institutions conforms to neorealist premises that only powerful states can endow institutions with binding procedures. Yet, counter to those premises, the consensus rule across both regions precluded would-be hegemons from advancing their agenda at the expense of other members.

Domestic models thus offer only a baseline for understanding institutional design, albeit an important one at that. East Asian regional institutions were not rigid and legalistic but, in Goldilocks fashion, "just right," accommodating diverse internationalizing models. Beyond shared commitment to "open regionalism," the coalitional logic provides internationalizers with wide-ranging institutional options. Consensus-oriented, informal means to advance confidence-building measures; the plethora of routine meetings endemic to East Asia; bilateral, plurilateral and multilateral free trade agreements; and unilateral liberalization enabling self-binding commitments that facilitate diffuse reciprocity, are all synergistic with efforts to enhance regional stability. From this standpoint, formal institutions may not be required. Yet Southeast Asia has not been completely inimical to legalizing verification and compliance mechanisms as evident in the Bangkok Treaty Nuclear-Weapon-Free-Zone allowing referral to the International Court of Justice and additional recent developments (Johnston 2008). The League, reflecting the entrenched inward-looking strategies of its makers, was antithetical to "open regionalism" but changes among some of its membership could alter older patterns in the future.

Finally, findings validate the hypothesis on institutional effects: all four institutions benefited their creators but only ASEAN and the League privilege domestic coalitions as explanations. The League largely delivered what its creators' intended: a non-intrusive institution that paid lip service to Arab unity. APEC and the ARF delivered little (in tandem with dominant coalitional preferences) although APEC arguably helped diffused normative consensus around "open regionalism" and market-driven liberalization (inextricable from coalitional preferences). ARF statements matched coalitional preferences for regional peace and stability but its institutional effects were marginal beyond developing "habits of cooperation," for instance in China (Johnston 2008). One might conceive of East Asian institutions as constructing an identity pivoted on global markets and institutions. Yet the empirical causal arrow goes in the other direction – from domestic preferences to institutions. Furthermore, standard constructivist studies have not emphasized internationalizing identities but rather (highly contested) uniquely "Asian values," sovereignty and non-intervention. Nor does relative power explain these institutions' emergence and evolution or why they were able to anchor, tame, or coopt would-be hegemons. Overall institutional effects were limited, yet hegemonic preferences changed from pre- to post-institutional settings for APEC and the ARF (Krauss and Pempel 2003). Furthermore, ASEAN-based institutions paved the way for ASEAN Plus 3, the East Asian Summit and other institutional contexts. Ironically, "Asianness" was an unanticipated regional by-product of internationalizing coalitions primarily oriented to the global economy.

In sum, for the cases under scrutiny the nature of dominant coalitions explains incentives to create institutions, mold them according to their preferences, and fine-tune their effects.[17] However, baseline forms of these hypotheses assume that institutional consequences for power, transaction costs, and norms are negligible or hard to estimate. Those conditions were not met about half of the time, when such consequences were sizeable. Furthermore, coalitional preferences were often compatible with different institutional outcomes and provided no more than permissive conditions for the emergence, design, and effect of institutions. While generally benefiting the domestic coalitions that gave them life, institutions also had unintended and unanticipated effects. Domestic models, while well-suited to explain incentives to create institutions, do not singlehandedly determine their design; power, ideas, and efficiency considerations can be relevant sources of institutional variation. Even with those caveats, findings question exclusive attention to power, transaction costs and norms in standard accounts of regional institutions, which obscure deeper drivers underlying their emergence, design and effects. Interpretations rooted in coalitional or other domestic frameworks provide more complete insights into why institutions emerge, in whose interest they operate, when they are allowed to play a significant role, and why they may not be vital to regional cooperation.

Above all, the hypotheses examined in Chapter 8 do not assume that domestic coalitional models self-evidently "dominate" other explanations. Indeed hypotheses stipulating scope conditions similar to the ones advanced here can be crafted with alternative analytical points of departure hinging on norms, power or efficiency. Studies along these lines can advance a comparative research agenda that puts extant literature to work in more productive and inclusive ways than do conventional paradigmatic studies of regional institutions. Findings also drive home the shared absence of formal legalized regional institutions that sets the EU apart from all other regions. Formal institutions may be less compelling under various conditions, including when members' time-horizons are long, gains from cooperation are repetitive, uncertainty about future benefits is rampant, imperfect information and incentives to defect are widespread, peer pressure is important, less public scrutiny is preferable, competing bureaucratic pressures can foil cooperation, and when flexibility is required to cope with changing conditions (Lipson 1991; Harris 2000). Many an international institution is designed with exactly those ubiquitous criteria in mind. Furthermore, ample information (pivotal to functional accounts) and robust trust (pivotal to norm-based accounts) can obviate the need for formal institutions. Regional institutions beyond the EU are thus no empirical anomalies but average practice.[18]

Chapter 9 examines another informal institution, joining together an internationalizing regional cluster (the EU) with a predominantly inward-looking Middle East/North Africa (MENA) region. The Barcelona Process Initiative emerged as part of a broader EU evolution in the post-Cold War era involving outward spatial and functional expansion in tandem with efforts to forge a common foreign policy. EU concerns with the fate of the Mediterranean basin (*Mare Nostrum*) stemmed from both classical security considerations regarding non-conventional weapons, terrorism, and natural resources as well as "new" security issues including migration, drugs, human rights violations, environmental degradation and others. In a wide-ranging 1991 survey of security dimensions of European integration, then President of the European Commission Jacques Delors identified the need for Europe's "Southern flank" (the Maghreb, the Mashreq and the Middle East) to develop economically as a prerequisite for achieving peace and stability in the region. The Barcelona Declaration or European–Mediterranean Partnership (EMP) launched efforts to institutionalize relations between the more affluent North (EU) and the effervescent South (12 MENA states) as a means to manage those wide socio-economic, political, and cultural differences.

Three main processes discussed thus far for other regions were crucially important for enhancing cooperation across this mixed regional cluster of internationalizing and inward-looking states. Internationalizing economic reforms, democratization, and the role of regional institutions were rather incipient in Southern Mediterranean states, with important implications for European states.

Hence the development of markets, democracy, and regional institutions provided the "triple logic" or foundational rationale for the joint EMP enterprise. The inherent wisdom, desirability, and motivations behind each of these logics were heavily contested largely because of their domestic distributional effects North and South of the Mediterranean. Different economic and political sectors in each state had different incentives regarding the opportunities and constraints of market reform, for instance. Specific sectoral (agricultural) and other interests also shaped competing agendas for EU states. The chapter examines some dilemmas embedded in the assumptions and performance of the Barcelona process, including the entrenched nature of inward-looking coalitions not only among radical Islamist challengers but also among secular regimes such as Syria's. Notwithstanding EU investments in this institutional framework, which in 2008 evolved into the Union for the Mediterranean, it would be difficult to argue that EU efforts played a major role in the 2011 Arab uprisings. The latter were the product of a much more complex set of factors brewing primarily out of the stagnation and exhaustion of inward-looking models described earlier. An internationalizing critical mass à la ASEAN can overturn the domestic coalitional competition within inward-looking regimes easing their eventual transformation and inclusion. There is much skepticism, however, regarding the odds that such critical mass can be achieved in the Middle East anytime soon. The "triple logic" or three pillars underpinning the EMP were incipient at the time of its creation and remain so today.

Regional security trajectories

Part 4 extends the explanatory framework, concepts and themes explored in previous sections to a different dependent variable: regional nuclear orders. Taking stock of findings from nine empirical chapters in *Nuclear Logics*,[19] the conclusions in Chapter 10 address two interrelated questions. The first takes up the broader theoretical debate on why some states have sought nuclear weapons since the Nonproliferation Treaty (NPT) entered into force in 1970 whereas other states have renounced them. The second extends the puzzle of diverging trajectories in the Middle East and East Asia to the nuclear arena.[20] Since 1970 several Middle East states sought nuclear weapons; by contrast, the ones alleged to have been most likely to do so in East Asia avoided them. North Korea, an anomaly in East Asia in the post-NPT era, acquired them; Egypt, a conspicuous anomaly in the Middle East given its leading regional role, abstained from doing so. Coalitional analysis helps explain motivations for or against nuclear weapons, diverging regional patterns and anomalies. Before deploying the approach to understand these two regions, however, the chapter reviews advantages and shortcomings of conventional explanations for why states acquire or refrain from acquiring nuclear weapons.[21]

Neorealist literature traces nuclearization to international structure, anarchy, self-help, relative power, and balance of power. The domestic nature of states, regimes, groups, or individuals, in that view, is irrelevant to nuclear decisions and outcomes. Yet the nine empirical chapters in *Nuclear Logics* suggest that neorealism fails to explain several cases, is incomplete in explaining others, competes in every case with alternative explanations in what should be its best arena of argumentation, suffers from under-determination (leads to multiple possible outcomes), and is unfalsifiable (too many options can be made to fit vague notions of security maximization a posteriori). Security predicaments may be important sources of nuclear behavior but reducing nuclear tendencies to this rubric leads to analytic overestimations of *state* security (rather than *regime* security) as *the* exclusive source of nuclearization. Concerns with existential security are never perfunctory reflections of structural considerations invariably leading to power maximization and nuclearization. Domestic filters convert those considerations into different policies even under similar structural conditions.

Several acutely vulnerable states have not acquired nuclear weapons. Even states whose rivals did acquire them did not always respond in kind, such as most European states but also Egypt, Taiwan, South Korea, Japan, Vietnam, Jordan, and many others. There are too many "dogs that didn't bark" or states that faced vulnerabilities but chose to forgo nuclear weapons. "Insecurity" – an elusive concept – is not a sufficient condition for acquiring them; many insecure states have not. Indeed insecurity may not even be necessary: states without *existential* threats have considered or pursued nuclear weapons (Argentina, Brazil, Algeria, Iraq or Libya in the 1970s). Changes in East Asia's power distribution over recent decades (the rise of China, North Korea's nuclearization) should have altered the region's nuclear map according to the theory; more states should have gone nuclear but have not done so. Some invoke the role of alliances or superpower coercion in explaining East Asian cases. However, hegemonic protection did not have similar effects in too many other cases. US, Soviet, and Chinese coercion did not succeed in North Korea, Iran, Israel, Pakistan, and, for many years, in Iraq. Coercion played virtually no role in nuclear reversals in Argentina, Brazil, and South Africa. Furthermore, states reversed nuclear ambitions even without superpower guarantees: Egypt, Libya (2003), South Africa, Argentina, Brazil. This non-trivial number of anomalies leads to two conclusions: acute vulnerabilities may be neither necessary nor sufficient for acquiring nuclear weapons; and hegemonic protection may be neither necessary nor sufficient to relinquish them.

How can one explain the dominance of neorealism on this issue given its analytical and empirical deficiencies? It stemmed partially from the broader dominance of the approach in security studies for many decades and its path-dependent legacy despite its noteworthy decline among competing intellectual paradigms (Vasquez 1998; Legro and Moravcsik 1999). It also stemmed from problems of evidence collection afflicting nonproliferation studies that may have led to biased inferences. Leaders and government officials have incentives to justify nuclear decisions in terms of "reasons of state," knowing that both domestic and international audiences consider them more legitimate than parochial domestic reasons. Analysts thus find more "evidence" for the role of neorealist variables in leaders' statements and justifications along those lines, and the secondary literature reinforces that focus. But in-depth analyses of North Korea, Iraq, Libya, post-1991 Iran and others clearly suggest that nuclear weapons programs were driven more by *regime* than state insecurity. Yet the latter, not the former, has been the staple of neorealist accounts of nuclearization. Cumulative conceptual and empirical challenges have helped overturn this once-dominant conventional wisdom. The most important frontier for understanding nuclear choices and outcomes is the relationship between domestic and external political survival.

So why would this be such a significant challenge for neorealism? Because, in addition to the shortcomings listed above, the theory's performance is deficient precisely in what should be its best arena of argumentation. Given its basic tenets, it follows that the ultimate strategic behavior (states' nuclear choices) must have an ultimate structural strategic source. If reality proves this expectation to be far more tenuous empirically or analytically than previously assumed, the theory's validity suffers. Another way to think of this is to underscore that nuclear behavior provides an easy ground for testing theories of relative power and state security under anarchy. Since nuclear weapons are presumably at the heart, the inner sanctum of states' security dilemmas, the study of why states acquire or renounce them is arguably the most favorable domain for corroborating neorealist canons. The topic loads the dice in favor of neorealism. Yet, the very fact that nuclear behavior as a subject-matter favors neorealism in principle, ironically does not make nuclear decisions an optimal arena for validating its canons, methodologically speaking. A good or crucial test of any theory is one that forces it to survive unfavorable conditions. A theory that can be confirmed despite adverse circumstances gains significant analytical traction. A theory that cannot be easily confirmed even under the best circumstances suggests serious problems.

Neoliberal institutionalist perspectives emphasize that states join institutions because they serve their interests and are less costly than relying on self-help. Accordingly, a rather unquestioned lore has assigned critical weight to the Nonproliferation Regime (NPR) as explaining abstention from nuclear weapons. The NPR has indeed performed some of the functions attributed to institutions that might influence the nuclear calculus of states. Yet the relationship between NPR rules and state compliance requires a deeper understanding of the domestic politics explaining disparate patterns of compliance with its injunctions. Furthermore, we do not have a systematic empirical foundation for assessing the extent to which the NPR has played a central role in most states' decisions to abstain from developing nuclear weapons. Collecting such evidence would entail a massive historical project gauging systematically the ways in which the regime changed the calculations of most states now party to the NPT away from nuclear weapons. What we do have is sometimes circumstantial – at other times more robust – evidence that it may have played some role in particular cases but not others ones. States may have joined the NPT for a wide range of reasons, including domestic ones. Whether more states would have opted for nuclear weapons in the NPT's absence remains an important counterfactual hypothesis.

Constructivist perspectives stress the effects of international institutions and norms as socialization processes. States join institutions because they share common purposes and beliefs, including presumed revulsion against nuclear weapons after Hiroshima and Nagasaki. Yet the approach cannot explain many historical choices for or against nuclear weapons. If a strong universal norm or taboo against nuclear weapons acquisition (as different from use) developed since Nagasaki, the theory must explain why many states still either acquired them or considered acquisition. At least thirty, and perhaps more, actively considered them (many after the NPT's conclusion); others violated NPT commitments; the South Asian and North Korean nuclear tests, and Iran's nuclear violations were met with widespread moral indifference. No systematic account validating the role of norms is yet available for all cases that considered or abstained from acquiring nuclear weapons.

Japan's "nuclear allergy" is often considered the poster child for normative explanations. An important pacifist movement undoubtedly sensitized Japan's leaders to such considerations. Yet fateful decisions in the 1960s–1970s may not be so easily traced to anti-nuclear norms. Japan took eighteen months to sign the NPT following its 1970 adoption (and longer since the agreement was reached in 1968); it attached an unusual addendum to its signature taking note of Article X of the NPT allowing legal withdrawal three months after notification; and it delayed ratification by nearly seven years. Furthermore, Japan conducted various studies on nuclear options since 1968 suggesting that nuclear weapons acquisition – although unlikely – was less than a taboo. Nor do surveys and archives suggest that nuclear weapons were "unthinkable." Most importantly, opponents of nuclear weapons regarded the US–Japan alliance as "embedded nuclearization," with Japan's defense resting on the US nuclear umbrella. Institutional restraints such as the Atomic Energy Law and Three Non-Nuclear Principles (which never became law) had significant force but there was continuous contestation over interpretations of Article 9 of the Constitution, which renounced the right of belligerency but not explicitly reliance on nuclear weapons. Premier Sato was awarded the Nobel Peace Prize for Japan's Non-Nuclear Principles but archival evidence suggests that he personally may have favored nuclear weapons for Japan.[22]

Japan was not alone in substituting US nuclear weapons for its own. South Korea and Taiwan also relied on US commitments, suggesting additional pragmatic compromises rather than principled condemnations of nuclear weapons. Indeed, all three countries encouraged the alliances and extracted repeated US pledges by occasionally insinuating that without them they might be forced to acquire indigenous deterrents. Common identity or ancestry (Chinese, Korean) were not dominant arguments against nuclear weapons. Nor were ethical considerations fundamental in other cases of abstention or reversal including Argentina, Brazil, Libya, South Africa, Egypt and various other Middle East cases, many of which had a poor record of compliance with WMD treaties in any event.

Do democratic institutions make a difference in decisions to develop or eschew nuclear weapons? Two potential generalizations can be made about the post-NPT era. First, no democracy appears to have considered or acquired nuclear weapons for the purpose of deterring other democracies. Two out of three non-NPT states are long-standing democracies – India and Israel – and they are surrounded by autocracies (India faces China and Pakistan, the latter an intermittent, unstable democracy). Second, most known NPT violators have been autocratic (Iraq, Iran, North Korea, Syria and Libya). Beyond that, the NPT and Nuclear-Weapons-Free-Zones were concluded by mixes of democracies and autocracies and sometimes in temporal and spatial domains with few democracies (Latin America, the South Pacific, Africa, and Southeast Asia). Moreover, autocratic leaders initiated unilateral denuclearization in Argentina, Brazil, Egypt, Kazakhstan, Belarus, Ukraine, South Korea, Taiwan, and other cases. And the vast majority of democracies and autocracies have abided by their NPT commitments. There is no record of democracies transferring nuclear weapons to terrorist organizations.

After reviewing the strengths and weaknesses of the four theories of international relations discussed thus far, Chapter 10 outlines the vital contributions of coalitional theory for explaining nuclear choices. Politicians and their supportive coalitions embrace different political-economy models of political survival with implications for nuclear choices. Internationalizers have incentives to avoid the political, economic, reputational and other costs of acquiring nuclear weapons because such costs impair a domestic agenda favoring economic growth via integration in the global economy. By contrast, inward-looking coalitions incur fewer costs and have greater incentives to exploit nuclear weapons as tools in nationalist platforms of political competition and survival in power. Under the specific "world historical time" incepted by the NPT (1970 onwards), the connection between models of political survival and nuclear choices finds support from systematic observations across different regional security contexts, diverse associations with hegemonic powers, and over successive leaderships within the same state. Rejection of nuclear weapons by states that had entertained them invariably entailed a domestic evolution toward internationalization. Such rejection has endured for decades even where the security context remains challenging, as in East Asia. Most defiant nuclear courses have been tools of choice of autarkic or inward-oriented models such as Perón's Argentina, North Korea's *juche*, India's *swadeshi*, and equivalents in Nasser's Egypt, Iraq, Iran, and pre-2003 Libya (and possibly Indonesia's Sukarno and Burma until recently).

Weak internationalizers have been more politically constrained in curbing nuclear programs, particularly in inward-looking regions. Whether a region's center of gravity is internationalizing or inward looking has implications for the range of possible choices. An internationalizing East Asia offered different incentives to coalitions in that region than a resilient inward-looking Middle East, which raised significant constraints for internationalizing models. US alliances made receptivity to denuclearization easier in some cases (Japan and South Korea) but this is different from arguing that alliances obviate nuclear weapons in a generic sense. US commitments to Japan, South Korea, and certainly to Taiwan were not absolute, inclusive, unlimited, or unconditional, never putting their security dilemmas to rest. Further, their choice for alliance over a self-reliant deterrent was made at particularly vulnerable times, with a US weakened by the Southeast Asian debacle and Nixon's diminished commitments to East Asian allies. Yet the requirements of internationalizing models made them more receptive to the alliance despite its deficiencies. Nuclear weapons would have seriously undermined economic growth, international competitiveness, and global access. Internationalizing models and alliances were thus mutually enabling. Inward-looking models were much less so: North Korea pursued nuclear weapons even under the war-tested protection of not one but two superpowers (China and the Soviet Union). One cannot understand why dilemmas of abandonment were so much more extreme in this case without dwelling on *juche*, the autarkic model of political survival nurtured by the Kims dynasty for decades. The role of formal alliances is mediated by the nature of domestic models, each with different receptivity to hegemonic inducements and coercion. Many internationalizers rejected nuclear weapons even in the absence of alliances or security guarantees.

In sum, models of political survival – at home and regionally – help explain competing nuclear preferences, why nuclear policies may vary over time in the same state; why different states vary in compliance with international legal commitments; why security dilemmas are more intractable in some cases than others; why some states ranked alliance higher than self-reliance or vice-versa; why nuclear weapons programs surfaced where security hardly justified them; and why they were avoided where one might have expected them. The omission of political-survival models in studies of nuclear proliferation has led to an overestimation of other causal variables. Its inclusion improves our understanding of the effects of security dilemmas, international norms and institutions. This is different from arguing that models are the only relevant variable; only that they enable a better understanding of the relative impact of other variables on nuclear choices (Sil and Katzenstein 2010; Solingen 2010b). The association between models of political survival and nuclear choices is not deterministic or inevitable; it suggests only a tendency: internationalizing models make the development of nuclear weapons less likely than inward-looking models. Or conversely, nuclear aspirants are more likely to emerge from domestic political landscapes dominated by inward-oriented models. These propositions are bounded, subject to regional scope conditions, and refutable. Nuclear behavior provides an extremely difficult arena for testing and validating the coalitional argument proposed here. The dice is loaded against it in many ways, which makes nuclear choices an ideal testing site. Theories must survive tough tests to gain validation and coalitional analysis does so even in this unlikely domain.[23]

Concluding reflections, regions in flux, a research agenda

The general framework for the comparative study of regionalism discussed in this volume offers some conceptual advantages. A single category (coalitions) incorporates other variables relevant to regional orders including globalization, nationalism, and patterns of military expenditures; operates at the vortex of international, regional, and domestic politics thus transcending levels-of-analysis; allows wide variation in the relationship between state and private actors across countries; grounds regional relations in a dynamic framework (coalitions develop, thrive, collapse, and reconstitute) as opposed to overly structural ones; has important implications for institutional expressions of regionalism; accommodates a wide range of methodological preferences yielding hypotheses testable through aggregate data or comparative cases; avoids overly-exceptionalist understanding of regions that render them incomparable; is no less suitable to the analysis of "great-powers" often considered a category of their own; and illuminates why regions may not be simply defined by basic geographical ontology. Coalitions subordinate (mutable) regional boundaries to their grand strategy. In other words, regions are in the eyes of coalitional beholders and therefore subject to continuous redefinition.

At the same time, even early versions of this framework recognized that the domestic impact of globalization is far more complex and unpredictable than stipulated by any single theory; that the coalitional cleavage stemming from globalization is ubiquitous and tends to attract others but is not the only important political cleavage; that the distance between Weberian ideal and empirical coalitional types can be extensive and hybrid forms abound; and that the argument could be persuasive in explaining the past yet less applicable under new scope conditions. While the basic features of the argument remain relevant today, new theoretical and empirical developments offer opportunities for further refinement, testing, qualifications and revisions. For instance, the evolution of regionalism and sub-regionalism in Africa over the last decade provides other contexts for gauging the argument's applicability.[24] The argument can also be extended backwards in history to explore why the nineteenth century wave of globalization could not stem the outbreak of World War I in Europe exactly 100 years ago.[25] This application provides an opportunity for testing assumptions regarding coalitional behavior under a different world-time, in the absence of the kind of international and regional institutions whose effects we can study today.

Contemporary tensions between China and Japan invite further exploration of the rise of hyper-nationalisms fueling a regional spiral. Such dynamics can become collectively stable in a regional cluster, feeding off each other and making it difficult to restore a prior equilibrium with lower conflict potential.[26] However East Asian nationalism competes with strong internationalizing currents that have profoundly transformed regional relations even in the presence of serious historical and territorial antagonisms (in the Korean peninsula, East and South China Sea and Taiwan Straits). A scenario of an inward-looking cluster growing dominant in East Asia and unleashing major war would align with theoretical expectations of the argument advanced here, as would the sustained absence of war under strong internationalizing coalitions. Two scenarios would challenge this framework's expectations: a strong inward-looking regional cluster that retreats from the global economy but deepens regional cooperation, and major war among strong internationalizers. As these scenarios make clear, expectations from coalitional analysis can be disconfirmed empirically. Furthermore, this open-endedness regarding coalitional futures separates this argument from teleological ones that consider internationalization to be linear and unproblematic, and inter-state wars outdated. The favorable global and regional circumstances that lubricated East Asia's model cannot be taken for granted; the model can be buffeted by shocks that deepen internal rifts and reverse coalitional balances. Although war has thus far been avoided, the ascent of nationalist leaders in Japan and stronger inward-looking constituencies in China may make armed conflict more possible.

The Great Recession is of particular relevance to a core argument that begins with domestic responses to globalization in order to draw some regional corollaries. Domestic coalitional landscapes are not merely derivative of global forces yet; international economic and security regimes influence those coalitional balances. As a natural (if unfortunate) experiment, the global crisis introduced a shock of major proportions with potential for affecting coalitional evolutions worldwide and, with them, regional outcomes. It was more difficult to imagine crisis scenarios of this sort while writing in the mid-1990s, a golden age of globalization. Yet the original chapters in *Regional Orders* noted the vulnerabilities of internationalizing models, later exposed in 2007–8.[27] They thus warned against severe unintended crises that might be triggered by an international environment that may seem generally favorable to internationalizing coalitions; by painful transitions and the burden of recessions, unemployment, and reduced public subsidies; by insufficient attention to highly concentrated benefits of some internationalizing models; and by financial structures and obsolescent capital controls that enable evasion and exit. The concluding chapter in *Regional Orders* (not included in this volume) made the case even more forcefully, warning against both myopic economic reforms and myopic inward-looking nationalism.

As these points make clear, the argument assumed that competing incentives would drive coalitions into diverging regional preferences which, in turn, would have implications for a regional cluster's overall proneness to conflict and cooperation. However, it made no generic assumptions regarding the association between coalitional type and "good governance," ethical standards, sensitivity to human rights, environmental policies or other outcomes.[28] It did point out that the survival of internationalizing coalitions required that the benefits from integration in the global economy be broadened through compensatory safety nets. It also suggested that significantly reduced military budgets would not only improve conditions for regional cooperation but would also extinguish a historical source of domestic political power in industrializing states (i.e. the military). Those considerations remain valid today.

Finally, models of political survival and the regional clusters they create diffuse within and across regions through rational learning, emulation, competition, socialization, and various other mechanisms, including international institutions. We have much more to learn about who learned or emulated, when and why (even if they did not succeed), who did not and on what grounds, and why the cycling of models recurs. The ideal-typical East Asian models described here were themselves partially the product of diffusion from within and beyond the region, as well as of internal legacies.[29] In turn, ruling coalitions from Turkey to Brazil adapted components of East Asian models whereas elsewhere in those same regions enduring inward-looking models erected firewalls against internationalization. Patterns of intra- and extra-regional diffusion are thus another research frontier in the comparative study of regions and regionalism. Particularly prone to intra-regional contagious diffusion is hyper-nationalism which, far from vanishing with globalization, continues to raise its hydra-like regenerative tentacles into the twenty-first century.

Notes

1 Solingen (1998). I use regionalism here to refer broadly to the organization of regional orders in economics and security along the conflict–cooperation spectrum. This usage subsumes what is sometimes labelled "regionalization" (increased regional economic and other exchange) as well as the analysis of regional institutions. It thus transcends a contested distinction between regionalization as driven by market forces and regionalism as driven by political forces which, although useful in some ways, also obscures the ways in which politics underlies regionalization and markets create conditions for the emergence and design of institutions. See also Higgott (1997).
2 Some works begin by acknowledging this trap but proceed nonetheless to undertake that very comparison.

3   Ironically, a leading theoretician of European integration, Ernst Haas, warned against applying the European integration model to other regions, arguing that "if regional integration continues to go forward in these areas [outside of Europe], it will obey impulses peculiar to them and thus fail to demonstrate any universal 'law of integration' deduced from the European example" (Haas 1961: 389). Moreover, Haas did not consider formal structures to be good guides for predicting outcomes, acknowledging instead the role of domestic interest group competition, perceived interests, capitalist social democracy and pluralism as drivers (Haas 1958; Ruggie et al. 2005).

4   For overviews, see Väyrynen (2003), Katzenstein (2005), Fawn (2009), Mansfield and Solingen (2010), Powers and Goertz (2011), and De Lombaerde and Soderbaum (2014).

5   Breuning et al. (2005); Johnston (2008).

6   Internationalization involves the progressive expansion of international markets, institutions and norms into the domestic politics of states. It is not simply about what [growing] percentage of a state's GDP is accounted for by international activities and about the political implications thereof, but also about what [growing] fraction of domestic issues becomes affected by international regimes, institutions, and values relative to the past.

7   The suffix internationalizing indicates a process, a path, an approximation that never quite matches the ideal-type. Earlier work in this volume uses the term statist-nationalist to refer to "inward-looking" coalitions.

8   For an overview, see Solingen (2009). See also Rosecrance (1986, 1999).

9   On the continental divide between the progressively more inward-looking Mercosur and the more internationalizing Pacific Alliance (Chile, Peru, Colombia and Mexico), see Malnight and Solingen (2014). On broader sources of regionalism in Latin America, see Tussie (2009).

10 For a detailed analysis of distinct trajectories of regime-type and models of political survival, see *Regional Orders* Chapter 4 (not included here). On democratic peace theory, see Solingen (2001a).

11 Kahler (1995, 2000) warned that more has been made of "common norms" in East Asia than is borne by reality and evidence.

12 On historical institutionalist, path-dependent dimensions of these trajectories, see Solingen and Wan (2014).

13 Dodge (2002). Of 48 militarized regional conflicts between 1965 and 2006, 41 involved Arab–Iranian, inter-Arab, and Turkish-Cypriot dyads. The Iran–Iraq, Iraq–Kuwait/Saudi Arabia, and Morocco–Polisario wars accounted for the bulk of casualties, the only interstate wars with over 10,000 casualties since 1973. Seven (of 48) militarized conflicts involved Israel; three of those against Syria and Hezbollah after 1973. Gulf Cooperation Council Secretary General Abdalla Bishara remarked that the basic threat to Gulf states were other Arab states, not Israel (Korany 1994: 66). More recently the Council defined Iran as the most serious threat. Iran was involved in five militarized incidents; the Iran–Iraq war alone – initiated by Iraq – resulted in 500,000 to 1 million deaths. Turkey was involved in 3 militarized conflicts; the 1974 Cyprus invasion – which pointedly preceded Özal's inception of export-led growth – involved thousands of casualties.

14 For a comprehensive overview of the multilateral regional process, see Solingen (2000).

15 On implications of internationalization for China's approach to sovereignty, sanctions, and regional relations, and on outstanding inward-looking challengers, see Solingen (2013 and 2014) respectively.

16 Kahler (2000) noted the compatibility between internationalizing coalitions and legalized institutions.

17 One would be hard pressed to conceive of counterfactual outcomes where, for instance, dominant inward-looking coalitions in East Asia would have converged on "open regionalism." Indeed the empirical evidence suggests that no such convergence emerged in earlier, inward-looking periods.

18 Enhancing information was not central even for the EU (Moravcsik 1998).
19 Princeton University Press (Solingen 2007c).
20 Chapter 1 in *Nuclear Logics* (not included here) discusses at least nine advantages from a focused comparison between the two regions that is sensitive to methodological issues in comparative analysis, case selection, and research design.
21 Approaches leaning on domestic sources of nuclear choices were a rarity in the early 1990s in a literature dominated by deterrence theory. For an early account of domestic drivers, see Solingen (1994a, 1994b). The latter explains the absence of a nuclear regime in the Middle East and the paths that could lead to one in the future, a timely topic in light of proposed contemporary schemes for a Middle East WMD-free zone. For further elaboration and critiques of various approaches to nuclear acquisition and abstention, see Wan and Solingen (forthcoming).
22 For further details, see Chapter 3 in Solingen (2007c: *Nuclear Logics*) and Solingen (2010a).
23 Potter and Mukhatzhanova (2008) find the argument to be "the cutting edge of nonproliferation research."
24 I thank Kathleen Hancock, who found preliminary support for the argument in African contexts, for this insight. The argument has also informed applications (not included in this volume) to the Europeanization and internationalization of Eastern European states; Turkey; Venezuela and the Southern Cone of Latin America; Southeast Asia and Northeast Asia (Petrovic and Solingen 2005; Solingen and Ozyurt 2006; Rosecrance, Solingen and Stein 2006; Solingen 2001c, 2004, 2005a, 2005b, 2006, 2012c; Malnight and Solingen 2014).
25 The 1914 strategic cluster arguably provides a most likely case for confirming inward-looking proneness to war (Solingen 2014).
26 Repeated neorealist predictions of impending war in East Asia for at least the last three decades have failed to materialize thus far, requiring further specifications of the additional structural variables that would account for war now but not earlier.
27 See Chapters 2, 3 and 4 in the current volume, including Table 2.1 in Chapter 2.
28 The United Nations Development Program's 2013 Human Development Report (p. 74) suggests that "there is no evidence that in the post-war period inward-looking economies have systematically developed faster than those that have been more open." It also points out that states that integrated into the world economy gradually and sequentially have also been best performers in socio-economic and educational criteria between 1990 and 2012.
29 Strategies of deeper engagement with the global economy in the latter part of the 20th century diffused within East Asia far earlier than among other regions (Solingen 2012d; Jetschke and Lenz 2013).

PART I
Globalization, economic reform, and regional relations

2
INTERNATIONALIZATION AND DOMESTIC COALITIONS

The theoretical framework outlined in *Regional Orders* (Solingen 1998) builds on the underlying assumption that the kinds of ties binding different domestic political actors to global processes affect the ways in which these actors identify their preferences, whether material or ideal.[1] Domestic considerations are, as is often recognized, most influential in the definition of preferences. Quite often, however, global and domestic processes are inextricable, as in the case of economic liberalization. Safeguarding a certain preference or value requires the formulation of policies that often span the domestic, regional, and global spheres. Political actors – institutions, interest associations, state agencies, political parties, religious groups, social movements – aggregate those preferences and cloak them in ideological cloth. Political entrepreneurs, individually or through institutions under their control, rely on their actual or potential organizational capacities and popularity in order to broker coalitions among relevant actors. They do so by logrolling – exchanging the mutual rights of partners to seek their most valued preference – using both material and cultural ingredients to define a political strategy. Politics is about brewing the right mix of ingredients, selling it, adapting it along the way, and disposing of the mix altogether if and when necessary; all these entail the ability to interpret the mobilizing capacity of prevailing norms, powerful identity concepts, and historical myths. Entrepreneurs are likely to craft coalitions that maximize their own power and control. Logrolled coalitions trading votes across issues compete against other coalitions.

---

[*] I am particularly grateful to Jack Snyder, Stephan Haggard, Joel Migdal and three anonymous referees for their comments on earlier versions of the entire manuscript. I would also like to thank Vinod Aggarwal, Jawad Anani, Bassam Awadallah, Steven Brams, Benjamin J. Cohen, Harry Eckstein, Richard Eichenberg, Albert Fishlow, Jeff Frieden, Peter Gourevitch, Robert R. Kaufman, Steve Weber, David Lake, Fawaz Gerges, Sung Chull Kim, Chung-in Moon, Manuel Pastor, Shimon Peres, Ahmed Qurie, Ira Sharkansky, and Abdullah Toukan. Any remaining errors are my own.

Actors – individual and collective – vary in the currency (the yardstick for measuring power resources) they bring to bear on prospective coalitions: the military can wield its ability to coerce; capitalists their potential to invest, employ, and exit; labor its option to strike; independent central banks their capacity to maintain macro-economic stability; threatened state bureaucracies their opportunities to foil the implementation of reform; "symbolic analysts" their technical skill to convert policy into outcomes; and religious fundamentalists their willingness to self-sacrifice in violent havoc. Political entrepreneurs use available rules and structures to translate interests and values into bargaining resources at particular sites, from legislative chambers to bureaucratic corridors, military headquarters, single-party command centers, corporate suites, the ballot box, the *diwan*, the battlefield, and the peace demonstration. Out of these bargains emerge grand strategies designed to pursue the most valued preferences of coalitional partners.

Based on these fundamental assumptions, this chapter advances the following argument:

1. The distributional consequences of internationalization and economic liberalization create two ideal-typical coalitions within states, one supporting it (internationalizing); the other opposing it (statist-nationalist, SN henceforth or SNC as a subcategory with a confessional component).[2]
2. Political entrepreneurs crafting these coalitions endorse contrasting preferences and observable instruments (a fiscal or tariff target, a foreign investment blueprint, a budget rule, borrowing ceilings, or the rejection of an international regime) that advance their material and ideal preferences.
3. Those preferences are aggregated into a "grand political-economic strategy" (grand strategy henceforth). Grand strategies reveal a coalition's definition of the state's relation to the global political economy, the domestic extraction and allocation of resources, and the regional context. Grand strategies can be explicitly stated – as in a party platform, a coup's pronouncement, a political pamphlet – but more often than not they are implicitly embedded in a wide range of policy positions. Though empirical referents can exhibit little coherence, the conceptual utility of this definition of grand strategy remains.
4. Once a coalition prevails politically – as a function of its size, cohesiveness, and effectiveness, and the institutional context within which it operates – its grand strategy becomes the *raison d'état*. Policy must now reflect the essential contours of that strategy, although the institutional context can hinder implementation. Grand strategies identify potential threats to the coalition's survival at home, regionally, and throughout the world, and formulate political, economic, and military means to counter those threats.
5. The grand strategy of internationalizing coalitions includes the pursuit of economic reform at home, the decimation of political opposition, and the maintenance of secure access to foreign markets, capital, investments, aid and technology. A cooperative (nonviolent) regional neighborhood serves all aspects of this synergistic strategy well. Regional stability – not regional economic integration – is the main conceptual link between regional and global dimensions of internationalizing grand strategies.

6   By contrast, the grand strategy of statist-nationalist-confessional coalitions seeks to preserve allocations to statist and military-industrial complexes, resist external pressures for liberalization, and weaken political adversaries advocating economic reform and internationalization. Regional insecurity and competition serves this grand strategy well, as does the fueling of national and religious myths that help justify the strategy.
7   The symmetrical attempt to weaken adversarial coalitions politically is an important component of respective grand strategies. Contingent on their relative power, domestic challengers can constrain ruling coalitions in their implementation of grand strategies.
8   International political and economic structures and institutions purposefully – but also unintendedly – influence the domestic coalitional interplay, strengthening internationalizing coalitions at times, empowering their rivals at others.
9   The outcome of ruling coalitions' policies affects its own standing vis-à-vis domestic adversaries, neighboring states, and the global political economy. Outcomes can reinforce, dilute, or replace strategies – and coalitions – altogether.

Figure 2.1 outlines this basic understanding of the reciprocal relationship between the global political economy, its coalitional effects, and grand strategies.

Polanyi's (1944) formulation of a dialectic "double movement" – global market expansion and the political response to it – encapsulated the essential logic behind the constitution of contending coalitions at one time. Yet it requires adjustments to the late twentieth-century "world-time," particularly following the 1989 transformations. The identification of coalitions must take account of their integrated interpretation of this economic – both market and institutional – and political-strategic context, one that many defined as leading not merely to price convergence but normative and institutional convergence as well. Specifying precise links between this

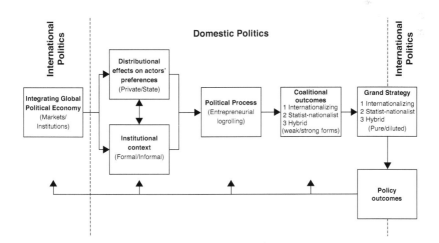

Figure 2.1 The global political economy, coalitional effects, and grand strategy
Source: Revised from Solingen (1998: 21)

evolving context and domestic coalitional configurations remains a crucial task into the twenty-first century. The remainder of this chapter identifies natural partners of internationalizing and SNC coalitions (parties, state agencies, the military, peak industrial organizations, labor, and confessional movements, among others) given their expected material and ideal gains and losses from internationalization. It also outlines their respective patterns of coalitional aggregation, articulation, and logrolling;[3] stipulates logical connections among components of each grand strategy; and reviews the impact of the global political economy and institutions on the relative strength and survivability of competing coalitions.

Internationalizing coalitions

Preferences, composition, and patterns of aggregation and logrolling

Coalitions can be characterized by their membership, which endorses observable policies under a given institutional context. Internationalization poses threats not merely to material interests but also to cultures, identities, and values, and to the interests of political entrepreneurs endangered by both types of threats. Thus, coalitions are constituted by competing approaches to economic liberalization as well as by integrated interpretations of how the political-economic and strategic context affects domestic coalitional balances. Nevertheless, a thorough understanding of "qui bono" (who gains) and "qui malo" (who loses) from economic liberalization is a good point of departure. Internationalization involves a series of steps geared to impose a market rationale on economic activities. Privatization, the contraction of state entrepreneurship, and openness to global markets, capital, investments, and technology are its central features. External liberalization affects individuals and groups in different sectors through changes in employment status, labor incomes, and returns on assets, through changes in the prices of goods and services consumed, and through the provision of public services.[4]

A common approach to mapping distributional impacts of liberalization relies on cleavages between tradable (internationally competitive) and nontradable (uncompetitive) sectors. Labor, management, and investors in protected industries stand to lose, at least provisionally, from eliminating protection. Owners of uncompetitive sector-specific assets have incentives to pressure governments to maintain protection; the higher the adjustment costs, the stronger those incentives. Export-intensive activities, by contrast, benefit from opening up the economy. Large banking and industrial complexes – particularly those already involved in foreign trade, investment, lending, and licensing – seek to increase openness as do workers and "symbolic analysts" employed by competitive firms, their suppliers, and consumers of imported products. The preferences of internationalizing coalitions transcend the domestic–international divide. The external orientation of overseas investors, competitive producers, and consumers of imported products is arguably translated into a preference for deflationary, internationalizing, or "monetarist" policies at home. Export-intensive sectors and liquid-asset holders are more receptive to structural adjustment policies and wary of confrontations with international financial institutions and investors.

Beyond these general expectations, however, identifying preferences for or against liberalization is less straightforward than suggested by export-oriented/import-competing cleavages. Firms with more diversified portfolios face more complex incentives regarding different aspects of the liberalization package such as stabilization – designed to restore macroeconomic balance – and trade policy. Moreover, quite often volatile conditions produced by liberalization induce high uncertainty across sectoral, class, institutional and occupational categories, particularly during the initial stages and when commitment to reforms (credibility) is hard to predict. Only after traversing "the valley of transition" (Przeworski 1991) may a wider political basis develop to support liberalization. Even when likely to organize politically, beneficiaries of economic reform can face significant resistance from beneficiaries of the status quo. Economic crises imposing short time-horizons are important – although neither necessary nor sufficient – for coalescing political pressure for reform.

Clearly, understanding expected distributional consequences of internationalization is only a first step. The institutional context within which coalitions operate plays an important role in defining their political wherewithal and the very fate of liberalization. Political entrepreneurs in "dirigiste" developmental states (Johnson 1982) can plan the direction, rate, and extent of liberalization in line with the interests and values of their supportive coalition. Thus liberalization from above – as in the classical cases of South Korea and Taiwan – relies on powerful states or strong bureaucracies imposing central priorities on private actors and setting the nature and pace of reform. This model can be exclusionary in political terms, particularly toward labor, but is not the narrow preserve of authoritarian regimes, as the experiences of democratic reformers in the 1990s suggest. Initial support for reform is rarely overwhelming but as integration with the global economy unfolds, its beneficiaries grow economically and politically stronger. At more advanced stages new political groups can burst the exclusionary mold and demand political reform. Institutional capacity may be necessary but insufficient for implementing economic reform, particularly absent the political will.

In contrast to top-down patterns, economic liberalization from below – much less frequent – begins with powerful societal actors that rely on typical bureaucratic allies in ministries of finance, independent central banks, and managers of export-processing zones. Ministries of trade and industry and the military-industrial-complex typically resist pressures from below. The ability of local and foreign-owned big business and investors to "vote with their feet" gives them an important voice in lobbying for reform. Political entrepreneurs logrolling internationalizing coalitions can also coopt organized labor through political pacts, safety nets, longer-term benefits in exchange for short-term restraint; and through rhetoric emphasizing putative benefits of economic reform. Studying this mobilizational rhetoric is as important as untangling actual and potential distributional effects of liberalization.

Internationalizing economic agendas should not be equated with "laissez-faire" policies across the board; they can retain selective protection, regulation, and industrial policy.[5] Liberalization is neither linear nor coherent; different sectors can be affected in different sequences. This selectivity and gradualism explain why "internationalizing" may be an appropriate label for coalitions moving along a spectrum while rarely reaching complete openness, in other words, it is an empirical approximation that never quite matches the ideal type. In different combinations and sequences, steps toward liberalization include export drives, opening domestic markets to foreign goods and investment, reducing state entrepreneurship and deregulating financial flows. Central to the economic program of internationalizing coalitions is the primacy accorded to macroeconomic stability, best reflected in typical lower tolerance for inflation among East Asian liberalizers. Whereas high inflation induces capital flight and lowers incentives for foreign investors, macroeconomic stability reduces uncertainty, encourages savings, and enhances domestic and foreign investment rates.

Where internationalizing programs prevail politically and are implemented effectively, protection rates decline markedly while foreign trade and private entrepreneurship accounts for growing shares of GDP. Actual policy success, however, is not the most reliable indicator of a coalition's *commitment* to reform, although success helps strengthen such commitment. Openness to foreign investment may be a prerequisite though not a guarantee that such investment will materialize. Success stems from a more complex set of factors including domestic and regional stability (as discussed in *Regional Orders* Ch. 3). Higher levels of trade openness may be a potential symptom but not a dependable measure of the dominance of internationalizing coalitions. South Korea's trade openness was under 15 percent in 1964 when President Park Chung-Hee launched his internationalizing strategy; it doubled by 1967, reaching nearly 72 percent by 1990 with his strategy firmly in place. High trade openness was the end product of a successfully implemented – if ruthlessly applied – internationalizing strategy.

Internationalization – and the coalitions that form in response to it – is not merely about trade orientation but also about a fundamental approach to an array of regimes, institutions, expectations and values within which it is nested. I turn now to these broader sources of coalitional mobilization and their impact on regional orders.

The grand strategy of internationalizing coalitions

The outlined agenda of internationalizing coalitions is served better by certain regional policies than others. Cooperative regional postures are often most efficient – from the standpoint of these coalitions – for their domestic, regional and global implications. Such postures are expected to free up resources to carry out reform at home; weaken competitors opposed to reform; and secure access to foreign markets, capital, investments, and technology.

Freeing up resources to carry out reform at home

Conflict-prone external postures require internal mobilization of resources for potential military conflict. From the perspective of internationalizers, such mobilization contributes to the expansion of state power; maintenance of unproductive and inflation-inducing military expenditures (MILEX); protection of state-owned enterprises under a mantle of "national security"; and perpetuation of rent-seeking patterns. Hence, internationalizing coalitions have incentives to avoid external conflict and inflated military budgets that increase budgetary deficits, raise the cost of capital, curtail savings and productive investment, deplete foreign exchange coffers, induce overvalued exchange rates, currency instability and unpredictability, and distort human capital formation.[6] The technology-intensive content of modern weapons multiplies those effects, rendering trade-offs imposed by MILEX even starker. In sum, high expected opportunity costs of such expenditures make internationalizers less prone to extract and mobilize societal resources for external conflict that might threaten their core macroeconomic objectives.

Two conditions are likely to hold when internationalizing coalitions do invest in weapons. First, their levels of MILEX are less likely to seriously endanger their dominant political-economy strategy or shatter the fiscal discipline essential to its success. This approach to MILEX is underpinned by a primary concern with economic growth and is thus compatible with both the capital formation model and the export-led growth model on the impact of MILEX on economic performance (Chan 1992). The former model stresses private investment as the key determinant of economic growth; the latter sees MILEX as depriving the most dynamic (export) sectors from important resources and skills. Declines in international competitiveness lead to a weaker currency, structural unemployment, chronic trade deficits, and a less attractive environment for international investments – all outcomes that are anathema to internationalizing coalitions. Where MILEX are kept at levels that avert such outcomes, hard political choices on guns-versus-butter can be deferred. Second, MILEX by internationalizers can be incurred as an insurance policy, particularly against neighboring SNC adversaries or generalized uncertainty. Broader foreign policy patterns can reflect this defensive posture as well. Yet the essential ingredient of internationalizing grand strategies is economic growth through global access, not military prowess. Successful internationalizers – many in East Asia – are better able to persuade domestic and foreign audiences that they can provide defense, growth, and welfare at once.

These two conditions are crucial for understanding the role of MILEX under internationalizing coalitions. Although subject to constant threats to its survival from North Korea, South Korea devoted 4–6 percent of GDP to the military in the 1970s–1990s (ACDA 1990). As GDP grew by 10 percent average between 1965 and 1989, MILEX declined as a percentage of GDP. Even during the consolidation of its export-led strategy (1962–1972) expenditures for economic development were higher than MILEX. By 1990 MILEX were 3.8 percent of GDP, comparable to Argentina's that same year, in a region characterized by much lower threat perceptions than East Asia. Taiwan allocated nearly 8 percent of GDP to defense on average (1961–1987), declining by the 1970s as the export-led model took root. MILEX in South Korea and Taiwan were far lower than in high-conflict regions like the Middle East where they amounted to 8–17 percent of GDP in the 1970s–1980s, reaching up to 20 percent in Syria and Iraq, or between three and four times higher than the world's average.[7] For all of internationalizing East Asia, MILEX was 4 percent of GDP in 1990–1991 (even less, excluding China) and 2.8 percent in Southeast Asia. Moreover, despite references to military acquisitions in Asia-Pacific as the prelude for armed conflict, there was neither an arms race nor an offensive build-up.

Weakening groups and institutions opposed to reform

The taming and resolution of regional conflicts often has an adverse impact on three main groups opposed to economic reform:

1 The military – which tends to inflate both budgets and threats (Snyder 1991; Van Evera 1993) – is weakened institutionally (in size and mission) and personally (trimmings in material and other prerogatives);
2 A large network of public and private enterprises – thriving on production and distribution of protected military and ancillary goods – loses its *raison d'être*;
3 Advocates of civic nationalist and/or confessional causes that prosper from regional conflict see their political legitimacy decline.[8]

These three groups thus have incentives to resist regional cooperation and economic reform that threaten their survival. Material interests of statist groups are safeguarded at the price of fiscally expansionary policies that engender inflationary spirals and currency weakness and instability. Statist-nationalist, ethnic, and confessional movements also typically connect internationalization with global (Western) institutions whose policy prescriptions they loathe because of perceived adverse effects on these movements' viability. Those institutions provide opponents of internationalization with a convenient ideological lightning rod for mobilizing support against internationalizers at home and across the border.

Securing access to foreign markets, capital, investments, and technology

Cooperative regional orders have positive global externalities for internationalizing coalitions, minimizing risk, enabling foreign investment, decreasing the likelihood of sanctions and penalties from external private and public actors, and reinforcing these coalitions' ties to economic institutions such as the IMF, World Bank, private banking and insurance, to which they endear themselves through reform programs.[9] By contrast, intransigent and uncertainty-inducing regional policies raise the propensity for conflict and risk for foreign investors, and may trigger denial of external aid, technology, and resources.

Internationalizing grand strategies are thus much broader than economic reform, entailing a particular approach to regional and global relations. Regional cooperation is not just the product of concessions to external pressures. Internationalizers do not merely trade the right to pursue the national interest regionally (whatever that means) for the right to enrich themselves, as their domestic adversaries often argue. Rather, internationalizing coalitions aim at shrinking state entrepreneurship but, if successful, end up strengthening the leaner state's institutional capacity for extraction, including – when necessary – for war.[10] These coalitions attract domestic actors that value the downgrading of militarized conflicts and upgrading of regional cooperation because they help advance economic reform; rein in adversarial forces at home; and secure international economic, financial, and political benefits including debt relief, export markets, technology transfer, food imports, aid, and investments. Those benefits, in turn, can be used to broaden domestic support and strengthen the institutional framework underpinning economic liberalization.

Where most positive externalities from regional cooperation are captured by a few groups with intense internationalizing preferences and equally intense political access, those groups are particularly active in advancing internationalizing agendas. Internationalizing entrepreneurs can rely on mythical effects of markets and leaner (presumably more effective) states to broaden support, sometimes also exaggerating the "peace dividends" expected from downsizing military-industrial complexes.

The empirical chapters in *Regional Orders* discuss a wide variety of internationalizing coalitions, from infancy to maturity. South Korea and Taiwan were pioneers in shedding inward-looking policies characteristic of the early 1950s in favor of substantial reductions in overvaluation and incentives toward export promotion. In time they became paradigmatic models of export-driven industrialization, guided by active states that nourished private sectors into competing internationally and displaced private initiative to a far lesser extent than import-substituting states in Latin America, South Asia, or the Middle East. South Korea's state enterprises accounted for 10–15 percent of total industrial employment and 25 percent of industrial output even during a brief statist-nationalist interlude in the 1970s. Corresponding Middle East averages were 50 percent of total industrial employment and 75 percent of industrial output.

Substantial threats to South Korea and Taiwan's physical existence required highly developed military-industrial sectors but these were not allowed to harm the integrity of internationalizing strategies. Bureaucrats cajoled military and industrial conglomerates (*chaebols*) in South Korea and Taiwan toward foreign markets, capital, technology, and investments.[11] Maintaining the strategy and economic stability required downgrading regional conflict, leading South Korean and Taiwanese rulers to shift from highly adversarial policies in the 1950s and early 1960s to much less confrontational ones despite an otherwise charged regional security context. Both renounced potentially expensive nuclear competitions since the 1970s, joining the nonproliferation regime despite their inherent ability to match (overwhelm in South Korea's case) their rivals in a nuclear race. Clearly, the texture of regional cooperation is contextual, heavily influenced by the depth of security dilemmas and the shadow of past militarized encounters. The relatively restrained behavior of South Korea and Taiwan must be assessed in this light. Other internationalizing coalitions have been far more embattled politically, as in the Middle East and South Asia. Relative newcomers to internationalization – Latin America's Southern Cone in the 1990s – made important strides in implementing domestic, regional, and global requirements of that strategy.

Statist-nationalist-confessional coalitions

Preferences, composition, and patterns of aggregation and logrolling

SNC coalitions encompass an eclectic group that colludes in challenging different aspects of internationalization. This joint challenge generally constitutes the most valued preference of each partner but can otherwise suppress profoundly different objectives including rejection of economic policies, security regimes or liberal norms. Not all potential partners to such coalitions are present everywhere, and those partners' relative strength varies across states and regions. SN coalitions have an inherent affinity with import-substituting models of industrialization and classical populist programs involving strong, active states that control prices, increase nominal wages, overvalue currencies to raise wages and profits in nontraded-goods sectors, protect state enterprises, allocate credit at low interest rates, and dispense rents to private industry by discriminating against imports competing with domestic products (through tariffs, import controls, and multiple exchange rate systems). In the Latin American context, populism was designed to mobilize support from organized labor, lower-middle-classes, and inward-looking industries against landowners, foreign enterprises, and large-scale domestic industrial elites (Kaufman 1989). Import-substitution provided an intellectual rationale easily manipulated in support of populism. Economic nationalists everywhere linked domestic production of goods to strategic logics. In their extreme form, inward-looking leaders advocated outright economic autarky and self-sufficiency even for very small national markets, such as the "hermit kingdom" of North Korea.

Constituencies receptive to this appeal included import-competing firms with close ties to the state (internationally uncompetitive "hothouse" industries); industrial bankers tied to protected firms, and sectors vulnerable to wide fluctuation in international markets, most of which employ urban unskilled, formal sector blue-collar and white-collar workers; state bureaucracies linked to planning, industrial policy, capital controls, and import licensing; state-owned enterprises and banks; politicians adversely affected by the dismantling of those enterprises and the erosion of their basis of political patronage; and underemployed intelligentsia. Some of these groups stand to lose irreversibly from liberalization while others face transitional hardships and uncertainty regarding the longer-term. State entrepreneurship can be widespread in the industrializing world but whereas it is *the* pivotal economic engine for SN coalitions (Iran, Pakistan, Egypt, Syria, Iraq) it is more commonly an instrument to facilitate private-sector development in internationalizing models. The first replaces the market, the second promotes it.

Military establishments are often adversely affected by liberalizing reforms that curtail military budgets and the proliferation of military and security agencies with overlapping jurisdictions which, though relying on external threats to legitimize their existence, make domestic repression and the survival of SN coalitions their core mission. Military-industrial complexes, often including a vast array of economic enterprises unrelated to military objectives (in food and consumer goods among others) also benefit from indirect rents such as state subsidies of important inputs, raw materials and energy, often justified for their presumed spin-offs. Even where it agrees with liberalization in some sectors, the military forcefully retains statist-protectionism within its military-industrial-complex. For all these reasons, the military resisted economic liberalization from Argentina to Brazil, Iran, Syria and Egypt, among many others. Internationalizers in South Korea and Chile, however, disciplined their respective militaries into supporting integration into the global economy. Turkey's military transformed itself from custodian of the post-independence statist-nationalist project to the main line of defense against SNC projects. More often than not, however, the interests of military factions differ, leading to wide variation regarding economic liberalization. In his study of internationalizing reforms, Díaz Alejandro (1983: 45) concluded prophetically that "the nature and laws of motion of the collection of men in uniform are the darkest black boxes in Latin American social science," given their ambiguous and inconsistent attitudes toward economic openness. Several decades later the military is less of a "veto player" in several Latin American countries but remains so in others (Venezuela, perhaps Brazil) and particularly in the Middle East and parts of Africa.

Given their makeup and preferences, SN coalitions are expected to reject fiscal orthodoxy and stabilization plans, particularly as imposed by the IMF and other financial institutions, and to favor more expansionary fiscal and monetary courses.[12] The policies of SN coalitions have been characterized by persistently high budget deficits, inflation, excessive borrowing, and overvalued exchange rates. The military, state enterprises, and their protected suppliers and clients have captured the lion's share of rationed foreign exchange. The latter's scarcity induced further controls on imports, capital flows, and foreign travel, to the detriment of export industries and other sectors that benefit from liberalization. The historical alignment of military institutions with SN coalitions turns dependencia-style arguments about an enduring alliance between global capitalism and local military establishments on their heads. Domestic allies of global capitalism can be the military's most powerful *adversaries*. Economic liberalization often brought about dramatic collapse in military budgets.

As argued, the volatility and uncertainty accompanying market reform leaves wide segments of society behind the "veil of ignorance," that is, unable to figure out where and how they will come out at the end of the reform process. This uncertainty makes constituencies in state-supported agencies and enterprises highly vulnerable to the promise of protection offered by SN populist ideologies against the material and spiritual onslaught resulting from marketization and internationalization. Many unemployed and underemployed scientists, scholars, teachers, and students in the Middle East and South Asia – heavily dependent on state support – fear the dislocations engendered by economic liberalization whereas their peers in private transnationally integrated networks have fewer reservations regarding reform.

SN coalitions cast the benefits from protection, statism, and a military-industrial complex as reaching relatively wide segments of the population, yet such benefits are often captured largely by public bureaucracies, inefficient producers, and military leaders with strong incentives to oppose reform. Furthermore, their ability to prevail politically is enhanced by their control of important state institutions and symbols. The economic costs of statism, militarization, and protection for diffuse interests in the population are low relative to the massive benefits that those policies yield to their beneficiaries. But inflation worsens income distribution, punishing labor and the middle class the most.

Civic nationalist and majority ethno-nationalist and confessional movements can be natural partners in SNC coalitions and important keys to mass political mobilization.[13] Such movements appeal to communal, "organic" values that are often threatened by the crude impersonality of market forces and their guiding principle of efficiency. Statist "*Völkisch* populism laden with racism and nationalism" (Gourevitch 1986: 27) is clearly not a new socio-political phenomenon in the twentieth-century. Indeed inward-looking bourgeoisies share some commonalities, such as uncritical nationalism and idealization of cultural values (*Innerlichkeit*), with the nineteenth-century German bourgeoisie.[14] Particularly during early stages of marketization, generalized uncertainty, insecurity, and widening social disparities puncture the mantle of solidarity encouraged by ties of nationality, ethnicity, religion, or language.[15] Nationalist and confessional responses to marketization have appropriated long-standing critiques of capitalism as wasteful and corrupting, pointing to beneficiaries of economic liberalization as exemplars of venal and unethical lifestyles, quite accurately in some cases, but applicable no less to some beneficiaries of SNC policies.[16]

Marketization and internationalization are not the only sources of nationalist and confessional mobilization but are certainly powerful ones, as Gellner (1983) suggests, particularly in the hands of skillful leaders able to identify effective antidotes to unwanted and painful change. As argued, expanding global trade exerts pressure toward convergence not just in prices but also in norms and social institutions. Rodrik (1997) points to the arbitraging effects of open trade, which induce stress on long-standing social contracts and norms. Threatened by this arbitraging effect, national and confessional memories and myths acquire a heightened mobilizing potential. As Cox (1986) argued, collective images of social orders – of the legitimacy of power relations, the meaning of justice – are not reducible to material capabilities. Yet economic, technological, institutional, and military configurations tend to encourage certain collective images. Memories of things past, and the potential of internationalization for superseding them, are very important in the political construction of ethnic and religious identity.

Economic liberalization has global referents. SNC movements thrive on popular resentment over externally imposed adjustment policies, reliance on foreign investment, and "Western" principles and norms embodied in most international regimes. In extreme cases, as with right or left revolutionaries and religious fundamentalists, the choices are presented more starkly, favoring a sharp delinking from the global political economy that helps establish their power and bring about a radical transformation in the domestic economy and polity (Díaz Alejandro 1983). A confessional solvent can be poured successfully into an objective context of crisis and deprivation. Highly organized confessional groups step in to provide safety nets against the compounded explosive impact of lingering populism under incipient liberalization. Ethno-confessional entrepreneurs mobilize social movements through welfare associations, schools, and professional networks, as throughout the Islamic world. Turkey's Nekmetin Erbakan relied on democratic procedures and a deep rift among liberalizers to turn his Welfare Party's 21.38 percent majority (1995 elections) into his springboard to power. The weakness of his political opponents – Erbakan declared – was their "strongly capitalistic economic program, which helps a very small elite and leaves the rest of our people in misery," their lack of identity and "sick" imitation of the West, and their secularism.[17] Erbakan's campaign speeches further illustrate SNC ideologies: "We will set up an Islamic United Nations, an Islamic NATO, and an Islamic version of the European Union. We will create an Islamic currency." In the context of the rise of confessionalism in Middle East politics, Erbakan was considered a moderate rather than a fundamentalist.

The material pillar of SNC coalitions against internationalization and liberalization is stronger at times, as where state enterprises and import-substituting interests are powerful. At other times, the confessional component becomes a driving force. Where possible, leaders logroll across both groups to reinforce their joint appeal, strengthening their ability to reach new groups, uncertain of their own post-liberalization fate. The apparent paradox of weakened statist-nationalist parties (such as Egypt's Socialist Labor party) or weakened Marxist parties (such as the Palestinian movement's PFLP and DFLP) allying themselves with confessional ones (such as the Muslim Brotherhood and Hamas) quickly dissolves when bearing in mind the potential advantages of challenging internationalizing coalitions jointly, in a marriage of convenience. A natural consequence of logrolling – allowing each coalitional partner to get what it wants most – can, however, infuse SNC coalitions with stress. Some protectionist, nationalist, or military segments may have to swallow their more secular outlook while confessional groups may have to compromise on religious injunctions where these threaten their partners' interests.

Islamist movements seek to capture the state to exploit its educational and indoctrinating capacity, as well as its material resources. Despite a presumed fundamental doctrinal affinity between Islam and small private entrepreneurship, the record of Islamist regimes so far suggests that, once in power, they do not dismantle the state economically while building its potential for indoctrination: they use the state's economic power, as in Iran, to service indoctrination. Not all confessional movements opposing internationalization embrace militarized strategies. Some are largely political movements (Algeria's Islamic Salvation Front), as opposed to primarily military organizations (Algeria's Armed Islamic Group), although it is not always easy to disentangle the intricate patterns of reciprocal support. As Salamé (1993) and Razi (1990) have argued, the political game played by moderates and militants alike mutually bolsters their bargaining power in practice.

Confessional movements can become allies of internationalizing coalitions in some circumstances, as when they benefit from international openness or become potential targets of hegemonic ethnic or religious movements, as has been the case with Lebanese and Egyptian Christians, Alevi Turks, and, to some extent, Rwandan Tutsis and Iraqi Kurds. Moreover, coalitions can embrace some economic liberalization without abandoning their political reliance on confessional mantles of legitimacy, as in Pakistan, Saudi Arabia, Arab Gulf states, Malaysia, and Indonesia, to widely different degrees. However, Islamic content is only pursued insofar as it does not impinge on internationalizing political-economic strategies. This is much less the case (so far and for the most part) for self-proclaimed "true" Islamic republics in existence – Iran and Sudan – and for the overwhelming majority of fundamentalist Islamist challengers closer to SNC models. Saudi Arabia's ruling coalition (its extensive royal family) is known more for its commitment to accumulation and consumption of wealth than for devotion to ascetic Islamic lifestyles.[18] It has thus relied on an internationalizing strategy that advances its most valued preference, subordinating other political instruments to that goal. Similarly, some internationalizing coalitions in Pakistan have gone along with selective application of *sharia* (Islamic law) that does not overturn the benefits of internationalization.[19] The Saudi military often finds ample justification for its appetite for arms in the need to counter radical SNC neighbors in Iraq and Iran. Pakistan is alleged to pursue a nuclear deterrent, nurtured by its own lingering SNC wing. Yet, while facing nuclear-capable India, incipient Pakistani liberalizers (Benazir Bhutto) advocated a nuclear-weapons-free zone in South Asia, and some even expressed interest in joining the Nonproliferation Treaty unilaterally (without India doing so), only to be subdued by a resilient SNC opposition.[20]

The fit between statism and protectionism on the one hand, and nationalism, militarism, and confessionalism on the other, is fairly powerful but not perfect. Political entrepreneurs may cater to nationalist-confessional and economically liberalizing constituencies at the same time, as did Israel's Prime Minister Benjamin Netanyahu during the electoral campaign of 1996. However, the inherent tension between the two strategies was evident from the significant flow of internationalizing constituencies away from Netanyahu's Likud-led coalition. Moreover, SNC partners within this coalition have – as of 1997 – overwhelmed a feeble liberalizing fringe (Finance Minister Dan Meridor's resignation is but one symptom of their victory). Reliance on populist, nationalist, and confessional votes has progressively submerged liberalizing elements within Likud. Each of these constituencies is inherently rent-seeking, demanding subsidies along socio-economic or religious lines, low cost housing, imperial infrastructural projects, and new settlements in the West Bank and Gaza, all of which can translate into a reality that transcends electoral promises of growth, stabilization and adjustment. Simply put, liberalization is not Netanyahu's most valued preference, and other aspects of an internationalizing agenda (such as regional concessions and harmonizing policies vis-à-vis international institutions) are anathema to most of his coalitional partners. Internationalizing constituencies in Israel are massively entrenched in Labor's political camp. As evident from a variety of cases from Latin America to Serbia, Israel, and South Asia, a single internationalizing finance minister does not an internationalizing agenda make. The implausibility of internationalizing reforms under statist-nationalist leadership is also evident in Syria, where some liberalizing goals were forfeited when core objectives of the military-industrial complex were at stake. President Assad thus proclaimed his commitment to "a stubborn pursuit of the national struggle against Israel even at the expense of economic development" (Hinnebusch 1993: 189). Syria also highlights the use of Arab nationalism, statism, and populism to deflect the reality of minority dominance by a confessional group (Alawites) over the Sunni majority.

As the last point suggests, the notion of logrolling – exchanging the mutual rights of partners to seek their most valued preference – is essential to understand why components of a statist-nationalist-populist and sometimes confessional coalition gravitate toward one another. Some aspect of an internationalizing agenda fundamentally threatens their interests, sometimes propelling them into coalitions with strange bedfellows. The consortium of old-styled statist-nationalist parties in the Arab world with Islamist parties and movements is but one example. The cooperation of fascists and communists in President Tudjman's nationalist Croatian Democratic Union is another. The convergence between Israel's confessional-populist Shas and other Likud constituents – despite Shas's earlier "conciliatory" positions on foreign policy – is a third. Identifying most valued preferences is rarely an easy feat but, as this overview suggests, neither is it always elusive, even as preferences shift over time.

Finally, this overview highlights a strong personalistic component in the logrolling of SNC coalitions (both for civic-nationalist and confessional variants), even in formally democratic contexts. Personalism can play an important role in internationalizing contexts as well, particularly in the initial logrolling on behalf of economic reforms. However, once the grand strategy becomes politically entrenched, the centrality of organizing entrepreneurs to the strategy's survival recedes far more frequently in an internationalizing context than in a SNC one.

The grand strategy of statist-nationalist and confessional coalitions

The preferences, composition, organization, and logrolling patterns of SNC coalitions make them prone to embrace certain regional policies that advance their grand strategy. Actors aggregated in these coalitions perceive regional cooperative outcomes as weakening them politically and economically, for many of the same reasons that internationalizing coalitions expect such outcomes to benefit them. From the vantage point of SNC coalitions, prospective peace settlements, cooperative regional contexts, and arms control agreements are generally detrimental for the following reasons: they legitimize downsized allocations to the military-industrial complex; they deprive the coalition of nationalist myth-making opportunities, a major source of political capital; and they weaken the coalition's ability to justify societal extraction to benefit SNC interests.

Downsizing allocations to the military and weapons-producing enterprises

A cooperative regional context weakens justifications for extracting societal resources for military purposes. Yet the military upholds its institutional mission of confronting external threats, and resists carrying out that mission with fewer resources. Moreover, where external threats are downplayed, maintaining export-oriented military-industrial complexes becomes less justifiable, as when the end of the Cold War arguably undermined the justification for such complexes (Posen 1984; Van Evera 1993). Militarization is not subsidiary to larger political-economic objectives but pivotal to the grand strategy of SN coalitions, for which military prowess constitutes a core basis of legitimacy, as in Iraq and North Korea. This is not to say that the military is invariably interested in actualizing its war-fighting potential. Indeed it sometimes seeks to avoid military showdowns that might endanger its leadership or integrity. Yet as an institution, the military is interested in maintaining (at a minimum) and broadening (where possible) its own share of budgets to guarantee its wealth, autonomy, and prestige.[21] Finally, external threats are efficient not only for increasing access to material resources but also for amalgamating the military internally, particularly where political, economic, confessional, or hierarchical cleavages threaten its unity.

Academic and policy analysts have often misread programs aimed at developing weapons of mass destruction in the industrializing world, considering those programs as products of a rational search for cost-effective security strategies (as in "more bang for the buck"). Yet in reality such programs have often become budgetary black holes employing several times the required number of scientists, technologists, and bureaucrats. Nuclear programs in particular have been ideal technological allies of SNC coalitions. First, they encourage construction of dense scientific, technological, industrial, and bureaucratic complexes that often dwarf other statist endeavors (Solingen 1996a). Second, this complex is often beyond formal budgetary oversight. Third, the actual or imaginary output of this large-scale provider of rents becomes itself a powerful source of myths. It is not entirely unexpected, therefore, that inward-looking nationalist regimes have exaggerated regional threats as pretexts for not joining or complying with the global nonproliferation regime or its regional pillars. This is different from arguing that nuclear programs in every region have similar origins, although an amazing number do (Solingen 1994a, 1994b).

Devalued role of myth-making

Myth-making – a major source of political capital – entails the ability to mobilize militant religious, ethnic, nationalist or cultural groups against actual or imagined regional adversaries (Snyder 1991). Myths may connect to reality but the connection is often flimsy. Self-reliance is a central myth of SNC coalitions, either in their secular or confessional form (e.g. North Korea's *juche*, India's *swadeshi*). SNC coalitions rely on legitimating symbols including sovereignty, geographical and territorial integrity, self-reliance, and confessional unity and purity. Reliance on conspiratorial theories goes hand in hand with protecting these symbols. Moreover, such coalitions are more likely to come to power by revolutionary means than are their internationalizing counterparts. The post-revolutionary regime often relies on mobilizing ideologies to stabilize its rule and establish its legitimacy. Myths of external threats are central to this legitimation. Reliance on myths for domestic consumption generates *real* external threats and even aggression, even if the revolutionary regime had no actual intention of launching a war (Walt 1996).

Eroding statist-nationalist and confessional privileges

A cooperative regional context with a devalued role for myths also undermines the entitlements of SNC interests. Iraqi and Iranian state enterprises (including Islamist "welfare" patronages) and military agencies derived significant advantages from external conflicts and heightened myth-making. "National security" myths have proven quite effective as a means to justify protection of state-owned enterprises. As Porter (1994) argues, no theory explains bureaucratic growth as consistently as war and military rivalry, evoking Tilly's (1985) notion of external threats as a racket to neutralize putative menaces.

Where most negative domestic externalities from liberalization and regional cooperation are captured by politically strong SNC constituencies with intense preferences, resistance to internationalization is likely to be stronger. Given their basis of political support, inward-looking coalitions – unlike their internationalizing adversaries – are also more resilient to coercive international intervention in regional conflicts, and excel in converting such interventions into domestic political capital. Hence SNC coalitions from Iraq and Iran to Serbia, Libya, and North Korea defied external sanctions while powerful import-substituting interests prospered from international closure; the military-industrial complex remained protected from the effects of sanctions; and sanctions strengthened state agencies and enterprises responsible for productive and distributive functions. These effects, however, can be short-lived and, over the long haul, can severely threaten these coalitions' survival (although one wonders how long the haul can be, given the experiences of Kim Il Sung, Muammar Gaddafi, Hafez al-Assad, Saddam Hussein or Fidel Castro). Political longevity has everything to do with ruthless grip on power. Yet the self-defeating (strategically suboptimal) outcome of these policies is reflected in politically weakened and delegitimized regimes.

Defiant behavior by extremist SN coalitions can be interpreted in five ways:

1 These coalitions may fail to act strategically because their immediate survival imposes short-term horizons and excessive rent seeking (Argentina's Leopoldo Galtieri, Serbia's Slobodan Milosevic, Azerbaijan's Abulfaz Elchibey);
2 They may act strategically in the belief that "standing up to the world" will secure future political benefits (Iraq's Saddam Hussein, Egypt's Nasser, Argentina's Perón);
3 They may be impermeable to learning (Libya's Muammar Gaddafi);
4 They may have no other choice, given their political makeup, than playing this all-out, risky (sometimes suicidal) strategy;
5 They may fail to estimate accurately the negative consequences of vote trading, as with Snyder's (1991) agents of imperial overexpansion.

These mutually compatible possibilities provide a rationale for the higher propensity for risk-acceptance of SN coalitions relative to internationalizing ones, a feature that permeates their domestic, regional, and global policies. Finally, where war is proximate to the revolutionary takeover, SN rule often becomes more nationalistic, radical, and centralizing as with Kim Il Sung, Nasser, Assad, Ayatollah Khomeini, and Castro.

The empirical cases in *Regional Orders* highlight the wide variety of SN coalitions, from most extreme to more moderate versions, with or without confessional elements. In the Middle East, populist-confessional challengers (fundamentalists, in their most radical variants) offer themselves as an alternative to an array of internationalizing coalitions (some secular, others royalist with a more pragmatic Islamist bent).[22] Their platform advances a political economy rooted in proclaimed Islamist principles, including rejection of international economic regimes and their perceived associated scourges of inequality, corruption, unemployment, and enslaving indebtedness. There is little room in their proposed socio-political order for regional reconciliation with "apostate" Arab regimes, let alone Israel. Iran, Sudan, and other Islamist challengers have legitimized the use of violent means to undermine the viability of domestic and regional internationalizing adversaries.

SNC coalitions in South Asia have also aggregated constituencies opposing economic reform and international regimes and upholding belligerent postures vis-à-vis regional rivals. This is evident in the platforms of Pakistan's radical Islamic party Jama'at-i-Islam and India's Hindu Bharatiya Janata Party (BJP), although BJP has used confessional themes more instrumentally. Instrumental use of such themes is also characteristic of Israel's Likud coalition, which has shared its tent with fundamentalist groups in spite of a fairly secular history. As argued, Likud represented free enterprise liberalism in earlier times but has played progressively populist, nationalist, and confessional cards in the last two decades (mid-1970s to mid-1990s). Politically captive to West Bank settlers, religious parties, developing areas, protectionist interests, and groups resisting the contraction of the military-industrial complex, Likud's Netanyahu and his political allies prevailed by a small margin in 1996 elections, largely by challenging Labor–Meretz peace initiatives toward Palestinians and Syria.

The dominance of statist-nationalism in the Southern Cone for decades precluded effective denuclearization and genuinely integrative regional frameworks. Of all the statist-nationalist coalitions dominating this region in the postwar era – from Perón onward – Argentina's were the least stable, continuously challenged by either competing SN factions (military or otherwise) or liberalizing factions, or both (Solingen 1996c). The "outbidding" among SN variants over that period crucially explains the extreme nature of Argentina's grand strategy in its internal, regional, and international dimensions, as well as the strategy's corollaries: military crises and mobilizations (Beagle conflict), war with the United Kingdom (Malvinas/Falklands), and a bid for nuclear supremacy against Brazil).

We can now sum up the relationship between coalitional type and grand strategy (see Table 2.1).

1   Internationalizing and SNC coalitions differ in: their preferences for domestic and international resource extraction and allocation; the state-society compacts they advance; their patterns of aggregation, articulation, and logrolling; their time-horizons; their risk acceptance in regional and international behavior; and the role of personalism.
2   SNC coalitions are oriented toward either what Barnett (1992) labels an "accommodationist" strategy of mobilization of societal resources for security objectives (a strategy that maintains the basic compact between a robust entrepreneurial "state" and societal interests) or toward a centralizing restructural strategy (increasing state control over the economy and society). Internationalizing coalitions, by contrast, aim at restructuring state-society relations by divesting state participation in productive activities while investing "virtual states" (Rosecrance 1996) with the task of developing a human and physical infrastructure that expands material wealth in an internationalized economy.
3   Successfully implemented and sustained internationalizing grand strategies lead to leaner states with meaner capabilities, as states can convert high levels of accumulated foreign exchange into military assets and maximize access to external inputs. Moreover, such states can rely on a wealthier tax base should deepened extraction of resources be required. Conversely, SNC grand strategies sap private and public resources in the long run and are unable to sustain high levels of societal extraction or MILEX. SNC coalitions create and

TABLE 2.1 Selected characteristics of competing grand strategies.

Selected characteristics of grand strategy	Statist-nationalist coalitions	Internationalizing coalitions
State-society compact	**Maintenance/expansion** of robust state entrepreneurship	**Divesting** state entrepreneurship; ushering of "virtual state"
Ratio of resource extraction to military allocations	**High** (*wehrwirtschaft* as core basis of legitimacy)	**Low** (subordinated to internationalizing economic requirements)
Short-term risks, and advantages	**Risks:** War	**Risks:** vulnerability to international markets; Economic crisis ("valley of transition"); and diminished military capabilities
	Advantages: High political mobilization potential	**Advantages:** High economic mobilization potential (particularly of international resources)
Long-term risks, and advantages	**Risks:** Economic collapse and sapped military strength	**Risks:** International political vulnerability
	Advantages: Higher (but not unlimited) resilience to international pressures	**Advantages:** Deepening of resource extraction and military capabilities
Implications for regional cooperation	**Cooperation threatens:** 1) viability of statist, inward-looking, military, and ethno-confessional enterprises and bureaucracies; 2) their associated myths, and hence; 3) undermines the very lifeline of the coalition	**Cooperation enables:** 1) economic reform at home; 2) the flow of international resources, and hence; 3) strengthens the coalition's political lifeline
Role of ethno-confessional card	**Logrolled to *buttress*** the coalition's rejection of an internationalizing strategy	**Logrolled to *tame*** ethno-confessionalism while subordinating it to an internationalizing strategy
Role of personalism	**Central** to both logrolling and long-term survival of the coalition's grand strategy	**Less central** to the long-term survival of an internationalizing grand strategy

Source: Revised from Solingen (1998: 47).

maintain a *Wehrwirtschaft* (war economy) that functions as their core political fulcrum. Internationalizing coalitions may invest in MILEX but prevent such expenditures from overwhelming domestic reform, regional stability, or global access.

4 Regional cooperative policies hold different payoffs for each coalition. Cooperation is expected to benefit internationalizing coalitions at home and abroad; cooperative regional orders enable economic reform while spelling transparency, predictability, good reputation, and the blessing of the international community. Cooperative regional orders weaken SNC coalitions: they undermine the viability of state agencies and enterprises linked with military functions and production, threaten with extinction the state's ability to disburse rents on national security grounds, and deprive populist entrepreneurs of a rich fountain of myths. External conflict ties different partners into SNC coalitions.

5 Internationalizing coalitions embrace domestic, regional, and global policies that may be politically risky in the short term (as with Israel's defeated Labor–Meretz coalition in 1996) but potentially rewarding over the longer haul (Argentina's Menem re-election in 1995). SNC coalitions rely on domestic, regional, and global strategies with short-term political payoffs but fundamentally counterproductive in the long run (Egypt's Nasser). Clearly, coalitional durability in either case is not merely a reflection of policy success but also of the presence of democratic institutions; their absence can make the long run longer. Both coalitional strategies have coexisted with democratic and authoritarian institutions, as discussed in Chapter Three of *Regional Orders*. Global market and institutional structures affect that durability as well, through a mix of threats and opportunities.

These are the general political contours shaping the grand strategies and regional policies of internationalizing and SNC coalitions. As contours, they portray more of the ideal type than real ones, which often approximate hybrids. Indeed the empirical analysis in Part Two of *Regional Orders*, like some of the examples above, suggests that many coalitions pursue hybrid strategies although some have more dominant profiles. The "purity" of the strategies and the extent to which they can be followed unhindered is contingent on the relative political strength of respective coalitions, to which I turn now.

Coalitional strength and the pursuit of grand strategy

There is no deterministic relationship between the character (composition, goals, and objectives) of a coalition and policy outputs, let alone outcomes. Coalitional policy preferences (aspirations) are important, but the actual constraints and incentives they face matter a great deal, shaping the probability that coalitional makeup and policies will indeed be aligned. The ability of either coalitional type to implement its preferred strategy in both its domestic and external dimensions is contingent on its cohesiveness and the size of the political resources it has amassed relative to its opposition. Among other things, resources help coopt groups otherwise inimical to some dimension of the ruling coalition's preferred policies.

A coalition's internal cohesiveness is related to the degree of macropolitical consensus reigning in its midst, reflecting widely shared preferences over macro-political goals among partners (Solingen 1996c). Macropolitical goals are those at the apex of a coalition's hierarchy of goals and means, and are typically gleaned from declaratory policy and informal statements, party platforms and legislative debates. Those goals may involve the pursuit of export-led growth and macroeconomic stability, or more egalitarian income distribution, or a confessionally-based new economic order. A coalition pivoted on politically powerful import-substituting producers and their associated dominant labor unions aggregating nontradable sectors is likely to converge against reform (Garrett and Lange 1996; Frieden 1991). The intensity of preferences and organizational skills of coalitional partners affects the likelihood that they will organize and demand policies attuned to their preferences. Institutional arrangements also influence the degree of coalitional cohesiveness. High macropolitical consensus and cohesiveness lower the costs of logrolling, produce internally consistent strategies, and strengthen coalitional stability.

The strength of coalitions is also a product of their ability to broaden their basis of support by compensating groups and institutions that might otherwise support competing coalitions, or those unable to assess the longer term impact of competing grand strategies. Inherited conditions such as economic collapse, fragile political institutions, and defeat in war tend to limit available compensating resources, as in many Middle East states. Cohesive and resourceful coalitions end up broadening their electoral appeal, legislative votes, and approval rates. Negative measures of coalitional strength (or weakness) include the incidence and scope of no-confidence votes, mass protests, threats of military coups, capital flight, terrorist bombs, labor strikes, and unrelenting political mobilization against a ruling coalition. Positive and negative measures of coalitional strength help estimate a coalition's ability to implement its grand strategy more or less coherently and expediently. The weaker a ruling coalition is vis-à-vis its opposition, the less coherent implementation is likely to be. An opposition that is largely consensual in its macropolitical objectives, that has considerable command over resources, and that is effectively organized can pose a formidable barrier to the implementation of ruling coalitions' grand strategies. Conversely, a divided and loosely organized opposition allows ruling coalitions greater latitude to avoid watering down the latter's favored strategy.

There is considerable variation in the way in which coalitional preferences are aggregated throughout the world, and institutions play a major role in that process. Democratic institutions can strengthen diffuse interests at the expense of concentrated ones. Proportional representation allowing each constituent group veto power can hinder economic stabilization measures, as was the case in Brazil (Alesina 1994). Parties, trade unions, ethnic and confessional movements can depict the consequences of economic liberalization in different ways – playing on uncertainties about distributional effects – to buttress policies they prefer. Whether political parties or their equivalent aggregate interests over broad sectoral categories or represent specific classes has consequences for the policies pursued and the outcomes obtained.[23] Whether organized labor is excluded, repressed, replaced by other sources of mass support, or drawn into coalitions can seal the fate of economic reform. Institutional resources are thus central for shaping the political field within which coalitions vie for political power.

States with different organizational capacities can embrace different mixes of market-conforming and interventionist strategies. The degree of lateral and vertical autonomy (from other state agencies and from the executive) and of insulation from societal political forces influences the ability of state agencies to implement reforms. However, lateral autonomy has also perpetuated extensive rents for military-industrial complexes and associated state and private enterprises. Highly autonomous institutions can amass considerable political power and sway the direction of reform. Although certain state bureaucracies are associated with either internationalizing projects (sometimes central banks) or SNC ones (often commerce ministries), the coalitional proclivities of state agencies are a matter of empirical investigation. Israel's Foreign Ministry became embedded in Labor's internationalizing strategy in the mid-1990s; Egypt's Foreign Ministry, or Brazil's, retained lingering imprints of earlier SN eras for some time. In the end, political entrepreneurs rely on available institutional infrastructures (including parties, bureaucracies, electoral systems, peak associations and labor unions) or attempt to fashion new institutions to build political support.

Ruling coalitions thus enjoy varying degrees of political cohesiveness, stability and longevity that affect the conduct of grand strategy. A conquering internationalizing coalition in the early 1990s enabled President Carlos S. Menem to revolutionize Argentina's decades-old grand strategy in its internal and external dimensions alike. Similar coalitions emerged in some East Asian countries, although not overnight and rarely under democratic sponsorship. Weaker ruling coalitions in Egypt since the 1970s and India since the early 1990s pursued less coherent strategies, binding their preferred policies to their immediate political survival in the face of powerful SNC opponents. The weaker the political foundations of internationalizing coalitions, the greater the pressures on them to: a) Dilute reform (as in Benazir Bhutto's Pakistan and pre-Narasimha Rao's India); and b) Gravitate toward themes, myths, and interests of challengers in order to survive politically (i.e., strengthen sharia law in Saudi Arabia and Pakistan, derail "desestatização"/state contraction under Fernando Collor de Mello in Brazil). In Van Evera's (1994) formulation, the temptation to engage in myth-making is inversely proportional to a coalition's legitimacy. Under such conditions, internationalizers are less able to downplay regional security threats or counter statist opponents in the military-industrial complex. Thus, although scapegoating external enemies is more frequently a tool of SNC coalitions, insecure internationalizers may use them too.

A high incidence of weak internationalizing coalitions evident from empirical chapters in *Regional Orders* begs the question of why internationalizers are prone to weakness. Clearly, economic reform unleashes painful processes, "valleys of transition." Yet inflationary cycles and widespread scarcities in SNC contexts can build political foundations for change. Moreover, the valleys of reform are deeper in some cases than others, and not always a function of pre-existing capital, educational, or infrastructural endowments. An important source of weakness for internationalizing coalitions may be their failure to distribute the spoils of reform more equitably, pursuing their short-sighted rather than enlightened self-interest. This phenomenon is widespread, with Egypt providing a classical case, given the longevity of reform efforts since the mid-1970s, their tentative nature, and meager successes. Accounts of market reform in Russia and Eastern Europe are rich in details of income concentration and widespread impoverishment, reminiscent of the experience of other industrializing countries. International conditionality requirements – imposing harsh fiscal and budgetary targets – have in some cases reinforced the natural tendency of these coalitions to focus on unfettered pursuit of wealth ignoring the risky political consequences of concentrated benefits. Stabilization programs often lead to recessions, reduced public subsidies and infrastructural investments while trade liberalization can exacerbate short-term unemployment. Food riots in Egypt, Sudan, Algeria, and Morocco followed reductions in staple subsidies, as did the conservative 1991 Russian coup. Shock-style therapy without safety nets and social insurance thus ends up weakening state and societal agents of economic reform while SNC-opponents offering sometimes unreal solutions-reap the political benefits.

The net result of the political dynamics of non-distributive internationalizing coalitions can be summed up in a paradox: prodded by international institutions, such coalitions may plant the seeds of their own destruction. Regional cooperation can – and has – become a collateral casualty as internationalizers fight for survival by moving toward more SNC instruments to build political support. In the Middle East and North Africa, all three incipient internationalizers threatened by powerful domestic Islamist opponents (Jordan, Yemen, and Algeria) moved to support Saddam Hussein during the 1991 Gulf War. Similar proclivities to gravitate toward less cooperative regional policies may loom on the horizon in Egypt, India, and Pakistan. Notably, where integration into the world economy evolved in tandem with more egalitarian income distribution, as in Taiwan and South Korea, internationalizing coalitions were gradually able to muster enough political support to make their grand strategy – at home, towards the region and the world – least reversible.[24] There was less regional adventurism and saber rattling once internationalizing strategies were in place. South Korea's cautious response to the vagaries of the North (including nuclear threats) in the 1970s–1980s, and Taiwan's restraint vis-à-vis militarized Chinese offensive threats in 1996 are symptomatic of relatively strong internationalizing coalitions.

SN coalitions also vary in political strength. At the height of their political dominance, they can implement their strategy almost unchallenged, as with Perón's Argentina, Nasser's Egypt, and the Ayatollahs' Iran shortly after their respective revolutions. Support whittles down once the strategy falters due to internal and external reasons, compelling them to revive the strategy just as resources have been all but consumed. The weaker the political base of SN coalitions: a) the stronger the pressures for economic liberalization; b) the harder the choice between overplaying external threats effectively and using scarce resources to coopt wavering groups at home; and c) the lower the capacity to transfer rents to the military-industrial complex. These conditions limit SN coalitions' wherewithal for implementing their grand strategy; even Perón, Iranian and Sudanese leaders begrudgingly and quietly followed IMF policies occasionally.

The sources of weakness of these coalitions are embedded in the very nature of their strategy: populist, self-reliant, statist, and military-intensive. Even with the fortuitous blessing of rich endowments (e.g. oil), the bonanza that enables both guns and butter can wither away. Redistribution can improve the chances of regime survival, as in Saddam Hussein's Iraq, but is often ultimately thwarted by higher ranking objectives, including gargantuan investments in military-industrial machines with little social overhead value. Iraq's nuclear program by itself is estimated to have absorbed $15 billion in the 1980s whereas arms imports reached $32 billion between 1982 and 1986 (against a total GDP or $47 billion in 1985). Iraq's military and related weapons programs are estimated to have absorbed $85 billion between 1980 and 1988.[25] The result was income disparities and creeping poverty, much as in myopic internationalizing contexts. Nationalist and confessional purity become devalued political instruments over time, as in Iran and Iraq by the mid-1990s. The compounded effect of defiant foreign policies, sanctions, deprivation, and external hostility dilutes rally-round-the-flag effects, weakening the regime further.

Overall, the terms of the bargain struck by SN partners may lead to Riker and Brams' (1973) "paradox of vote trading," where logrolling leaves partners worse off than they would have been without trading votes, as some Likud politicians found out regarding Netanyahu's 1996 coalition. Partners in SNC coalitions in the Middle East – from former Marxists to humanist and moderate Islamist groups – occasionally ponder about such unintended effects, particularly when widespread violence transcends the boundaries of coalitional camps, as in Algeria since 1991. At the regional level, Saddam's coalition – including the then-PLO and radical Islamist factions spanning the Arab world – experienced dramatic losses from their joint venture in the Gulf crisis. The ensuing regional decline of SNC coalitions infused new life into nascent internationalizing platforms.

There are instances of stalemate when the competition between contending coalitions fails to yield a clear victor. Three main scenarios obtain from such domestic coalitional equipoise. Under the first, the rough balance of forces leads to highly unstable coalitional successions with none able to hold power for any significant time. Postwar Argentina's stop-go cycles in the four decades leading to the early 1990s is a paradigmatic case. In the second scenario the two coalitions find enough room to rule as a condominium, dividing up the state and policy areas into coalitional fiefdoms. This can happen under democratic rule (e.g. Israel's national unity government, 1984–1990) or authoritarian sponsorship (Iran's Ruhaniyat and opposing Ruhaniyoun in the 1980s–1990s). Neither of these two scenarios holds much promise for implementing coherent grand strategies at home or abroad.

Under the third scenario contending coalitions find no grounds for mixed-motive games enabling limited cooperation. The security dilemma is now internalized into domestic politics. Such zero-sum conditions prevail in some African states where violent competition – civil war – has led to the collapse of a central government, as in Somalia, Rwanda, and Ethiopia under Mengistu Haile Mariam. The domestic power vacuum can precipitate regional conflict when neighboring ruling coalitions scramble to minimize negative externalities. The absence of a ruling coalition and intractable domestic coalitional strife become preludes for regional conflict. Such conditions may offer an opportunity for external intervention, as in Cambodia, geared to promote broad-based reform and regional cooperation. Interventions are extreme cases of intrusion by the global context on domestic coalitional power struggles, to which I now turn.

The global context: Impact on the domestic coalitional interplay

The constitution, orientation, and competition between internationalizing and SN coalitions are not carried out in a global vacuum. Domestic politics are never too far removed from systemic incentives and constraints. Potential coalitional partners anticipate – with different degrees of accuracy – how external structures and institutions may aid or thwart their favored policies. In the words of Brazil's former president Fernando H. Cardoso (1995: 5) "the exercise of politics in the modern world requires that we dovetail domestic and international considerations." This section explores the impact of nested international political, economic, and security structures on coalitional dynamics. Though unable to anticipate which coalitions are likely to seize power when and for how long, this overview helps explain global influences on the emergence and durability of coalitions.

International economic, security, and normative structures and institutions purposefully but also unintendedly influence the domestic coalitional interplay, strengthening internationalizing coalitions at some times, empowering their rivals at others. Different international regimes (institutional clusters around an issue-area) privilege the interests of one coalition over another. Accordingly, in the 1970s SN coalitions sought a global regime more compatible with their grand strategy. This New International Economic Order (NIEO) favored authoritative statist mechanisms over market-oriented ones (Krasner 1985), and was conceived to both gain leverage over rival coalitions at home and maximize collective gains vis-à-vis the industrialized world.[26] The former Soviet Union provided powerful practical and ideological support for statist import-substituting paradigms and wars of "national" liberation, particularly in the early Cold War era. The United Nations General Assembly and other UN agencies beyond the control of Western powers provided a convenient site for the coordination, elaboration, and diffusion of SN platforms in their domestic, regional, and international dimensions. Superpower competition in different regions privileged – indeed gave life in some cases – to many a military-industrial complex, even where regional threats were remote. The post-1989 collapse of SN regimes, particularly in the Soviet sphere, dealt a heavy blow to their collective ability to advance compatible international institutions.

International economic structures and regimes at the end of the twentieth century favor internationalizing coalitions worldwide to an extent never evident before. By providing credit and defining the terms of trade and investment, public and private international institutions are central to the political longevity of these coalitions. The World Bank and the International Monetary Fund (IMF) have become ever more powerful in shaping the economic orders of industrializing states, particularly following the 1982 debt crisis (Stallings 1992). Externally induced structural adjustment policies have frequently strengthened institutions in charge of reform (particularly finance ministries, central banks, export-promotion bureaus, and export-processing zones) at least initially. Several rounds of trade liberalization through the General Agreement on Tariffs and Trade (GATT) resulted in a progressively more open trading system, leading to the creation of the World Trade Organization (WTO) in 1995. WTO membership consolidates access to international markets while binding members to economic reform at home. New institutional layers such as the Group of Seven leading industrialized states (G7) include in its agenda the need for a "currency early warning system" to prevent crises – such as Mexico's 1995 "Tequilazo" – that threatened embattled internationalizing coalitions. Formal pronouncements of the G7 in 1997 affirmed the goal of realizing the full benefits of globalization. The G7 has grown to define these challenges in ways that transcend macroeconomic coordination, focusing on the embedded nature of economic, social, and security regimes. War-prone and terrorism-prone SNC regimes have become frequent targets of opprobrium by the G7.

New structures of international production (multinational administrative hierarchies) and financial intermediation (obsolescent capital controls) have made it easier for internationalizing firms and investors to pursue strategies of evasion and exit, helping these firms prevail over state agencies seeking capital controls or stiffer capital taxation. The ability of such firms – local and foreign-owned – to influence domestic investment patterns and transfer capital abroad thus increases their political leverage in shaping adjustment policies (Goodman and Pauly 1995). These same international structures have posed formidable challenges for SN coalitions. Dwindling external financing has disabled populist strategies and preferential credit programs; foreign direct investment has altered domestic coalitional balances by injecting jobs and technology at some points and not others; the critical role played by a dynamic technological edge in the global economy has favored symbolic analysts most enmeshed in international markets – via networks and "strategic alliances" – at the expense of those in state bureaucracies and domestically oriented firms; educational institutions and other international training agencies in industrialized countries have reinforced the ranks of internationalizing state and private technocrats, experts, and symbolic analysts whose skills are essential for implementing economic reform.

International economic structures and regimes have also undermined the viability of military-industrial complexes and military establishments – frequent partners in SN challenges to economic liberalization. Structural adjustment often threatens these complexes as does the demand for greater domestic and external budgetary accountability and transparency. Disagreements on evidence related to guns-versus-butter tradeoffs notwithstanding, economic stagnation exacerbates such tradeoffs, and they are most salient for developing countries under severe financial constraints. International investors understand those tradeoffs, and the World Bank has begun addressing more directly than ever the size and transparency of military budgets. The fact that these international institutions' interlocutors are often central banks and finance ministries (rather than military agencies) is a double-edged sword. It can undermine the domestic legitimacy of those interlocutors on the one hand, often accused of taking cues from foreign institutions. But it can also be used to shift the blame for downsizing "national" symbols such as the military sector unto external actors, highlighting positive economic, social, and political outcomes of reduced MILEX.

The international economic environment, otherwise generally favorable to internationalizing coalitions at the end of the century, can also lead to unintended consequences and severe crises of the kind endured by Mexico in 1995 and East Asia in 1997. Structural adjustment, stabilization programs, and economic liberalization more generally entail painful transitions for large sections of society bearing the burden of recessions, unemployment, and reduced public subsidies and infrastructural investments. As argued, external conditionality reinforces the tendency of internationalizing coalitions to pay insufficient attention to highly concentrated benefits of liberalization during initial stages and to the risky political consequences of such inattention. Weakened agents of internationalization – and the potential erosion of democracy itself – are the unintended consequences. Regional cooperation can be a collateral casualty as internationalizers fight for survival by embracing SNC instruments. Conditionality requirements imposed by international donors on the new Palestinian Authority (PA) have hurt it to some extent, as its inability to meet those requirements has slowed down financial aid. Donors have argued that early conditionality might help the PA avoid statist and rent-seeking patterns in the longer term; the state-in-the-making would thus be internationalizing at birth. However, reduced international aid and investments have resulted in growing challenges to the PA leadership from SNC constituencies.

The survival of internationalizing coalitions requires that the benefits from economic liberalization be broadened beyond the concentrated interests that may sustain these coalitions initially. Providing compensating resources, export incentives, targeted subsidies, and training can minimize domestic opposition to liberalization. Organization for Economic Cooperation and Development data reveal a remarkably positive correlation between trade openness and social spending (Rodrik 1997). Resources for upgrading social insurance can be marshaled (at least partially) from funds freed by contracting military budgets, thus increasing support for reform within civil society while extinguishing a historical source of political power for military establishments. Shifting the style of external institutional intervention toward effective consultation and enhancing industrializing states' participation in international institutional decisions can deflate nationalist resentment (Kahler 1992). The other side of this coin is the power of internationalizing coalitions to use SNC threats to extract concessions from their international partners and alleviate conditions for continued credit and investment. This "reverse conditionality" can be an effective bargaining strategy in the hands of struggling internationalizers, a strategy for which Egypt is said to have written the manual, with Russia's Yeltsin improving on it.

Protected markets in the industrialized world are another global challenge for internationalizing coalitions. Whereas the prospects of trade concessions and access to wealthy states' markets strengthen the appeal of liberalizers, protectionism undermines such appeal, as South Korea's President Park learned in the early 1970s. To a large extent, therefore, internationalizing coalitions find themselves at the mercy of global processes of economic liberalization that are not entirely irrevocable but rather intermittently threatened by the possibility of cyclical "shifting involvements" (Hirschman 1982). Where global processes contribute to unsuccessful stabilization and uncontrollable external balances, economic reform is more likely to flounder and their political agents with it. The resurgence of neomercantilistic tendencies could thus undermine what Cox (1986: 234–235) labels the "transnational managerial class" of multinational executives, finance ministries, and internationally oriented labor and symbolic analysts. Notwithstanding these potential developments, appropriate external support for internationalizers does improve their political credibility and performance. Such support has become ever more critical with respect to financial crises fueled by currency speculation.

The dominance of industrialized liberal democracies – the US in particular – within international security power structures and regimes is virtually unchallenged. Moreover even though power hierarchies generally breed resentment, the overwhelming majority of states at century's end share in the fundamental principles upheld by these regimes. The most powerful states can operate through international institutions that invest their own preferences with greater universality and legitimacy.[27] These principles include progressive disarmament, nuclear nonproliferation, anti-terrorism, banning nuclear testing and prohibiting the production, trade, and use of chemical and bacteriological weapons. These regimes advance the domestic agendas of internationalizing coalitions for reasons specified throughout this chapter. Western countries and international institutions at times provide concrete military, moral, and political support for internationalizing coalitions under assault by rivals at home or in the region. Support can range from dispatching military forces to the Persian Gulf in 1991 to a massive international presence at Israel's Prime Minister Yitzhak Rabin's funeral, signaling support for a "summit of peacemakers" threatened by terrorist challengers. International intervention poses yet another challenge to military establishments claiming a monopoly over military power on their territory. While the military – particularly under SNC regimes – regards external intervention in peacekeeping, export-control regimes, and on-site inspections as puncturing national sovereignty, civil societies welcome international guarantors offering physical protection from their own national military.

The fact that international regimes strengthen the influence of the most powerful states that created them is not lost on constituencies in industrializing states. Even internationalizing coalitions in those states raise issues of international equity and hegemonic prerogatives. Full implementation by powerful states of commitments such as the reduction and eventual elimination of nuclear arsenals according to Article VI of the Nonproliferation Treaty, helps prevent erosion in the legitimacy of internationalizing coalitions. Toward the late 1990s even "zero-option" nuclear futures emerged among some security experts, notably former US Defense Secretary Robert McNamara. The conclusion of a 1996 Comprehensive Test Ban Treaty and a 1997 Chemical Weapons Convention further strengthened the legitimacy of a multilateral order that reduced the rationale for SNC military-industrial complexes.

In sum, international economic and security regimes influence domestic coalitional balances of power; their second-order effects help shape regional orders, as we shall see in Chapter Three. International institutions and regimes can make a difference, a subject of much debate in international relations. The extent to which they weigh more or less heavily is largely contingent on the nature and strength of domestic coalitions. In designing a grand strategy, coalitions face choices regarding external allies, including the risk of conflict with international economic, political, or military actors. Internationalizers are generally more sensitive to international injunctions and conditions than their SN counterparts. This is different from arguing that international institutions determine the fate of economic reform, domestic political change, or regional orders. Domestic coalitional balances are not merely derivative of global forces. Studies point to the inability of external actors to tip the political scale in favor of reform in unfavorable domestic institutional and coalitional environments (Kahler 1992; Haggard and Kaufman 1995). International pressures for trade liberalization and macroeconomic adjustment did not bear fruit for many years in inward-looking contexts such as Argentina and India. Syngman Rhee resisted macroeconomic reform in the late 1940s and 1950s even as South Korea was under virtual US occupation while Park introduced his "deepening" program despite US and World Bank opposition. Saddam Hussein's military-industrial complex continued its nonconventional weapons production for years notwithstanding the most stringent UN on-site inspections regime in history. Outcomes are the product of changing dynamics between "the force of epochs" (world-time) and "the force of national trajectories" (Gourevitch 1986: 217). Global influences vary in their domestic effects although growing capital mobility has deepened their impact on coalitional balances, rewarding or punishing policies at home, regionally and worldwide virtually overnight.

It is worth reaffirming that the domestic impact of economic liberalization and international institutions is far more complex and unpredictable than stipulated by any single theory; that the coalitional cleavage around economic liberalization is not the only political cleavage but is certainly a common and prominent one; that this cleavage tends to attract other cleavages that often cluster along its fundamental fault lines; and that the distance between Weberian ideal and empirical coalitional types can be extensive and hybrid forms abound. Most importantly, strong versions of each coalition are likely to be better positioned to implement their grand strategies – other things being equal – than their weaker counterparts. Among those crucial "other things" is the identity of neighboring coalitions. The nature of – and strategic interactions with – ruling coalitions in the region and their domestic challengers are thus important intervening variables. The next chapter analyzes why the regional context is endogenous to understanding coalitions' ability to implement preferred grand strategies.

Notes

1   See Gramsci's (1988: 200) conception of historical blocs, where "material forces are the content and ideologies are the form, though this distinction between form and content has purely indicative value, since the material forces would be inconceivable historically without form and the ideologies would be individual fancies without the material forces." On ideology as the instrument injecting collective purpose and realms of agreement into coalitions, see Gourevitch (1986).

64 Globalization, economic reform, and regional relations

2   On the origins and evolution of each coalitional type see Chapter Four. Subsequent work substitutes "inward-looking" for SN.
3   On the relationship between democracy and coalitional type, see *Regional Orders* (Ch.4).
4   Important work informing this section includes Baldwin (1988); Milner (1988); Kaufman (1989); Frieden (1991, 1995); Haggard and Kaufman (1992); Nelson (1992); Bates and Krueger (1993); Frieden and Rogowski (1996); Keohane and Milner (1996).
5   Thresholds for protectionism are contested (Rodrik 1994) but declines in average tariffs from 100 to 12 percent – as in parts of Latin America in the 1990s – signal growing trade openness.
6   No general "guns-versus butter" theory is postulated here; those tradeoffs vary across states, time, and macroeconomic conditions and have different implications for competing coalitions. On military-industrial-complexes, MILEX and external debt, see West (1992). On why domestic constraints on resource extraction lead to restrained foreign policy, see Lamborn (1991).
7   Average MILEX/GDP for developing states (1970s–1980s) was 4–6 percent (West 1992). US military aid to South Korea and Taiwan facilitated relatively low MILEX but those levels persisted once US aid subsided.
8   On the affinity between economic nationalism and a "national security" ideology, and on the proneness of statist-protectionist coalitions to belligerent stands, see Gilpin (1987).
9   Cooperation and openness to foreign investment may be preconditions, not guarantees that foreign investment will indeed flow. On links between security threats and business risks, see Rosecrance and Schott (1997).
10 On economic reforms as explicitly strengthening states by expanding the tax base, effective collection, and basic services, see Haggard and Kaufman (1995).
11 Taiwan's foreign trade amounted to about 85 percent of its GNP in 1985 (Chan 1988). On how Taiwan's export drive, fiscal conservatism, and high rate of savings relative to consumption enabled it to contain inflation despite a heavy defense burden, see Chan (1992b).
12 On the preference for inflationary, weak-currency, nationalist, or "fiscalist" policies by uncompetitive, domestically bound, and nontradable producers, see Frieden (1995).
13 On the historical connection between the rise of nationalism, massive increases in armed forces and taxation, and the growth and centralization of nation-states, see Tilly (1994) and Rasler and Thompson (1989). On how nationalism and religious fundamentalism converge in the Middle East, see Leca (1994).
14 Johnson (1993: 220); Craig's preface to Kehr (1977: xi).
15 On reliance on ethnic ties as a logical means to overcome security dilemmas, see Posen (1993).
16 In the words of Mehdi Bazargan, first Prime Minister of the Islamic Republic of Iran, "the scale of corruption [in Iran] is breathtaking" (Sanger 1995).
17 All citations here from "Islamic Leader Is First Non-Secular Turk Premier in 75 years." *New York Times*, 29 June 1996: p. 5.
18 At the same time, the regime's distributive efforts may have foiled the decades-long prediction – so far falsified – of its imminent demise. Where the benefits are relatively more widely distributed there is less need to rely on external scapegoating. Despite earlier short-sighted financing of infamous radical groups, Saudi policy in the region has been generally more restrained than that of other Islamist and secular nationalist regimes.
19 Nawaz Sharif, representing Pakistani industrial interests backed by pragmatic Islamist groups, lamented the political energy invested in debates over Islamization "while the world is marching fast to meet the challenges of the twenty-first century" (Mayer 1993: 131). Some Islamist groups do not see inherent tensions between international economic exchange, technological modernization, and Islamist principles.
20 *Eye on Supply*. Monterey Institute of International Studies No. 6 (Spring 1992: 11).

21 As a brigadier in command of Brazil's Aerospace Technical Center put it, "we wished [tensions with Argentina] had continued, because we would have received a higher allocation for our work [on military nuclear technologies]." *Veja*, quoted in Joint Publications Research Service, Latin America. Springfield, VA: National Technical Information Service (22 March 1993: 20).
22 I follow As'ad AbuKhalil (1994: 677) here in using "Islamic fundamentalism" to refer to "all those movements and groups that aspire to the complete application of Islamic laws, as interpreted by leaders of the movements, in society and the body politic." Some Islamic, Jewish, and other fundamentalists share common objectives to create theocratic states, whether or not they choose democracy as appropriate means.
23 Haggard (1995). Populist parties within relatively polarized party systems in Latin America mobilized urban labor movements that resisted anti-inflationary stabilization efforts. Weak representation of rural interests mutes their support for adjustment (Nelson 1992).
24 On equitable land distribution, equitable wages and salaries distribution, and East Asian growth, see Amsden (1991).
25 International Institute for Strategic Studies (1995: 265).
26 International institutions in the 1940s–1950s foiled alternatives to import substitution and rigorous exchange controls (Díaz Alejandro 1983).
27 Ruggie (1993). Cox (1986) explains this legitimacy as the product of Gramscian hegemony, where the powerful make concessions to secure the acquiescence of the weak. For Buzan (1991) great powers have established at the dawn of the twenty-first century a multipolar, ideologically cohesive security community of capitalist states that lays the ground for an international society with common goals and values.

3
COALITIONS, STRATEGIC INTERACTION, AND REGIONAL OUTCOMES

The regional behavior of domestic political coalitions (in and out of power) is highly responsive to the identity and strength of the actors it faces throughout the region. Put differently, the nature of a ruling coalition in country A creates regional externalities or spill-overs for country B's ruling coalition (and its opposition) as well as others in neighboring countries. Thus, the coalitional preferences of domestic publics in country A have strategic implications for the region. In some cases actors are more conscious of such implications than in others, but a general increase in that awareness seems evident at the end of the twentieth century.[1] Clearly, the interactive regional context influences the electoral appeal, behavior, and policies of coalitions, in both their domestic and external expressions. This chapter spells out the ways in which the identity (internationalizing or SN) and political strength of coalitions in neighboring states influence a coalition's behavior and policies in a particular state. The ontogeny (individual development) of a domestic coalition – e.g. internationalizing – is intimately linked to that of its regional group development, or phylogeny. *The degree of coalitional homogeneity / heterogeneity at the regional level influences the scope and nature of regional conflict and cooperation. Thus, higher and more extensive levels of cooperation can be expected where internationalizing coalitions prevail throughout a given region than where SN, or competing internationalizing and SN neighbors, face one another.*

Cooperation implies active attempts to adjust policies to meet the demands of others under conditions of discord or potential discord. Such attempts involve the willingness to repeatedly forsake the unilateral pursuit of one's own interests and to undertake commitments on a basis of diffuse reciprocity.[2] These commitments run the gamut of substantive issue areas. Very often, security and economic cooperation are linked not merely because of economies of scope but because of the complementary role both play in the grand (domestic, regional, and global) strategy of different coalitions.[3] The broader the scope (issues), the more *extensive* the cooperative framework. The deeper the level of commitments, the more *intensive* is cooperation expected to be. Highly extensive and intensive cooperative relations yield a pattern akin to a pluralistic security community.[4] The willingness to undertake commitments based on diffuse reciprocity and to forsake routinely the pursuit of self-interest declines as we move toward the other end of the spectrum. This decreasing disposition often transcends most issue areas and, in its extreme case, is evidenced in the open articulation of the war option as inevitable and even desirable. Although fundamental patterns of cooperation and war-proneness may be easily identifiable in some cases, the meaning of behavior cannot be separated from the security context in which it takes place. The shadow of the past filters the interpretation of a given behavior, rendering the definition of purely "objective" categories equivocal and vague. Knowledge about the depth and longevity of regional security dilemmas is essential for interpreting cooperation in different regional milieus. The mere existence of a direct dialogue entailed meager cooperative achievements in the Southern Cone for decades whereas such dialogue implied a revolution in cooperation in the Korean peninsula, China–Taiwan relations, and the Arab–Israeli context. Initial security conditions do matter, and coalitions differ across regions in terms of their starting points for the construction of regional orders.

To explore the interactive dynamics among coalitions throughout a region, Figure 3.1 provides a schematic plotting of all the possible coalitional combinations for the simplified case of a single dyad, states A and B. The schema takes note of our discussion in Chapter Two of the centrality of a coalition's political strength at home, by differentiating between weak and strong coalitions in states A and B respectively. As argued, positive and negative measures of a coalition's strength relative to its domestic challengers provide us with important information regarding the likelihood that such a coalition can implement its grand strategy in a more or less coherent and prompt fashion. The other side of this coin is, of course, that an opposition that is sizable in resources, largely consensual in its macropolitical objectives, and effectively organized is likely to pose a more formidable barrier to the implementation of a ruling coalition's grand strategy. Weaker ruling coalitions are likely to have shorter time-horizons than stronger ones.

Both states A and B may be ruled by a weak or strong, internationalizing or SN coalition, defining four basic possibilities for each state. In a dyadic situation, this matrix yields twelve possible coalitional combinations (notice that cells 2 and 3 involve analytically indistinguishable combinations, with only the identity of the coalitions reversed). The darker the shaded areas in Figure 3.1, the more cooperative the bilateral relationship is expected to be. Cooperation declines as we move to mixed cells 2 and 3 – where internationalizing and SN coalitions face each other – and declines even more in the lighter-shaded areas depicting relations between SN dyads. The remainder of this chapter explains the logic behind this pattern.

Zones of stable peace: Converging grand strategies in strong internationalizing orders

Cells 1_{I-IV} capture situations where both A and B are ruled by internationalizing coalitions. Despite variations across them, the four quadrants ($_{I-IV}$) portray the most extensive and intensive cooperative relationships in Figure 3.1. Quadrant 1_I reflects

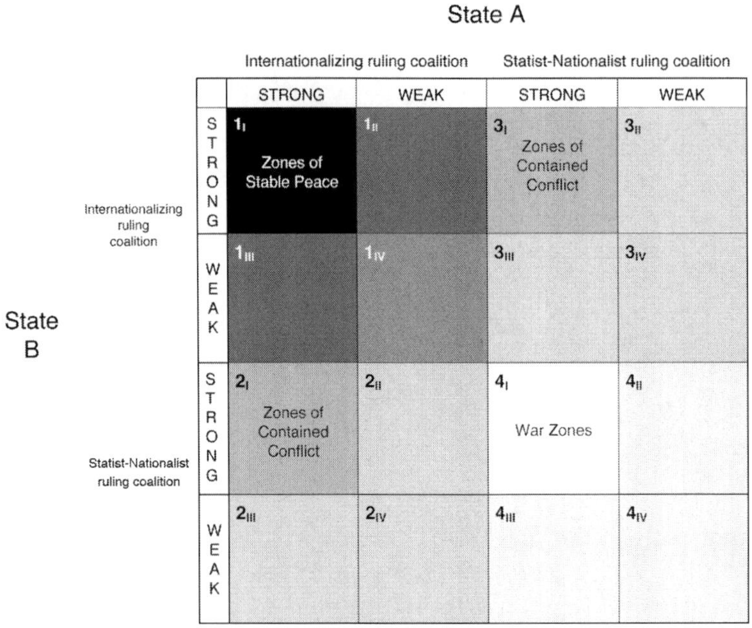

State A

		Internationalizing ruling coalition		Statist-Nationalist ruling coalition	
		STRONG	WEAK	STRONG	WEAK
Internationalizing ruling coalition	STRONG	1_I Zones of Stable Peace	1_{II}	3_I Zones of Contained Conflict	3_{II}
	WEAK	1_{III}	1_{IV}	3_{III}	3_{IV}
Statist-Nationalist ruling coalition	STRONG	2_I Zones of Contained Conflict	2_{II}	4_I War Zones	4_{II}
	WEAK	2_{III}	2_{IV}	4_{III}	4_{IV}

State B (row label)

Figure 3.1 Coalitional combinations and regional orders
Source: Revised from Solingen (1998: 64)

zones of stable peace, whereas quadrants 1_{II} and 1_{III}, and particularly 1_{IV}, portray largely cooperative relations but less robust and stable than quadrant 1_I (due to the weak versions of internationalizing coalitions represented in the three other quadrants). The synergies between economic and security cooperation across cells 1 become evident when one recalls the domestic implications of regional policies described in the previous chapter.

In the realm of security, relations between internationalizing coalitions are characterized by the following features:

First, domestic considerations of political survival drive economic rationalization – and military downsizing – as much as external factors. There is therefore a virtual built-in guarantee that fellow internationalizing coalitions – all things being equal – will be reluctant to defect through militarized strategies. This is not to say that internationalizing dyads never have long-standing disputes, territorial, confessional, and otherwise. However, the primacy of their grand strategies tames those disputes, rendering reliance on militarized means highly unlikely. For internationalizing dyads and clusters, de-escalation is dominant in managing their disputes. The potential for armed conflict and extensive military build-ups threatens their economic and political fundamentals – fiscal conservatism; macroeconomic, political, and regional stability; access to capital, technology, and markets – required by internationalizing agendas.[5] Internationalizing preferences and strategies function, in essence, as tacit self-binding commitments that do not always require formal alliances. These symmetric conditions alleviate what might otherwise become prisoner's dilemmas (as in most arms races). Furthermore, they help internationalizers defend their endorsement of economic reform, contained or shrinking military complexes, and cooperative regional postures from attacks by domestic challengers. *The domestic programs of internationalizing coalitions, in sum, create positive security externalities in the region.* As Jusuf Wanandi, one of Indonesia's leading strategic analysis argued, "If each [ASEAN] member nation can accomplish an overall national development and overcome internal threats, regional resilience can result, much in the same way as a chain derives its overall strength from the strength of its constituent parts."[6] This statement lays out the logic of regional requirements for the fulfillment of domestic internationalizing agendas.

Second, the mutually reinforcing domestic and interactive regional inducements to allay conflict also reduce transaction costs in relations between internationalizing coalitions. Agreements on issues under dispute are easier to reach and there is less need to monitor or punish compliance or improve information. This transparency is highest when internationalizing grand strategies are more fully in place and their political agents more strongly entrenched – conditions that are, of course, inter-related. Thus, internationalizing coalitions beget the conditions for self-sustained, rather than externally imposed, regional cooperation, as in the Southern Cone in the 1990s. Even where external actors (powerful states or international institutions) do play a facilitating role in conflict management or conflict resolution – as in the Middle East – the engine of regional cooperation is progressively more internal if and when internationalizers grow stronger. Conversely, their political deterioration requires more active external intervention. The historical breakthrough between the PLO and Israel's Labor–Meretz coalition in 1993, known as Oslo I, bypassed the formal process of negotiations in Washington, DC, under (mainly) US sponsorship. Similarly, the Jordan–Israeli rapprochement of July 1994 and the subsequent peace treaty revealed a strong internal and regional logic reflected to some extent in public meetings held by King Hussein and late Prime Minister Rabin at their mutual border, even prior to the White House lawn routine. The US played an important role as moderator and guarantor in most Middle East peace negotiations, but more so as internationalizing coalitions came under strain or in relations between mixed dyads, as in Syrian–Israeli interactions even under Labor–Meretz or Jordanian–Israeli interactions under Netanyahu. Strong internationalizers have not found a place in the Middle East thus far.

In the realm of economic cooperation, where internationalizers take a firmer hold throughout a region than in the budding case of the Middle East – as with the paradigmatic European Union (EU), or the still-evolving cases of ASEAN, the Southern Cone's Mercado Común del Sur (MERCOSUR), and the Gulf Cooperation Council (GCC) – their domestic political-economic strategies are often transferred to the regional institutional arena.[7] New regional cooperative and integrative regimes emerge that serve the purposes of strengthening the internationalizing model at home while disabling its opposition, and lubricating external ties to the global political economy. Establishing markets requires harmonization of product standards and legal and administrative infrastructures, which, in turn, deepens the institutional links among internationalizing coalitions in different countries, as well as their mutual interdependence. These coalitions embrace trade-creating schemes that emphasize positive regional and global externalities, largely compatible with "open regionalism."[8] The progressive expansion of bilateral and regional trade benefits the domestic economies directly and strengthens the flow of outside investment, creating pressures for further – more generalized – liberalization.

Although an absolute increase in regional trade and investment often results from interaction among ruling internationalizing partners in neighboring states, regional economic integration is not always required for cooperative relations to develop. For instance, when competitive – rather than complementary – economies are involved, the drive for integration is initially weaker, as with ASEAN or the GCC.[9] Extensive intra-regional economic exchanges are not a necessary condition for embarking on a cooperative regional order. The 1979 Egyptian–Israeli peace agreement exemplifies why, even in the absence of dramatic economic benefits from bilateral economic interactions, internationalizing coalitions might still find it in their interest to maintain cooperative relations. The underlying logic of economic liberalization is global: regional arrangements may become stepping-stones subordinated to that logic. Put differently, nation-to-system interdependence is the engine of regional cooperative arrangements, in both economics and security.[10] This is quite different from arguing – as in classical interdependence theory – that the expectations of bilateral economic gains fuel broad-based cooperation between or among regional partners. Yet, where the international credibility of internationalizing agendas throughout the region is questionable – as was the case in the Southern Cone and continues to be in the Middle East – formal regional arrangements in the direction of freer trade can, of course, signal a more believable commitment to extra-regional investors. ASEAN and early internationalizers in South Korea and Taiwan embraced a global focus at the outset. Indeed ASEAN's intra-regional trade as a percentage of total trade declined in the 1980s.

Thus far I have discussed Cell 1 in a general way although, as is clear from the examples, the variance between interactions among strong and weak internationalizing partners – across cell 1 quadrants – can be significant. The most extensive and intensive levels of cooperation within Cell 1 can be expected when both A and B are ruled by strong internationalizing coalitions (quadrant 1_1). The regional orders created by such combination – particularly when enjoying relatively long time-horizons – have elements of what Keohane (1984) defines as "harmony." In these situations policies are pursued to advance a unilateral self-interest thus facilitating the attainment of similar goals by the other side, without a constant need to adapt policies to take into consideration the other side's interest. However, even these orders require cooperation, or adjusting one's policies to facilitate the goals of others or to reduce the negative consequences of one's policies on others. To some extent, cooperation in strong internationalizing contexts assumes the form of an assurance game, where the benefits from joint cooperation are higher than those from unilateral defection, and where assurance comes from the domestic incentives of internationalizing coalitions. The compatibility and synergies of their domestic agendas minimize "the balance of threat:" internationalizing partners perceive their own political resources as growing in tandem with those of their internationalizing neighbors. The level of cooperation in quadrant 1_1 is high enough to ensure stable zones of peace, such as the European Union. Even in North America, where peaceful relations among the US, Canada, and Mexico have been a constant for much of this century, the deepest levels of cooperation were not forged until the strongest version of an internationalizing coalition in Mexico's history came to power, that of former President Carlos Salinas de Gortari.

Levels of cooperation decrease somewhat where a weak internationalizing coalition faces a strong internationalizing neighbor (quadrants 1_{II} and 1_{III}). In the Southern Cone, a weak internationalizing coalition in Brazil under pressure from SN challengers was more tentative about bilateral cooperative process launched in 1991 – in economics and security – than its counterpart in Argentina. The ascent of Itamar Franco to Brazil's presidency in 1992, his wooing of a SN constituency and of the military, his attacks on international institutions and their domestic "allies," and his statements on Brazil's sovereignty in nuclear matters, all temporarily tamed but did not eliminate the drive toward a new, more cooperative regional order. The stronger Argentine internationalizing coalition at the time, under President Carlos S. Menem, continued to push forward an agenda of privatization, low inflation, downsized military expenditures, and balanced budgets, complete with a commitment to unilateral accession to the Nonproliferation Treaty (not contingent on Brazil's accession), a step that Argentina had resisted for decades. Some of this dynamic was also evident in Egyptian–Israeli relations during 1993–1995, at the height of an internationalizing interlude in Israel. Egypt's cooperative approach to the peace process at the time – in both their bilateral and multilateral venues – was far more tentative than Jordan's, for King Hussein had managed to deflect the opposition to economic liberalization and regional accommodation more successfully than his Egyptian counterpart had during that period.

Under the circumstances prevailing in quadrants 1_{II} and 1_{III}, the relatively stronger internationalizing coalition (in A for instance) faces a dilemma: if it maintains its liberalizing program, it helps its weak internationalizing neighbor (in B) uphold cooperative postures. However, at the same time, it risks raising domestic doubts – fueled by a lingering if weakened SN opposition – about giving in to an unstable partner. The weak internationalizing coalition in B is, of course, at the mercy of a stronger SN domestic opposition. This opposition, in turn, exploits the asymmetry (between a strong liberalizer in A and a weak liberalizer at home), accusing the weak liberalizers in power of yielding to the regional "adversary." President Yasir Arafat endured this delicate position since the inception of the Palestinian Authority (PA), even when Labor–Meretz enjoyed a strong political base. The asymmetry under these conditions can become unstable, as the weakness of the weak liberalizer in B spreads to the hitherto stronger liberalizer in A. This is largely a result of the stronger opposition in B begetting a stronger opposition in A, a situation that led to the progressive weakening of Labor–Meretz in Israel and its eventual replacement by its SNC rival in 1996. High and consistent levels of asymmetry are thus not very conducive to maintaining concessions that might broaden the scope of diffuse reciprocity.

Within the largely cooperative Cell 1, cooperation is even more tentative and unstable when two rather weak internationalizing coalitions face one another (quadrant 1_{IV}). This is so because, despite risking accusations of sellout, a weak internationalizing coalition in B finds it easier to survive politically while pursuing compromising regional policies in situations where A is steered by a strong internationalizing coalition, as when Brazil's Franco faced Argentina's Menem. As argued, A's pursuit of state-shrinking policies, lower military budgets, and easier access to international markets, capital, and technology makes it easier for B's weak internationalizing coalition to justify its cooperative posture vis-à-vis A when facing its domestic opponents. Where B's weak internationalizing coalition faces a similarly weak one in A, however, it is likely to encounter greater domestic resistance to accept the risks of downsizing military endowments and engaging in diffuse reciprocity. Time-horizons are shorter here. Accusations of SN challengers resonate far more effectively when they can point to frail reforms and strong SN-confessional counterparts in the neighboring state.

This effect is particularly evident in the difficulties encountered by incipient internationalizing Indian and Pakistani coalitions since 1991. Their respective political fragility at home made it harder for each to transcend old patterns of domestic and regional enmity. In a sense, the domestic weakness of such dyads raises issues of more discounted future payoffs and involuntary defection. Under such conditions, the benefits of an alleviated security dilemma are more likely to be dismissed than in the case of strong internationalizing interlocutors. Even where they face serious challenges at home, however, weak internationalizing coalitions are on stronger ground to cooperate when they face an internationalizing interlocutor than when they do not. The most cooperative Arab dyads – relative to others in the region – historically fall under this category, including Egypt and Jordan (1980s), Egypt and Tunisia (1970s–1990s), and Egypt and Saudi Arabia (particularly since the 1980s). However, as these cases suggest, bilateral relations between weak internationalizing coalitions – as those between mixed dyads – cannot be taken out of a broader regional context where SN-confessional coalitions might dominate. Such context affects the ability of an internationalizing dyad or cluster to transcend militarization, and compels it to balance coalitional adversaries in the region, frustrating many components of its grand strategy.

The multilateral Middle East peace process of the early 1990s was, to a significant extent, the product of incipient quadrant 1_{IV} conditions. Variants of nascent internationalizing coalitions were beginning to emerge throughout the region, from the financial, tourist-based, commercial-agriculture, and *munfatihun* economies in Egypt and Jordan to the oil-exporting industries in the Gulf and the Arabian Peninsula and the high-tech export-oriented sectors in Israel. Egypt had pioneered a regional rapprochement since the mid-1970s, when Sadat embarked on an effort to replace Gamal Abdel Nasser's import-substitution strategy with a policy of liberalization (*infitah*), accumulation, and growth.[11] Liberalizing agendas had overtaken even important factions of the Palestine Liberation Organization (PLO) once the convulsive energy of the late 1980s *infitah* (uprising) had spent itself out. At the time of the 1991 Madrid Conference most participants were under extremely fragile and highly diluted versions of internationalizing coalitions shackled by strong SN and confessional opponents. Core participants such as Israel and Syria – who attended Madrid largely under forceful prodding by the US – were dominated by SN coalitions under strain. The conference's immediate results were limited. As incipient PLO liberalizers grew stronger and attracted unprecedented international support, they also articulated unprecedented cooperative principles by 1993. Meanwhile, in the 1992 Israeli elections Labor–Meretz won a mandate for socio-economic renewal at home and territorial compromise with the Palestinians. This convergence led to the historical Oslo agreements in September 1993. A stronger set of region-wide internationalizers was able to transform the multilateral working groups born in Madrid in 1991 into more viable cooperative undertakings after 1993.

Internationalizing coalitions throughout the region laid out the foundations of a brand new regional order, both at the bilateral level (Palestinian–Israeli and Jordanian–Israeli) and in multilateral negotiations over economic, security, environmental, water, and refugee issues. Superseding decades of regional and global power balancing, these coalitions planted the seeds of what might, in time, become multilateral collective security arrangements.[12] Each coalition, however, continued to be threatened by the specter of intransigent and violent domestic SN-confessional oppositions. As of 1996 the short time-horizons of these weak coalitions had become a major barrier to deepening cooperation, and their contagious domestic fragility eventually stalled both bilateral and multilateral cooperation, particularly following the ascent of a SNC coalition in Israel. Incipient cooperation among internationalizers had created a new balance of power in the region, between the partners to the peace process on the one hand, and SNC coalitions – mainly in Iran, Iraq, the Palestinian Islamic Resistance, and Sudan – who chose to remain outside the process, on the other. That cooperative frameworks can have negative security externalities for third parties is not startling. Neither is it unexpected – given the coalitional logic outlined so far – that the new regional coalitional balance was largely shattered after 1996, in tandem with Israel's new domestic coalitional balance-emerging in response to Palestinian terrorist attacks that strengthened SNC forces.

War zones: Balancing power and myths in statist-nationalist (SN) orders

What forms do regional orders take when SN coalitions face each other in a region, as in Cell 4? In principle, where they confront a coalitional clone supported by similar political and economic interests across the border, one might expect cooperation – even attempts at political and economic integration-to be more likely. The history of SN (mostly military) Arab regimes during the 1960s and 1970s provides many examples of this scenario, as with the Ba'athist coalitions in Syria and Iraq. Yet cooperative schemes among Nasser's Egypt, Gaddafi's Libya, Hussein's Iraq, and Assad's Syria were invariably brief, even when their respective SN coalitions were quite strong.[13] This is not entirely unexpected bearing in mind the fact that SN coalitions thrive on regional competition. Integrative efforts have the potential of forcing many of those coalitions' natural constituencies literally out of business. Furthermore, collective security arrangements or integrative schemes weaken SN rationales for maintaining high levels of unilateral military preparedness. At best, the presence of internationalizing coalitions in the region might justify the maintenance of a common military effort. Yet such effort implies a division of labor among SN allies that could undercut the military-industrial constituencies in each SN ally. These constituencies are often very large, demanding between 15 and 25 percent of GDP or over three times the world's average. Even levels of cooperation lower than integrative schemes have the potential of alienating confessional (and territorially irredentist) groups whose aspirations often fuel hitherto dormant territorial disputes. Eastern and Central Europe are an abundant source of examples for this as are South Asia and the Middle East. As a result of all this, SN coalitions facing each other in a region are prone to embrace hyper-nationalist (or hyper-confessional) postures designed to accentuate rather than blur their differences.[14]

Given the constituents or political pillars of SN coalitions, their domestic program itself (emphasizing extensive state entrepreneurship and militarization, economic closure, and national or confessional purity) often has negative security externalities throughout the region.[15] Differentiation along national or confessional lines and insistence on territorial aspirations are defining characteristics of SNC coalitions and integral parts of their survival strategy. Sovereignty over disputed territories acquires a centrality and zero-sum quality that differentiates SN interactions from all others. Sovereignty over Shatt al Arab, for instance, was far less subject to negotiation for the Iranian–Iraqi SNC dyad than was the case with the West Bank and Gaza for Israel's Labor–Meretz and the PA, despite the greater centrality – indeed the existential status of these territories for both Palestine and Israel. Notably, intractable approaches to territoriality are crucial features for this last pair's respective domestic opposition, historical Likud, Hamas, and their allies. This comparison highlights the contrast between cells 4 and 1. In cell 4, relatively smaller security threats – an area separating two territorially massive rivals such as Iran and Iraq – could produce a war zone of vast proportions. In cell 1 a dramatic reciprocal vulnerability, overlapping claims over the same territory, and a deep historical security dilemma do not always preclude dialogue and compromise under internationalizing interlocutors.

The centrality of national symbols, territoriality, and self-reliance among SN dyads tends to foil attempts at pan- or trans-regional movements, even among otherwise "natural" allies such as Nasserite and Ba'ath-ruled regimes, Kampuchea and Vietnam, or the Islamic Republics of Iran and Sudan. Weaker SN coalitions can be expected to be more tempted than stronger ones to rely on integrative efforts – particularly with a strong SN partner that shares its political platform – in order to strengthen their own delicate position at home. Yet such efforts involve the risk of being absorbed by the stronger partner and, consequently, of impairing the weak coalition's position even further, as Syria's Ba'athist officers quickly realized after the aborted United Arab Republic with Egypt. Military alliances between or among SN coalitions are thus ephemeral. The presence of neighboring SN coalitions heightens the "balance of threat" for these coalitions no less – and in some cases even more – than would internationalizing coalitions. In sharp contrast to internationalizing clusters, a heightened balance of threat at the border offers SN coalitions opportunities to thrive politically and advance their grand strategy. Their rhetoric is imbued with contradictory assertions that their adversaries posit awesome security threats but are essentially inert "paper tigers."[16]

Thus, in the realm of security, SN coalitions further their parochial interests by creating a climate of risk, instability, conflict, and competition. At the same time, they are not invariably interested in actualizing their war-fighting potential, that is, in resorting to war. Yet the logic of their political-economic strategy (particularly extensive militarization) and their risky posturing often lead – or make them stumble into – armed conflict.[17] At times, even while trying to avoid showdowns that might endanger their leadership or physical integrity, war becomes an unintended consequence, as Iran discovered in 1980. The individual proneness to brinkmanship in a regional context dominated by balance-of-threat strategies explains the high incidence of militarized conflict, war zones, and regional overexpansion, evident in Kim Il Sung's attack and ejection from South Korea, Nasser's encroachment in Yemen, Begin's encroachment in Lebanon, Galtieri's Malvinas/Falklands debacle, and Saddam Hussein's fiascos in Iran and Kuwait.[18] The idea of multilateral conflict management (or of forsaking the unilateral pursuit of their own interests) is oxymoronic for regimes thriving on myths of self-reliance, military prowess, sovereignty, and national or confessional purity. Saddam Hussein could thus submit to his own domestic public that the most compelling response to the putative aggressive intentions of Shi'ite Islamic Iran was to counterbalance its ruling coalition first, and defeat it next.

If all these conditions were not enough to exacerbate conflict, an additional characteristic of SN coalitions is expected to intensify the hostility typical in such dyads/clusters. These coalitions are often held together by strong leaders sometimes worshiped as virtual deities, adding a personalistic adversarial touch – and an important source of myths – to cross-border SN relationships.[19] The personalistic element tends to fuel – rather than repress – the slippery slope into war zones. Though not unique to SNC coalitions (or to non-democratic contexts), the incidence of personalism is higher and its role more integral to the strategy than for internationalizing coalitions. Even where authoritarian leaders spearhead internationalizing strategies, once the strategy is in place it often transcends the original leadership, as in South Korea, Taiwan, and Chile. In contrast, the actual or prospective death of SN leaders often creates disarray regarding the coalition's survival, as in North Korea, Iraq, Sudan, Libya, and Argentina at the time of Juan D. Perón. This uncertainly renders personalistic transitions within SNC regimes particularly vulnerable to temptations to lash out in external aggression as a means to rescue the coalition from the instability created by the loss of a coalescing leader. Diversionary wars as a first resort are risky but nonetheless a viable instrument in the grand strategic kit of these coalitions.

The scope of regional devastation in war zones resulting from encounters between SN coalitions is widespread and, in the aftermath of much bloodshed and destruction, those coalitions' political exit is far from assured. Indeed, wars can further strengthen the political pillars of SN regimes. Particularly where democratic institutions are absent, these coalitions manage to retain strongholds on remaining political, economic, and organizational assets. Put differently, there is no simple transitivity between the folly of war and the folly of political defeat. As Salamé (1994: 17) argued, military defeats have arguably strengthened rather than weakened dictatorships in the Arab-world, archetypical SN types. The popularity of challenging an adversary compensated for the opprobrium of defeat. This phenomenon helps explain why such coalitions are less likely to shy away from war. Democratization surely forces greater accountability for regional adventurism but tends to face special challenges under regimes ruled by SN coalitions, as developed in Chapter 4 of *Regional Orders* (not included in this volume). Finally, the relatively higher affinity of SN coalitions with risky and potentially devastating regional policies is evident in their typical pursuit of weapons of mass destruction (WMD). Indeed, such coalitions have stood at the vanguard of nuclearizing regions, with expensive nuclear and other WMD programs playing a central role in the call for "redeeming" solutions to regional threats (threats that in some cases – South Asia – were perhaps more realistic than others, such as the Southern Cone).

Historical examples of strong SN coalitions include those headed by Pakistan's Zulfiqar Bhutto, Iran's ayatollahs, Egypt's Nasser, Libya's Gaddafi, North Korea's Kim Il Sung, Iraq's Hussein, Argentina's Perón, and Brazil's Getúlio Vargas. With few exceptions, these coalitions helped create some of the most conflict-prone regions. Particularly bloody were encounters between strong SN rivals (quadrant 4_I) such as South and North Korea (1950s), Kampuchea and Vietnam (1978–1979), India and Pakistan (1948, 1960s), Iran and Iraq (1980s), and Israel and Egypt, Syria, and Iraq (1950s–1960s) among others. The Serbian–Croatian–Bosnian debacle of the 1990s falls largely under this category as well. Territorial issues – highly malleable material in the construction of myths – are almost invariably central to these disputes.

Pairs of weak SN coalitions (quadrant 4_{IV}) and mixes of weak and strong SN ones (quadrants 4_{II} and 4_{III}) are similarly prone to slide into militarized confrontations, such as those between Indonesia and Malaysia (1960s), Somalia and Ethiopia (1977–1978), Israel and Syrian-occupied Lebanon (1982), and South and North Yemen (1979, 1994). In all three cases (quadrants 4_{II}, 4_{III}, and 4_{IV}) a weak SN coalition is particularly constrained domestically, and can hardly afford to engage in "appeasement" exercises vis-à-vis its equally weak SN neighbor. Domestically embattled coalitions are more concerned with short-term survival than with potential benefits in an uncertain future. This is not merely the case for leaders constrained by democratic electoral cycles but also for those led by authoritarian entrepreneurs challenged by competitors, particularly those logrolling even more extremist SNC partners – frequently fellow military officers. In sum, weak versions of SN coalitions are likely to be more affected by this competitive outbidding effect, which tends to radicalize the rhetoric and actions of competing factions even within the same SN coalitional camp.

In the realm of economic arrangements, SN coalitions face conflicting incentives. On the one hand, satisfying the domestic economic constituencies that sustain them may involve a measure of regional economic cooperation, for instance where such cooperation broadens the protected market for import-substituting firms. This pattern of preferential trading blocs largely characterized many of the efforts at regional integration in Latin America, including LAFTA (Latin American Free Trade Association), CACM (Central American Common Market), and the Andean group.[20] ECLA (UN Economic Commission for Latin America) provided the regional institutional foundation of this model, one that resisted integration into the global economic system because of its alleged exploitative nature.[21]

Intrabloc trade among COMECON (Council for Mutual Economic Assistance) partners and regional schemes in Africa and Asia also exemplified efforts at import-substitution writ large. Quite often, economic cooperation among these coalitions resulted in trade-diverting schemes with negative externalities for third actors in the region and beyond.

On the other hand, private and state monopolies threatened with competition from regional counterparts resist lowering trade barriers. Where such monopolies play a critical role in sustaining SN coalitions, they strive to maintain a regional system of competing rather than complementary economies. As fundamental pillars of such coalitions, protected sectors balking at cooperative undertakings likely to threaten their niches generally prevail under these conditions.[22] In the Middle East at twentieth century's end, some SNC coalitions propose political economies putatively rooted in Islamist principles, largely rejecting many tenets of international economic regimes.[23] These coalitions have only attained full power in Iran and Sudan, and have proven willing to drown the benefits from regional economic exchange in a politically more rewarding sea of confessional radicalism, at least initially.

A SN coalition in control of a large regional power can avail itself of the imperial commercial strategy so aptly described by Hirschman (1945). It thus seeks to import goods for which there are no substitutes at home (or only poor and expensive ones) and goods required for its war machine, relying on the supply effect of foreign trade. It also uses foreign trade to increase its regional power and influence, inducing maximum dependence by its neighbors through various means: exporting industrial goods in which it has a monopolistic position; diverting its trade to weaker trade partners (particularly poor and small ones) for whom the utility of trade is higher; increasing the others' adjustment difficulties of discontinuing trade; actively deindustrializing weaker potential competitors in its export markets; creating "exclusive complementarities" (products with little demand elsewhere) within the targeted trading partners; and purchasing some of their products at uncompetitive and stable prices to drive them out of alternative markets. SN regional powers can also rely on exports of abundant commodities (e.g. oil) to reinforce bilateralism, dependence, and domination. Nazi Germany in the late 1930s and early 1940s provides the textbook case of an imperial commercial strategy; less successful SN hegemons have tried their hand at it as well, as Iraq with Jordan.[24] Such strategy allows the hegemon to maximize economic profit, military power, and regional influence, all of which sustain and reproduce its ruling SN coalition. Although the strategy weakens neighboring states, it may strengthen some SN partners who benefit economically (as monopolies and monopsonies) and politically from the coercive trade practices of the powerful neighbor. SN coalitions thus put their commercial regional strategies to work by seeking subservient political accessories across the border.[25]

SNC forces in Israel and South Asia rode the crest of a political backlash against internationalization in 1996. The opposition to Israel's Labor–Meretz coalition's efforts at internationalization and regional peace settlements gravitated toward Likud and its partners on the religious and secular nationalist extremes. Returning to power in 1996, this opposition had sustained significant losses with the achievements of a Labor–Meretz government and regional breakthroughs with the

PLO (1993) and Jordan (1994). However, the SN camp was revived from this political knockout primarily by bloody radical Islamic attacks on Israeli civilians, and by the political reorganization of a populist-confessional camp resisting economic liberalization (the doubling of Shas seats in the 1996 Knesset was a symptom of the latter). SNC coalitions in Israel and Palestine feed on each other's success, as evident from the growing political difficulties facing the PA. This relationship exemplifies the dynamics of regional diffusion of SN confessionalism and heightened likelihood of military confrontation. At time T the radical SN opposition to the PA shifts (a) the coalitional balance within Israel toward its own SNC camp through terrorist activities against Israeli citizens and (b) the coalitional balance within Palestine via competitive outbidding with the PA. At time $T+1$ the political reinvigoration of SNC forces in Israel gives new life to its Palestinian counterpart, no longer marginalized by the peace process and by prospects of regional economic cooperation. Indeed, the opposition to the PA has consistently foiled such prospects, inducing political and economic insecurity and triggering – via terror – Israeli closure of the territories, which deprives many Palestinians of work possibilities in Israel. Even Labor–Meretz succumbed to the flawed logic of territorial closure in response to the massive assault by SNC opponents. The fury of that assault was such that it gave life to extremist corollaries such as the assassination of Israel's Prime Minister Yitzhak Rabin – the architect of Oslo – in November 1995. At $T+2$ the bilateral and multilateral peace processes had reached their deepest valley, reversing the achievements of the internationalizing interlude of 1993–1995. As of 1997, many fear the region has shifted toward Cell 4.

In South Asia, the platform of India's fundamentalist Hindu Bharatiya Janata party (BJP) proposed a two-pronged approach to India's predicaments: banning foreign loans, investments, and imports on the one hand, and deploying nuclear weapons on the other.[26] This coalition draws support from import-competing industries (food-processing, automobile, banking, and communications), a large and influential sector of Brahmins, a broad base of public-sector employees, and some rural sectors opposed to economic reform at home or vis-à-vis the global economy. BJP won a plurality of votes in a highly fragmented contest in 1996 but proved unable to organize a viable coalition and was forced to surrender power within two weeks. Pakistan's radical Islamist Jama'at-i-Islam is somewhat of a mirror image of Hindu fundamentalism, although BJP uses confessional issues more instrumentally (as does Israel's Likud). Jama'at challenged Western-style modernization policies of Prime Ministers Nawaz Sharif and Benazir Bhutto, exploiting primordial confessional passions and combative policies vis-à-vis India. Coalitional dynamics here, as in the Middle East, portray weak internationalizers intermittently challenged – and sometimes replaced – by SNC rivals, a cycle that has precluded any significant cooperative breakthroughs in South Asia. Indeed South Asia lagged behind the Middle East in the early 1990s, despite arguably better initial conditions and a more manageable number of states needed for convergence on cooperation.

SNC backlashes in these two regions raise the issue of transitivity between SNC positions advanced while in the opposition and their actual policies once in power. The reigning assumption holds that shifting from opposition to government has moderating effects. Two factors call into question such expectations: the political logic that sustains these coalitions and the historical legacy and contemporary empirical record of SNC coalitions in power. [The empirical chapters in *Regional Orders* dissect the political logic and empirical record of such coalitions in detail.].

In sum, *SNC regional orders strengthen the internal consistency of the individual grand strategies that create them.* External threats (in the form of neighboring SNC coalitions) give coherence to a program of domestic militarization, expansion of state entrepreneurship and intervention, and myth-making. The presence of internationalizing coalitions in such regions challenge the collective consistency of SN grand strategies in ways I explore next.

The paradox of contained conflict: Grand-strategic equilibria among strong mixed dyads

Cells 2 and 3 depict mixed dyads, where alternative internationalizing and SN coalitions face each other. I first consider the general case for all four generic variants of mixed dyads (eight, when reversing their identities). These conditions lead a SN coalition in B to use the neighboring internationalizing ruling coalition in A as a lightning rod for both regional tensions and its own domestic difficulties. SN leaders in B thus depict A's efforts to liberalize its domestic economy only through its negative fallouts; portray A's overtures to liberalize regional trade as hegemonic designs; and interpret A's greater affinity with international regimes and institutions as complete capitulation to dictates of foreign powers. This portrayal of internationalizing coalitions often includes labels such as "lackeys," "flunkeys," "paper tigers" and "puppets" – notably in the Middle East – or *sadaejuui* (puppets) in North Korea.

A's ruling coalition provides yet another arena for carrying on B's domestic battle against its own internationalizing opposition. This phenomenon is evident, for instance, in the Middle East, where secular SNC challengers in Iran, Iraq, Sudan, and Libya offer themselves as alternatives to various internationalizing coalitions (some royalist, some secular, some with pragmatic Islamic bents). SN coalitions exploit the presence of internationalizing rivals in neighboring states to kindle domestic support for their own programs. By rejecting religious or economic "apostasy," "moral decadence," and "cosmopolitan" values, SNC leaders expect to reinvigorate their camp. Their internationalizing rivals are thus more constrained domestically in their ability to pursue cooperative regional postures. Moreover, the task of contracting military-industrial complexes becomes more difficult where adversarial SNC coalitions promote regional threats and instability. The basis for a stable cooperative framework is missing throughout Cells 2 and 3, in varying degrees. In "mixed" regions, alternative coalitions create negative externalities for, or impose costs on, their neighboring adversarial coalitions. This is mostly so when (a) a neighbor's model can be credited with undeniable achievements (as with South Korea's "miracle") or (b) when, in the absence of such achievements, the neighbors' defiant regional postures place serious barriers on the implementation of domestic goals. Mixed dyads are not likely to develop extensive trade relations, given the inherent economic closure and adversarial ideology of SN models and the primarily global orientation of internationalizing ones. This does not preclude instances of unilateral or mutual dependence on markets and raw materials, where the benefits of trade are carefully channeled to the respective coalitional beneficiaries, statist-protectionist or internationalizing.

Where strong adversarial coalitions (internationalizing and SN) rule in A and B (quadrants 2_I and 3_I), cooperation is undermined because both sides are compelled to reaffirm the political-economic strategy that sustains and legitimizes them, while keeping their adversary at bay. Yet despite this intense ideological competition, the coalitions' respective strength allows them to achieve a certain modus vivendi, a "live-and-let-live" framework, an ersatz cooperation less tainted by short-term considerations of political survival than among weaker counterparts. Despite the strength of the SN coalition, imperial commercial schemes are out of the question under the circumstances of a strong, successful internationalizing neighbor with access to the rest of the world. To be sure, strong mixed dyads are not friendly – hardly the stuff that evolves into security communities. Although wars remain a definite possibility, preliminary empirical evidence in Part Two of *Regional Orders* supports expectations that quadrants 2_I and 3_I do not elicit as many examples of extensive bloodshed as quadrants in Cell 4. A methodological difficulty arising in these quadrants is the overall scarcity of strong internationalizing coalitions ruling industrializing states until very recently. This scarcity limits the number of mixed dyads involving a strong internationalizing and a strong SN coalition. A brief examination of a few cases, however, illustrates the dynamics of strong adversarial coalitions.

South Korea evolved from a SN phase in the 1950s under Syngman Rhee into a pioneering internationalizing model by the 1960s. North Korea, by contrast, has provided one of the most durable instances of SN coalitions in power, largely held together by the near-mythical figure of Kim Il Sung. The Korean War – launched by the North – unfolded against a background of parallel efforts at SN strategies in North and South, although the North had attained revolutionary consolidation. By the late 1960s Park Chung-Hee's new export-led model in South Korea and the North's inward-looking model (*juche*) were firmly in place. Ever since, the rivalry between the two has created a regional context of tension and mistrust but not full armed conflict. The absence of war might be considered particularly remarkable given that the postwar armistice of 1953 was never replaced by any formal instrument indicating cessation of a state of war.[27] Indeed an unprecedented dialogue between these fierce opponents was under way by the 1970s, even as the North persisted in its aggressions against the South, including the assassination of President Park's wife, South Korean cabinet ministers, and civilians. This incremental cooperative pattern, embraced by the South despite its greater economic power vis-à-vis the North, was a natural extension of the former's grand political-economic strategy premised on domestic and regional stability and peaceful change, key to the survival of an internationalizing project. This helps explain the absence of major war between strong versions of an adversarial dyad even in a regional context of intermittent threats and high ideological polarity. The unfriendly but war-free modus vivendi of these two decades, however, was altered by changes in North Korea that eroded the SN grip on power by the early 1990s. This was no longer a strong adversarial dyad, but one involving a strong internationalizing coalition in the South facing internal instability in the North. This new coalitional structure unleashed a different regional dynamic best described in the next pattern.

A weak SN coalition confronting a strong internationalizing counterpart (quadrants 2_{III} and 3_{III}) faces a hard dilemma: On the one hand, it can pursue a cooperative regional policy with its internationalizing neighbor at the risk of finding itself weakened even further domestically, because such policy alienates its natural constituencies. On the other hand, it can pursue an aggressive regional policy that tends to the political needs of those natural constituencies but that also involves two main risks: (1) providing political ammunition to internationalizing challengers at home, who can accuse the ruling coalition of fabricating security threats where there are none, and (2) forcing the neighboring internationalizing coalition to deepen its own military preparedness. The strength of the neighboring internationalizing coalition is likely to derive from a successfully implemented grand strategy that has now begun to yield substantial resources, both to maintain the strategy in place and to buttress military capabilities if required. As a result, the weak SN coalition misses the opportunity of a regional modus vivendi, and instead finds itself weakened further externally – as it confronts a stronger internationalizing neighbor – and internally. The strong internationalizing neighboring coalition offers cooperative opportunities, having a built-in proclivity to lower conflict, downsize the state and the military-industrial complex, and to upsize its international status as a stable and reliable target of investments.

A weak SN coalition facing both a budding internationalizing coalition at home and a strong internationalizing neighbor at its borders is thus caught in a double whammy, vulnerable to concerted political challenges by both. With some internationalizing constituencies growing stronger in the early 1990s, Syria's Assad faced this dilemma at the height of incipient internationalizing convergence in Arab–Israeli relations (1993–1995). North Korea's SN regime, though with far more feeble internationalizing forces at home, confronted a comparable dilemma in a region where internationalization had diffused widely by the 1990s. Reliable information on tensions between the two camps, their exact composition and relative strength, remains extremely scarce. However, few observers doubt the existence of political competition between supporters of the SN *ancien regime* and those endorsing transformations that might build up regime legitimacy, as in China. Relations between North and South in the 1990s have borne the imprint of this tension in the North, as proto-internationalizing North Koreans endorse cooperative approaches only to be undone by dominant SN adversaries. Given the regime's personalistic nature, Kim Jong Il likely holds the key to an evolving coalitional balance as he straddles both camps.[28] Internationalizers in the South – now arguably stronger by virtue of having invested their strategy with democratic legitimacy – could duck the North's provocations, including vague (presumably nuclear) threats to engulf Seoul "in a sea of fire." Despite lingering SN protests in the South enhanced by the economic crisis; stresses in its internationalizing strategy; and the consequences of conversion from authoritarianism to democracy, vast constituencies supportive of internationalization endorse a "soft-landing" approach to the North's predicament to secure a peaceful – and economically less exacting – transition in the peninsula. South Korean conglomerates increasingly interested in shifting their labor-intensive operations to the North were a pillar of this strategy in the 1990s.

A situation where a strong SN coalition faces a weak internationalizing neighbor (quadrants 2_{II} and 4_{III}) overturns the previous double-whammy scenario, allowing the SN coalition to ride roughshod over the weak internationalizing opposition at home and across the border. These conditions are likely to whet the appetite of hegemonic SN coalitions for physical aggression and imperial commercial practices, everything else being equal. Cashing in on its own solid domestic support and the neighbor's weakness, the strong SN coalition faces optimal conditions for implementing its grand strategy, including the preferred regional policies of its core constituents. It is better able than in most other circumstances to extract vast resources from society and to convert them into a powerful military machine. This machine, in turn, is enabled (and emboldened) to extract vast resources from the neighborhood as well, through threats and imperial fiat. The weak internationalizer across the border is now afflicted with the double-whammy syndrome of a politically strong SN challenger at home and in the region. It is highly constrained in implementing its domestic reform program; translating economic efficiency and growth into an effective military deterrent; and retaining internationalizing postures that lubricate foreign trade and investment. It is thus under pressure to adopt some of the themes of its own opposition for the sake of advancing its short-term survival, and to embrace policies that run counter to its long-term interests at home and abroad. At the same time, unless it is prepared to yield to the demands of its strong SN neighbor, this coalition becomes an easy target of external attack, turning quadrants 2_{II} and 3_{III} into ones with highest potential for militarized hostilities in Cells 2 and 3.

Some of the dynamics of quadrants 2_{II} and 3_{III} were evident in Syrian–Lebanese (1970s), Libyan–Moroccan (1980s), and Algerian–Moroccan (1960s) relations. Similarly, Nasser's rise drew rivals from the House of Saud in Saudi Arabia and Hashemites in Jordan and Iraq to coalesce under the "King's Alliance," to stem Nasserite inroads in their own yard.[29] Closer to the textbook case are Iraqi–Kuwaiti relations, outlined in Chapter Seven of *Regional Orders*. Iraq has been an archetypical SN highly militarized regime held together tightly by Saddam Hussein's strong leadership. Iraq swallowed Kuwait whole in August 1990 in an attempt to use Kuwaiti oil assets for maintaining and expanding a SN strategy that devoted $85 billion (1980–1988) to military programs. With a weak internationalizing domestic opposition, a weak and wealthy internationalizing Kuwaiti neighbor whetted Saddam's appetite for bellicose and risky adventurism. Alas, this "mother of all statisms" – Iraq – proved the "mother of all battles" – the Gulf War – to be yet another instance in a list of unproductive SN brinkmanship, much as the Korean War, the Six-Day War and the Malvinas/Falklands War, among others. Kuwaiti rulers relied on powerful international allies with strong interest in the preservation and deepening of internationalizing forces in the Arabian Peninsula and the Gulf. As argued in Chapter Two, the international context is not precisely neutral to domestic and regional coalitional balances; in this case it applied its military might to reverse Saddam's designs.

The final scenario of mixed dyads pits a weak ruling SN coalition against a weak ruling internationalizing neighbor (quadrants 3_{IV} or 2_{IV}). The weak SN coalition in A faces a formidable opponent at home, ready to challenge any deepening of resource extraction and continued expansion of state controls and activities, including military expenditures. Conditions for promoting either its domestic or regional SN interests are largely curtailed. The weak internationalizing coalition in B, in turn, is fettered domestically by SN opponents that resist reforms and warn against cooperating with a competing SN neighbor. This situation resembles the interaction between Jordan and Israel during the 1991–1992 hiatus between the post-Gulf War and the electoral defeat of Likud in 1992. A nascent internationalizing coalition in Jordan – emboldened by the defeat of SN supporters of Saddam – faced a weakened SN adversary in Israel under Prime Minister Shamir, fiercely opposed to compromise with the PLO. This environment of weak adversarial coalitions with short time-horizons created little incentive for reciprocal concessions and devalued the expected future benefits of cooperation. By contrast, Israel's 1992 internationalizing shift bolstered its Jordanian equivalent, paving the way for the historical mutual recognition and diplomatic normalization between Israel and Jordan in 1994. Elsewhere, the Ukraine's weak SN coalition under Leonid Kravchuk and Russia's weak internationalizing coalition under the early Yeltsin presidency were unable to reach an accommodation that would become possible in 1995, with a much-improved political context for internationalizing agendas.

From dyads to regional dynamics

Figure 3.1 depicts a simplified regional system, mapping interactions between ruling coalitions in two states. In many cases this bilateral interaction is critical in determining a region's level of conflict or cooperation.[30] For instance, the Argentine– Brazilian relationship has largely defined the nature and scope of regional rivalry and cooperation in the Southern Cone, although other bilateral interactions between these two and others in the region (notably Chile) are not necessarily derivative of the main dyad. The Middle East involves a more complex situation where larger numbers of states define the regional order. Yet, as the many examples reviewed in this section suggest, Figure 3.1 retains its utility in accounting for such situations.

We may think of A as "the regional environment" facing coalition B, or as an aggregate measure of the relative strength of internationalizing versus SN coalitions. An internationalizing regional environment is one in which a more or less homogeneous group of internationalizing coalitions holds power; the reverse is true for a SN (and confessional, where relevant) regional environment. Converging internationalizing grand strategies in a given region are collectively stable, creating an environment least propitious for SN strategies.[31] The more internationalizing the region's center of gravity, the higher its reliance on concerts (at a minimum), collective security, and multilateralism. Concerts convey situations where partners do not perceive immediate threats from each other; do not consider aggressive steps toward each other; accept the status quo in matters pertaining to territorial sovereignty; and assist any member subject to threats or aggression.[32] Regional concert arrangements enable simultaneous implementation of the domestic components of internationalizing grand strategies, setting in motion a cooperative ratchet. An internationalizing regional order, in economic terms, makes statism and populist-expansionary and military-oriented policy particularly hard to pursue, as attested by the Vietnam and Myanmar experiences once the ASEAN regional order began to consolidate. Collective achievements of a region's inter-nationalizing model threaten SN holdovers through demonstration effects, as in North Korea. The 1997 East Asian financial crisis reveals a vulnerability of inter-nationalizing strategies as depicted in Table 2.1 (Chapter Two). Yet some interpret the crisis as a result of deficiencies in the "economic fundamentals" of their internationalizing model – widespread corruption, distorted financial markets – that might have been avoided under a fuller implementation of the model. Responses to the crisis have largely followed internationalizing prescriptions, suggesting that collective regional strategies of cooperation may be maintained.

Internationalizers seek to broaden the sphere of regional stability by coopting and transforming residual SNs in the region where possible, and without endangering the collective stability of their own grand strategy. Where cooptation and "soft-landing" strategies are not viable, or where internationalizing coalitions are not strong enough at home and throughout the region, they cooperate among themselves to protect their own domestic survival against assaults from neighboring SN rivals. GCC (Gulf Cooperation Council) states, comprising Saudi Arabia, Bahrain, Qatar, Oman, the UAE, and Kuwait, excluded strong SNC regimes in Iran and Iraq at the outset. Similarly, ASEAN initially excluded Vietnam, Kampuchea, and Laos. After years of deriding ASEAN as a "puppet of the Western imperialists," Vietnam incepted economic liberalization (*doi moi*) and acceded to ASEAN's Treaty on Amity and Cooperation in 1992.

The association between internationalizing coalitions and reciprocal cooperation appears, prima facie, to challenge Maoz and Russett's (1992: 257) finding that rapidly growing states are more likely to fight each other than would be expected by chance alone. However, such a tendency between 1946 and 1986 was mostly evident among non-OECD states, largely ruled by SN coalitions, particularly in the earlier decades. In the early postwar period, some SN regimes spawned both considerable economic growth and waged wars against each other. Even weak (let alone strong) internationalizing coalitions were quite rare beyond OECD states at the time, as discussed in Chapter Four of *Regional Orders*. Once internationalizing coalitions took root in industrializing states such as South Korea, Singapore, Hong Kong, Taiwan, Thailand, Malaysia, Indonesia, Chile, Brazil, Argentina, and Israel), they unleashed both unprecedented rates of growth and cooperative ventures. Where these coalitions were both strong domestically and dominant in a region, armed conflict was generally eluded, even in regions with a long history of wars and rivalries. ASEAN has a record of defusing internal disputes and its members have managed to conduct an effective diplomacy on regional matters, notably on Kampuchea.[33] Empirical findings of an inverse relationship between trade openness and international conflict provides indirect support for the expected behavior of internationalizing coalitions.[34] The latter typically underplay nationalism and ethno-confessionalism for their potential to derail internationalizing models domestically and regionally.

Regional environments dominated by SN coalitions multiply the inherently conflictive logic identified for SN dyads. This is a multipolar balance-of-threat system par excellence that strengthens the logic of expanding statist entrepreneurship and control, deepening military-bound resource extraction, and developing baroque weapons. This logic willy-nilly lowers barriers against military conflict and places SN coalitions in a position of having to consider war options more frequently than they might otherwise prefer. Converging SN grand strategies are collectively stable, feeding on each other's existence, often creating war zones most immune to internationalizing strategies, at least in the short term. SN war zones prevailed across the Middle East following independence, and continue to dominate those sub-regions resisting internationalizing shifts (the Iran–Iraq–Syria triangle in particular). Weak internationalizing coalitions such as Lebanon's in the 1970s and Jordan's intermittently for decades found it hard to survive in a regional environment dominated by strong SN coalitions. Thus, they either adapted by embracing the themes of their own opposition (Jordan), or died in internal warfare (Lebanon). War zones also dominated in Indochina (1950s–1970s) and the Korean peninsula in the 1950s. A mutating global context and demonstration effects from other regions can eventually undermine immunity to change in SN war zones. Ultimately, however, it is the domestic political and institutional prism that determines such shifts and their durability.

In regions where alternative coalitions vie for the legitimacy of their respective models we might expect (1) less cooperation and a higher incidence of balance-of-threat mechanisms than where ruling internationalizing coalitions share common agendas, but also (2) lower levels, incidence and scope of military confrontation than in SN war zones. The Middle East of the 1990s seems to exhibit this tendency. The cooperative impasse within the Arab Maghreb Union (Algeria, Libya, Mauritania, Morocco, and Tunisia) and the Arab Cooperation Council (Egypt, Jordan, North Yemen, and Iraq) can be similarly traced to competing ruling coalitions where internationalizers face heavy domestic and regional challenges from SNC challengers. As argued in Chapter Two, competition between the two ideal-typical coalitions within a state fails to yield a clear victor that can effectively hold on to power. Conditions of rough domestic parity between competing coalitions generally yield most erratic patterns of regional behavior, as in North Korea in the late 1980s-early 1990s and Algeria in the 1990s. Policies become ridden with unwieldy inconsistencies over time and across issue areas. Under such conditions, a highly homogeneous cluster of neighboring coalitions can play a central role in swaying the domestic impasse in one direction or another, depending on whether the cluster is internationalizing or SN. Conversely, a regional coalitional balance can also exacerbate domestic coalitional competition.

Finally, for every regional variant described in this section, the relationship between external policy risk and internal political risk varies. Lamborn (1991: 56) defines such a relationship as positively interdependent (policy failure damages the coalition politically, or policy success builds the coalition up) or negatively interdependent (low policy risk involves high political risk, or high policy risk is associated with low political risk). Policy and political risks can be positively or inversely interdependent in the short run and inversely or positively interdependent in the long run. For SN orders, (1) cooperative regional policies are politically risky in the short run (given their constituent's incentives specified in Chapter Two); and (2) aggressive regional postures are quite risky in the short and longer term (they can slide into wars). Yet those policy risks are less positively interdependent with political risk, particularly in nondemocratic contexts, than in alternative regional orders. In mixed orders, cooperative regional policies are less risky where strong coalitional variants enjoy considerable domestic support. In internationalizing orders, cooperative postures carry positively interdependent (low) policy and political risks.

Broader theoretical implications

Before turning to the impact of the democracy variable on coalitional interactions, it is time to take stock of several implications of interactive regional effects on coalitional dynamics and regional orders. The implications of strategic interaction among coalitions in a region include:

1 Domestic ethno-confessional diversity per se is not an efficient indicator of states' proneness to conflictive or cooperative behavior vis-à-vis neighbors. The coalitional pattern available to ethno-confessional actors at home, the relative political strength of the coalition they join, and the identity and strength of the coalitional cluster they face at the border provide more proximate gauges of their potential behavior. Thus, even a region ridden with domestic and regional ethno-confessional cleavages – ASEAN for instance – can exhibit high levels of cooperation under strong internationalizing coalitions.

2 The degree of regional homogeneity/heterogeneity of political regimes per se does not provide enough information on the likelihood of conflict and cooperation, as some theories suggest. Knowledge about the identity and strength of a regional coalitional cluster is essential: highly homogeneous internationalizing clusters exhibit higher levels of extensive and intensive cooperation; highly homogeneous SN clusters exhibit higher levels of military conflict; and heterogeneous clusters span a wide range of conflictive-cooperative behavior that does not typically reach high values at either end. Driven by different approaches to the global political economy, coalitional clusters create regional "identities" and shared expectations about conflict and cooperation. Paradoxically, Asia's Asianization is the result of the globalization of its economy, as noted by Funabashi (1993). And internationalizing strategies have done more to build MERCOSUR than have decades of regional "self-reliance" discourse.

3 Internationalizing clusters are more likely than SN or mixed clusters to rely on broader definitions of security (including economic) than on military confidence-building measures and arms control. This expectation derives from the logic of self-binding commitments that internationalizing agendas engender, particularly the unilateral interest in avoiding unwanted levels of militarization that threaten core macroeconomic objectives. This logic also explains why codification (treaties) and high institutionalization are not always necessary, and in effect can lag behind praxis, as with ASEAN's Regional Forum, created in 1994. In contrast to internationalizing clusters, the highly heterogeneous group of states that converged around CSCE (Conference on

Security and Cooperation in Europe) emphasized security confidence-building measures and codified CSCE guidelines prior to their implementation.[35]
4 Military expenditures relative to GDP and central government outlays are likely to be higher among SN and mixed clusters than internationalizing ones. An internationalizing coalition in the midst of a SN regional environment is likely to spend more on defense (relative to GDP) than it would otherwise. Military expenditures of the SN Middle East cluster reached sometimes 20 percent of GDP and over 40 percent of central budgets. The mixed Northeast Asia region spends 600 percent more in defense than ASEAN countries do, although South Korea's internationalizers have maintained military expenditures comparable to industrializing world averages even in a region ridden with security dilemmas.[36]
5 Internationalizing clusters, particularly with domestically robust ruling coalitions, are less likely to develop nuclear weapons than SN and mixed ones. Preliminary support for this expectation stems from the fact that, of all states considering a nuclear option in the last three decades (beyond the original five nuclear powers), not one embraced a nuclear weapons-free zone under a SN coalition. Furthermore, only internationalizing clusters undertook effective nonproliferation commitments and complied with those international legal obligations (Solingen 1994b).
6 An internationalizing coalition surrounded by SN neighbors is likely to face significant difficulties in implementing its grand strategy domestically and regionally. To avoid being exploited, such a coalition is forced to expand its military infrastructure and to deny its rivals the advantages of cooperation. This recalls Axelrod's (1984) principle that only a minimal number of cooperative (nice) strategies can overcome an environment of "meanies." Below that threshold, internationalizing coalitions may be more prone to mirror SN strategies. Precluded from embracing their preferred strategies, internationalizing islands in SN seas are less likely to survive in power. Most propositions thus far clearly suggest only general tendencies, which make deviant cases such as Costa Rica particularly attractive for understanding their survival amidst militarized SN neighbors.
7 A SN coalition surrounded by internationalizing neighbors is likely to find it progressively more difficult to maintain its traditional domestic base of support or use external threats to prop itself up. The region's reigning grand strategy – economic liberalization, growth, cooperative relations – particularly when successful, is likely to doom the legitimacy of SN policies, as ASEAN neighbors like Vietnam discovered.
8 SN regional clusters are collectively stable, creating environments resistant to internationalizing strategies in the short term, but not completely immune to mutating – globalizing – international and regional pressures in the longer haul. Predominantly internationalizing regional clusters are collectively stable as well, creating environments resistant to SN strategies but not completely immune to unintended effects of globalizing pressures – such as currency crises – or to global mutations in protectionist directions. Notwithstanding this chapter's special attention to regional interactive effects, the latter are only one

input into a coalition's relative domestic strength. Independent and parallel domestic dynamics in different states can add up to changes in the existing regional coalitional center of gravity.

9 Coalitional analysis thus highlights how numbers may affect cooperation, a concern raised in game-theoretic and collective-action approaches that regard large numbers as encumbering cooperation. Low ratios of internationalizing coalitions to the total in a region can make cooperation difficult, but not so low ratios of SN coalitions. High regional ratios of internationalizing coalitions bolster cooperation whereas high ratios of SN ones burden it. Numbers and ratios, however, matter only when we gain a proper understanding of coalitional identities and dynamics.

The basic hypotheses outlined in this chapter and the additional implications examined in the concluding section are falsifiable. The empirical behavior of internationalizing, SN and mixed clusters can depart from the expectations outlined here. A particularly strong challenge could come in the form of strong clusters of internationalizing coalitions that exhibit highly conflictive and militarized patterns, particularly when few SN rivals remain in the region. Another strong challenge could come from observations of extensive, intensive, and highly stable cooperative patterns in SN clusters. These propositions are the subject of in-depth analysis in empirical chapters of *Regional Orders*, which also explore a variable formally omitted thus far from this discussion: the impact of democratic institutions – or their absence – on coalitional formation, durability, and regional interaction.

Notes

1 Chapter Six in *Regional Orders*, for instance, documents how Israel's high-tech entrepreneurs voted massively for the Labor–Meretz coalition in 1992 and 1996, with an eye on the domestic, regional, and global windfalls from prospective regional cooperation.
2 Keohane (1986). In the security realm, behavior oriented to initiate, maintain, and/or exacerbate armed conflict – such as a direct attack or blockade, threats to use force or invade a territory, mobilizations and swaggering near the borders – is considered to be conflictive. Behavior oriented to resolve disputes and to avoid armed confrontations is considered cooperative. Issues of perceptions and thresholds are incorporated, as will be clear throughout this chapter, in the analysis of coalitional type.
3 On the complementarity of economic and security policies, see Gowa and Mansfield (1993). On how economies of scope lower transaction costs involved in negotiating, monitoring, and enforcing agreements, see Lake (1997).
4 The term, first used by Deutsch *et al.* (1957), points to sustained and widespread institutional practices that build dependable expectations of peaceful change.
5 These coalitions need not be blind to potential regional threats to their own survival, and may even acquire weapons to protect themselves, but they also restrain their MILEX so as not to endanger their grand strategy. Their MILEX are often in line with the world's average (about 4.5 percent of GDP in the 1970s and 1980s) even in high-conflict regions, in contrast to those of SN coalitions, which are three and four times higher.
6 Quoted in Mack and Kerr (1994: 135).
7 On ASEAN , see Solingen (2004, 2005a, 2005b, 2007a, 2008). On MERCOSUR see *Regional Orders* (Chapter Five) and Malnight and Solingen (2014).

8 Trade-creating schemes are those in which trade replaces home production or results from increased consumption. Trade-diverting schemes replace trade with third parties by trade between partners to the scheme (Cable and Henderson 1994; Bhagwati 1993). Viner (1950) is the locus classicus.
9 The GCC established a free trade area in 1983, but its implementation has been slow and intermittent. Imports from other GCC states account for very small fractions of their respective total imports.
10 On the importance of extra-regional trade for each of the emerging trading blocs, see Lawrence (1995: 411–412).
11 In this process Egypt reduced its military expenditures from 52.4 percent of its GNP in 1975 to 13 percent in 1979 while foreign exchange from tourism, workers' remittances, and canal revenues (activities made possible by peace with Israel) grew from $700 million in 1974 to about $9 billion in 1981 (Karawan 1993: 17). On *munfatihun* economies attempting to increase "openness" to the global economy, see Waterbury (1983) and Barkey (1992).
12 On these incipient multilateral institutions, see Sayigh (1995) and Solingen (1995).
13 On the failure of alliance formation among these similar regimes, see Walt (1987).
14 On hyper-nationalism as involving a belief in the inferiority of other national groups and in their threatening nature, see Van Evera (1993).
15 On how states characterized by small export sectors are more prone to choose war, see Domke (1988). On emphasis on "groupness" as inherently threatening and constitutive of security dilemmas, see Posen (1993: 30).
16 Snyder (1991). The behavior of these coalitions is compatible with Walt's (1987) view that states sharing certain ideologies are more likely to compete than to form durable alliances.
17 On war as the "waste by-product" of the military's pursuit of growth, wealth, and prestige, see Van Evera (1984), Posen (1984), and Snyder (1991). On how international disputes accompanied by arms races are much more likely to induce wars than those in which arms races are absent, see Chan (1992a).
18 Overexpansion can be estimated a priori by considering the heightened security and economic costs associated with expansion relative to the security and economic benefits (Snyder 1991: 60).
19 Weber (1978) identified this extreme form of patrimonialism as "sultanism," a highly nepotistic regime in which the public sphere overlaps with the sultan's private domain.
20 Notably, even in the relatively benign Latin American system, conflict and wars in the last fifty years or so often involved inward-looking, nationalist rivals, with territorial issues looming large in their regional postures. As Mares argues (1997), it would be inappropriate to define that system as a security community throughout those years of import-substituting industrialization and powerful military institutional presence with strong emphasis on "national sovereignty."
21 ECLA was less favored by Chile's strong internationalizing coalition post-1973, which favored elimination of common external tariffs and lowering effective protection.
22 Liberalizing forces rather than protectionist ones propel regional trade agreements as building blocks toward global openness (Lawrence 1995). On liberalizing effects of preferential agreements, particularly when domestic biases toward closure are significant, see Oye (1993).
23 Sahliyeh (1990); Kuran (1993).
24 Economic sanctions on Iraq in the 1990s reversed somewhat Jordan's dependence on its neighbor's economy via "transit trade" effects, which are otherwise presumed to benefit the imperial strategy of regional hegemons (Hirschman 1945: 33–35).
25 This pattern of attempted regional influence is not very different from that of internationalizing coalitions, although the structure of regional trade policies is. Hirschman (1945: 29) depicted these efforts at transnational political activation of "vested interests" well: "In the social pattern of each country there exist certain powerful groups the support of which is particularly valuable to a *foreign* [original italics] country in its power policy; the foreign country will therefore try to establish

commercial relations especially with these groups, in order that their voices will be raised in its favor."
26 *New York Times* (24 January 1993). The BJP leader endorsed a nuclear deterrent though there was no party consensus. On supporters and detractors of economic liberalization, see Kohli (1990).
27 Official talks to that effect would not start until mid-1997, a development compatible with the coalitional dynamics explored in Chapter Seven of *Regional Orders*.
28 This brinkmanship is depicted in greater detail in Chapter Seven of *Regional Orders* and Chapter Six of *Nuclear Logics*.
29 Walt (1987).
30 On why the most efficient group of contributors to the management of regional relations is often smaller than the group of potential contributors, see Lake (1997).
31 On collective stability as a measure of a strategy's robustness against invasion by other strategies, see Axelrod (1984).
32 Job (1997); Jervis (1982). A less benign definition of concerts emphasizes their enforcement through strong power collusion and their conditional postponement – not suspension – of balance of power mechanisms (Betts 1993). On concerts and collective security, see Kupchan and Kupchan (1991) and on multilateralism Ruggie (1993).
33 On the weakness of populist challenges in East and Southeast Asian countries in the 1980s, see Haggard (1995a: 455). On ASEAN institutional deepening into security issues, see Solingen (1999, 2004, 2005a, 2005b).
34 Gasiorowski (1986); Domke (1988); Oneal and Russett (1997).
35 This does not mean that internationalizing coalitions never opt for security confidence-building measures or institutionalization but, rather, that neither is required for cooperation to come about. When defense has the advantage (offense is too costly for the ruling coalition) arms controls are less necessary, and unilateral defensive policies result (Glaser 1994/95; Jervis 1982b).
36 International Institute for Strategic Studies (1992); ACDA (1990); World Bank (1996).

4

MAPPING INTERNATIONALIZATION

Domestic and regional impacts

International relations still lack universally accepted propositions with unchallenged empirical status regarding the precise links between a state's level of economic openness and its general approach to conflict and cooperation. Furthermore, until recently the literature has been overwhelmingly concerned with the impact of bilateral trade interdependence, and much less so with how overall openness to the global political economy may affect state choices for conflict or cooperation. Some studies have focused largely on great powers (Rosecrance 1986), but we are still bereft of a more universal understanding of this relationship. Yet, growing levels of internationalization force greater attention to the links between openness, domestic distributional effects, and ensuing strategies for managing external threats and opportunities. This article seeks to contribute to the task of conceptualizing the effects of internationalization on domestic and regional politics.

Section 1 (entitled "Internationalization: Definition and signals") provides a working definition of internationalization while laying out an analytical scheme for mapping the domestic impact of both material-economic and normative dimensions of internationalization. Section 2 (entitled "Implications for regional orders: Ideal-typical coalitions and strategies") derives three ideal-typical domestic coalitions; outlines their respective grand strategies (domestic, regional, global); and develops a set of expectations about their regional effects. Section 3 (entitled "An empirical application") provides quantitative evidence from five regions (the Middle East, South Asia, Latin America's Southern Cone, and East and Southeast Asia) including ninety-eight coalitions in nineteen states. Section 4 (entitled "Conclusions") outlines paths for further research on the impact of internationalization on domestic and regional politics.

---

* This research was assisted by an award from the Social Science Research Council-MacArthur Foundation Fellowship on Peace and Security in a Changing World. I would like to thank Randall Gibbs for excellent assistance with data collection and processing, and helpful comments from Matt Evangelista, Cecelia Lynch, Jerry Cohen, John Odell, Mark Lichbach, John Oneal, Barry O'Neill, and two anonymous reviewers.

Internationalization: Definition and signals

Internationalization involves the expansion of global markets, institutions, and certain norms, a process progressively reducing the purely domestic sphere of politics.[1] This expansion provides signals – displaying opportunities and constraints – for different actors, who join coalitions with different proclivities to embrace or reject internationalization. Although not a brand new phenomenon, our knowledge about this complex process is still limited. It is not simply about what [growing] percentage of a state's GDP is accounted for by international activities and the political implications thereof, but also about what [growing] fraction of local identity issues becomes affected by international regimes, institutions, and values relative to the past. Internationalization thus threatens interests, cultures, and political leaders endangered by its advance; leaders, in turn, forge coalitions advancing competing interpretations of the international political, economic, and strategic context. The essential logic behind the constitution of contending coalitions in response to internationalization is encapsulated in Polanyi's (1944) dialectic "double movement" – global market expansion and political responses to it – but does not end there and requires adjustments to the new millennium.

With respect to *economic incentives and threats* from internationalization, the analysis begins with an understanding of who gains and who loses from external liberalization, given different institutional configurations. Openness to global markets, capital, investments, and technology affects individuals and groups via changes in employment status, labor incomes, and returns on assets; in prices of goods and services consumed; and in the provision of public services (Nelson 1992). A common approach to map distributional impacts relies on the cleavage between tradable (internationally competitive) and nontradable (uncompetitive) sectors. Accordingly, export-intensive industries benefit from openness whereas laborers, managers, and investors in uncompetitive industries stand to lose from openness and have incentives to pressure governments for continued protection (Bruno 1988). Related approaches emphasize large banking and industrial complexes already involved in foreign activities that favor openness (Frieden and Rogowski 1996; Milner 1988). Liberalization is also presumed to benefit competitive industries (firms), their workers and suppliers, and consumers of imported products. International economic institutions – the World Bank, IMF, WTO, and others – encourage openness.

The same international context can trigger different responses even by comparable domestic political economies. The economic and political impact of internationalization is neither simple nor uniform; differential effects dominate beyond some broadly similar impacts (Keohane and Milner, 1996). Variations emerge from contingencies including actors' ability to read signals under uncertainty and institutional efforts to block relative price signals or freeze old coalitions. As argued, leaders can play a major role in forging coalitions that favor or reject internationalization. Yet political-economy models often ignore other actors' responses to internationalization, such as those of the military and ethno-confessional leaders.

Internationalization also poses *normative opportunities and threats* stemming from the intrusion of international institutions and normative frameworks that favor values of some groups against those of others. A vast constructivist literature addresses this nexus between transnational and domestic actors and their impact on state preferences, values, and behavior (Klotz 1995; Risse-Kappen 1995; Finnemore 1996; Katzenstein 1996; Finnemore and Sikkink 1998). Mechanisms at work here emphasize persuasion and socialization more than exchange and cost-benefit calculations. "Norm leaders" promote acceptance or aversion to free trade, war, slavery, or torture. Internationalization multiplies the range of identities individuals can embrace, deepening the methodological difficulty of isolating core identities that might explain a given behavior. Whereas social identities of early rural social formations were relatively easier to map, the identity of a late twentieth century Hindu/software engineer/mother-of-two/pacifist/born in a Bihari village/ currently residing in dynamic Bangalore is defined by a far more complex social and institutional context that now also includes international regimes in telecommunications and nonproliferation.

Just as there is no simple formula for estimating the political-economy impact of expanding global markets, our understanding of international normative effects remains open-ended. Domestic responses to international institutions span a broad spectrum of issue-areas from classical (military) security to human rights and the environment. In an effort to simplify a much more complex reality, Figure 4.1 focuses on two clusters: economics and security.[2] The schema can accommodate a

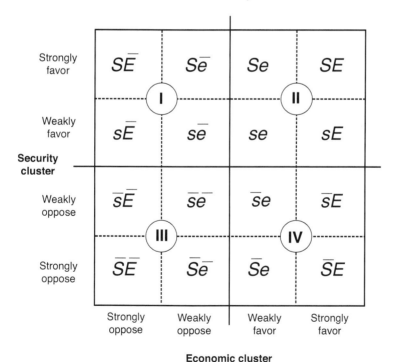

Figure 4.1 Positions regarding international economic and security regimes
Source: Solingen (2001b)

more complex cluster, however (e.g. there is considerable overlap among social movements that campaign against nuclear weapons, environmental degradation, and human rights abuses). But support for regimes advancing those values does not necessarily overlap with attitudes toward economic liberalization. There can be tensions between freer economic exchange and environmental regulation although there are also synergistic effects between contracting state budgets, reducing defense expenditures and weakening the military politically (which often enhances human security). Figure 4.1 thus leaves out for future exploration the complexities introduced by other issue areas. The (vertical) economic cluster is itself a simplification that clusters global markets and institutions in trade, technology, capital flows, and others. The (horizontal) security cluster also aggregates across security regimes on WMDs and ancillary prohibitions.

We can map domestic constituencies according to their position on both clusters, allowing for various levels of commitment to support or reject a cluster. Actors may feel strong about a certain issue but not others. Figure 4.1 outlines sixteen political spaces ranging from the northeastern corner (cell SE) of quadrangle II, where there is strong support for both clusters, to the southwestern corner (cell $\bar{S}\bar{E}$) of quadrangle III, where there is strong opposition to both. Capital letters signify positions that are strongly held (e.g., S for strongly favoring security regimes and $\bar{S}$ for strongly opposing it). Lower-case letters represent weakly held or ambivalent positions. Cell $\bar{s}E$ thus reflects weak opposition to a security regime and strong support for economic openness. Instead $s\bar{e}$ reflects weak support for security regimes and weak opposition to economic openness.

Consider the hypothetical dilemma of an Indian partner to a multinational venture with a US firm. The Bharatiya Janata Party (BJP)-led coalition's nuclear test in 1998 – an affront to the nonproliferation regime – may touch a nationalist chord that might position her as "weakly opposed" to that regime. However, the potential costs for her business and her strong commitment to economic openness are likely to loom large on her motivations to replace or support India's government. She could thus find herself gravitating from $\bar{s}E$ to quadrangle II (to sE for instance) as potential costs of nuclear tests for her own business rise. A hypothetical Indian minister that once decried the nuclear program may now favor such tests, along with his large support base among Rashtriya Swayamsevak Sang nationalists. Once positioned in the horizontal space between $s\bar{E}$ and $s\bar{e}$ he is now entrenched in quadrangle III or IV. Our two imaginary examples may find themselves supporting competing coalitions in the battle over internationalization.

Leaders rely on available institutional contexts (democracy, autocracy) to broker coalitions across these cells through logrolling, or exchanging the mutual rights of partners to seek their most valued preference. They employ both material and cultural themes to develop the right blend, selling, adapting, and disposing of it altogether when necessary. This process requires an ability to interpret the mobilizing capacity of prevailing norms, identity, and historical myths no less than the mobilizing capacity of promises and myths about global markets. In crafting coalitions, politicians combine different power resources that prospective partners may command, such as the military's coercive capabilities; industrialists' potential to invest, employ, and exit; labor's option to strike; central banks' imputed independence; organizational advantages of threatened state bureaucracies; or threats of violence from ethno-religious zealots. Politicians thus fashion coalitions that maximize their own relative power and control over resources; they rely on available rules and structures to translate interests and values into bargaining resources at particular sites, from the ballot box to legislatures, street protests, bureaucracies, military barracks, and corporate boardrooms. Out of these bargains emerge their grand strategies – of domestic, regional, and global reach – designed to pursue most valued preferences of coalitional partners.

Implications for regional orders: Ideal-typical coalitions and strategies

Based on these sources of coalitional mobilization, three archetypal domestic coalitions can be identified out of a richer empirical menu. The 16-cell matrix accommodates myriad combinations fitting political and institutional landscapes in different states. Yet three ideal-types capture typical responses to internationalization.

- *Internationalizing coalitions* aggregate primarily constituencies from quadrangle II and are often driven by the most dynamic sectors favoring openness including those tied to international finance and their associated labor force; consumers of imported products; state agencies entrusted with economic reform (independent central banks, finance ministries, managers of export-processing zones); and competitive agricultural exporters among others. The military joins them when openness does not threaten them financially or institutionally or when politicians can purge expansive military-industrial complexes.
- *Inward-looking (statist-nationalist) coalitions* are primarily entrenched in quadrangle III, comprising sectors threatened by external liberalization including protected private and state-owned enterprises and banks; uncompetitive blue-collar labor; state employees and agencies vulnerable to reform (i.e., capital controls or import licensing); typically the military and associated industrial complex; internal security agencies and opponents of international regimes that curtail "national sovereignty." Civic-nationalist, ethnic, and confessional politicians wary of withering away with internationalization are natural partners in these coalitions. As communal, "organic" values threatened by crude market forces are important levers for mass mobilization, those leaders appropriate long-standing critiques of international capitalism as wasteful and corruptive, and defy "Western" international institutions.
- *Hybrid coalitions* span quadrangles I and IV, are much less clear-cut in their composition, and can bring together strange bedfellows (e.g. Patrick Buchanan and Lenora Fulani).[3] Military-industrial complexes are expected to oppose international security regimes that put them out of business, typically placing them in quadrangle III. However, the more exit options available (e.g. private-sector jobs created by economic reform) the more likely they are to gravitate into quadrangles II or IV. Peace, environmental and human security movements

endorse international regimes that expand political and legal rights. Yet some are lukewarm at best – and sharply critical at times – of economic aspects of internationalization, making them natural dwellers of quadrangle I, though not invariably so. The more heterogeneous the hybrid coalition, the more likely it is to be affected by internal distributional conflicts.

Patterns of logrolling and grand strategies

Politicians of all stripes compete for the allegiance of constituencies in quadrangles I and IV and may themselves dwell in hybrid quarters when neither internationalizing nor inward-looking quadrangles hold much promise. "Positive logrolling" is more likely between those who feel strongly positive about one cluster but ambivalent about the other (sE and Se). Some human-security movements with strong ties to international regimes compromise on economic issues to advance their primary mission. "Negative logrolling" is likely between those who feel strongly negative about one cluster but ambivalent about the other (cells $\bar{S}$e and s$\bar{E}$). Fervent economic nationalists might suppress sympathy for international regimes in other issue-areas to join strong opponents of international security regimes who mildly support economic reforms. This invokes a classical convergence between economic and security nationalists (Gilpin, 1987). High uncertainty about the effects of internationalization concentrates constituencies in quadrangles I and IV. With wide segments of society behind the "veil of ignorance" – unable to envisage where and how they will fare along the process – leaders' rhetoric can be particularly powerful. Imputed, not real, effects of internationalization become the raw material for political platforms. Leaders of all stripes can use the state to advance their programs; at times they compete to capture different state agencies making the state itself the battlefield over internationalization.

Politicians aggregate coalitional partners's policy preferences into "grand political-economic strategies" defining positions vis-à-vis the global political economy and institutions, the domestic extraction and allocation of resources, and the regional strategic context. Grand strategies can be stated explicitly in party platforms or pronouncements but are often embedded implicitly or developed along the way. They identify potential threats to coalitional survival – at home, in the region and beyond – and devise political, economic, and military means to counter them. Grand strategies become the *raison d'etat* once a coalition prevails politically.

Internationalizing grand strategies include adjusting the domestic political economy to the requirements of internationalization; weakening opponents; and securing access to foreign markets, capital, investments, and technology. Cooperative (stable and nonviolent) regional orders serve this strategy well as does macroeconomic stability (low inflation), which reduces uncertainty, encourages savings, and enhances investment. If successful, the strategy leads to declining protectionism as foreign trade, investment and private economic activity account for growing GDP shares. Internationalizers resist mobilizing resources for potential military conflict in order to (1) avoid unproductive, inflation-inducing investments and budgetary drains under the shroud of "national security" and (2) undercut inward-looking beneficiaries of state rents. Military expenditures, typically restrained to protect the strategy, are incurred only as insurance, lest they lead to costly arms races. Cooperative, stable, and non-militarized regional environments have positive global externalities as well; they minimize risk, enable foreign investment, decrease the likelihood of sanctions, reinforce ties to international economic institutions, and enhance internationalizers' reputation in the global order.

Inward-looking grand strategies seek to preserve state leadership and military-industrial allocations; resist pressures for economic liberalization and putative intrusions on sovereignty; and undercut internationalizing adversaries at home and abroad. Regional insecurity and competition is a natural side-effect – at times a central contributor – to the viability of this strategy. Regional cooperation threatens inward-looking coalitions, scaling back military imperatives; eroding statist privileges; and devaluing nationalist and confessional myths as political currency. Intransigent and uncertainty-inducing regional policies raise the propensity for conflict and risks for foreign investors, potentially triggering denial of external resources. Inward-looking coalitions thrive with such outcomes, in the short and medium terms, given their inherent affinity with state and military leadership, import-substitution, classical populism, price controls, nominal wage increases, overvalued currency (to raise wages and profits in nontraded-goods sectors), and import controls through tariffs and multiple exchange rates (Dornbusch and Edwards 1991). Inward-looking strategies rebuff fiscal orthodoxy and stabilization plans imposed by the IMF and other international regimes portrayed as "Western" diktats.

All coalitions are constrained internally by the relative strength of their domestic challengers, leading to different degrees of coherence in their grand strategy. *Pristine* grand strategies are most feasible where there is massive support for both internationalization clusters (quadrangle II dominates) and where there is massive rejection of both (quadrangle III is the political center of gravity). Either case allows freer implementation of coherent strategies closer to the ideal-type. *Diluted* grand strategies are more common when leaders must attract support from quadrangles I and IV. Internationalizing leaders pivoted in quadrangle II, for instance, may reach out to constituencies strongly positive regarding one cluster but mildly opposed to another ($\bar{s}E, S\bar{e}$). Inward-looking leaders may reach out of quadrangle III to attempt "negative logrolling" between those strongly opposed to one cluster and ambivalent about the other (cells $\bar{S}e, s\bar{E}$). Either effort leads to diluted grand strategies. *Defiled* grand strategies result from logrolling difficulties or the small size of cells $\bar{s}E, S\bar{e}, Se$ and $s\bar{E}$. This scenario forces politicians to court cells $\bar{S}E$ and $S\bar{E}$; they can do so sequentially or inter-temporally (as in Hirschman's "shifting alliances") endorsing/rejecting one cluster at time t and another at $t + 1$. These "Voodoo politics" (Williamson 1994) and "bait-and-switch" strategies (Drake 1991) involve promises made with full knowledge that they might be betrayed. Politicians can also attempt ambitious schemes that require vastly disparate constituencies to converge in a joint endorsement – or joint rejection – of both clusters, a scenario Hirschman (1963: 289) labels "*mutual sacrifices*." This maneuver isolates diehard SE and $\bar{S}\bar{E}$; often requires wielding the threat of national collapse, and underlies efforts to craft national-unity governments and grand coalitions. Politicians who hitherto engineered such threats or advanced unsuccessful or tension-ridden grand strategies later wield those threats to survive politically.

In sum, *logrolling efforts, sequential courting,* and *ambitious unifying maneuvers* can strain a strategy's internal coherence. On the one hand constituencies may be unaware or dismissive of internal tensions, dissonance and trade-offs induced by logrolling. On the other hand, politicians – particularly risk-prone ones – miscalculate their ability to have their cake (e.g. favorable Moody's credit ratings) and eat it too (e.g. aggressive regional policies). They may be able to maintain inherently unstable mixed strategies for some time, as Israel's Likud and India's BJP coalitions have. In time, however, deep tensions in that strategy force coalitional reshuffles and reformulation of the strategy.

A typology of regional orders

Coalitions are also constrained externally by regional coalitional balances of power. The latter reflect the identity and strength of competing coalitions in neighboring states, which produce three main ideal-typical regional orders.

1. *Zones of Stable Peace* flourish where most states in the region (and extra-regional powers with a strong regional presence) enjoy coalitional majorities in quadrangle II. The potential for armed conflict and military build-ups threatens the fundamentals of their grand strategy: macroeconomic, political, and regional stability; and global access. Domestic considerations drive economic rationalization and military cuts as much as external factors. Such policies act as tacit self-binding commitments, assurances against militarized strategies, and inducements to diffuse disputes. De-escalation dominates under symmetric regional conditions, assuaging potential prisoner's dilemmas such as arms races. This reciprocal restraint helps leaders ward off inward-looking domestic criticism of economic reform, shrinking militaries, and cooperative regional policies. Synergies across domestic and regional policies translate into reduced transaction costs, facilitating agreement on disputes and moderating the need to scrutinize compliance and enhance transparency. Internationalizing orders require regional cooperation but not necessarily economic integration: their underlying logic is global. They can lead to absolute increases in regional trade and investment and trade-creating schemes sensitive to an "open regionalism" that lubricates ties to the global economy. Strong, symmetrical quadrangle II coalitions in a region are more likely to exhibit pristine internationalizing strategies. More diluted versions can be expected where coalitions straddle quadrangles I, II, and IV, due to logrolling and sequential courting. Time-horizons are shorter, self-binding and symmetric commitments at the regional level less credible, and cooperation and diffuse reciprocity more tentative and unstable. Paradoxically, formal regional arrangements liberalizing trade seem more compelling here, as tools to weaken recalcitrant inward-looking quarters and to signal more believable commitments to international investors.

2. *War Zones* prevail where most states in the region (and extra-regional powers with a strong regional presence) are led by leaders aggregating primarily quadrangle III constituencies, emphasizing economic self-reliance, military prowess, sovereignty, and national or confessional purity. Here coalitional symmetry (across states) operates to heighten power balancing and competition: leaders rely on civic-nationalist or ethno-confessional themes condemning both internationalization as

well as inward-looking leadership across the border. This symmetry fuels risk, instability, and conflict that – even unintendedly – lead to armed conflict. The pursuit of WMDs is symptomatic of risk-prone strategies imbued with parochial symbolism that also caters to inward-looking – civil and military – economic nationalists. Military-industrial and ancillary scientific-technological constituencies loom large in those orders, foiling collective security arrangements that threaten their own existence. Integrative economic schemes are similarly ill-fated, lest they drive key constituencies – private and state monopolies – literally out of business. Inward-looking leaders attempt imperial commercial strategies (Hirschman 1945) that maximize economic profit, military power, and regional influence, all of which sustain and reproduce their power at home. The more embattled inward-looking leaders and the more strenuous their efforts to court quadrangles I and IV, the more diluted their grand strategies. Competing inward-looking leaders – at home and in the region – outbid each other in radicalizing the strategy, leading to spiraling conflict domestically and across the border.

3. *Zones of Restrained Conflict* reflect regional coalitional competition among internationalizing, inward-looking, and hybrid leaders, where no pure coalitional type dominates across the region. Inward-looking leaders depict internationalizing or hybrid opponents at home and in the region as "lackeys," executors of Western imperial designs. They portray economic reform only through its negative fallouts and efforts to liberalize regional trade as hegemonic designs. This regional environment constrains internationalizers' ability to cooperate and undertake self-binding commitments regarding military investments. Yet their incentives to de-escalate conflict that might foil internationalizing agendas irreversibly remains. Regional instability harms investments and makes economic reform more costly politically. The inherent asymmetry in these orders – closure versus openness – enhances discord and instability and undermines regional trade. Benefits from trade are channeled to respective coalitional beneficiaries at home. Stronger internationalizing and inward-looking leaders in hybrid regions – less encumbered by domestic pressures – can reach a certain "live-and-let-live" framework, an *ersatz* cooperation less tainted by the short-term considerations afflicting weaker versions. Embattled leaders have strong incentives to strengthen their coalitional namesakes across the border. Stronger internationalizing neighbors enable greater coherence in the strategy of peers across the border. Likewise, stronger inward-looking neighbors enable greater coherence in inward-looking strategies. Regionally hegemonic coalitions in hybrid orders (Nasserism circa 1960s) dominate the fate of regional coalitional balances, shifting them toward their own type.

An empirical application

Classifying coalitions

The conceptual framework developed thus far gained sharper definition toward the late twentieth century, but its referents are of longer gestation. The empirical application that follows, therefore, spans most of the postwar era, identifying leaders that logrolled ninety-eight coalitions in nineteen states across five regions: the Middle

East, East and Southeast Asia, South Asia, and Latin America's Southern Cone. These regions account for much of the industrializing world, sharing high levels of what neorealism describes as anarchic, self-help, historical contexts, poorly endowed with effective regional institutional infrastructures that might facilitate cooperation.

The design and available data make this a particularly hard test for exploring coalitional effects on grand strategy empirically. Indeed the statistical analysis excludes those years when internationalizing effects were strongest (1990s) and would have sharpened their impact on coalitional type.[4] Homogeneous data for most dependent variables is only available up to 1993 at the time of this writing. Nonetheless, confidence in this analytical path may be enhanced if, even under less auspicious eras for internationalizing strategies than the 1990s, one could still discern different behavioral patterns across coalitions that match the framework's expectations. The analysis is confined to economic openness and military security; prevailing authoritarianism and the Cold War environment help explain the relative marginality of peace and human rights movements as ruling coalitional partners during most of this period.

Following the general argument outlined in Figure 4.2, the empirical analysis begins by identifying coalitions – the independent variable – according to their composition, or logrolled partners. I rely on extensive qualitative research including public and private statements, press accounts, memoirs, party platforms, parliamentary debates, legislative proceedings, and personal interviews with politicians, business and military leaders, diplomats, bureaucrats, officials from peak associations, labor, and political parties. A vast literature in comparative politics and political economy also enabled better specification of coalitional composition.[5] Where democratic institutions allowed a free press and political expression, coalitional classification was made easier; democracies are allies of political analysis but do not necessarily correlate with any grand strategy. Politicians of all stripes rely on democratic or authoritarian institutions.

No ideal-typical coalition, by definition, has perfect empirical referents but some approximate ideal-types more than others. Internationalizing politicians craft coalitions primarily from quadrangle II constituencies, and I and/or IV when needed. Inward-looking leaders mobilize coalitions largely from quadrangle III, and I and/or IV when needed. Hybrids rely on mixed coalitions across quadrangles, either concomitantly or sequentially. The resulting classification of coalitions is in Appendices I, II, and III. Appendix IV lists all coalitions chronologically, by country and type. Beginning dates reflect a coalition's inception, which frequently coincides with a particular leader's ascent to power. End dates correspond to a coalition's unraveling; for some cases 1993 marks the last year for which data are available. Leaders may start out with one coalition but replace it in light of new coalitional opportunities or crises (Park Chung Hee 1961 vs. 1963; Sadat 1970 vs. 1974). Hybrids are particularly prone to shifts; they may start with unclear coalitional makeups and end up leading diehard coalitional types (Videla and Galtieri). Successive leaders in a single state holding together a continuous coalitional arrangement are listed together (Lee Kuan Yew–Goh Chok Tong 1965–1998; Yitzhak Rabin–Shimon Peres 1992–1996).[6] Coalitions vary in size from a few key individuals and institutional actors, largely under dictatorships, to more inclusive democratic representation.

Grand strategies in action

Against this threefold identification in coalitional composition, behavioral differences in grand strategies can be gauged through policies regarding economic liberalization, military investments, and regional and international security. Cases vary along a continuum. Policies are seldom linear or coherent but purer types reveal greater consistency and sharper trajectories than hybrids.

Economic openness

Approaches to the economic cluster can be derived from (1) statements of intention regarding fiscal or tariff targets, budget rules, foreign investment blueprints or borrowing ceilings, *inter alia*; and (2) concrete steps such as actual removal of quantitative import restrictions, tariff elimination, unification of import tariffs and export subsidies, and reduced state control over credit allocation, freer interest rates, removal of subsidies and barriers to entry, and bank privatization (Bruno, 1988; Kahler, 1998). External liberalization is a matter of degree. No case fits "laissez-faire" policies across the board; most retain selective protectionism, regulation, and industrial policy. Furthermore, policy outcomes can be at odds with initial intentions and concrete steps; coalitions' relative strength/resources are important intervening variables. Policy success is thus not a wholly reliable indicator of policy commitment; yet success can strengthen commitment to the policy. Openness to foreign investment is only a prerequisite, not a guarantee that investments will

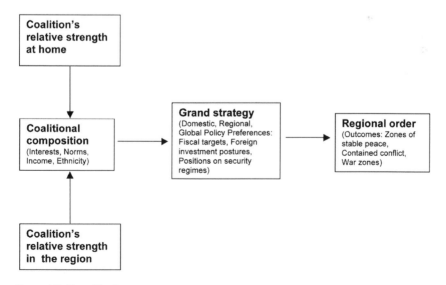

Figure 4.2 Causal logic

materialize. Success is the daughter of more complex conditions including regional stability. Hence, rising trade openness (TO) may be a symptom, not a reliable measure of the presence of an internationalizing coalition; it does, however, indicate a significant probability that internationalizing policies have been implemented.

No single indicator of TO is free of problems and each captures different dimensions of trade policy.[7] A commonly used measure is "imports plus exports as percentage of GDP." Although many other considerations affect this index, it offers the advantage of providing the most comprehensive data base.[8] Data aggregated yearly for each coalition (N=572) yields a mean TO value of 88 – the highest – for internationalizing coalitions; 38 for inward-looking; and 52 for hybrid (Appendix V). Mean internationalizing TO values is over double those of inward-looking and higher than hybrids (differences in means across coalitions significant at the .01 level). A test of multiple comparisons shows a mean difference of 50 between internationalizing and inward-looking and 36 between internationalizing and hybrid (both significant at <.001). Only the mean TO difference between hybrid and inward-looking is statistically insignificant, entirely in line with the anticipation that hybrids can gravitate toward inward-looking policies based on coalitional opportunities. Internationalizing coalitions increase their TO by 1.9 percent per year and hybrids by 1.1 percent; inward-looking coalitions decrease TO by 0.23 percent yearly averages.

These aggregate contrasts are quite suggestive but ignore initial conditions, country-specific considerations (larger states have smaller trade shares), and peculiar policy dynamics. Longitudinal comparisons of successive coalitions in a single state provide more controlled assessments of coalitional impact. Disaggregating the data in Appendix IV, Chile suggests a dramatic imprint of coalitional changes on TO values. Allende's coalition reduced average TO from 29 percent over the preceding decade to 23 in 1972 ($8 bn 1970 GDP); TO grew from 29 percent (1973) to 53 (1975) and 66 in 1989 (GDP of $25 bn) under Pinochet, more than doubling Allende's average. Democratic internationalizers Patricio Aylwin and Eduardo Frei averaged 60 percent (1990–1996).

No less dramatic is South Korea, with TO levels below 13 percent under Syngman Rhee's coalition of a profligate military, Liberal Party (opposing tight fiscal and monetary policies), bureaucrats, and import-substituting firms. Park Chung Hee's 1964 internationalizing revolution nearly doubled TO by 1968 from 20 to 38 percent; quadrupled it by 1974 reaching 67 percent of a rapidly growing GDP; rising to 73 (1980s) under Chun Doo Hwan. Despite more favorable initial natural and industrial resource endowments than its southern nemesis, North Korea's Kim Il-Sung regime gave real meaning to an inward-looking strategy. Foreign trade, very low throughout, still amounted to only 13 percent of GDP by 1994. Taiwan's Chiang Ching-kuo and the Kuomingtang's internationalizing strategy trebled TO from 30 percent (1960) to 89 (1973), reaching 99 averages by the 1980s. Indonesia's 21 percent average TO under inward-looking Sukarno declined to 18 (1960–1965), rising sharply after Suharto's coup from as low as 10 (1964) to 33 ($6 bn 1966 GDP) and over 50 percent by the late 1970s ($78 bn 1980 GDP). Suharto's TO average – 47 percent – more than doubled Sukarno's.

Compare these trends with the Middle East. Egypt's TO declined from over 53 percent prior to the 1952 revolution to 37 average under Nasser ($4.4 bn 1965 GDP) and Sadat's early (inward-looking) rule. Following Sadat's 1974 *infitah* (economic opening) revolution, TO climbed from 33 (1973) to over 61 (1975) and 78 percent (1979), replacing Nasser's 37 average with 66. Under Mubarak's initial hybrid coalition, TO halved from 82 (1981) to 41 percent (1986) climbing to 60 (early 1990s) once economic liberalizers began asserting themselves politically. In Syria's relatively small economy ($1.4 bn 1965 GDP, $13 bn 1980, $17 bn 1995), TO declined with the ascent of inward-looking Ba'ath and 1960s nationalizations from over 50 percent (late 1950s) to 38 average. It reached 48 averages (1980s), perhaps reflecting a more vigorous political presence of Damascene merchants favoring *infitah*, even under dominant control by the Ba'ath and its military-industrial complex. Iraq's TO declined from 64 percent ($2.4 bn 1965 GDP) in the early 1960s under Ba'ath rule to 55 average (late 1960s, early 1970s) and 71 (late 1970s) with expanding oil revenues and incipient reforms by Saddam Hussein's circumstantial coalition against Ba'ath rivals. Soon thereafter, however, TO declined to 47 percent (mid-1980s), when Saddam's regime pivoted heavily toward an inward-looking militarized economy. Sanctions after 1990 render TO measures less useful for this analysis.

Israel's TO under decades of hybrid coalitions from Ben Gurion onwards, doubled from 38 percent in 1960 ($4 bn 1965 GDP) to 83 (1977), following embryonic economic reforms in the 1960s. TO increased to over 90 percent with Menahem Begin's ascent but declined to 73 by the end of his tenure, as he relied more heavily on inward-looking constituencies. TO declined – from 80 (1984) to 64 percent (1991 – under the hybrid national unity government. Replacing inward-looking Yitzhak Shamir, Labor's internationalizing coalition brought an initial TO of 65 percent (1992) to 80 by 1996 ($92 bn GDP). Pakistan's TO averaged 28 percent ($9 bn 1970 GDP) under inward-looking Zulfiqar Bhutto, increasing to 34 under hybrid Zia and 36 percent under hybrids Benazir Bhutto and Nawaz Sharif, both shackled politically by inward-looking Islamist fundamentalism and the military-industrial complex.

As for larger economies, Brazil's TO increased from 12 percent average in the early 1960s ($19 bn 1965 GDP) to 18 in the 1970s ($35 bn 1970 GDP). A hybrid succession maintained TO at 15 percent average into the 1990s, rising soon after the accession of internationalizers Collor de Mello and Fernando H. Cardoso. Argentina's TO remained below 15 percent ($16 bn 1965 GDP, $77 bn 1980) for decades – under inward-looking and hybrid rule from Perón to Alfonsín. Under inward-looking Peronist coalitions (early 1950s, mid-1970s) TO was lowest. Under Menem's 1990s internationalizing revolution TO rose to over 18 percent in a much larger economy ($281 bn 1995 GDP), reaching Argentina's highest levels in 50 years. Trade in goods relative to goods/GDP grew from 23 (1986) to 44 percent (1996). India's TO under inward-looking coalitions from Jawaharlal Nehru to Indira Gandhi averaged 10 percent ($172 bn 1980 GDP). With Morarji Desai's incipient liberalization (1977) TO rose to nearly 16 percent (1979); surpassed 20 only in 1992 following N. Rao's reforms; and reached 27 in 1995 ($325 bn GDP), more than doubling I. Ghandi's average. In an economy highly dependent on oil exports, Iran's TO under (Mohammed Reza Pahlavi) Shah's hybrid rule averaged

34 percent in the 1960s ($6 bn 1965 GDP) rising to 71 in 1974 ($11 bn 1970 GDP) with Shah's incipient reforms. With the latter's replacement by an inward-looking Islamic Republic, TO plummeted from 61 percent (1977) to 9 (1986). The rise of a "pragmatic" Islamist faction helps explain a slight recovery (early 1990s) with TO reaching over 30 ($64 bn 1994 GDP). The Islamic Republic more than halved Shah's average TO (46) to 20 percent. Thus, even in large economies though more pronouncedly in smaller ones, coalitions appear to have left significant marks on TO levels notwithstanding different geography, natural endowments, and historical trajectories.

Another measure commonly used to gauge internationalizing policies is *export growth/GDP*. Díaz Alejandro (1983) considered export growth rates, particularly for nontraditional exports, the best TO index for industrializing states (better than effective rates of protection and subsidization). Mean yearly export ratios for internationalizers neared 44 percent, almost threefold the inward-looking mean of 16 and nearly double the hybrid mean of 25 (Appendix V).[9] Mean changes in exports/GDP reflect 1.3 percent yearly increases for internationalizers; 0.45 for hybrids; and average yearly declines of 0.27 for inward-looking coalitions.

Beyond global coalitional averages, over-time coalitional variations within the same state are even more revealing. South Korea's exports/GDP under internationalizers grew from below 8 percent (1965) to 26 (1976) under Park to 35 average under Chun and Roh Tae-woo. Under Taiwan's internationalizers, exports/GDP grew from below 16 percent (1965) to 52 (1977) and higher thereafter. Indonesia's ratio under Sukarno averaged below 19 percent, doubling under Suharto to 39 (1973). Under Mahathir Mohamad's more inward-looking phase (1980–1987) Malaysia's exports/GDP were below 55 percent average, rising to over 77 with liberalization (1987 onwards). Singapore's already high ratio (115 percent, late 1960s) rose to over 200 by the 1990s under Lee Kuan Yew. Chile's exports/GDP average under Allende (11 percent, 1971–1973) grew to 23 (1976) under Pinochet, averaging 27 for his entire period and rising to 33 percent under his internationalizing democratic successors. Israel's exports/GDP under hybrids averaged 25 percent, rising to 29 under Begin and 33 percent under a national-unity government (1984) but far more sharply under the internationalizing Labor – Meretz coalition. Nasser's 20 percent average rose to 24 with Sadat's *infitah* but remained at 21 averages under Mubarak's hybrid era.

In larger economies, Argentina's ratios under decades of inward-looking and hybrid coalitions were lower than 9 percent (5 in the 1970s under inward-looking Isabel Perón) rising slightly under internationalizing Menem's first two years to 11 percent despite an overvalued peso.[10] Brazil's averaged only 7 percent under hybrids, rising to 12 under internationalizing Collor. Rao's liberalization in India may be credited with rising export ratios from 5.5 averages under I. Gandhi to nearly 10 percent (1996). Iran's 11 percent averages under Shah plummeted to 4 with the inward-looking Islamic revolution. As with other measures, actual export success is not a flawless indicator of efforts to expand exports; global and internal micro and macroeconomic factors affect performance. Overall, however, efforts to internationalize via exports vary significantly across coalitional variants.

Yearly-aggregated data on *foreign direct investment* (FDI) growth provide yet another measure of changing openness. Mean yearly FDI for internationalizing coalitions was $712 million, slightly less for hybrids ($655M), and only $38M for inward-looking ones.[11] Looking at variances between each coalitional pair, it is possible to reject the hypothesis that there is no difference between means for internationalizing and inward-looking cases ($p=.014$), but (only at the .5 level). Differences between hybrids and the other two categories are not statistically significant. Internationalizers increased FDI inflows by $110M on average and hybrids by $33M; inflows decreased by $25M under inward-looking coalitions.

Intra-state over-time variations provide further evidence compatible with expectations. Argentina's FDI inflows were $10M under inward-looking Isabel Perón and remained below $512M average under hybrids until 1988. Menem's internationalizing shift trebled FDI from $1.8 bn (1990) during his first year in office to over $6 bn (1993), averaging $3.7 bn yearly. Average FDI inflows under Brazil's hybrids (1960s–1970s) were $1.5 bn, declining dramatically under Franco but leaping to $10 bn (1996) – the combined total of the preceding three years – under Cardoso's internationalizing strategy. India's post-independence inward-looking and hybrids discouraged FDI. Desai's brief interlude incepted FDI flows ($3M by 1980), averaging $50M under I. Gandhi (early 1980s), rising to $237M under Rajiv Gandhi's hybrid coalition. Internationalizer Rao trebled FDI from $148 to $435M from 1991 to 1992. These are still relatively low levels considering India's size. Singapore's FDI averaged $1.7 bn under Lee Kuan Yew, nearly doubling from $5.5 bn (1990) to $9.4 bn (1996) under Goh Chok Tong. In Chile, negative flows under Allende were followed by $299M averages under Pinochet and $428M under internationalizing democratic successors. Relying largely on grants and loans, FDI flows into South Korea were rather low ($68M average under Park) but grew significantly by the late 1980s reaching $2.3 bn by 1996. FDI averaged $9M under inward-looking Z. Bhutto, rising to $104M under hybrids Zia, Benazir Bhutto ($194M), and Nawaz Sharif ($319M). Israel's FDI remained low – $78M – under successive inward-looking and hybrid coalitions until the 1980 reforms. Labor's internationalizing strategy expanded inflows dramatically from $300M under inward-looking Shamir (1991) to nearly $2 bn (1995), representing 7.3 percent of gross domestic investment, up from 1 percent in 1980.[12] Netanyahu's initial hybrid coalition reversed this pace by 1998, when investments became affected by political and security uncertainty that "makes it harder to utilize the opportunities embodied in the globalization process."[13] Egypt's FDI more than doubled following Sadat's *infitah* (1974–1976), averaging $599M but declining to $169M under Mubarak's hybrid period (1980s), rising again in the 1990s with a revamped proto-internationalizing coalition.

Shifts from inward-looking to internationalizing coalitions and vice-versa thus correspond with expected changes in yearly FDI flows for the overwhelming majority of cases. Yet FDI is responsive not merely to host-country policies but also to coalitions' credibility and regional (in)stability. Greater stability following the Oslo peace process partially accounts for higher FDI flows into the Middle East. The prospect that greater stability will enhance FDI is, of course, central to the calculus of internationalizing coalitions.

The military-industrial complex

Military expenditures (MILEX) were overall high during the Cold War, particularly in regions most directly affected by it. One might thus argue that the dice is loaded against finding effective differences across coalitional variants. Furthermore, several internationalizers – notably in East Asia – were particularly engulfed by Cold War threats and regional corollaries that might have neutralized efforts to tame MILEX. Nonetheless, contrasts across coalitional variants are clear. Internationalizers generally prevented MILEX from overwhelming domestic economic reform, regional stability, or global access. Inward-looking coalitions, in contrast, made a *Wehrwirtschaft* (war economy) pivotal to their grand strategy. Wide variance in mean MILEX relative to GDP (MILEX/GDP) is evident: it was more than double for inward-looking (9.53 percent) than for internationalizers (4.59 percent), with hybrids in-between (7.58).[14] MILEX/GDP declined by 0.15 percent yearly average for internationalizers and 0.07 for hybrids, but rose by 0.62 percent for inward-looking coalitions. Data on MILEX/central government expenditures (MILEX/CGE) reflects a similar pattern.[15]

These findings confirmed restrained MILEX by internationalizers, particularly considering their threatening regional environments. Taiwan's MILEX/GDP was 8 percent (1961–1987 average) declining to 6 (1970s–1980s) as internationalization took root, and 4 percent (1990s). Averages for internationalizing Southeast Asia were 2.8 percent (1990–1991). Thailand's MILEX halved from 5 (1985) to 2.6 percent (1994). Malaysia's declined from 5.6 to 3.9 percent (1985–1994), Singapore's and Brunei's from 6.7 to 4.8, and Vietnam's from 19.4 to 5.7 percent. Growth in Southeast Asia's MILEX lagged behind GDP growth by 50 percent. MILEX/CGE also reveals overall decline under internationalizers from 27 percent under Park to 15 under Kim Young Sam, and 25 percent under inward-looking Sukarno to 13 under Suharto. Notwithstanding routine military acquisitions, arms races and offensive build-ups were avoided.

South Korea deserves special attention because external and internal conditions weighed heavily in favor of expansive MILEX. Yet General (President) Park subdued pressures from a statist military-industrial complex that threatened his grand strategy (Haggard and Kaufman, 1992). Relying on technical and economic experts, he checked "the arbitrariness and rashness of military officers;" cultivating national strength, he argued, meant "doing away with those activities that tend to drain or waste our natural resources in a broad sense" (Park, 1976: 107, 171). Park reduced MILEX/GDP from 5.5 percent average under Syngman Rhee (1960–1962) to 4.6 (1963–1970). Despite sharp declines in US military assistance since 1969, MILEX/GDP remained at 5 percent (US grants ceased completely in 1978). Inflation and government expenditures remained relatively low and budget deficits relative to GDP declined in the late 1970s. At 5 percent, MILEX/GDP was comparable to the industrializing world's average (1970s–1980s) and far lower than in other high-conflict regions, notably the Middle East (15–25 percent). Moreover, while South Korea's GDP grew by 10 percent (1965–1989 average), MILEX/GDP remained largely constant, declining to 3.6 percent by the early 1990s.

Paradoxically, this last figure was comparable to Argentina's (late 1970s–early 1980s) in a region characterized by low threat perceptions. At its peak South Korea's MILEX accounted for 26 percent of the budget (1960s–1970s), down to 15 percent (early 1990s), whereas Brazil allocated 20 percent (1967–1973).[16] Entrenched military-industrial complexes in Argentina and Brazil during inward-looking and hybrid decades help explain this paradox. Even MILEX/GDP above 2 percent was too high for a low-conflict region, and Argentina's reached over 6 percent (early 1980s). "Internal security" can hardly be summoned to explain such expenses since most autocracies – including South Korea's – built police states. Argentina's puzzle lies in a long succession of strong inward-looking coalitions interlocked with state and military enterprises. The latter's eventual demise under Menem's internationalizing revolution drove MILEX to all-time lows – 1 percent (1992) – ending universal conscription altogether. Brazil's internationalizer Collor slashed MILEX/GDP below 1 percent (0.30) and MILEX/CGE to 4 percent, denied military salary raises, and purged officers from the bureaucracy. Cardoso endorsed similar trends. Chile's MILEX/GDP rose slightly to 3.5 after the 1973 Pinochet coup. Yet, notwithstanding his abominable human rights record, Pinochet avoided military build-ups and external confrontations – triggered by Argentina – to protect his economic reform program. With a much smaller economy from which to draw resources than Argentina's, even higher MILEX/GDP yielded smaller absolute military resources for Chile. Yet Pinochet reduced MILEX when stabilization efforts required it (1975–1976, 1981), unlike inward-looking Argentine military counterparts.

Coalitional shifts help explain evolving MILEX/GDP patterns even in Israel, which faced potential combined attacks by Arab states during most of the period under consideration. A high 1948–1977 average – 20 percent – clearly mirrored a regional cauldron of war fueled by inward-looking regimes. Yet the average declined to 7 percent (1960s) when Premier Levy Eshkol and Finance Minister Pinhas Sapir attempted a proto-internationalizing shift, foiled by external (Nasser and the Six Day War) and internal inward-looking forces. Very high MILEX/GDP averages after the 1973 surprise combined Arab attack declined to 18 percent (1985–1989) following structural adjustment by a hybrid national unity government under Labor's Shimon Peres as Finance Minister. The first truly internationalizing coalition (Labor–Meretz) brought MILEX down to 9 percent in 1992, dramatically downsizing and privatizing defense firms.

Other Middle East hybrids and would-be internationalizers maintained lower MILEX/GDP than most neighbors. Morocco's remained below 3 percent (1960s), nearly doubled when conflict with Algeria flared up (late 1970s), but declined to under 2 percent (1990s). Tunisia's MILEX was consistently lower than 2 percent except for a brief rise in the early 1980s. MILEX/CGE for Morocco and Tunisia were 3 percent in a region that averaged nearly 40 percent. MILEX/CGE declined in Jordan from 44 percent (1960s–1970s) to 24 (1990s) with incipient internationalization; MILEX/GDP dropped from 15 to 8 percent in the same period. Most dramatic was Sadat's contraction of MILEX from 52 (1975) to 13 percent (1979), a 3.86 percent yearly decline. Egypt's pre-1970s high ratios lead naturally to the next coalitional profile in MILEX performance.

MILEX/GDP averages of 9.64 percent and mean yearly increases of 0.63 percent provide support for inward-looking coalitions' hypothesized priorities. MILEX/CGE averaged 40 percent. The high incidence of such coalitions in the Middle East explain high regional averages (nearly 19 percent for 1970s–1980s), over three times higher than industrializing world averages. Iraq's reached over 50 percent (1973–1985), 10 times that global mean. MILEX/GDP under Nasser and Sadat's inward-looking period (1970–1973) reached 24 percent, and Syria's under Hafez al-Assad was 16 (1973–1985) declining below 10 after 1988 under embryonic economic reforms. PLO's MILEX/CGE neared 70 percent. Israel's hybrid coalition slid toward more inward-looking constituencies (1996), reversing MILEX/GDP decline under internationalizers. Despite favorable regional strategic conditions Netanyahu increased MILEX as his first budgetary priority. Iran's Islamic Republic might seem an exception. However, reported MILEX/ GDP of 6 percent average (early 1980s) – rising sharply to 34 percent during the Iran–Iraq war and declining below 3 (1990s) – underestimate actual expenditures according to SIPRI. MILEX/CGE of 30 percent are much closer to the region's average. Kim Il-Sung's MILEX/GDP resembles the Middle East, averaging 25 percent (1985–1994) and perhaps much higher according to SIPRI, astonishing levels given basic subsistence needs and foreign debt that kept North Korea at the world's bottom in credit standing.

Not every inward-looking coalition exhibits such high MILEX/GDP although most have higher ratios than internationalizers in the same country. India's 3.3 percent average under I. Gandhi declined to 2.5 percent (1990s) with Rao's liberalization, rising sharply under hybrid Hindu BJP-led coalition (1998) to near 4 percent and more sharply after its nuclear tests and Kargil war. BJP tamed inward-looking economic proclivities to capture constituencies in quadrangle IV but heeded nationalist and military pressures for higher MILEX. MILEX/CGE averaged 18 percent (1960s to early 1980s), declining slightly under hybrids to 15 and 13 percent under Rao's incipient internationalization. Inward-looking Z. Bhutto doubled Pakistan's MILEX/GDP from 3 percent average in the previous decade to 6.2 (1970s), maintained by successive hybrids (1980s–1990s). Inward-looking and hybrids in Brazil retained comparable ratios over decades – below 2 percent – slightly higher for inward-looking variants. Argentina's MILEX/GDP climbed to 6 percent with nationalist militarism leading to the Falklands/Malvinas war. Aggressive military build-ups were typical for quintessential inward-looking Juan Perón (1946–1955); a second Peronist administration increased MILEX/GDP (relative to military predecessors!) to 2.5 percent (1973). Allende increased Chile's real MILEX/GDP slightly from 2 percent (1960s average) to 2.77 (1970–1972). Sukarno's averaged 5.4 percent (early 1960s); Suharto's internationalizing drive slashed it to 3 percent (1970s–1980s) and 1.2 (late 1980s–early 1990s). MILEX/ CGE fell from Sukarno's 25 percent to Suharto's 13 average.

In line with theoretical expectations, hybrids facing powerful inward-looking constituencies domestically and regionally exhibit higher mean MILEX/GDP (7.7 percent). Jordan's King Hussein was a paradigmatic case, forced to suppress internationalizing tendencies to accommodate domestic and regional inward-looking pressures. MILEX averaged 16.5 percent (1960s–1970s) while participating in major wars. Ratios declined to 12.5 (1980s average) and – under incipient reforms – 8 percent (1990s). MILEX/CGE nearly halved in the latter period. Egypt's Mubarak faced similar pressures; his hybrid coalition reduced MILEX/GDP from high inward-looking levels to 5 percent (1994) and lowered MILEX/CGE. Iran's MILEX/ GDP averages below 7 percent under Shah (1960s) rose slightly (early 1970s) but remained lower than hybrid averages.

Regional and international behavior

Extensive militarization, economic closure, and emphasis on civic nationalism or confessional purity are expected to have negative regional security externalities. Relying on civic, ethnic, or religious differentiation, territorial aspirations, sovereignty, and self-reliance as mobilizing themes contribute to a climate of risk, instability, conflict, and competition. The logic of this strategy – particularly militarization, nationalist brinkmanship, and heightened balances of threat – has often led willy-nilly into armed conflict. Kim-Il Sung's attack on South Korea, Nasser's encroachment in Yemen and quarantine of Israel, Sadat's 1973 War, Begin's invasion of Lebanon, Assad's threats to Israel and invasion of Lebanon, Arafat's threats to Jordan and Lebanon, Perón's intimidations of neighbors, Galtieri's Malvinas debacle, repeated Indo-Pakistani military encounters and nuclear swaggering, Iran's Islamic Republic threats to Iraq, and Saddam's invasions of Iran and Kuwait, are all instances of this logic. Unsurprisingly, many among these inward-looking cases also brandished WMDs, an "upgrading" in military prowess fueling challenges to "Western-dominated" international regimes.

The Korean War unfolded against the background of parallel efforts by Rhee – promoting the aggressive motto "Let us march North" – and Kim Il Sung, committed to invade the South and overthrow Rhee. Kim emphasized *juche* and *chajusong*" (all-round independence) and *minjok tongnip* (national or ethnic independence). Rhee's coalition included extreme nationalists, notably Minister of Defense Yi Pom Sok who exalted the nation, the state, and racial purity while opposing reliance on foreigners. Sukarno launched aggressive regional policies and removed Indonesia from the UN. Zulfiqar Bhutto sought an "Islamic bomb" even if Pakistanis must "eat grass." India's inward-looking coalitions fueled wars against inward-looking China (1962), Pakistan (1965, 1971), and Sri-Lanka (1987–1990). India (and China) opposed international regimes such as the NPT as crowning examples of colonialism and fueled nuclearization (1974) under strong domestic pressures to offset Congress party's responsibility for India's defeat by China. Fundamentalist Hindu BJP-led coalition exacerbated regional tensions that had subsided under Rao and tested nuclear weapons in 1998 while rallying a fissiparous and unwieldy domestic coalition.

Inward-looking coalitions' involvement in Middle East wars is extensive. Seeking regional hegemony, Nasser intervened in Yemen against Saudi Arabia with chemical weapons; closed the Tiran Straits and expelled UN peacekeepers only to be defeated by Israel; and launched another "war of attrition" along the Suez Canal. Syria's Ba'ath aggressive pan-Arab bent accounts for its reputation as "the beating heart of Arabism," calling for war to liberate Palestine, war against "reactionary" pro-Western kingdoms, and the revival of Greater Syria (Lebanon, Jordan, and Palestine). Its most radical version peaked in 1966–1970 – leading to the Six Day War – but even more moderate ones under Hafiz Assad maintained a stranglehold over Lebanon. Fatah – the PLO's dominant political faction since the 1960s – embraced a national-populist strategy advocating total war on Israel and "pro-Western" Arab regimes until the 1990s. Threatened leaders in Jordan and Lebanon waged wars against PLO efforts to undermine them from within. Spasmodic war erupted between Iran's Islamic Republic and Iraq (1980–1988), leaving one million people dead and two million wounded. Saddam's efforts to restore his coalition's resources led him to invade Kuwait. Staggering allocations to WMD infrastructure employed 20,000 scientists and technologists while resisting UN-mandated inspections.

Israel's inward-looking and hybrid politics progressed from milder versions (Begin in 1977 but not 1982) to less moderate ones (Yitzhak Shamir, 1980s-early 1990s; Netanyahu, 1996–1998), including fundamentalist and civic-nationalist parties exalting self-reliance and high distrust for international institutions. In the words of minister Rafael Eitan "what the world thinks does not matter at all" (Getzler 1998). Begin's coalition was cajoled into accepting Sadat's Camp David initiatives but also unleashed war on Lebanon. Shamir's was dragged into the Madrid Peace Conference by the US but maintained intransigent demands. Netanyahu obliterated most progress in Arab–Israeli reconciliation since the Oslo process, regarding it as a child of internationalizing interlocutors in the region. Netanyahu exemplifies the inherent instability of hybrids with strong inward-looking components. Despite some initial support from economic reformers (quadrangle IV) his coalition pivoted fundamentally toward quadrangle III: "greater Israel" constituencies (religious, settlers, civic-nationalists), populist, developing areas, protected business and labor opposed to the economic consequences of peace with Arab neighbors, and Russian immigrants reliant on state subsidies. Internationalization was not this coalition's *most valued* preference; it was rather the product of broader political support for this process that run counter to inward-looking priorities.

Argentina's inward-looking policies shared traits with its Middle Eastern namesakes, including statist militarization, nationalism, populism, regional aggressiveness, and anti-Western rhetoric. Both brands resulted from a competitive outbidding among rival inward-looking factions appealing to large populist, bureaucratic, and military-industrial constituencies mobilized by Perónism and Nasserism. Perón challenged most international regimes and announced – misleadingly – Argentina's mastery of nuclear fusion. Successive unstable and short-lived coalitions extended Perón's grand strategic blueprint for decades. This coalitional makeup turned a relatively peaceful region into one with militarized confrontations (Chile, Beagle dispute), full-fledged war (Great Britain, Malvinas/Falklands), and persistent nuclear competition (with Brazil). Outbidding among inward-looking factions overwhelmed weak hybrids entangling Argentina in militarized initiatives. Brazil's own succession of hybrids avoided aggressive expansionism but retained nuclear competition.

Internationalizers are expected to endorse cooperative regional relations that enable economic reform, military downsizing, and accommodation with international security regimes that minimize risks and sanctions, facilitate foreign borrowing and investment, and reinforce global economic access. The evidence suggests that this proclivity remains even in regions with entrenched security dilemmas, prone to foil internationalizing strategies. South Korea's Park abandoned Rhee's aggressive policies, seeking to reduce tension: "Unification...must never be pursued by means of violence or military force"; proposing "peaceful competition between our free system and [North Korea's] to determine which system can give the people a better life"; and warning that "unless a policy of high economic growth is sustained, there will be no way to meet increased defense spending" (Park 1976: 94–96, 125). Park's Open Door Policy sought to improve South Korea's global access. Even as the North developed nuclear weapons Park signed and ratified the NPT as part of his internationalizing thrust, assuaging two major guarantors of his grand strategy (the US and Japan). Roh's "Economic Commonwealth" policy was backed by powerful *chaebol*, interested in shifting labor-intensive operations to the North, strengthening cooperation (Nordpolitik), and deepening global trade and investment. The relative moderation of security policies is brought to relief by three considerations. First, staying an internationalizing course entailed no small domestic political cost for a country engulfed geographically by powerful inward-looking adversaries – North Korea, China, the Soviet Union – particularly given North Korea's repeated attacks on South Korean civilians. Second, South Korea's renunciation of its alleged best survival option – nuclear weapons – given its extreme vulnerability, runs counter to expectations from neorealist theory. US security guarantees were never fool-proof for many South Koreans; US coercion worked only because of the coalition's internationalizing priorities (it failed in various other instances – see Chapter 10). Third, nuclear renunciation was particularly remarkable for a military regime with unquestionable capacity to overwhelm North Korea in a nuclear race, as the North threatened to turn Seoul into a "sea of fire." Internationalizing goals dominated competing incentives.

Facing a similar regional predicament, Taiwan's record is comparable to South Korea's in its pursuit of accommodating regional policies and nuclear renunciation despite questionable US commitments after normalization with China and the abrogation of the Washington–Taipei Security Treaty. Taiwan's internationalizers responded with aplomb to China's 1996 threats. Further South, ASEAN members declared "the concept of free enterprise" as their philosophical basis, arguing that the alternative to free trade is not just poverty but war.[17] The internationalizing cluster worked to diffuse inter-state disputes to tend to domestic challenges and enhance collective appeal to foreign investors. Global access – not defensive intra-regional trade – was their core objective. Suharto suppressed East Timor at home but reversed Sukarno's aggressive regional policy and restored Indonesia to the UN. The Bangkok Treaty created a Nuclear Weapons Free Zone among ASEAN states in 1995.

The Southern Cone's internationalizing revolution of the 1990s unleashed historical foreign policy reversals as well. Menem embraced international regimes shunned by Argentina for decades, scrapping missile projects, ratifying the NPT, joining the allies' naval contingent in Iraq, renewing diplomatic relations with Britain, welcoming EU investments, and obtaining formal US non-NATO ally status. Regional initiatives complemented these policies, including MERCOSUR's common market and nuclear agreements with Brazil renouncing nuclear weapons and establishing mutual verification and inspection procedures. Cooperation with internationalizing Chile deepened as well.

Internationalizers' cooperative strides were even more remarkable in Arab–Israeli relations, given a violent history. Sadat reversed Nasserism, signing the first ever Arab peace agreement with Israel. Lingering inward-looking pressures throughout the region explain frequent challenges to this agreement. Similar pressures affected King Hussein until Iraq's 1990 defeat discredited inward-looking opponents. Jordan and Israel established diplomatic relations soon after a historical breakthrough by an embryonic, fragile internationalizing dyad, Israel and the PLO. Backed by urban professionals, middle-class, highly skilled labor, export-oriented industrialists, cooperative agriculture, and a vast pool of technical, scientific, service, managerial, and entrepreneurial groups, Israel's Labor–Meretz coalition won a mandate for socio-economic renewal within pre-1967 borders and territorial compromise beyond that line, enabling Oslo's mutual Palestinian–Israeli recognition. Economy Minister Yossi Beilin highlighted the coalition's internationalizing logic: a peaceful regional transformation that would enable Israel to deepen its ties with the global marketplace, an objective that required becoming "a more welcome member of the international club" (*Haaretz*, November 5, 1995, B2).

Incipient internationalization may also account for Palestinian evolution toward Oslo. Chief negotiator Ahmed Quray became Economy Minister and head of a National Council for the Encouragement of Investment. Another leading Oslo participant and eventual Minister of International Cooperation, Nabil Sha'ath, enunciated the Palestinian Authority's global orientation and regional cooperative policies. External actors – the US, European Union, World Bank, and others – nurtured the PA's internationalization. Morocco, Tunisia and Gulf countries joined a supportive regional network – the Multilateral Peace Process – tasked with resolving outstanding security, economic, and other issues. The unprecedented cooperative strides of 1993–1995 collapsed under inward-looking reactions in both Israel and Arab countries.

As expected, hybrids' records are mixed. Where they could isolate diehard inward-looking fringes in quadrangle III, wars were avoided even if deep regional cooperation never materialized. This is true even for democratic variants – Argentina's Alfonsín and Brazil's Franco – who never reached the higher levels of cooperation attained subsequently by internationalizers. Where hybrids slid into radical inward-looking variants – Videla and Galtieri's intertemporal courting of economic liberalizers first and extreme nationalists and protectionists later – wars ensued even in the least threatening regional environments. Iran's Shah asserted Iranian identity regionally but carefully avoided conflagrations of the kind that later engulfed the Islamic Republic. Jordan's hybrids could hardly avoid wars with Israel under Nasserism's heyday. Israel's hybrids often failed to reach peace agreements – except Camp David 1979 – under inward-looking pressures. Mubarak's intertemporal and sequential logrolling of hybrid coalitions resulted in policies asserting intermittently Egyptian, Arab, and Islamist themes. Hybrids in India and Pakistan failed to advance cooperation despite mild attempts by Rajiv Ghandi, Benazir

Bhutto, and Nawaz Sharif. Hybrids that worked hardest at attracting quadrangle II constituencies (e.g., Morarji Desai) also went furthest in cooperative regional overtures. Those efforts never went as far as Rao's, his Finance Minister Manmohan Singh, and Pakistan's former World Bank vice-president Moeen Qureshi, who headed a brief internationalizing interlude.

Given this overview it is hardly surprising that, over the period under study, inward-looking coalitions initiated over 30 international crises, hybrids about 17, and internationalizers only 2 (Brecher and Wilkenfeld 2000, Appendix V). Of all crises initiated, inward-looking coalitions account for 62 percent, hybrids for 34, and internationalizers for 4 percent. The mean number of crises initiated by inward-looking coalitions was 1.40 but only 0.11 for internationalizers and 0.94 for hybrids.

A coalition's domestic and regional strength, and the nature of logrolling across quadrangles, create notable differences even within coalitional categories. Inter-regional comparisons suggest that different coalitional mixes in a region create and reproduce typical regional orders and, conversely, are influenced by them. Where internationalizers reached a critical mass, they relied more on concerts, collective security, and multilateralism, avoiding aggressive steps, assisting members subjected to threats, and compromising on territorial disputes. ASEAN produced peaceful stability on the ashes of earlier wars; incipient Arab–Israeli internationalizers converged on the Oslo agreements; and their Southern Cone counterparts made MERCOSUR and denuclearization a reality. Ascending "zones of peace" challenge lingering inward-looking coalitions in the region and their grand strategy, from the merits of economic closure to the advantages of militarization. ASEAN had that effect on Vietnam and Cambodia, easing their eventual inclusion in the regional framework. Middle East internationalizers have been far more fragile, overwhelmed by inward-looking constituencies, and achieved limited success at economic openness relative to other regions. With shorter time-horizons, less credible commitments, and widespread coalitional asymmetries across the region, cooperation and diffuse reciprocity have been more tentative and unstable.

Conclusions

This article maps constituencies according to their position regarding internationalization. From myriad constellations three ideal-typical coalitions emerge – internationalizing, inward-looking, hybrid – as the product of logrolling efforts, sequential courting, ambitious unifying maneuvers, and leaders' manipulation of uncertainty. The three ideal-types differ in preferences over domestic and international resource extraction and allocation, time-horizons, and regional and international behavior. They thus advance different grand strategies with synergistic domestic, regional, and global effects. The coalitions' relative domestic and regional strength condition how pristine or diluted those strategies are likely to be. Strong internationalizers create more cooperative regions than strong inward-looking clusters. Hybrid coalitional equipoises, diluted strategies, and mixed regions create unstable regional orders that elude extensive cooperation or warfare.

Evidence from the industrializing world confirms significant behavioral differences across the three coalitional types regarding economic openness, military investments, international regimes, and regional policies. Aggregate data suggest that these differences are statistically significant for trade openness, exports relative to GDP, FDI, MILEX, and crisis initiation.[18] As expected, differences between internationalizing and inward-looking coalitions are more pronounced than differences between inward-looking and hybrids. Disaggregated longitudinal analysis of successive coalitions in single countries offers more detailed evidence – taking into account initial conditions and country-specific considerations such as size – validating expectations of coalitional differences beyond geography, natural endowments, and historical trajectories. The analysis of MILEX suggests that different coalitions filter regional security dilemmas through the requirements of their favored grand strategy. Thus, inward-looking coalitions can overspend even where security dilemmas are relatively low, and internationalizers can tame MILEX relative to their available resources and security dilemmas. Inward-looking coalitions initiated over 10 times as many international crises as internationalizers, and are far more prone to risky competition and instability that begets war, particularly in inward-looking-dominant clusters.

These results are particularly significant given reliance on quantitative data sets that pose hard tests for discerning coalitional effects. The inclusion of post-1993 data would have arguably sharpened those effects for internationalizers as would the inclusion of data on Taiwan. Yet behavioral differences across coalitional categories are clear even under more inauspicious eras for internationalizing strategies. The focus here was on economics and security; coalitional proclivities regarding human rights, environmental regimes or social equity are beyond the scope of this article. Further research may well suggest alternative coalitional patterns altogether.

The evidence also supports hypothesized synergies across domestic, regional, and global pillars of a "grand strategy." Internationalizers are more prone to deepen trade openness, expand exports, attract FDI, tame profligate military-industrial complexes, initiate fewer international crises, eschew WMDs, defer to international economic and security regimes, and strive for regional cooperative orders that reinforce those objectives. Pristine and coherent grand strategies of any sort are rare but the links between commitment to internationalization and regional cooperation are evident. By contrast, inward-looking coalitions are found to restrict and reduce trade openness and exports, curb foreign investment, build expansive military-industrial complexes and WMDs, initiate international crises, challenge international regimes, and exacerbate civic-nationalist, religious, or ethnic differentiation by emphasizing territoriality, sovereignty, militarization, and self-reliance. The risks and externalities of those policies make war more likely even when they may not be the most favored option. Hybrids straddle the grand strategies of their purer types, intermittently striving for economic openness, contracting the military complex, initiating international crises, and cooperating regionally and internationally, but neither forcefully nor coherently.

Coalitional effects are evident even under changing global circumstances ("world-time") over the last four decades. Global trends can have profound effects on domestic coalitional balances of power. The Cold War may have provided more supportive global structures for inward-looking strategies, from economic closure to militarization and regional conflict. This might help explain the relative weakness of internationalizers over that period and their sometimes diluted grand strategies. The post-Cold War era, by contrast, provided an international economic and institutional environment far more favorable to internationalizing strategies, up to a point. Unintended effects of IMF, World Bank, G8, and other conditionality programs have sometimes weakened internationalizers and, on occasion, their cooperative regional initiatives. Fears that the 1997 Asian crisis might have similarly detrimental effects were dispelled; internationalizers stayed the course. Yet protected markets in the industrialized world, volatility unleashed by global capital liberalization, and tendencies to approach reform with myopic disregard for safety nets and equity considerations remain dangerous challenges for internationalizing coalitions.

This framework and its findings have several implications for theory. First, they defy notions of linear progression toward economic liberalism and regional cooperation, allowing for possible cyclical patterns and "double movements" (Polanyi, 1944). Second, the focus moves from classical interdependence theory's emphasis on bilateral economic gains to international openness as an engine of regional cooperation. Third, extending the framework outlined in Figure 4.1 can help capture international effects of import to constructivist research insofar as ideas, identities, and evolving "cultures" find their way into the domestic politics of coalition formation. Coalitional accounts can benefit from deeper understanding of how and why domestic constituencies become socialized into international ideational structures. Fourth, coalitional arguments provide more tractable venues for assessing when, how much, and why international institutions play a role domestically, and consequently, in foreign policy. Fifth, the effects of coalitional balances of power can override structural power theories. The shadow of security dilemmas may benefit inward-looking coalitions over internationalizing ones, affecting the speed, viability and shape of regional cooperation. Yet structural power categories are under-determining, requiring deeper knowledge of domestic and regional coalitional configurations for explaining outcomes. The absence of genuine security threats does not guarantee regional cooperation. Nor do genuine security threats place insurmountable barriers. Favorable regional *coalitional* balances of power can condition the effects of classical neorealist power considerations. Whether or not such balances emerge in troubled regions is contingent on how domestic constituencies approach internationalization and its corollaries.

Notes

1 That increasing dimensions of domestic politics are exposed to external phenomena does not necessarily imply that domestic responses are uniform. Internationalization involves reduced barriers to international flows of goods, capital, and ideas but not necessarily global convergence, at least not in the short to medium terms.
2 Figure 4.1 builds on Hirschman's (1963: 285–291) simpler but inspiring account of parliamentary debates over economic reform.
3 Quadrangle I includes strong and weak opponents of economic openness who otherwise endorse security regimes strongly or weakly. Quadrangle IV includes weak and strong proponents of economic openness who oppose security regimes strongly or weakly.
4 The next section offsets this data deficiency by including some post-1993 data – where available – in longitudinal discussions of individual cases.

5   See the original article published in *International Studies Quarterly* in 2001 for an extensive list of sources.
6   This grouping collapses 98 coalitions into 55 entries.
7   Most indices build on limited samples and time periods (Edwards 1997). No existing data bases cover the entire period and countries for most measures.
8   For 1950–1992 data is from Heston and Summers's *Penn World Tables* (1991/1995), supplemented with the UN Statistical Yearbook (1999) for 1993–1998. The longitudinal analysis below also builds on World Development Indicators for 1992–1996 (World Bank, 1998: 310) and World Development Report (World Bank, 1991–1997). Scarce data for North Korea, the PLO/Palestine, various Arab states, and the 1950s generally compels greater reliance on qualitative sources.
9   The hypothesis of equal variances across the three groups can be rejected at the .01 level; differences in means across coalitions are statistically significant at the .01 level.
10 The inward-looking average would have likely been lower had data for Juan D. Perón's presidency been available from the same data set.
11 $F=4.075$, significant at $<.018$; differences in coalitional means for FDI significant only at the .05 level. FDI data for inward-looking and hybrid coalitions are extremely scarce (118 inward-looking cases – of 144 – largely missing), perhaps confirming theoretical assumptions regarding these coalitions.
12 Israel, Central Bureau of Statistics. Available from www.cbs.gov.il/lmse.cgi.
13 Israel's independent Central Bank Director (Bank of Israel, www.bankisrael.gov.il).
14 F statistic of 26.19 significant at the $<.001$ level. Regarding variance between dyads, mean differences between internationalizing and inward-looking (4.9) and internationalizing and hybrid (2.9) are significant at $<.001$, and between inward-looking and hybrid only at the .05 level.
15 MILEX/CGE averaged 20 percent for internationalizers, 31 for inward-looking and 22 for hybrids. The mean difference between internationalizing and inward-looking was 11 and between inward-looking and hybrid 7, with little significant differences between internationalizing and hybrid. MILEX/CGE declined by nearly 0.4 percent yearly average for internationalizers and 0.15 percent for hybrids, but rose by 0.9 percent for inward-looking coalitions (Appendix V).
16 In another region subject to Cold War tensions, the Middle East, MILEX/CGE averaged 40 percent.
17 Lee Kuan Yew, "Survey: Asia, A Billion Consumers," *The Economist*, Oct. 30, 1993: 329.
18 The only variables significant at the .05 level (rather than .01) are FDI – for which there is scarce data – and crisis initiation.

PART II
Regional effects of democratic institutions

5

PAX ASIATICA VERSUS BELLA LEVANTINA

The foundations of war and peace in East Asia and the Middle East

The dawn of the twenty-first century exposes two dramatically different regional circumstances in East Asia and the Middle East. Despite a background of deadly wars (Korea 1950s, Vietnam 1960s), enduring resentment over aggression and colonial domination (mainly by Japan), and persistent historical, ethnic, religious, and territorial cleavages, there have been no major wars in East Asia for several decades. Indochina has been at peace for two and a half decades, maritime Southeast Asia for four, and Northeast Asia for five. Existing disputes have been restrained as never before in recent history, and major powers have normalized diplomatic relations despite continued tensions, mainly over Taiwan and the Korean peninsula. Military modernization has not undermined macroeconomic and regional stability. Military expenditures relative to GNP have declined from 2.6 percent (1985) to 1.8 percent (2001), lower than world averages of 5.4 percent (1985) and 2.5 percent (2001), with parallel declines – in most states – in military expenditures relative to central government expenditures. Extra regional trade and investment expanded dramatically, intra-Asian exports grew from 30 percent (1970) to 55 percent (2004), and incipient and informal – but inclusive – regional institutions (APEC, ASEAN Regional Forum) have emerged. This sustained absence of war and deepening of cooperation help envision a "Pax Asiatica" in the East Asian region.[1]

In sharp contrast, the Middle East has hardly been peaceful. The highly conflictive 1940s to 1950s were superseded by more inter-state wars, militarized interventions and mobilizations, invasions, shows of force, border clashes, and

---

* I thank the Social Science Research Council-MacArthur Foundation for a Fellowship on International Peace and Security that spearheaded this comparative project. I would also like to acknowledge support from an S.S.R.C./ Abe Fellowship, and helpful suggestions from the *American Political Science Review* editor, three anonymous reviewers, Leonard Binder, Steph Haggard, Miles Kahler, Giacomo Luciani, T. J. Pempel, John Ravenhill, Maurice Schiff, and Beth Yarbrough. Wilfred Wan provided excellent research assistance. I also thank Maryam Komaie, John Altick, and Phil Potter.

covert (violent) cross-border subversion involving Egypt–Yemen/Saudi Arabia (1962–1967), Syria–Jordan (1970), North–South Yemen (1972), Arab states–Israel (1967, 1973), Libya/Algeria–Morocco (1970s), Libya–Chad (1973–1987), Morocco–Polisario (1975–2000), Syria–Lebanon (1980s–2005), Iran–Iraq (1980–1988), Israel–Lebanon (1980s–1990s, 2006), and Iraq–Kuwait/Saudi Arabia (1990–1991), among others (see Table 5.1).[2]

Despite dismal economies, arms races continued to attract the highest levels of military expenditures/GNP worldwide, 17.3 percent (1985) and 7.7 percent (2001) averages, nearly three times the global average. Trade and investment remained bleakly low and regional institutions hopelessly marginal; inter-Arab trade has accounted for 7 to 10 percent of total trade since the 1950s (Arab Human Development Report [AHDR] 2002: 26). The region also exported terrorism in scales unmatched by other regions. Protracted "Bella Levantina" (Middle East wars) have led to its common characterization as a "cauldron of war," holding 7 percent of global population while accounting for 35 percent of armed violence in the last 55 years (Military Balance 2001–2002). Halliday (2005) stipulates that:

> the international relations of the Middle East have long been dominated by uncertainty and conflict. External intervention, interstate war, political upheaval and interethnic violence are compounded by the vagaries of oil prices and the claims of military, nationalist and religious movements.

Although turmoil characterized both regions in the two decades following World War II, since 1965 the incidence of inter-state wars and militarized conflicts was nearly five times higher in the Middle East. There were five major Middle East wars with at least 10,000 casualties since 1965, but only two in East Asia. Excluding US military participation, four major wars were waged between/among local actors in the Middle East as opposed to only one in East Asia. Moving from regional to state-level measures, involvement in militarized conflict becomes even more striking. Disaggregating regions into component states reveals that five East Asian states (of 19) accounted for most militarized conflicts, whereas every single Middle East state (of 19) was involved in them. Beyond indicators included in Table 5.1, many assassination attempts on neighboring leaders in the Middle East contrast with their virtual absence in East Asia. Since 1973, ballistic missiles have been used in battle 10 times, with Middle East states accounting for eight instances; East Asia, for none (Karp 1995). Egypt, Iraq, Iran, Libya, and arguably Iran used chemical weapons in inter-state wars; no East Asian states are known to have done so since World War II. Cross-border efforts to undermine neighboring regimes have been legion in the Middle East but rare in East Asia. All these indicators reflect the actual – rather than potential – higher incidence and severity of Middle East inter-state conflicts.

Why is this contrast puzzling, and why does it deserve attention? First, these differences are perplexing considering that both regions shared common initial conditions in the 1950s to early 1960s: colonialism as formative experiences, comparable state-building challenges, economic crises, low per-capita GNPs, heavy-handed authoritarianism, low intra- and extra-regional economic interdependence, and weak or nonexistent regional institutions capable of organizing

TABLE 5.1 Differences in the incidence of militarized conflict: East Asia and the Middle East (1965–2006).

East Asia	Middle East	
Vietnam War (1965–75)	Egypt–Yemen–Saudi Arabia (1962–67)	Libya–Egypt (1980)
Vietnam–Cambodia (1975–79)		Libya–Malta (1980)
China–Vietnam (1979)	Jordan/Israel (1966)	Syria–Jordan (1980)
Vietnam–Thailand (1984)	**Arab states–Israel** (1967)	Libya–Tunisia (1980)
China–Vietnam (1984–88)	Turkey–Greece, Cyprus (1967)	**Iran–Iraq** (1980–88)
Laos–Thailand (1984–88)	Israel–Jordan (1968)	Israel–Iraq (1981)
China–Philippines (1995)	Iran–Iraq (1969)	Israel–Syria (1982–83)
China–Taiwan (1996)	Egypt–Israel (1969–70)	Libya–Sudan, Egypt (1983)
North Korea–South Korea (1996)	Saudi Arabia–South Yemen (1969–70; 73)	Sudan–Ethiopia (1984)
Myanmar–Thailand (2002)	Syria–Jordan (1970)	Libya–Sudan, Egypt (1984)
	North–South Yemen (1972; 1979)	Libya–Tunisia (1985)
	Oman–South Yemen (1972)	Libya–Egypt (1985)
	Libya–Chad (1972–87)	Qatar–Bahrain (1986)
	Iraq–Kuwait (1973; 1976)	Iran–Saudia Arabia (1987)
	Arab States–Israel (1973)	**Iraq–Kuwait and Saudia Arabia** (1990–91)
	South Yemen–Oman (1973; 1976)	Iran–Iraq (1992)
	Turkey–Cyprus (1974)	Iran–UAE (1992)
	Morocco, Algeria, Mauritania (1975–80)	Iraq–Kuwait (1992)
	Morocco–Polisario (1975–83)	Saudia Arabia–Qatar (1992)
	Syria–Lebanon (1976–2005)	Egypt–Sudan (1992)
	Iraq–Syria (1976)	Iraq–Kuwait, Saudia Arabia (1994)
	Libya–Sudan (1976)	Sudan–Egypt (1995)
	Egypt–Libya (1977)	Turkey–Syria (1998)
	Israel–Lebanon (1978–2006)	Syria–Lebanon (2005)
	North–South Yemen (1978–79)	

Sources: Solingen (2007b: 777). This list builds on the International Crisis Behaviour Online database (Wilkenfield and Brecher www.cidcm.umd.edu/icb) but excludes those entries falling outside the definition of militarized conflict as well as conflicts between regional actors and outside powers. Only conflicts between two or more regional actors are included. These criteria also eliminated some entries from the Militarized Interstate disputes database (Ghosn, Palmer and Bremer, 2004). Interstate wars with over 1,000 casualties are from the COW database (Sarkees, 2000). Between 1965 and 2002 Wilkenfeld and Brecher found 46 interstate crises in the Middle East, 5 in Northeast Asia and 25 in Southeast Asia (6 of them connected with the Vietnam War, and 18 involving Vietnam or continental Southeast Asia neighbors).

Notes: **Bold**: Wars with more than 10,000 casualties. The long list of militarized incidents in the Middle East involved armed attacks, artillery fire and border-crossing by tanks and aircraft, partial invasions, or major military standoffs at the border. The first state listed is usually imputed with having started hostilities, although war initiation is sometimes hard to assess (such as the long series of Lebanon/Israel raids and retaliations). There were 8 different militarized incidents between Syria and Chad, grouped here as a single protracted conflict according to Wilkenfeld–Brecher criteria because of significant continuity. Similarly, Israel–Lebanon and Syria–Lebanon conflicts could have been disaggregated further but were included as two protracted conflicts. The Yemen protracted conflict involved 6 militarized conflicts/wars. Disaggregating just these three conflicts and others into discrete crises would have made the list of militarized conflicts for the Middle East much longer. Furthermore, the list does not include many cross-border coups *unless* they were militarized (it thus excludes several coups sponsored by Muammar Qaddafi against Anwar el-Sadat and several other Arab and African leaders, a 1981 coup sponsored by Iran in Bahrain, coups sponsored by various neighbors against King Hussein of Jordan, and many others).

cooperation. Indeed, these initial cross-regional similarities invoke Mill's method of difference where, despite many common features, some crucial explanatory variables account for differential outcomes. Second, despite enormous intra-regional diversity, states in both regions emphasized family, literacy, and community. If these cultural variables explain East Asia's rapid development, as some argued, they would have had comparable effects in the Middle East. Instead, East Asia's economic transformation entailed changes in the content of education and the inclusion of women that have dramatically eroded educational gender gaps. Third, whereas intra-regional diversity arguably heightens barriers to cooperation, a far more internally diverse East Asia – in language, ethnicity, religion, development levels, and regime type – generated more cooperation. Much of the Middle East shares Arabic language and culture and an overwhelmingly Islamic character, despite ethnic, tribal, and communal diversity. Fourth, both regions faced comparable international opportunities and constraints during the Cold War regarding economic and security choices. Given these four considerations the dearth of systematic comparisons across these two regions is baffling, and perhaps explained by a tendency toward "exceptionalism" in respective regional scholarships.

I begin with an overview of conceptual alternatives explaining differential levels of inter-state conflict, distilled from hitherto disconnected literatures addressing Pax Asiatica and Bella Levantina respectively. For neorealism, anarchy and self-help lead only to tenuous or contingent cooperation, blurring cross-regional differences. Nor can regional institutions explain the emergence of East Asian cooperation or the permanence of Middle East war. "Asian values" accounts and their Middle East counterparts suffer from woolly definitions, underspecified theory and causal effects, inability to explain change, and presumed regional uniqueness. Domestic-politics explanations are puzzlingly rare or underspecified as a systematic framework for comparing these divergent regional trajectories.

I undertake the challenge of developing such a framework by tracing contrasting inter-state relations to distinctive domestic models of political survival. *Leaders in most East Asian states pivoted their political control on economic performance and integration into the global economy whereas most Middle East leaders relied on inward-looking self-sufficiency, state and military entrepreneurship, and nationalism.* This core argument compels both backward exploration of antecedent – permissive and catalytic – conditions explaining divergent models of political survival, and forward examination of these models' consequences for regional conflict. Whereas many states within each region shared a common model, I explore some anomalies and aborted efforts to adopt alternative models within each region. Both models relied on authoritarianism, state institutions, and the military as key allies for securing political control but differed in the nature of that reliance, with diverging consequences for inter-state relations. Observations for these disparate outcomes span the regional and state levels of analysis; different decisions by the same state over time (under different leaders); and different historical periods. Variance across and within regions and states, and over time, provide many observable implications of the core argument (King, Keohane, and Verba 1994; George and Bennett 2005). I end with conceptual and methodological conclusions.

Four candidate explanations

Neorealist accounts challenge the very premise of a Pax Asiatica. The universal logic of power distribution reigns over all regions, leaving none immune from cyclical war predicaments. By this logic, the presumed Pax Asiatica is merely a hiatus in war-making (Friedberg 1993/94). Robust, bipolar, and symmetric distribution of nuclear weapons – had it existed – might have explained a lull but, in the absence of such conditions, neorealism can hardly explain the absence of war. Indeed changes in power distribution – China's rise, Japan's normalization, North Korea's nuclearization – should have made war more likely. That has not happened yet. Furthermore, fluctuations between US hegemonic assertion and defection have not altered East Asia's peaceful progression. One crucial difficulty with power-based explanations is stipulating whether East Asia has been multipolar, bipolar, or under US hegemony. The Middle East has been more straightforwardly enmeshed in self-help, with no hegemon capable of enforcing a Pax Levantina, and multiple poles of power – external and internal – fueling security dilemmas. Iraq, Libya, Israel, Egypt under Nasser, and Iran arguably sought nuclear weapons with attending asymmetric and destabilizing results. However, in the final neorealist analysis, the same asymmetries exist in multipolar East Asia, with several declared nuclear powers. Both regions were multipolar yet different levels of conflict obtained, undermining polarity as an important explanatory category.[3]

Other neorealist variants trace East Asia's stability (not "peace") to bilateral US commitments; yet the latter mysteriously had different effects in the Middle East. Moreover, bilateral alliances may partially explain Pax Asiatica but compete with alternative accounts irreducible to US fiat (discussed below). Nor can most militarized Middle East conflicts be traced to Soviet or US initiatives. While both often supported different sides, most incidents began as schemes by regional actors sometimes opposed by respective patrons, from Iraq's wars to Gaddafi's defiance and some Arab–Israeli wars. Nor did the US presence in East Asia prevent major wars (Korea, Vietnam, Sino-Vietnamese) or North Korean military incursions. All these points question exclusive attention to polarity or hegemony in explaining disparate inter-state conflict levels across the two regions. Furthermore, neorealist perspectives differ over whether the Middle East has indeed been more prone than East Asia to inter-state conflict. Above all, neorealist accounts cannot argue both that (1) levels of conflict have been comparable across the two regions, and (2) the United States accounts for lower levels of conflict in East Asia. Only one statement can be true. Finally, hypotheses rooted in geopolitical considerations could trace Middle East conflict to land borders whereas waterways presumably kept East Asian adversaries at bay. Yet waterways did not preclude wars in earlier periods even at lower technological levels of maritime warfare; and land borders are not inevitable precursors of war, as evident in South America.

Neoliberal-institutionalist approaches would trace differential inter-state conflict levels to regional institutions presumed to reduce transaction costs and enhance cooperation. However, Pax Asiatica preceded legalized institutions envisioned by functionalist frameworks. Institutions emerged only after remarkable expansion in markets, investment, and cooperation and remained minimalist, informal, and consensus based (Solingen 2005). Nor did the Arab League's emergence in 1945 as the first regional institution worldwide preclude extensive Middle East conflict. Thus, comparable initial conditions – very low regional economic interdependence and weak or nonexistent regional institutions – led to different levels of inter-state conflict. Regional institutions were neither necessary for the emergence of East Asian cooperation nor sufficient for preventing Middle East conflict (Barnett and Solingen 2007).

Cultural interpretations too are beset by difficulties. First, both hegemonic religious/cultural identities – Islam (Middle East) and Confucianism (Northeast Asia) – emphasized family, literacy, and community but coexisted with different levels of inter-state conflict across regions. The same cultural construct could not explain both an earlier period of militarized conflict in East Asia and a subsequent Pax Asiatica. The ancient "Oriental wisdom's" penchant for consensus, harmony, unity, and community did not produce Pax Asiatica in earlier times. Second, historical memories remain alive in both regions yet found different mechanisms of expression or sublimation. Memories of Japan's World War II cruelty or repeated aggressions against Vietnam by successive powers did not preclude extensive economic, political, and diplomatic rapprochements. Third, better Middle East endowments in shared language and culture did not yield more cooperation; indeed, some trace common culture to conflicts over the normative content of Arabism (Barnett 1998). Conversely, extremely diverse East Asian cultures did not preclude cooperation. Fourth, some norms labeled "Asian values" and "ASEAN way" are not too different from those characterizing the Arab League, including informality, incrementalism, building on personal and political relations, saving face, emphasizing process over substance, constructive ambiguity, and relegating divisive issues to future resolution once they achieve ripeness or become irrelevant (Almonte 1997–1998). Fifth, even if shared norms do exist in East Asia – a disputed premise – they failed to have similar (cooperative) effects prior to the region's economic transformation.

Domestic political explanations could explain Pax Asiatica versus Bella Levantina but studies comparing the two are uncommon if not virtually inexistent. One approach, "democratic-peace" theory, is inapplicable because Pax Asiatica preceded a growing cluster of democratic states, and indeed still operates in a region hosting several non-democracies. Neither can "democratic-peace" theory explain Bella Levantina; joint democratic dyads/clusters were largely absent in the Middle East. Ephemeral cooperation during the Oslo process did not involve democratic dyads. Middle East conflicts are often explained by the predominance of autocracies (except for Israel within 1967 borders, and Turkey more recently); yet a fairly autocratic cluster spearheaded more peaceful conditions in Southeast Asia. Another approach builds on Rosecrance's (1986, 1999) seminal notion of "trading states," which indirectly led the way in its implicit contrast between Middle East atavisms and growing East Asia cooperation. While forcing attention to markets and trading states – a novel analytical move in a field hitherto dominated by balance of power theory – it compelled further work on how trading states came about. Who reads international incentives and constraints differently and why, and how does this reading affect the evolution of trading or territorially oriented

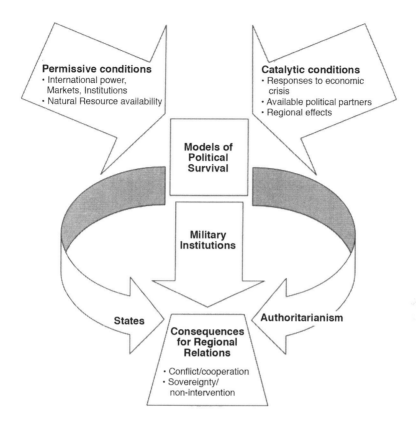

Figure 5.1 Causal sequence
Source: Solingen (2007b: 761)

war-prone states? Solingen (1998) traced the texture of regional relations to "grand strategies" of competing domestic coalitions: internationalizing coalitions favoring global economic and political access create conditions for regional cooperation whereas their inward-looking counterparts burden cooperation.

This article builds on these insights but goes beyond them, advancing that distinctive domestic models of political survival were critical drivers explaining variation in regional outcomes.[4] This requires better specification of four critical relations crucial to a focused comparison between the two regions: (1) the permissive international, regional, and domestic contexts that enabled the rise and maturing of respective models of survival; (2) the more immediate incentives and constraints leaders faced when adopting one model over another; (3) the consequences of each model for the nature of states, military, and authoritarian institutions; and (4) the implications of the latter three for inter-state relations. Efforts to endogenize models of survival (1 and 2 above) entail subsidiary propositions, as do efforts to derive implications of different models for domestic institutions (3 and 4 above). Figure 5.1 maps the complete theoretical structure or causal sequence that ties all the article's sections together: permissive and catalytic conditions as antecedent variables affecting models of political survival; each model's respective implications for states, military and authoritarian institutions as intervening variables; and the consequences of these institutional features for the fabric of inter-state relations in each region.

Models and choices: Permissive and catalytic conditions

No effective understanding of cross-regional differences is possible without identifying the respective models of political survival and the political-economy on which they rested. Institutional innovations, as North (1981) noted, often come from rulers who seek to maintain or legitimize their hold on power. East Asian rulers pivoted their survival on economic performance, export-led growth, and integration in the global political economy. These required vigorous embrace of export-led models capable of both satisfying domestic constituencies mobilized for this effort and yielding enough resources to compensate those disadvantaged by it. East Asian models emphasized macroeconomic stability; controlled budgets and external debt; and high rates of savings, investments, and literacy, particularly technical education (Noland and Pack 2005). By contrast, Middle East rulers perfected inward-looking models emphasizing statism and self-sufficiency (Arab Human Development Report 2002). Rents from expropriations and closure enabled populist patronage initially, yet with their exhaustion, nationalism and military prowess became core instruments of political survival.

As a product of competing models, average per-capita growth rates for 1950 to 2004 (2000 constant prices) surpassed 3 percent in 11 of 18 East Asian states but only in 3 of 18 Middle Eastern states (Lebanon, Tunisia, UAE) despite extensive oil endowments throughout much of that region (Table 5.2). Indeed long-run trends in the Middle East point to economic decline since the 1960s for both oil and non-oil producers (Sala-i-Martin and Artadi 2003). Considering population growth (1975–1998), real GDP was stagnant in the Middle East but rose nearly 6 percent in East Asia (Arab Human Development Report 2002: 86–88). Poverty rates did not decline nearly as much in the Middle East as in East Asia. Trade openness (constant prices) increased dramatically in nearly all East Asian states, but decreased significantly or stagnated in several Middle East states, particularly in the 1960s. Non-oil exports declined or stagnated in at least 10 Middle East states but rose in most East Asian ones (Table 5.2).

Were these trajectories preordained? Why were leaders willing and able to adopt different models despite sharing common colonialist legacies, state-building challenges, economic crises, and low per-capita GNP in the 1950s? The Confucian construct presumed to underpin the "Asian miracle" – authoritarianism, family-based entrepreneurship, commitment to education, and community over individualism – had comparable referents in the Middle East yet led to the adoption of different models. Five drivers influenced the fateful choices and respective viability of models. Two permissive conditions enabled particular models in each context: (1) international power, market, and institutional considerations; and (2) the political-economy implications of natural resource availability. Three more immediate, catalytic conditions reinforced, magnified, and in some cases derived

Table 5.2 East Asia and the Middle East compared.

	US Aid (mil $) (a)		Agricultural, Manufacture, Food Exports (% of GDP) (b)				Fuels, Ores & Metal Exports (% of GDP) (b)				Real GDP growth rate per capita) (c) (% in 2000 constant prices) (c)						Military Expenditures/GNP (d) M.E./ GDP (e)						Military Expenditures/ CGE (d)				
	1956	2005	1960 1969	1970 1979	1980 1989	1990 1999	2000 2004	1960 1969	1970 1979	1980 1989	1990 1999	2000 2004	1950 1959	1960 1969	1970 1979	1980 1989	1990 1999	2000 2004	1963 1969	1970 1979	1980 1989	1990 1999	2000 2004	1963 1969	1970 1979	1980 1989	1990 1999
East Asia																											
Australia	123.4		9.4	7.99	7.2	8.58	8.3	1.62	3.31	4.5	5.09	5.87	1.8		1.76	2.03	2.13	1.77	4.28	2.91	2.58	2.24	1.88	16.7	10.3	9.3	9.04
Brunei	0																										
Cambodia	2849.9			2.58	8.98	17.9	46.1	0.01	0.07		1.22	1.09			6.38	−5.81	−1.21	1.25			10.2	4.5	6.6		23.3	12.5	28.8
China	200.8		9.31				23			2	2.44	2.04	4.82		−8.18	−2.16	2.1	5.05	4.47	14.7		4.32	2.62	30.3	67.2	6.6	28.8
Hong Kong	44.7		52.5	62.5	82.6	108	130	1.04	0.85	1.71	8.82	9.43		0.55	4.63	7.61	9.49	7.64	10.8	12.7	6.55		2.53		43.5	28.6	28.3
Indonesia	6592		5.25	6.68	7.31	17.5	22.5	4.87	13.4	15.9				7.9	6.74	5.54	1.93	3.22									
Japan	1362.8		8.42	10.3	11.2	8.69	10.1	0.13	0.16	0.16	0.14	0.2		1.14	5.87	3.16	2.65	2.51	2.95	3.43	2.48	1.33	1.025	29.5	17.3	10.7	7.36
Laos	2600.7												6.97		4.06	3.07	1.29	1.01	0.91	0.9	0.98	1		6.87	6.63	5.48	5.66
Malaysia	315.1		25	30	36.3	70.9	90.7	12.3	10.8	14.9	8.79	11.3	0.91	3.57	−1.35	4.09	0.15	2.71	13.6	9.4	6.8	5.28	2.05	40.7	45.1	16	20
Myanmar	372.8														6.79	3.36	5.28	2.86	3.14	4.23	4.31	2.8	2.28	12.7	14.5	11.4	10.5
New Zealand	4.3		18.9	18.6	20.4	20.6	21.1	0.18	0.84	1.43	1.59	1.37	0.78	3.33	0.49	1.25	1.53	2.47	6.16	4.54	3.14	8	1.8	32.9	28.6	20.5	99.8
North Korea	887.2														9.58	6.6	−2.39	0.74	2.03	1.75	2.1	1.5	1.12	6.97	5.05	4.76	4.02
Papua N. Guinea	31		14.6	16.6	18.1	16.4		15.7	18.7	25.3	43.4		4.47	1.59	12.8	−0.77	3.47	−1.48	12.8	21.3	24.4						28.5
Philippines	7624.8		12.1	9.81	22	42.2		1.48	2.95	2.08	1.38	1.38			3.02	0.04	0.94	2.83	1.28	2.01	1.78	1.77	2.28	9.8	14.6	11.1	4.86
Singapore	25.6		80.5	71.5	97.3	117	138	24.6	30.3	34.4	17	15.5	1.26	3.01	7.19	4.33	4.36	1.53	3.14	5.43	5.2	4.85	4.92	22.6	28	18.8	9.32
South Korea	13366.1		4.72	19.9	29.4	25.1	30.8	0.65	0.59	0.74	1.01	1.94	2.45	2.57	7.09	6.25	5.48	4.82	3.9	4.83	5.18	3.36	2.44	22.8	27.2	26.7	21.9
Taiwan	3983.4														8.17	6.6	6.49	2.75	10.7	8.09	6.31	4.88	2.44	49.6	39.1	41.9	16.8
Thailand	3486.3		11	13.1	18.8	33.2	52.6	1.52	1.62	1.17	0.73	2.14		4.54	6.49	5.47	4.17	3.34	2.36	3.23	3.66	2.39	1.36	14.2	19.1	19.2	30.6
Vietnam	23936.7												−1.12	5.1		5.18	4.49	4.82			11.3	3.9				76.1	13.8
Middle East																											11.2
Algeria	226.5		6.57	2.23	0.41	0.94	0.98	14.7	24	21.7	23.3	35.1		1.78	3.09	0.54	0.06	1.69	2.65	2.3	3.17	3.02	3.48	6.17	8.03	8.99	9.55
Bahrain	346.3				40.4	29.3	8.77		46.6	45	61.9	61.9			7.24	−1.38	1.19	2.05		3	5.93	8.45	3.48		7.1	15.3	21.4
Egypt	61195.4		10.2	9.46	4.93	3.21	3.05	0.62	1.99	7.07	2.98	2.62	1.26	3.01	2.47	3.4	3.1	1.84	8.36	17.8	11.4	3.17	2.78	22.9	33.8	21.1	9.19
Iran	1849.6									14		21.2	2.45	5.74	2.85	−4.13	3.87	2.44	6.04	11.5	7.43	3.48	4.76	27.4	30.5	31.7	15.5
Iraq	19125.2														7.52	−1.42	7.74	−15.1	11.5	15.3	44.2	5.88		33.6	31.9	40.5	
Israel	93987.5		12.3	18.3	22.7	21.4	28	0.62	0.39	0.55	0.41	0.47	3.42	5.54	2.77	1	2.89	0.32	13.1	17.2	20.1	10.3	8.82	40	40.9	26.9	21.6
Jordan	8826		3.65	6.78	10.7	18.1	24.2	1.75	2.74	4.96	6.11	4.03	7.16	1.57	−0.89	−0.15	−0.24	−0.94	14.2	23.4	18	8.98	8.6	42.2	40.5	36	26.5
Kuwait	1.7			5.71	22.8	3.84	3.31		63.4	27.4	34.9	45.6			−4.81	−5.1	2.43	0.99	2.43	4.51	4.73	30.2	7.76	7.7	12.2	12.4	46.8
Lebanon	1026.7																7.77	−0.57	2.7	3.78	5.98	3.76	5.0333	19	17.9	20.6	12.3
Libya	218.4		0.6	0.15	0.53	1.68		48.9	56.9	44.6	28.7								1.85	6.82	12.8	5.78	5.0333	6.3	18	30.1	17
Morocco	3484.2		9.11	7.77	10.3	15.4	18.7	5.26	6.14	4.72	2.62	2.3	−0.24	6.13	2.88	1.71	0.56	2.04	2.88	4.53	5.94	4.4	4.24	12.2	14.5	17.4	13.7
Oman	569.1			1.15	23	7.93	9.97		44.8	25.1	36.2	44.9			1.2	2.63	1.86	0.69		27.7	23.9	18.3	11.84		45.8	44.8	39.7
Qatar	1.5														−1.09	−6.61	1.27	3.07		5.21	9.3	11.3			10.8	20.1	25.3
Sudan	4391.5		13.8	10.6	5.58	5.93	3.07	0.13	0.23	0.14	0.04	10.4			1.26	−0.65	−0.39	4.69	2.48	3.11	3.35	6.16	3.5	14.8	16.2	22.4	53.3
Syria	628.4			4.75	5.22	9.68	6.05		9.37	8.75	16.6	19.6		4.67	4.89	−1.25	2.77	0.28	9.45	13.1	17.5	7.5	6.6	36.7	34.1	41.9	29.9
Tunisia	2237.2		8.78	9.21	14.3	24.9	28.9	4.12	8.82	9.49	3.48	3.61		2.92	4.45	2.18	3.25	3.13	1.39	1.85	3.43	2.25	1.62	5.3	5.88	8.48	6.43
Turkey	18718		2.48	3.3	9.04	11.2	18.3	0.21	0.29	0.81	0.51	0.8	5.4	2.43	2.36	1.82	2.23	1.97	4.71	4.81	4.31	4.05	4.26	22.7	20.6	19.2	16.4
UAE	4.8			4.05	48.4	26.5	16.9		57.9	13.3	43.2	52.9			24.5	−5.82	3.05	5.29		2.38	6.81	5.03	3.2	49.9		42.4	47.8
Yemen	947.4					3.13	2.31				29.8	27.2					0.71	1.59				8.39	6.4333				24.5

Sources: (a) Greenbook. USAID; (b) World Bank Group. World Development Indicators Online. http://devdata.worldbank.org/dataonline; (c) Alan Heston, Robert Summers and Bettina Aten, 43 Penn World Table 6.2, Center for International Comparisons of Production, Income and Prices at UPenn, 9/06; (d) U.S. Arms Control and Disarmament Agency, World Military Expenditures and Arms Transfers 1963–1973, 1967–1976, 1986, 1996, 1999–2000; (e) Information from the Stockholm International Peace Research Institute (SIPRI), http://first.sipri.org/non.first/milex.php

from those permissive conditions: (1) responses to economic crises; (2) the nature and strength of available domestic coalitional partners; and (3) modal regional patterns, or the relative incidence of particular models in each region.

A core argument distilled from those five conditions suggests that: following the exhaustion of import-substitution, differences in oil resources and land reform led to distinctive options, each relying on different coalitions of state and private interests. On the one hand, abundant natural resources hindered the prospects for competitive manufacturing; enhanced patronage funds for beneficiaries of import-substitution; and eroded private sector wherewithal in the Middle East. On the other hand, natural resource scarcity and effective land reform favored proponents (and weakened opponents) of labor-intensive manufacturing and private entrepreneurship in East Asia. Once in place, each model reinforced the state and private coalitional networks that benefited from each path. The regional context strengthened respective models through hegemonic coercion (e.g. Nasserism and Ba'athism), diffusion (second-order "Dutch disease" effects in the Middle East, "flying geese" in East Asia), and emulation (Japan in East Asia).[5]

Some East Asian states retained selective import-substitution and, though clearly not laissez-faire, most were market-friendly and emphasized performance in international markets as yardsticks for success (Haggard 2004). The contrast with Middle East patterns is clear (Hakimian 2001). Despite differences between the two, evident from Table 5.2, Southeast and Northeast Asia shared some basic patterns (Solingen 2004; Doner, Ritchie and Slater 2005). The Middle East-Southeast Asian comparison is in many ways an easier test of the argument advanced here. The Middle East-Northeast Asian comparison constitutes a harder, i.e. potentially more fruitful test. Neither model characterizes the universe of cases in each region but each captures ideal-types. The latter are heuristic devices in the imputation of causality, conceptual constructs rather than historical or "true" realities applicable to all cases equally or indeed to any particular case wholesale (Weber 1949; Eckstein 1985; Ruggie 1998b).

Permissive conditions

International power, institutions, and markets

Can international circumstances explain why East Asia's leaders embraced export-led models in the 1960s (Taiwan, South Korea, Singapore) and 1970s (Malaysia, Thailand, Philippines, Indonesia) and why Middle Eastern counterparts retained inward-looking ones? In the 1960s investment capital was plentiful, Eurodollars easy to borrow, interest rates and trade barriers against manufactures from industrializing states relatively low and labor-intensive competitors scarcer (Chan 1990). Trade grew faster in the 1960s–1970s than subsequently. Market-based incentives for export-led growth were thus strong. International institutions promoted state intervention but not suppression of private capital. Hence, intervention took different forms across the industrializing world, from regulating and promoting private markets to virtually eradicating them. Only in the 1980s the IMF and World Bank provided stronger signals to restructure economies, minimize state intervention and tariffs, and promote exports. But even then international institutions were far from determinative, their guidelines a constant against which states responded variably. The ability to impose reform through conditionality agreements was limited, mediated by the strength of prior *domestic* commitments to reform (Kahler 1989). Thus, both regions faced comparable international market and institutional incentives and constraints. Both models were feasible though many states – emboldened by the New International Economic Order favoring state entrepreneurship over market mechanisms – opted for import-substitution

(Krasner 1985). But others did not, including many in East Asia and latter Turkey, Chile, and others.

Were Cold War structures more constraining, discouraging states under US or Soviet influence from embracing rival models? Each superpower certainly sought to do that. Furthermore, US alliances exposed East Asia's partners to significant threats from Cold War dynamics. Yet that was also true for Middle East partners (Saudi Arabia, Jordan, the Gulf sheikhdoms, and Lebanon). Indeed strategic rents in the Middle East (aid, loans, transit fees) did not evaporate even after the Cold War as much as they did in East Asia. Several observations question the tendency to reduce models of survival to US imposition. First, not all US allies embraced export-led models. Far from it: most did not, even in Latin America (presumably under tightest US control) until the 1990s. Second, even under US occupation, Syngman Rhee ignored US conditioning of assistance to South Korea on macro-economic reform, privatization, realistic exchange-rates, ceilings on armed forces, and anti-inflationary stabilization. Third, Park Chung-Hee rejected US pressures too (1961–1963) and returned to industrial "deepening" (1970s) despite US and World Bank opposition. Fourth, Taiwan's Chiang Kai-shek embraced import-substitution in the Kuomintang's (KMT) early years, superseding it only in the 1950s with a new model of survival geared to avoid mistakes perceived to have led to Nationalist defeat in 1949. Many have underestimated the KMT's young technocrats' commitment to this model, and overestimated the efficacy of US coercion (Jacoby 1966). Fifth, the United States provided a market for agricultural and industrial goods during the Vietnam War and considerable foreign aid to Korea and Taiwan, albeit much less to other East Asia states. Had US aid constituted the main determinant of export-led models, Vietnam and the Philippines – the largest per-capita recipients – would have been strong instances of such shifts, but they were not. Finally, the United States applied similar pressures to encourage export-led growth on Middle East states, with mixed (often meager) success. The differential and dynamic domestic receptivity to US incentives and aid is often understated. Five Middle East states received over $8 billion in cumulative total aid (Israel, Egypt, Jordan, Turkey, and Iraq) but only two in East Asia (Vietnam and South Korea). For the same period (1956–2005) Sudan's $4.4 surpassed Taiwan's at $4 billion (Table 5.2). Notably, Egypt received more economic aid than Israel between 1956 and 1965, $760 million as opposed to $525 million.

Following radical nationalist revolutions in the 1950s, Middle East leaders sought Soviet arms and economic aid that reinforced these revolutions' orientation toward state capitalism, import-substitution, heavy industrialization, and bartering agricultural exports for weapons (Waterbury 1983). Soviet terms of aid were generally far more favorable than Western offers. US grain shipments fed substantial segments of Egypt's urban population until the mid 1960s but the United States remained suspicious of Nasser's domestic programs, Soviet courting, and armed intervention in Yemen. Remarkably the value of US economic aid was higher than Soviet aid, and Nasser cleverly played off both superpowers against each other to extract concessions while advertising his independence from the West. However, when the World Bank refused to finance the Aswan Dam, Nasser nationalized Suez and foreign firms. Egypt's agricultural exports shifted to Eastern European markets without altering Egypt's overall reliance on raw materials exports. South Korea's Park was no less sensitive to dependence on US aid than his Middle East counterparts but created alternative sources of foreign exchange through exports, foreign direct investment (FDI), and normalization with Japan.

Domestic receptivity to US incentives was much higher in East Asia than the Middle East due to respective models of survival. Thus, Middle East states were not coerced into inward-looking models by Soviet hegemony. Rather, inward-looking praetorian revolutions propelled leaders toward policies attuned to Soviet models (Heikal 1978). As Halliday (2005) suggested, "if this was a master-client relationship, it was not clear which one was the master." Nasser's Free Officers adopted import-substitution "in the name of national independence and economic sovereignty," platforms responsive to militant political forces on left and right (the military, import-substituting and petite-bourgeois interests, civil servants, rural notables, peasants), some of which had helped triggered the 1952 military revolution (Binder 1988; Waterbury 1983). Domestic and external vectors pushed in the same direction, toward export-led growth in East Asia and inward-looking models in the Middle East. Both regions faced roughly comparable international market and institutional opportunities and constraints, and neither superpower could impose models in the absence of domestic receptivity. Reducing choices to superpower designs is fraught with difficulties; only a proper understanding of domestic backdrops can help explain choices of one model or another.

Natural resource endowments

Natural resource endowments provided a second set of permissive conditions. In oil-abundant Middle East economies, high wages, high imports, high inflation, and overvalued currencies constituted structural barriers favoring nontradable goods and investments in consumption and infrastructure. Agriculture and manufacturing were thus subsidized and protected. In classical "Dutch disease" fashion, resource abundance sometimes reduced economic growth and export competitiveness in other goods. "Rentier states" used abundant oil revenues to coopt populations without taxing them, turning many into rent-seekers dependent on state subsidies in exchange for political acquiescence. This model had detrimental effects for democratic institutions. The expansion of omnipotent states with uncompetitive industries, suppressed labor, and undemocratic structures fueled by oil windfalls is at the heart of the "oil curse." Beblawi and Luciani (1987) found that rentierism afflicted most Arab states despite different endowments, including Jordan, Yemen, Lebanon, Syria, Egypt, and Sudan as recipients of aid or remittances from oil states. I refer to these as "second-order" effects of "Dutch disease" on non-oil producers. Only Morocco, Tunisia, Turkey, and Lebanon (until recently) derived little or no rents from oil. Structural differences in oil resources across the two regions thus affected the proximate context – examined below – within which leaders opted for one model or the other.

Catalytic conditions

Responses to economic crises

Crises of import-substitution afflicted states in both regions. Chiang Kai-shek's import-substitution led to expansion of private firms yet by the mid-1950s the crisis became evident: saturated markets, sluggish growth and investment, and balance-of-payments difficulties (Chan and Clark 1992). Some KMT officials favored state entrepreneurship and deepening of import-substitution to stem the crisis, yet an export-oriented model emphasizing small-medium private enterprise was in place by 1960. The foreign-exchange crisis helped younger KMT technocrats empowered by Chiang Kai-shek push for tight fiscal and monetary policy, high real interest rates, stable foreign-exchange rates, export promotion and fewer import restrictions. South Korea's Park, who had promoted import licenses, high tariffs, and multiple exchange rates in 1961, responded to severe inflationary and balance-of-payments crises in 1963 by incepting a new model. In the absence of oil resources, the exhaustion of import-substitution provided few options throughout most of East Asia. Stagnation, slow growth, and unevenly distributed benefits from growth increased poverty, left intractable problems of nation-building unresolved and contributed to foreign aid fatigue (Rothstein 1977, 1988).

Elsewhere (Latin America, South Asia, the Middle East) leaders were slow in recognizing the end of the brief "easy" period of expansion under import-substitution, and continued to spend heavily leading to inflation, balance-of-payments crises and further economic decline (Hirschman 1968). Natural resources, where available, provided both cushions against weak performance in other sectors and patronage resources for beneficiaries of import substitution. Not so in East Asia, where choices were constrained, with balance-of-payments deficits and inflation forcing different responses. Park (1979) read his regime's survival script on the wall: "For a country like Korea, un-endowed by nature and saddled with minuscule markets, only an external-oriented development strategy, making full use of the abundant human resources but aimed at exports, appeared relevant." Park popularized his strategy with the motto "Nation Building through Exports" and "Think Export First!" (Ogle 1990,40). Singapore's Lee Kwan-Yew and other East Asian leaders echoed similar calculations.

Because oil endowments offered more options for Middle East leaders, they weathered crises of import-substitution (1950s–1960s) by "deepening" statist inward-looking models rather than replacing them. Acute balance-of-payments and financial crises forced King Saud to yield power to Faisal who expanded the size and nature of state enterprises in oil and subsidiary industries, leaving local industry and agriculture behind protective barriers. Egypt's paltry exports did not resolve balance-of-payment crises resulting from capital goods imports, military adventurism in Yemen, permanent war preparations against Israel, and exhausted windfalls from Nasser's nationalizations (Barnett 1992). Throughout most Arab states, subsequent crises rarely led to reversals of the model that had entrenched its beneficiaries ever more deeply against reform, a point that leads directly into the second set of catalytic conditions shaping the adoption of different models in each case.

Available political partners

Adopting or maintaining a given model, or shifting from one model to another, alienates some constituencies and attracts others. The relative strength of groups endorsing or opposing models at critical junctures are thus decisive factors influencing such decisions. East Asian leaders could promote private capital oriented to the global economy because potential opponents of that model were weakened. World War II decimated agrarian elites and undercapitalized and disorganized industrial groups (Stubbs 1999). Taiwan's brief import-substitution prevented encroachment by beneficiaries, facilitating export promotion and unified exchange-rates in the absence of strong agrarian or import-substituting opposition (Chan 1988). An evolving and transparent KMT consensus could disable the opposition and decrease domestic and international uncertainty about its new program (Jones and Sakong 1980). The military felt initially threatened by the new model's emphasis on economic sufficiency and implications for war preparedness. Yet the military was completely subordinated to the KMT, whose overriding concern with macroeconomic stability curtailed rabid militarism and channeled it into "an evermore absorbing interest in economic growth" (Cheng, 1990: 155).

Syngman Rhee's unimpressive import-substitution created nascent South Korean firms weakened by stagnation and uncertainty and pliable to Park's 1964 shift to export-led growth (Haggard 1990). Favorable results reinforced support for the model. Repression of weak labor movements facilitated steadfast implementation and macroeconomic stability. Labor repression in and of itself lacks significant explanatory weight because it was common to both models. Nasser hanged workers upon the first strike following the revolution; his indirect taxation burdened the masses more than the upper classes; and a highly paid and corrupt state bourgeoisie implemented his model (Migdal 1988). Labor mobilized under longer and deeper import-substitution in Middle East states might have opposed alternate models forcefully. Yet Luciani (2007) finds Arab middle classes – largely public sector employees – to have been the strongest opponents of open economies and architects of a strong populist-nationalist discourse. Borrowing from Binder (1978), Luciani defines these "scribes" as the "second stratum," co-opted and mobilized as vital pillars of inward-looking models. Small and medium enterprises remained notoriously minute, with very limited influence, and so intertwined with the state that many bureaucrats could foster their own small business.

Regarding the rural sector, US military occupation ended large landholders in Japan, and land reform following decolonization from Japan eliminated large landholders as a powerful class in Korea and Taiwan (Woo-Cumings 1998). The KMT's reforms, designed to coopt peasants, stimulated agricultural production and undermined indigenous (Taiwanese) landlords, steering them toward manufacturing (Chan and Clark 1992). North Korea's invasion of the South reduced the economic base of landowners pushing them to urban activities. By contrast, landed aristocracies from Iraq to Egypt lingered despite revolutions. Nasser's land reform aimed at empowering poor and landless peasants but benefited middle and rich ones, achieving limited redistribution and failing to eliminate landed wealth politically (Binder 1978). State monopolies controlled agricultural inputs and marketing of major crops at fixed prices. State accommodation with rural strongmen enabled resource transfers from rural to urban throughout the Middle East (Owen and Pamuk 1999). By 1960 inequality in land distribution was much higher in Egypt than in South Korea, with Gini coefficients of 0.67 versus 0.39 respectively (Rivlin 2001). Whereas Nasser's reforms excluded nearly all landless wage earners, South Korea had no more landless peasants by the 1940s. Only in oil-poor Jordan, Morocco, and Tunisia were market- and export-oriented capitalist farmers stronger and more influential politically (Waterbury 1989).

In sum, whereas East Asia's leaders sought rural support through effective land reform, investment in agriculture and rural infrastructure, the Middle East countryside – particularly in revolutionary states – was forced to support and subsidize narrow urban coalitions (Campos and Root 1996). Hence, rural interests placed few political barriers to East Asia's export-led models and land reform helped level income distribution (Wade 1990). Middle East regimes deflated threats of peasant insurgency through state monopolies; East Asian ones did so through effective land reform and export-led growth.

Regional effects

Small internal markets reinforced export-led models in East Asia but less so in the Middle East due to first- and second-order effects of "Dutch disease" and three reinforcing regional factors:

1. Nasser threatened and subverted economic reform efforts by small, resource-poor Jordan and Lebanon among others. He recommended Jordan's expulsion from the Arab League, portraying it as an enemy of Arabism and decrying King Abdullah – assassinated in 1951 – for his association with Western powers. Upon learning of the proposed "Baghdad Pact" between Western powers and Iraq, Nasser mobilized pan-Arab nationalism, leading to the imprisonment of King Hussein. In 1960 Nasser declared that the UAR would not rest until it destroyed Hussein, adding that all Arabs wanted to poison him. Riots and near civil war compelled Hussein to yield to emboldened Nasserism writ-large throughout the region. Syria's and Iraq's Ba'ath threatened Jordan as a monarchical vestige inimical to their own revolutions. Jordan's Premier Wasfi al-Tall's efforts (1960s) to contract the state bureaucracy and military expenditures were suppressed by neighbors' subversion. Tall was assassinated in Cairo. Lebanon's export orientation – steered mainly by dominant Christian (Maronite) elites – also faced Nasserite and Syrian challenges. Lebanon's trade/GDP ratio was much higher than Egypt's or Syria's. By the 1970s, internal defiance by radical Palestinian groups, intercommunal strife, and Israel's interventions facilitated Syria's occupation of Lebanon for over 30 years. Syria placed limits on Lebanon's 1990s efforts to revive an export model. Syrian involvement in the assassination of Rafiq Hariri, the architect of Lebanon's economic revival, reflected older cross-border subversion patterns. Morocco – more removed geographically – was less subject to Nasserite diktats than Jordan and Lebanon.

2 Regional diffusion of "Dutch disease" from oil-rich to oil-poor states – second-order rentier effects – reinforced inward-looking models and state entrepreneurship in recipient states. Petrodollar transfers strengthened protectionism, industrial and exchange-rate distortions, weakening incentives to shift to alternative models. By the mid-1970s oil transfers reinforced Jordan's inward-looking policies. A decade later the state employed 60 percent of the labor force. Reduced oil transfers after the 1991 Gulf war and containment of inward-looking Iraq revived other options. Regional influences in East Asia were the mirror image of those in the Middle East. Postwar Japan's export-oriented model diffused to Taiwan, South Korea, Hong-Kong, Singapore, Malaysia, Thailand, China, Indonesia, and Vietnam. Famously captured by the "flying geese" analogy, Japanese capital and technology spread through FDI and bank loans to successive "tigers" and "dragons." Cooperative regional institutions reinforced the model informally, taming protectionism (Ravenhill 2000). APEC advocated "open regionalism" compatible with global trading rules and inclusive membership. ASEAN encouraged mutual support for domestic and regional stability to attract FDI and secure access to export markets. Economic growth and common resilience (*ketahanan*) was the motto. Middle East models – and the Arab League – could hardly promote "open regionalism."

3 Defeat in war and serious external threats fueled crises and catalyzed departures in models of political survival. South Korea, Taiwan, Southeast Asia and major Arab states endured wars in the late 1940s to early 1950s, followed by import-substitution experiences. However, East Asian leaders later turned to export-led growth in line with the political-economy considerations discussed earlier as well as lessons learned from defeat in war. The KMT linked its 1949 defeat by mainland Communists to its own record of hyper-inflation, hyper-inequality, and hyper-corruption. The KMT thus pivoted its new model on price stability, egalitarian income distribution, and decentralized (small-medium) private entrepreneurship. Park's lessons from North Korea's 1950 overrun led him to reject the coalition of absentee landlords and corrupt import-substituting industrialists that backed Rhee's model. The KMT's complete ejection from the mainland and South Korea's nearly complete invasion by the North were arguably far more devastating territorially than the Arab states' 1948 defeat, which could partially explain the need for more robust states in the East Asian cases. By contrast, the 1948 war initiated by Arab states after rejecting UN partition of Palestine did not result in as nearly complete a territorial defeat as Taiwan's and South Korea's, at least initially. However, the *Nakba* (cataclysm) dealt a severe blow to Palestinian and pan-Arab aspirations, coloring the political models of the 1950s. Despite its depiction as a "victory," the loss of 1 percent of Israel's population in a war fought under an arms boycott also left a legacy of inward-looking self-reliance among first-generation Israeli leaders. Sadat portrayed the 1973 October War as an Egyptian victory, enabling him to launch *infitah* (economic opening) in 1974, reversing Nasser's model. In sum, leaders defined victory and defeat in self-serving ways. Defeat in war was common across both regions and not

necessarily a long-term driver of inward-looking models or perennial conflict. Leaders manipulated external debacles in ways that reinforced domestic conditions favorable to one model or another. Threats of peasant-based Communist revolutions emanating from neighboring states (mainly China) are invoked to explain East Asian leaders' economic choices. Rural reform and broad economic growth helped deflate such threats. However similar revolutionary pressures (sometimes backed by Soviet encroachment) did not lead to similar choices in the Middle East.

Figure 5.2 disaggregates the causal sequence outlined in Figure 5.1, focusing on permissive and catalytic conditions leading to alternative models of political

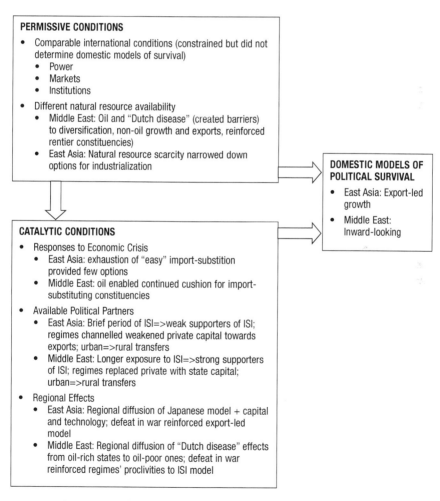

Figure 5.2 Permissive and catalytic conditions
Notes: ISI = import-substitution-industrialization.

survival. Two main propositions sum up these conditions. *Early and effective land reform, relatively brief import-substitution, and natural resource scarcity weakened domestic political opposition to export-led growth in East Asia. Regional effects reinforced export-led strategies.* By contrast, *late, inefficient or nonexistent land reform, longer exposure to import-substitution underpinned by extensive statist and military entrepreneurship, and abundant oil resources empowered opponents of export-led growth throughout much of the Middle East. Regional effects reinforced inward-looking models.* Put differently, in the Middle East stronger beneficiaries of relative closure, import-substitution, and natural resource monopolies – mostly within the state itself – constituted powerful barriers against alternative models.[6]

Path dependency, anomalies, and aborted shifts in DMPS

The relative incidence of particular models in each region cast its shadow on domestic decisions favoring one model over another, through emulation, socialization, and/or coercive external interventions. The political and economic successes of East Asia's model reinforced their progressive diffusion to most states in the region. Conversely, entrenched inward-looking Middle Eastern models reinforced domestic barriers against competing models requiring different sources of legitimacy – and new relations with international markets and institutions – hardly countenanced by 1950s to 1960s-style pan-Arabist politics. Some trace this profound suspicion of external influences to colonial domination and exploitation. However the latter did not preclude East Asia's transformation, including China's (a victim of unequal colonial arrangements) and Vietnam's (a victim of even more recent colonial brutality by Japan, China, France, and the United States). Clearly, political forces unleashed by Nasserism and rentier economies constituted formidable barriers to change. Beblawi and Luciani (1987: 16) trace reluctance to change to "a perception of a lack of any politically accepted alternative, or sheer shortsightedness." Chatelus (1987) emphasized overwhelming incentives by dominant groups to retain rents and disincentives to shift to productive activities. Path-dependent politics, lasting legacies including reproduction of political forces invested in extant institutional arrangements, and self-perpetuating mechanisms of exclusion go far in explaining stasis. Path dependency entails self-reinforcing feedback loops or "increasing returns" whereby actors reinforce the model's original logic, alternatives are dismissed, and institutions magnify existing patterns of power distribution (Krasner 1999; Thelen 1999; Pierson 2000). Thus, the long-term effects of temporal sequences in the intersection of domestic and international politics can be hard – but not impossible – to reverse. Furthermore, regional agglomeration of models creates "neighborhood effects" or network externalities that infuse new life into those models.

One might argue that rejecting export-led growth in the 1960s was not unusual, and that East Asia was the anomaly. Although this may be the case, most Middle East leaders declined subsequent opportunities including the 1980s crises and the 1990s widespread transformation of planned into market-oriented economies (Owen and Pamuk 1998). Capital flows in the 1990s "became almost indiscriminate torrents in search of emerging markets," with FDI to developing countries growing from about $20 billion (1990) to $170 (1998) (Henry and Springborg 2001: 44–45). Extraordinary world trade expansion offered unprecedented incentives often met with lethargic reform in the Middle East, whose share of FDI to developing countries (excluding Turkey) declined from 11.6 percent (1990) to 2.1 percent (1994–1996) and 1 percent (2001) (Arab Human Development Report 2002). Political instability, bad governance, and inadequate education thwarted FDI inflows while $1.5–$4 trillion was invested overseas (Halliday 2005). Capital flight from wealthy rentier states sharply contrasted with Japan's FDI investments throughout East Asia. Declining oil windfalls in the 1980s denied Middle East leaders resources available erstwhile to avoid adjustment; yet path-dependent legacies burdened change. The Middle East remains the region least integrated into global trade and finance after sub-Saharan Africa.

Some Middle East leaders slowly introduced elements of alternative models, suggesting that "critical junctures" and learning can be mechanisms for change even in processes heavily burdened with path dependency. Sadat used crisis to introduce *infitah* facing incalculable political risks, struggling to reverse Nasserism and enhance growth, foreign investment, exports, military conversion, and new relations with international markets and institutions. Sadat's assassination and the political landscape he inherited continued to trump Egypt's transition under Mubarak. Non-oil producers with fewer choices (Morocco, Tunisia, Turkey) began promoting private sectors in the 1980s and signing bilateral investment treaties to stimulate and protect foreign investments. By 1996 four Middle East states (Morocco, Tunisia, Turkey and Egypt) had signed at least 11 such treaties; half of the eight East Asian states that had done so. Monarchies had experienced less protracted colonial influences than praetorian states like Egypt, Syria, and Iraq, which mobilized revolutionary nationalist-populist zeal and swept competitive private capital more forcefully, raising barriers to reform beyond those imposed by rentierism (Henry and Springborg 2001). By 2000 Jordan, Morocco, Tunisia, Turkey, Egypt, and five gulf kingdoms had joined the WTO, but not Syria, Iraq, Saudi Arabia, Algeria, Yemen, and Syrian-controlled Lebanon. Even WTO members retained high tariff barriers and state enterprises.

Although Turkey and Israel embraced import-substitution for many years, they were neither subject to pan-Arab pressures to retain the model nor afflicted with second-order effects of "Dutch disease." Israel's departure from import-substitution and heavy-handed statism began tentatively in the late 1960s, under forceful resistance by protectionist constituencies including the powerful labor-union *Histadrut* (90 percent of eligible labor force), the inward-looking Manufacturers Association and the Ministry of Commerce and Industry. Isolated in its region and with neither oil nor a large internal market, free-trade-areas with Europe and the United States became ever more vital to the political-economy strategy of Israeli leaders. The mid-1980s crisis forced more decisive reforms. Israel was one among few Middle East states to reduce government consumption significantly – from 39 percent of GDP (1970s) to 27 (1990s) – largely due to declining military expenditure (Owen 2001). Following decades of statist expansion and import-substitution, high inflation, mounting external debt, and political violence in the 1970s, Turkey's military brutally altered the relative strength of societal forces in the early 1980s, enabling civilian Premier Turgut Özal to consolidate an export-led growth model (Waterbury 1983). The European market was a chief incentive, as was the absence of oil, and Turkey could count on a robust business class fostered under Kemal Atatürk. Government consumption shares of GDP declined far below most other states in the region.

An anomaly amidst rentier states, Dubai's more limited oil endowments led the ruling family to diversify its economy in the 1970s. Crown-prince Sheikh Mohammed bin-Rashid al-Maktoum and his three businessmen-advisors emulated Singapore and Hong-Kong, turning Dubai into a regional trading hub; financial, shipping, and media center; and tourist destination with an open stock exchange and outward-oriented appeal to foreign companies (800 from the United States alone by 2006). Dubai developed 13 free-trade zones, welcomed 5 million tourists annually, and reduced oil dependence to 6 percent of state income. Yet nearly 85 percent of its population is foreign-born, largely unskilled, sometimes indentured, and denied citizenship (Fattah 2006). Over the last decade Qatar, Abu Dhabi, Bahrain, and Kuwait introduced changes as well. Even Saudi Arabia, where 90 percent of government revenue derives from oil, joined the WTO and begun diversifying and privatizing segments of the economy while relaxing foreign ownership rules.

These experiences questions deterministic views that domestic configurations pose insuperable barriers to the introduction of alternative models. Differences in oil endowments and private-firm incentives provide different opportunities. Sadat forged and advanced new opportunities in the fairly constraining context he inherited. Özal leaned on allies in key state agencies and private conglomerates to launch an export-drive supported by constituencies wary of the 1970s political violence and economic disarray (Waterbury 1983). Sheikh al-Maktoum used oil endowments to imitate Singapore in Dubai. Ironically, East Asia's competitiveness – stemming from earlier decisions – compounded the barriers faced by Middle East leaders (Noland and Pack 2005). Amsden's (2001: 286) reformulation of Gerschenkron's theory has potentially ominous implications for inward-looking models: "the later a country industrializes in chronological history, the greater the probability that its major manufacturing firms will be foreign-owned." Such prospects did not deter Eastern European or East Asian newcomers but seem far more politically threatening for Middle East leaders. As Binder (1988: 83) noted regarding the Middle East, "no other cultural region is so deeply anxious about the threat of cultural penetration and westernization." Yet this section suggests that such difficulties are not always insurmountable. As Waterbury's (1983: 261) study of Egypt and Turkey suggests,

> economic and class structures… acted as retardants to processes of change but did not determine or cause them. …Rather, narrowly based political leadership, assisted by insulated change teams, drove forward both the import-substitution strategy and the subsequent introduction of market-conforming policies.

Models of political survival: Implications for states, the military, and authoritarian institutions

The two competing models shared three important features. First, both relied on state institutions as key allies for securing political control; yet differences in the nature of that reliance had diverging effects on the respective evolution of states. Second, both models relied on authoritarianism but each foreshadowed differential paths regarding democratization. Third, military institutions played important roles in both models but the military itself underwent different transformations under each model. Figure 5.3 summarizes the implications of alternative models for evolving institutions – states, the military, and authoritarianism – in each case.

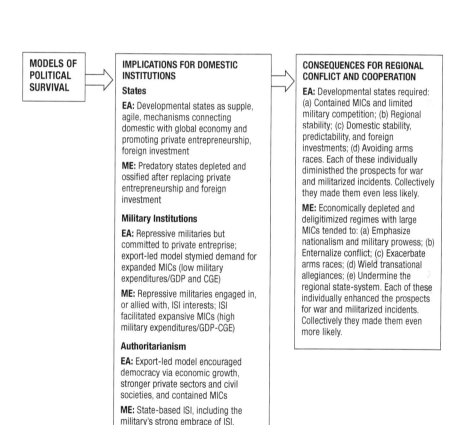

Figure 5.3 Domestic institutions and regional effects
Notes: ISI = import-substitution industrialization,
EA = East Asia, ME = Middle East, MIC = military-industrial complex

States

States played central roles in both models but the extent to which states replaced or enhanced private capital differed significantly. East Asian leaders mandated state institutions to provide lending, subsidies, and other incentives to private firms that met performance goals. Although certainly not *laisse-faire*, the model's dependence on export-led growth steered state intervention toward macroeconomic stability, new markets, investment in growth areas, and stable political-economic environments for foreign investment (Noland and Pack 2005). Japan's "minimalist state" – in overall size, despite extensive intervention in the economy – was significantly different from states in Taiwan, Hong-Kong, South Korea, Singapore, Malaysia, Thailand, China, Indonesia, and Vietnam (Pempel 1998). The KMT exposed "greenhouse capitalists" to the rigors of the market, phasing out protection, enforcing export quotas, and limiting state entrepreneurship (Evans 1995). The private sector's share of industrial production reached 80 percent by the early-1970s. Extensive consultations between businesses and government were common in East Asian cases, although leaders enjoyed significant autonomy in the initial phases (MacIntyre 1994). Subsequently, firms – not states – made most decisions about resource allocation (Stiglitz 1996). States were not heavy-handed: they supported export-oriented industries without micro-managing them; provided credit and promoted technical skills transferable across industries; selected initial industries and subsidized declining ones without thwarting private enterprise. East Asian states were active lenders and regulators but significantly less active entrepreneurs than their Middle Eastern counterparts.

Massive nationalizations of oil, banking, industry, and the Suez Canal accompanied import-substitution in the Middle East. Proceeds channeled to states as monopoly rents enabled leaders to introduce expansive yet unsustainable populist programs. Redistribution dissipated a decade after Egypt's revolution. Import-substitution's compelling logic and inherent weaknesses (Hirschman 1968) entailed income transfers from agriculture to infant industries under state aegis. State expansion and suppression of private firms eliminated economic and political competitors to the state (Anderson 1987). In rentier states "there was, in effect, no such thing as a private sector" (Halliday 2005: 278). States – not exposure to the global economy – sapped private capital of economic and political strength, albeit to a lesser extent in Jordan, Morocco, Lebanon, and Turkey than in Egypt, Syria, and Iraq. The former had lowest percentages of public employment whereas the latter had the highest.

Many states adopted import-substitution in the 1950s and 1960s but few embraced as comprehensive statist controls, entrepreneurship, and bureaucracies as in the Middle East. The Egyptian state owned most modern sectors of the economy under Nasser, contributing 90 percent of value-added by plants employing 10 or more workers, accounting for 91 percent of gross fixed investment, and consuming nearly 50 percent of GNP (Owen and Pamuk 1999). Syria and Iraq reached comparable levels of statization. State enterprises accounted for 48 percent and 57 percent of economic activity in Sudan and Algeria. Although most Middle East states displaced private firms, praetorian regimes in Egypt, Iraq, Syria, Algeria,

Sudan, Yemen, and Libya decimated private capital more thoroughly than the monarchies or Lebanon (Henry and Springborg 2001). The oil bonanza strengthened state sectors even further.

East Asian leaders vigilantly steered states toward macroeconomic stability and proper conditions for sustained export-led growth. States thus became relatively supple, agile mechanisms connecting the domestic and global economies. Middle East leaders crafted states adept only at internal repression; bound to deplete and ossify; presiding over current account and budget deficits, inflation, scarce foreign exchange; and ultimately unable to exert control over society except through force. East Asia approximated ideal-typical *developmental* states whereas the Middle East epitomized *predatory* ones. "Developmental" states were handmaidens of industrial transformation; "predatory states" undercut development even in the narrow sense of capital accumulation (Evans 1995). The former relied on Weberian-style meritocratic bureaucracies effectively extracting resources from society; rentierism inhibited meritocracy in the latter. Both types exhibited cronyism and corruption but only the former delivered collective goods. Southeast Asian states circa 1950s were at comparable or lower developmental levels than most Middle East states. Yet export-led models reduced government consumption in East Asia to 10–11 percent of GDP (early 1970s) while consumption remained three times as high in the Middle East (1970s–1980s). East Asian government deficits of 3 percent of GDP (1970s) became surpluses (1980s) in contrast to resilient Middle East deficits. Military expenditures help explain some of these differences. Finally, both models made states vulnerable, albeit to different challenges. East Asian states were more susceptible to global supply and demand and evolving risks of capital liberalization. The 1997 crisis – a major test – also offered proof of their resilience. Middle East states became vulnerable to the exhaustion of import-substitution, balance-of-payments, inflation, unemployment, inefficient industries, growing inequality, and weak private enterprise.

Military institutions

Military institutions played important roles as repressive mechanisms of political control in both cases and military expenditures (MILEX) were overall high during the Cold War. Yet each model bore different implications for both the relative size and the short- and longer term viability of expansive military-industrial complexes. Though ubiquitous such complexes varied widely in size and in the extent to which they replaced private enterprise; in the Middle East they entailed far more than armament production. Sprawling networks of military-controlled state enterprises controlled activities well beyond military purpose or natural resource exploitation, replacing private firms, creating captive import-substituting sectors, supplying inputs to military and civilian enterprises, and maintaining high tariffs and protection (Waterbury 1983). North Korea and Burma resembled this model. By contrast, export-led growth required stable macroeconomic policies, predictable environments, and downsizing inflationary MILEX that could endanger the model's core objectives.

MILEX shares of GNP and central government expenditures provide measures of sensitivity to such concerns (Table 5.2). MILEX/GNP reached 5 percent average (1970s) in Southeast Asia (excluding Indochina) during the Cold War; export-led models reduced them to 2.8 percent (1990). MILEX relative to budgets reflect similar declines. Northeast Asian states were relatively restrained except for inward-looking North Korea. A decade after surviving North Korea's attack, South Korea reduced MILEX/GNP from 6 percent under Rhee (1960–1961) to 4 percent (1963–1975) under Park's export-led model. Extensive US military assistance declined to less than 50 percent of total MILEX (early 1970s); military grants ceased completely in 1978. MILEX/GDP halved between 1980 and 2000, and declined from 27 percent to 17 percent of government budgets. Taiwan's MILEX declined from about 10 percent of GDP (1960s) to 2.5 percent (2000s), and from 50 percent to 31 percent of budgets over that period. The United States was reluctant to build Taiwan's military, discouraging it from challenging China. KMT leaders – controlling the military in Leninist fashion – were reluctant to finance expensive indigenous weapons' industries that might imperil export-led growth. Taiwan's MILEX/GDP played minor and indirect roles in growth, export expansion, and improving income equality (Chan 1988). Despite its existential predicament Taiwan ranked 52 in MILEX/GDP worldwide more recently. Growing economies enabled higher absolute MILEX yet East Asia's moderation is suggested by their lag after GNP growth; lower percentages of GDP and budgets than industrializing states' averages; and MILEX shares that were typically only one fourth of Middle East averages.

The Middle East exhibited the highest ratios of MILEX/GDP and government expenditures in the industrializing world, and the largest-sized militaries relative to population. Average MILEX/GNP reached 15 percent to 25 percent (1970s–1980s), several times the industrializing world's mean (5 percent), and much higher than any East Asian state except North Korea. Egypt's averaged 18 percent of GDP (1970s), Iraq's 44 percent (1980s), and Syria's 17.5 percent (1980s) and reached over 32 percent of budgets on average for Iraq and Syria and over 21 percent for Egypt (1960s–1980s). Israel's MILEX/GDP averaged 20 percent (1960s–1970s) declining to 9 percent under the Labor–Meretz coalition which halved military budgets from 40 percent to 22 percent for that period. Jordan's MILEX/GNP was also halved from 16 percent average (1960s–1970s) to 8 percent (1990s) with incipient economic reform. Iran's averaged 8 percent under the Shah. Lower shares under the Islamic Republic underestimate *bonyad* (state foundations) and Revolutionary Guards' contributions beyond budgetary control (SIPRI Yearbooks 1986–99). Notably, the few Middle East states with lower MILEX also pursued export-led models, including Morocco (averaging 4 percent of GNP, 16 percent of budgets) and Tunisia (below 2 percent and 7 percent respectively). Mubarak reduced MILEX/GNP from highs of 18 percent (1970s) to 3 percent (1990s), and from 34 percent to 9 percent of budgets. Middle East states still account for six of the highest eight MILEX/GNP spenders worldwide, averaging twice those of East Asia (Halliday 2005). North Korea's MILEX/GNP approached Middle East levels – 25 percent (1985–1994) – despite its world's bottom credit standing. The military-industrial complex remains the Kim's family most important partner in a model that remains the starkest anomaly in East Asia.

In sum, both models relied on the military for political control but their partnerships underwrote fundamentally different political-economies. Export-led growth stymied demands for expansive military-industrial complexes or enabled (restrained) compensatory transfers to the military. Backed by a "sword-won" coalition of military and civilian technocrats and industrialists, Park suppressed military officers demanding a large-scale import-substituting complex that might jeopardize export-led growth (Cheng 1990). Park (1971: 107) relied on technical and economic experts able to scrutinize, in his words, "the arbitrariness and rashness of the military officers." The model's success yielded resources for military modernization without risking mainstay economic objectives or imposing Draconian guns-versus-butter tradeoffs. The military thus joined other beneficiaries of economic expansion, purged antagonistic elements, and supported private enterprise as the engine of export-led growth (Amsden 1989; Cumings 1984). Finance ministries "review(ed) defense budgets with a much more skeptical eye than has probably ever been true in the Middle East" (Calder 1996: 2), where vast complexes replaced private capital as part of states' evisceration of political-economic competitors. Import-substitution supported those complexes' expansion into vast realms of economic life. Leaders endowed military-security apparatuses with gargantuan budgets and perks as key pillars of *mukhabarat* (intelligence) states. Massive armies consumed vast resources – 15 soldiers per 1,000 people against 5 in East Asia – and attracted nearly 15 percent of GNP and 37 percent of budget averages – against 2 percent and 11 percent in East Asia respectively. As chief guarantors of this model, Middle East militaries were most resolute opponents of changing state-controlled economies and import-substitution (Picard 1990). Egyptian economist Amin (1980), although critical of economic liberalization, listed MILEX as the foremost source of Egypt's development failure.

Authoritarian institutions

Although both models relied on authoritarian institutions, the implications of each for the role of the military and private entrepreneurship differed, and with them the implications for authoritarianism. East Asia's export-led models were not designed to advance but to curb democracy, fueling specious theories that authoritarianism was better at implementing painful reforms through repression.[7] Yet these models' unintended effects encouraged democracy via three mechanisms. First, they fostered stronger private sectors and civil societies that eventually overturned authoritarianism in most cases. Second, requirements for macro-economic stability and reduced state entrepreneurship limited military complexes and undermined the military's ability to accrue independent resources, forcing it into professionalization and lower hostility to groups underwriting outward-oriented growth. Third, the models led to unprecedented economic growth; since democracy is assumed to be least reversible at annual per-capita incomes above $6,000 (Przeworski *et al.* 1996), growth may help explain democracy's resilience in these cases, including Japan's postwar decades. At lower income levels, economic growth with low/moderate inflation – an important ingredient in East Asian models – heightens democracy's probability of survival. These three mechanisms operated in Taiwan, South Korea, Philippines, Thailand, and Indonesia, which evolved into democracies, with Malaysia's a somewhat truncated variant, particularly under Mahathir Mohamad. China and Singapore remained chief outliers; Indochinese states endorsed export-led models more recently with yet unclear effects for democratic transitions. Anomalies notwithstanding, East Asia's modal trajectory helped transform export-led growth into democratic polities.

By contrast, Middle East models created two built-in barriers to democratic development. First, by undermining independent private sectors they deprived democratic movements from key potential allies; weakened civil societies could not rely on capitalists' demands for political reform. Furthermore, Binder's (1988: 343) statement that "the rhetoric of political liberalism in Egypt does not include capitalism" applied more broadly. Consequently, efforts by Middle East leaders to adopt export-led models, as Sadat's *infitah*, had to contend with well-entrenched protectionist private interests resistant to overturn partnerships with military and state enterprises, particularly strong in Syria and Iraq. Second, import-substitution involved a far more fatal embrace with the military and its vast economic fiefdoms, beyond those emanating from state budgets. Repressive militaries thus remained staunch guardians of the authoritarian status-quo (Bellin 2004). Unsurprisingly, the only – very modest – steps toward democratization materialized where both protected entrepreneurs and military complexes were weakest (Jordan, Morocco, Lebanon, and selected Gulf states). "Democratic efficiency" theories aver that authoritarian leaders are better-off democratizing – even if at slow rates – as they engage in economic reforms (Maravall 1994).

In sum, the models of political survival adopted by most Middle East leaders decades ago had distinct implications for the nature and evolution of states, military, and authoritarian institutions. They also magnified other barriers to transformation, creating much lower employment, literacy (particularly female), and educational levels in most MENA states than their East Asian counterparts (Arab Human Development Report 2002).

Models of political survival: Implications for regional conflict

The intended and unintended consequences of political survival models for states, military, and authoritarian institutions had, in turn, important implications for regional conflict (Figure 5.3). First, recapitulating, Middle East states became instruments of import-substitution intended to achieve rapid industrialization, robust entrepreneurial states, and decreased reliance on international markets. Yet import-substitution unintendedly also depleted states' resources and ossified the political machinery that controlled them. Leaders of drained and entropic states were unable to deliver resources and services to constituencies previously mobilized through revolutionary or nationalist fervor. External conflict and nationalism became effective substitutes for maintaining political support and deflecting opposition. Middle East states were "certainly 'fierce' states, but not necessarily strong ones" (Dodge 2002: 177). They could deploy violence at home and abroad but lacked institutional power and legitimacy domestically and regionally. This fragility – hidden behind pan-Arab rhetoric – fueled mutual assaults on sovereignty. Acting in the name of state sovereignty (*wataniya*) was bad form and bad politics (Barnett 1998). Colonialism was blamed not for incorrect border demarcation but for conceiving of borders at all (Gause 1992). Yet unsuccessful drives for unity as means to counter perceived external threats (the West, Israel) paradoxically weakened the Arab state-system, and struggles for pan-Arab leadership increased opportunities for conflict (Kerr 1971). States exhausted by import-substitution and militarization were not the highest locus of political identification and legitimacy (Ibrahim 1995). Hence, violations of state sovereignty were more frequent, from militarized border conflicts and intervention in neighbor's domestic affairs to calls for political unification that undermined existing state boundaries, to violent efforts at ideological homogenization.

Second, entropic states could only engage in beggar-thy-neighbor economic exchanges compatible with import-substitution, severely restricting regional economic exchange (Halliday 2005). Common markets and integrative schemes among Egypt, Syria, Iraq, Libya, Algeria, Sudan, and Tunisia remained largely declaratory. Regional economic barriers remained among the highest worldwide, inter-Arab trade never rising above 7 percent to 10 percent of total trade since the 1950s. Dodge and Higgott (2002: 24–25) connect this lack of regional economic cooperation to the historical fragility of state sovereignty due to leaders' calls for supra-national schemes. This legacy, they argue, partially explains why war continues to be so prevalent in that region, with the Arab-Israeli conflict itself rooted in rejection of norms of sovereign non-interference and of borders themselves. Territorial disputes among states in the Arabian Peninsula and on either side of the Gulf also point to the continuous prominence of territoriality and military force in the Middle East. Noble (1991: 75) summarizes the texture of regional relations: "Arab governments relied primarily on unconventional coercive techniques," including "strong attacks on the leadership of other states, propaganda campaigns to mobilize opposition, and intense subversive pressures, including cross-frontier alliances with dissatisfied individuals and groups. The aim was to destabilize and ultimately overthrow opposing governments." Many among the 46 cases of militarized conflict (Table 5.1) fit well within this analysis.

A third vector fueling external conflict involved military-industrial complexes that remained strongly wedded to import-substitution and state entrepreneurship, replacing private capital as economic and political competitors. Inward-looking private sectors protected their partnerships with those complexes, without which their own viability was at stake. This strong convergence among state, private, and military institutional interests around import-substitution perpetuated sprawling and inefficient industrial complexes. Import-substitution also facilitated the latter's expansion under the aura of nationalism and pan-Arab symbols (Bill and Springborg 2000). Pan-Arabism (*qawmiyya* or *raison de la nation*) and state nationalism (*wataniyya* or *raison d'etat*) were convenient tools for camouflaging minority control of military and state institutions by Syria's Alawi, Saudi Arabia's Sudairi, Jordan's Hashemite, and Iraq's Tikriti minorities. Strong import-substituting military, state, and private industrial complexes unsurprisingly led to higher MILEX/GNP and government expenditures than most other regions, even after the Cold War, leading to recurrent arms races. Arms races are estimated to lead to war within five years (Sample 1997) and to displays of military capabilities at border incidents. Arms races are also more likely to lead to war when domestic interests rather than external threats drive military build-ups (Glaser 2000).

A fourth vector emphasizes external conflict as enhancing the military's *raison d'etre* and its prerogatives to gargantuan resources that trump alternative socio-economic objectives. Nasser prompted war on Yemen amidst severe economic crisis to justify a 30 percent increase in military budgets. Oil-rich monarchies were chief targets of Nasser's internal and external revolutionary order; Yemen thus provided an opportunity for weakening internal and external competitors. Sadat justified massive military budgets in the early 1970s on war preparations against Israel; with the 1973 war enhancing his legitimacy at home, Sadat was in better position to replace Nasserism with the *infitah* model. Saddam Hussein pointed to external threats to develop the largest Arab military-industrial machine, putting it to work against Iran and Kuwait, expecting these wars to enhance his domestic survival while expanding control over the Arabian Peninsula. Hafiz el-Assad protected MILEX while threatening Jordan militarily, attacking Israel, and occupying Lebanon. Praetorian states (Egypt, Iraq, Syria, Algeria, Libya, Sudan) decimated private capital, built more massive military complexes, and were far more involved in instigating militarized threats than were Arab monarchies. Libya and Egypt were involved – mostly pro-actively – in at least 10 militarized conflicts of the 46 in Table 5.1; Iraq and Syria in 7, including protracted ones. Jordan, Morocco, Kuwait, and smaller Gulf sheikhdoms were tangled – mostly reactively – in 1 to 3 of those conflicts, Saudi Arabia in 5.

As guarantor of leaders' political survival and authoritarian *mukhabarat* states, the military was a related, final vector contributing to Middle East propensity to externalize conflict. "National security" states protected domestic regimes primarily yet were portrayed as responses to external threats, leading to both internal and external conflict (Tripp 2001: 225). As Halliday (2005: 291) argued, "in terms of the historical sociology of Charles Tilly…Middle Eastern states are in essence … based on the use and threat of force." This brand of authoritarianism reinforced reliance on externalization of conflict as a tool to stifle domestic dissent. With the rapid exhaustion of patronage assets from import-substitution, military prowess and nationalist myths became even more crucial for political survival. Delegitimized *mukhabarat* states with mammoth military-industrial complexes influenced both inter-Arab and Arab-Israeli relations. Yet Israel provided a far more legitimate target from a pan-Arab viewpoint, and its own military-industrial complex, prowess and excesses was skillfully used by neighbors to maintain military complexes.[8] Nasser closed the Tiran Straits to Israeli navigation and ordered UN troops removed from the border while threatening war and victory, leading to the Six-Day War. Jordan's 1967 attack led to Israel conquest of Palestinian territories under Jordanian control, illegally occupied since. Egypt and Syria launched surprise attacks on Israel in Yom Kippur 1973. Since Sadat's inception of a new model, however, Egypt never initiated war against Israel again. Several Arab leaders attempting new models established diplomatic or trade relations with Israel.

Of 48 militarized regional conflicts, seven involved Israel; three out of the seven involved primarily inward-looking Syria and Hezbollah after 1973. The remaining 41 conflicts – from large-scale wars to massive mobilizations and cross-border battles – involved Arab–Iranian, inter-Arab, and Turkish-Cypriot dyads. The Iran–

Iraq, Iraq–Kuwait/Saudi Arabia, and Morocco–Polisario wars accounted for the bulk of Middle East casualties, the only inter-state wars with over 10,000 casualties since 1973. Gulf Cooperation Council Secretary General Abdalla Bishara went as far as remarking that the basic threat to Gulf states were other Arab states, not Israel (Korany 1994: 66). More recently the Council defined Iran as the most serious threat.[9] Iran was involved in five militarized incidents; the Iran-Iraq war alone – initiated by Iraq – resulted in high casualty numbers (between 500,000 and 1 million deaths). Turkey was involved in 3 militarized conflicts; only the 1974 Cyprus invasion – which pointedly preceded Özal's inception of export-led growth – involved thousands of casualties.

Quite different states, military, and authoritarian institutions developed in East Asia, with different implications for inter-state relations. Leaders advancing export-led models granted primacy to macroeconomic stability and predictability, deemed beneficial for attracting foreign investment. Domestic instability and regional tensions had kept investments away from East Asia (1950s) until the growth of local entrepreneurial expertise and relatively skilled labor forces (Chan 1990). Export-led growth also mandated stable regional environments unburdened with unproductive and expansive military budgets that increased deficits and the costs of capital, depleted foreign exchange, and stymied foreign investment.[10] Thus, no arms races or offensive build-ups threatened stability or investments; as discussed earlier, even Taiwan and South Korea's MILEX/GNP declined. Leaders vigilantly steering export-led models fostered agile states able to compensate adversely affected constituencies. Pivoted on economic growth, the model encouraged common resilience, stability, and "prosper-thy-neighbor" policies. At the height of their worst collective debacle, ASEAN's summit (1997) adopted plans for "a concert of Southeast Asian nations, outward-looking, living in peace, stability and prosperity, bonded together in partnership in dynamic development and in a community of caring societies…," while reiterating resolve "to enhance ASEAN economic cooperation through economic development strategies…which put emphasis on sustainable and equitable growth, and enhance national as well as regional resilience" (www.aseansec.org).

The maturation of East Asia's model led – in the longer run – to militaries weakened as political institutions and industrial complexes, largely coopted into export-led growth, regional cooperation and stability. Internationalizing policies strengthened private sectors, middle classes, and labor associated with exports. Invigorated civil societies demanded greater transparency and accountability, pushing the military further away from politics. In positive feedback fashion, more professionalized militaries extended support for policies underwriting export-led growth. Externalizing conflict would have endangered those models' core objectives and their supportive constituencies in developmental states, private sectors, and the military.[11] Even declining MILEX/GDP ratios remained adequate for modernizing military forces without wrecking the model's broader objectives. Declines in militarized conflict began in tandem with export-led growth, incepted by both democratic and authoritarian regimes. No "democratic-peace" effects were at work initially; authoritarian leaders were as constrained by the model's requirements to cooperate regionally, enforce nonintervention in neighbors' affairs, and tame ethno-religious revivalism and border disagreements. Economic growth helped consolidate more democracies, leading to even greater incentives to control MILEX and avoid conflict to channel resources to new constituencies. Notably, major wars in East Asia preceded 1980 and most militarized incidents involved inward-looking, often autarkic militarized rivals in Vietnam, Cambodia, Laos, Myanmar, North Korea and China. Notwithstanding historical, territorial, and border disputes, militarized confrontations remained rare as internationalizing models grew stronger. In contrast to East Asia's spatial and temporal concentration of militarized conflicts – five states (of 19) accounted for the bulk of them – every single Middle East state (of 19) was involved in them during the period under study.

In sum, as Figure 5.3 suggests, in their effort to divert attention from failed domestic models, economically depleted, entropic, crisis-prone, and de-legitimized Middle East regimes with large military-industrial complexes were prone to emphasize nationalism and military prowess; externalize conflict; exacerbate arms races; wield transnational allegiances and regional assertion; and undermine the region's state-system. Each of these vectors individually enhanced the prospects for war and militarized incidents; collectively they made them even more likely. War itself might not have been these regimes' preference but mobilizations, overt subversions, and cross-border invasions were certainly intended, though not always controllable. The logics behind the five vectors created a structural tendency toward conflict that willy-nilly slid into militarized incidents even when they may not have been the preferred outcome. By contrast, East Asia's developmental states required contained military-industrial complexes; limited military competition; regional stability; domestic stability, predictability, and foreign investments; and avoidance of arms races that might affect all these goals. Each of these requirements individually diminished the prospects for war and militarized conflict; collectively they made the latter even less likely.

Conclusions

Different models of political survival among East Asia and Middle East states had varying implications for states, military, and authoritarian institutions; the latter three, in turn, had intended, unintended, and unforeseen effects for external conflict. Significant synergies existed among state forms, military institutions, and authoritarianism, and among those three and proclivities toward inter-state militarized conflict. Domestically fragile regimes with low legitimacy – a legacy of enduring import-substitution and rentierism – led to a fragile Middle East statesystem and continued violations of sovereignty masked by pan-Arab or pan-Islamic rhetoric. By contrast, more robust East Asian states – underpinned by internationalizing models – led to stronger adherence to state sovereignty and lower incidence of militarized sovereignty violations. Sprawling military-industrial complexes helped block alternative models in the Middle East for decades, magnifying arms races, opportunities, and incentives to exercise militarized options. By contrast, export-led models restrained military burdens on state finances and politics, providing the military with incentives to professionalize and acquire stakes in regional stability. Inward-looking Middle East authoritarianism created higher barriers to democratization and compounded leaders' incentives to offset low legitimacy by externalizing conflict. Export-oriented models in East Asia improved conditions for democratization and incentives for external cooperation and stability, pivotal ingredients for economic growth, foreign investment, and electoral viability. Middle East models exacerbated the incidence of – and prolonged – clashes, militarization, and conflict-inducing challenges to sovereignty. East Asian models alleviated tensions, tamed militarization, and enhanced cooperation and mutual respect for sovereignty. These differences spilled over into the nature of regional institutions which, while lowly legalized in both cases, were more attuned to "open regionalism" in East Asia than in the Middle East, where the Arab League maintained rigid, identity-based criteria for membership (Solingen 2008).

These contrasts are particularly puzzling because states across both regions shared relatively similar initial conditions in the 1950s to the early 1960s, including ethnic diversity, state-building challenges, and involvement in militarized conflicts. The Korean and Indochinese wars, Sukarno's military *konfrontasi* against Malaysia, and the latter's expulsion of Singapore, among others, reveal a higher incidence of such conflicts in earlier times; this points to within-region variation in the dependent variable, dismissing essentializing penchants for war or peace in any region. Shifts away from militarized conflict in East Asia, corresponding with shifts in models of political survival, point to over-time variation. Most states in each region conformed to a general pattern but there were also anomalies. All these features, including comparable initial conditions, render the Middle East and East Asia particularly useful empirical domains for understanding evolution away from wars, militarized conflict and interventions. Conditions in Latin America were quite different, less relevant to the tight comparison offered here: scarce wars in over a century – little variation in the dependent variable – preceded changes in the political-economy variables of interest. Inward-looking models were certainly not the only precursors of war and militarized conflict in East Asia and the Middle East, but one that has been largely neglected, particularly in macro-regional comparisons.

This retrospective account identifies different models of political survival as key sources of *Pax Asiatica* and *Bella Levantina*. The analysis might be reasonably persuasive in explaining the past yet less applicable in the future. For instance, the beneficial economic and political circumstances of the 1960s that enabled East Asia's experience may not be replicable for the Middle East 50 years later (Noland and Pack 2005). Nonetheless, the broad argument helps estimate future probabilities. The inception of export-led models in the Middle East is expected to enhance the prospects of *Pax Levantina*. Conversely, the inception of inward-looking models in East Asia – though improbable in the near future barring major economic shocks – should increase the likelihood of *Bella Asiatica*. Both circumstances would provide confirming evidence of domestic models as important drivers of external behavior, as would the continuation of current patterns leading to a more peaceful East Asia and more conflict-prone Middle East. However, were internationalizing models in East Asia be visited by high incidence and severity in cross-border militarized conflict, our confidence would be undermined. Leaders advancing internationalization in the Middle East have similar incentives as those observed in East Asia. Were a far more widespread and serious deepening of internationalizing models throughout the entire region to be accompanied by high levels of militarized conflict, or, conversely, were hardened inward-looking models to fashion a Middle East peace comparable to East Asia's, the argument's utility would be questioned.

This effort to understand contrasting evolutions in the two regions builds on Tilly's (1984) strategies for comparative research, deployed in different sections of this article. First, a "variation-finding" strategy calls for locating common permissive and causal conditions leading to different outcomes across regions. This analytical path helps transcend entrenched academic traditions of regional exceptionalism. Second, an "encompassing comparative strategy" seems unavoidable in order to control for world-systemic effects or enabling conditions residing in global historical circumstances or "world-time." Finally, within-region variation and anomalies place limits on "universalizing comparisons" that assume the same internal causal sequence recurs in all regions. History and path-dependency warn against temptations to overemphasize invariant common properties across all regions. Path-dependence illuminates the role of critical junctures, why specific patterns of timing and sequence matter, and why a wide range of outcomes can evolve from similar initial conditions (Thelen 1999). "Increasing returns" (self-reinforcing or positive feedback processes) point to one form of path-dependence where preceding steps in one direction induce social actors to move in the same direction and not others (Pierson 2000). This results in institutions that magnify patterns of power distribution and heighten the costs of switching to alternative models because of large fixed costs, learning, coordination effects, and adaptive expectations (betting on the right horse). Under such conditions, rulers' short time-horizons militate against change but do not render it impossible. Small but significant steps in that direction are increasingly evident from Morocco to Jordan, Tunisia, and some Gulf states, (notably mostly monarchies, rentier and non-rentier).

The presence of Middle East outliers, and others in East Asia (North Korea and Burma), provide further support for the relationship between models of political survival and external conflict. Outliers sought alternative models to those prevailing in their region and exhibited dissimilar conflict behavior. Outliers question the scope of micro-phenomenological theories emphasizing local cultural origins and regional uniqueness. Above all, the incidence of outliers counters deterministic views about inevitable outcomes in any region. Contrasts between Southeast Asian and Middle East states also highlight wide variation among Moslem countries. The former, once labeled the "Balkans of the East" (under Sukarno's inward-looking model), were subsequently able to transform rentier political economies, reinforce a more flexible and "modern" Islam, and spearhead cooperative regional institutions.

Future research may probe further the generalizability of East Asia's model as harbinger of peace. As argued, the favorable global and regional circumstances, political and economic, that lubricated the inception of East Asia's model should not be taken for granted. Such models have been cycled elsewhere in different temporal and spatial circumstances, with different degrees of success; major upheavals sometimes forced their retrenchment. Indeed, some predicted that the 1997 Asian crisis would have such effect; although it did not, such potential should not be discounted. The relationship between domestic models of political survival and external conflict could arguably hold only up to a certain point. A key quandary in East Asia is whether the archetypical model is robust enough – particularly in China – to reproduce the low levels of militarized conflict that led to *Pax Asiatica* in recent decades. A key quandary in the Middle East is whether US intervention in Iraq has made the region's archetypical model less robust or whether, instead, it is likely to reproduce *Bella Levantina*.

Notes

1. I include Southeast and Northeast Asia in the East Asian region. The inclusion of Southeast Asia only – where peace appears far more stable – would have made it easier to corroborate the main argument. Adding Northeast Asia posits a tougher – and hence perhaps even more persuasive – test. Stipulated World Bank regional definitions include comparable numbers of states for both macro regions (Table 5.2). The Middle East and North Africa (MENA) includes 19 states (excluding Djibouti and Malta but adding Turkey) as does East Asia (excluding East Timor and smaller island-states).
2. Table 5.1 lists militarized conflicts since 1965, subsuming militarized inter-state disputes and militarized crises but excluding minor incidents (Ghosn, Palmer, and Bremer 2004; Wilkenfeld and Brecher n.d.).
3. For a deeper analysis of the doubtful utility of international power distribution for explaining differences between the two regions, see Solingen (2007c).
4. "Political survival" entails efforts by political leaders to gain or maintain power against domestic and external threats (Bueno de Mesquita, Smith, and Siverson 2003).
5. Emulation of Japan's growth model in the region may be interpreted as an instrument for enhancing – through economic strength – the state's external security and internal efficiency, as well as the political resources and survival of ruling coalitions. The three are largely synergistic, hence it is difficult to identify which impulse was stronger, a matter to be settled through further empirical research.
6. Major beneficiaries of import-substitution included middle- and upper-income consumers, organized labor in state and protected industries, and the state's managerial class (Richards and Waterbury 1990).
7. Authoritarian advantage theories looked at economic success cases only, comparing best – rather than average – practices (Przeworski *et al*. 1996). Many authoritarians tried but few succeeded.
8. This is different from arguing that Arab military-industrial complexes were mere by-products of this factor, as is clear from the analysis of permissive and catalytic conditions driving this model. Israel "provides both a cause and an excuse for distorting the development agenda," serving "to solidify the public against an outside aggressor" (Arab Human Development Report 2002: 2).
9. *Khaleej Times Online* (May 23, 2006).
10. Stabilization aims at restoring macroeconomic balance through short-term measures to reduce inflation, balance-of-payments and government deficits (Przeworski 1991). This involves reducing aggregate demand through fiscal and monetary measures often accompanied by devaluation (Nelson 1990); these force restraint in MILEX that can otherwise deprive the most dynamic export sectors of resources and skills. Declines in exports can lead to weaker currencies, structural unemployment, chronic trade deficits, and reduced international investments (Adams 1992; Chan 1992).
11. Riad Al-Khouri (1994: 110–111, 115) draws links among military expenditures, foreign investment, and propitious conditions for export-led growth: "Jordan's economic hopes are riding on the peace process…A resolution of the conflict with Israel would also allow reduction of the country's defense budget…more than 30 percent of government spending…The lingering Arab–Israeli conflict [makes it] almost impossible to attract [foreign] investors."

6
DEMOCRATIZATION IN THE MIDDLE EAST

Quandaries of the peace process (1996)

The notion that democracies rarely wage wars against each other has gained remarkable acceptance in scholarly and policy circles. At the same time, observers have expressed concern that incipient democratization in some Arab countries may pose a threat to the nascent peace between Israel and its neighbors. Are democratization and peace mutually exclusive or mutually supportive in this region? What are the dilemmas each process poses for the other?

The democratic-peace theory has found significant – but not unchallenged – acceptance among academic experts, who compete to explain why democracies are unlikely to wage wars among themselves (Solingen 1996, 1998). Some trace it to a Kantian conception of citizens' consent: the legitimacy granted by the domestic public of one liberal democracy to the elected representatives of another is said to moderate tendencies toward violent solutions among democracies. Others aver that free speech, electoral cycles, and the public-policy process restrain the ability of democratic leaders to pursue extreme policies toward fellow democracies. Reciprocal transparency – the joint availability of abundant information on each other's domestic evaluations of a policy – is also expected to stem war. Moreover, democracies respect the rule of law and undertake more credible and durable commitments to each other, which strengthen their reputation as predictable partners. These reinforcing normative, institutional, and instrumental restraints, however, operate only among democracies. In their relations with autocracies, the latter's lack of popular accountability, legitimacy, transparency, and credibility cancels out the moderating effects of institutional checks and balances that prevail among democracies.

The absence of democratic partners in the Middle East for many decades correlated with extensive military conflict, in the Arab–Israeli, inter-Arab and Arab Iranian arenas. However, Egypt and Israel shifted gears with the Camp David agreement, and later the Palestine Liberation Organization (PLO) and Israel, and Israel and Jordan, established diplomatic relations or negotiated peaceful resolution of conflicts. These developments cannot be traced to the interaction of fully democratic partners; Israel has generally been considered, with some caveats, to be the only democracy in the region. Nor do these developments invalidate the democratic-peace theory, which only claims to create sufficient conditions for the absence of war, but not to be a necessary prerequisite for the outbreak of peace. Thus democracy may not have been necessary for the birth of peace, but will democracy prove a key to its survival? Alternatively, could democratization in the region endanger the cooperation achieved so far?

Experiences with democratization

Democratization throughout the Arab world has been uneven, slow, and relatively recent, compelling a cautious characterization of this process as incipient. Yet even incipient democratization enables differentiation among regimes with varying degrees of democratic attributes, over time (in the same country) and across countries. Democratization involves movement toward "polyarchy" (Dahl 1989) with elected officials, free and fair elections, inclusive suffrage, the right to run for office, freedom of expression, alternative information protected by law, and associational autonomy. These institutional characteristics are universal (even if their strength and mix are not), and cannot be modified by relativist and exceptionalist concepts derived from different religious, cultural, or other doctrinal sources. Democratization involves the incremental attainment of these characteristics: the more elements of this formula present in a given polity, and the more fully they operate in practice, the farther the polity is on the path to democracy. I use the terms "nondemocratic" and "authoritarian" interchangeably to indicate a state that has not yet attained such characteristics, even if it has entered some of the initial transitional phases.

By these standards, Israel is the only democratic country in the region but only within its 1967 borders. Continued Israeli control over the Palestinian population in the West Bank and Gaza has been at odds with most of Dahl's criteria. Progressive withdrawal from these areas following the Oslo and Taba agreements and arrival at a final settlement of the conflict would remove an important qualifier to Israel's democratic character. Within Israel proper, some radical religious and nationalist minorities wage an unrelenting campaign to undermine democratic standards; the electoral system and coalition politics help them achieve significant successes. With these important caveats, Israel remains a democracy – and quite a vibrant one.

Although no Arab state meets most of Dahl's criteria (Turkey and Cyprus are not Arab states), movement toward some democracy is evident in several countries of the region. Morocco was a pioneer in its tolerance for freedom of the press and of association, and its civil society (a strong one by regional standards) has placed some limits on the monarchy. The 1993 parliamentary elections were the freest since the 1960s. Until the civil war in the 1970s, Lebanon embodied elements of pluralistic competition rare elsewhere in the region; in 1992 it held its first parliamentary elections in 20 years despite Syrian military control of the country. Egypt began taking uncertain steps toward democratization with its return to multiparty politics in 1976, but has restricted political participation through electoral laws that heavily favor the ruling National Democratic Party. Jordan has experienced competitive parliamentary elections since 1989 and a lively – but sometimes restrained – press debate over domestic and foreign policy. For the most part, tentative democratization in Jordan, Tunisia, Morocco, Kuwait, Egypt, and Yemen is a phenomenon of the late 1980s and early 1990s. The January 1996 Palestinian elections are arguably the most advanced if imperfect instance of democratization in the Arab world. Despite President Yasir Arafat's control over lists of candidates from his Fatah party, and intimidation by Fatah's security arm against an independent press, international observers pronounced those elections generally free and peaceful.

Syria, Iraq, Iran, Sudan, and Libya are highly resistant to democratization. Hafiz Assad's Syria, a highly personalistic authoritarian state, responded to demands for democratization with extraordinary brutality. The Ba'ath-dominated National Progressive Front won two-thirds of parliamentary seats in 1991 elections that restricted political competition mostly to rival groups within the dominant elite. Iran's legislative elections regulate the rivalry between competing power blocs. Candidates without a "practical commitment to Islam and to the Islamic government" are barred from running, a Council of Guardians checks the "credentials" of prospective candidates, and women and non-Muslims lack full political rights. Repression and violence are central instruments of state policy in Iran, even if there is fairly open parliamentary debate. The brutal regimes of Saddam Hussein in Iraq and Muammar Gaddafi in Libya have made no efforts at democratization except for patently fraudulent referenda. The coalition of military officers (led by General Omar Hassan Ahmed El Bashir) and the National Islamic Front (NIF, led by Hassan Turabi) that has ruled Sudan since 1989 has reversed democratization, replacing it with harsh authoritarianism. Democratization in Saudi Arabia and smaller Gulf countries has been minimal following the inception of the Saudi Consultative Council (Majlis al-Shura).

Patterns in the Arab world

Two basic quandaries characterize patterns of democratization in Arab countries:

1 First above, then below?

In sharp contrast to Eastern Europe, the Middle East has mostly seen democratization from above, launched by state elites with varying degrees of support from powerful societal actors, in efforts to coopt influential elites while carefully controlling the expansion of political rights. Egyptian presidents Anwar Sadat and Hosni Mubarak launched incremental democratic reforms while Tunisia's president Zine al-Abidine Ben Ali and Jordan's King Hussein gathered key figures in "national pacts" outlining ground rules and limits to oppositional activity. The Saudi Majlis – 60 members chosen by the king – was established in 1993 but arrests of dissident *ulema* and other opposition made the narrow boundaries of political openness clear. Kuwaiti elections for its National Assembly in 1992 launched limited political reform. Regimes in Tunisia, Algeria, and Egypt kept control over the content of political programs and party policies, party registration, and permits for meetings and rallies. Government-engineered electoral landslides are a far cry from real democratization. A partial exception to the general trend of democratization from above may be found among Palestinians, where pressures from below – within and outside the PLO – influenced the highly centralized leadership that also negotiated pacts with relevant elites.

What implications flow from this pattern of democratization from above? Cross-regional research suggests that elite pacts are a fairly successful formula for peaceful transitions to stable democracy. Peaceful mass mobilization is similarly promising, but violence and insurrection have rarely led to stable democratic outcomes (O'Donnell, Schmitter, and Whitehead 1986; Karl and Schmitter 1991; Waterbury 1994). Such evidence should not be taken as a firm basis for predicting democratic stability but it does suggest that Jordanian and Palestinian pacts may bode well for stable democratic openings. However, as Przeworski (1991) warned, political pacts that protect embryonic democratic institutions can also become exclusionary cartels of incumbents.

2   First democracy, then theocracy?

Perhaps the most excruciating problem for ruling coalitions throughout the region has been uncertainty about whether democratization will lead to democracy or to fundamentalist Islamic theocracy.[1] Words and actions of radical Islamist regimes and movements are not encouraging: the Islamist governments of Iran and Sudan rolled back democratization, left little room for dissent, limited women's rights, and remain high on rankings of states that violate minority rights (Kurds, Bahais, Christians, animists), assassinate and torture political dissenters. Radical Islamist movements challenging incumbents uniformly declare the establishment of Islamic states as their central objective. "Palestinian Islamists, including Hamas, dismiss democracy as a Western concept with no place in a Muslim society," notes Ziad Abu-Amr (1993: 18). The editor of the widely circulated *Al-Hayat*, Jihad al-Khazen (1995: 71) argues that "Muslim fundamentalist parties are undemocratic, no matter what they say." With few exceptions, preachers from Algeria's Islamic Salvation Front (FIS) openly disdained Western democracy while campaigning for the 1991 elections, refusing to guarantee future elections once in power. The record [as of 1995] speaks against the existence of a strong democratic current among Islamist challengers, beyond tactical reliance on elections as a springboard to power. Yet support for those genuinely committed to both an Islamic and democratic way of life – such groups do exist – should not be abandoned. The 1995 Algerian elections illustrate the constructive potential of groups that blend Islam and democracy while rejecting violence. Democratic inclusion can both strengthen *and* moderate such movements.

Even if democratic tendencies within Islamist movements are weak, it is important to consider the possibility that democratic inclusion may result in fundamentalist electoral strength no higher than 30 percent of the vote. Jordan's 1989 elections for the 80-seat Lower House yielded 22 seats for the Muslim Brotherhood (al-Ikhwan) and 12 for independent Islamists; their numbers declining to 16 and 6 seats respectively by 1993. The FIS won 25 percent of Algeria's eligible votes in 1991 (48 percent of actual ballots; 40 percent of voters abstaining); the moderate Movement for an Islamic Society – participating under threats from radical Islamists – carried 25 percent of the vote in 1995. President Liamine Zeroual won 61 percent of the vote with 75 percent voter turnout in elections considered "fair and representative" even by senior FIS officials. The Ikhwan won no more than 20 percent of the vote in Egypt's 1987 elections. Sudan's NIF never garnered more than 20 percent; Turabi himself was never able to win truly democratic elections. Tunisia's Hezb al-Nahda captured only 14 percent of the vote in 1989.

Such levels of electoral strength are compatible with the "balloon theory" of radical Islamist movements, holding that their rank-and-file are "remarkably mobile in terms of granting and withdrawing their allegiance."[2] Results from the 1993 Jordanian elections, the 1995 Algerian elections, and the 1996 Palestinian elections support this view. Political inclusion appears to lead to diminishing returns for Islamist movements, reducing their appeal to voters while sharpening their internal divisions. Strong institutional arrangements designed to protect the integrity of the democratic system can help prevent even a small plurality of votes (Islamist or otherwise) from undermining democratic continuity. Tentative steps toward democratic inclusion of Islamist constituencies have yielded the forceful eradication of militant groups in some cases. Egypt has tried physical elimination of extreme Islamist leaders; detention of Ikhwan members accused of supporting violence; and suppression of fundamentalist candidates for the legislature and professional unions. The armed forces in Algeria, Yemen, Bahrain, and Oman have arrested Islamist extremists and coopted more moderate groups.

Democratization and peace

Having outlined the general contours of democratization in the Middle East circa mid 1990s, I turn to the relationship between democratization and peace, especially in the context of the Arab–Israeli peace process. Only tentative propositions can emerge from very embryonic changes in the democratization variable. An influential study argues that former authoritarian states with rising democratic participation are more likely to engage in wars than are stable democracies or stable autocracies (Mansfield and Snyder 1995). Moreover, states that make the biggest leap from autocracy to mass democracy were found to be about twice as likely to fight wars in the decade after democratization as states that remain autocracies. At first glance, the implications seem ominous. Yet an analysis based on patterns of incipient Middle East democratization paints a more nuanced – perhaps more hopeful – picture:

1 First democracy, then theocracy, then war?

Mansfield and Snyder have persuasively identified the triad of democratization, belligerent nationalism, and war as an inauspicious historical pattern. Although they focus on the former Soviet empire, the pattern could apply to the Middle East if the "First democracy, then theocracy" sequence unfolds. At issue, however, is whether the democracy/theocracy/war sequence is as inevitable as one widely held viewpoint suggests: when radical Islamist movements hijack democracy and establish theocracies, peace withers along with democracy. Article 12 of the 1993 Charter of the Palestinian Islamic Resistance Movement (Hamas) expresses the affinity between nationalism and radical Islamism: "Nationalism, from the point of view of [Hamas], is part and parcel of religious ideology. There is not a higher peak in nationalism or depth in devotion than jihad when an enemy lands on the Muslim territories…The woman is allowed to go fight without the permission of her husband and the slave without the permission of his master."³ Turabi similarly emphasizes the link between nationalism and religion: "The only nationalism that is available to us, if we want to assert indigenous values, originality, and independence of the West, is Islam. ...It is the only doctrine that can serve as the national doctrine of today" (Viorst 1995: 54–55).

The operational content of this nationalism is outright opposition to the Arab–Israeli peace process, reinforcing a common view of radical Islamist movements as intractable, violent, and war-prone. Even the more moderate Ikhwan in Egypt and Jordan have thus far condemned every step in the direction of reconciliation, from the Camp David accords through the Madrid process, the 1993 Oslo agreement and other initiatives. Radical Islam is not only at the vanguard of opposition to the Arab–Israeli peace process but has also fueled regional conflict within the Arab and Muslim worlds. The Islamic Republic of Iran has exacerbated conflict in Lebanon and the Gulf, incited subversion and terrorism within the region and beyond, and built up weapons of mass destruction. The Bashir–Turabi regime funded violent opponents of the Arab–Israeli peace process, launched a war against Sudanese Christian and animist dissidents, escalated conflict with Egypt, and armed anti-government guerrillas in Uganda. Sudan is in virtual state of war against all its neighbors.

A key issue for some of those who emphasize violent tendencies of radical Islam is not whether peace and Islamic thought are compatible (they may well be). It is rather that current political conditions in the region, in their view, make radical Islamist regimes and movements implacable foes of reconciliation. Such movements evoke promises of redemption from both dreadful material conditions and unfulfilled spiritual aspirations through scapegoating and rejection of "the alien." This is certainly no more than a promise since there is no evidence that either Islamist economics or the politics of rejection have resulted in more just, more equal, or more productive societies (Roy 1994; Kuran 1995).

Others challenge the proposition that Islamist movements invariably subordinate religious and ethical considerations to political payoffs. Movements advocating a virtuous way of life, religious tolerance, and willingness to compromise are perfectly viable in their view, except perhaps for peace with Israel (Esposito 1992). Yet absent their combative, messianic, and radical overtones, it is hard to predict the political appeal of Islamist movements. The more tolerant and democratic Islamist movements seem to have been silenced by militant groups until recently. Yet past performance ought not to serve as the only predictor of future behavior; opportunities to recognize and encourage change could be missed. Sections of the Islamist opposition to the Palestinian Authority (PA) opted to participate in Palestinian elections counter to directives from foreign Islamist leaders. It remains unclear, however, how much support there is for suspending terrorist activities against Israeli civilians among the PA's Islamist opponents. One poll (Shikaki 1995) found 18.3 percent of Palestinians surveyed in the West Bank and Gaza supporting armed attacks against Israeli civilians. Over 69 percent expressed support for attacks on Israeli settlers – higher than the 67 percent who favored assaults against armed Israeli targets. Renewed Hamas bombing of Israeli civilians in buses, restaurants, and streets in 1996 exposed a virulent and uncompromising strain of radical Islam that claimed many innocent civilian lives; it also doomed Israel's dovish ruling coalition that had negotiated the Oslo agreements. A fully democratic and peaceful Islamist opposition seems a distant hope in 1996 although any stirrings in that direction deserve full attention. In Jordan, for example, the Arab Islamic Democratic Movement, a small group that includes women and Christians on its steering committee, declared its support for the peace process.

To summarize, political realities in the region in the mid-1990s point to at least four possible scenarios connecting democratization, radical Islam, and the peace process:

1   Democratization leading to radical Islamist takeover and autocratic/theocratic regimes as in Iran or Sudan: prospects for peace evaporate.
2   Democratization allowing political expression to Islamist movements that subsequently "deflate" and fragment, as in Jordan and Palestine: continued incumbent support for the peace process remains likely.
3   Democratization selectively coopting previously excluded important secular groups while keeping Islamists at bay, as in Tunisia: likely to sustain commitment to regional peace but under greater constraints than Scenario 2.
4   Democratization that fails to coopt important secular groups and eliminates violent Islamist opponents to the peace process, as in Egypt: likely to fail to broaden political support for the peace process even while maintaining a commitment to it.

The PA, betting on Scenario 2, won the 1996 Palestinian elections, providing support for the "balloon theory." Hamas formally abstained from presenting its electoral list but some members ran as candidates and many followers went to the polls, particularly in Gaza. Yet Islamist groups won only six representatives to the 88-member Palestinian Legislative Council (75 percent of seats went to Fatah and the remainder to independents). Arafat won the presidency with 88 percent of the vote, confirming estimates that the appeal of Hamas and its allies had declined significantly between 1993 and 1995. Indeed, given that the 1996 elections placed Palestinians at the forefront of regional democratization, the appeal of radical Islam arguably reached its lowest ebb where democratization was at its highest. Most important, the prospects for resolving the putative stark dilemma between democratization and peace improved. As the only Arab political entity to ever regain Palestinian land – succeeding where 21 Arab states with 200 million people and vast standing armies had failed for decades – the PA was in a position to consolidate popular support and defeat its extremist opponents. Palestinian statehood is now closer than ever to becoming a reality, no meager achievement. However, terror by Islamist groups influenced the outcome of Israel's May 1996 elections; Benjamin Netanyahu's coalition is likely to burden the PA with new challenges.

The sequence democracy/theocracy/war has generally been less of a concern in the Israeli case, where a vast secular majority could always be counted on to prevail in elections. Nonetheless, certain features of Israeli democracy – and the 1996 turnover of political power to a Likud-led coalition – have amplified concerns regarding the impact of Israel's fundamentalist groups on democracy and peace alike. Coalition politics have long distorted the basic secular center of gravity of Israeli politics, granting small religious parties disproportionate weight. The radicalization of religious parties advocating Greater Israel since the Six-Day War turned them into natural partners of Likud's nationalist camp. The threat from extreme messianic ultranationalist movements not only to peace but also to democratic institutions became painfully evident in November 1995, when a radical Orthodox Jew committed to Israeli ownership of the West Bank assassinated the architect of the Oslo process, Prime Minister Yitzhak Rabin. Rabin's dedication to the peace process was the imputed motive but his assassination revealed a deeper tendency among anti-democratic religious nationalists to extract intractable postures toward Israel's neighbors.

While Israel's electorate is overwhelmingly secular, political support for such radical movements has risen. Three heterogeneous religious parties captured a combined 20 percent of the vote and 23 of 120 Knesset seats in 1996. A hard core of religious hyper-nationalists with a disturbing penchant for violent dissent lurks in the background, seeking to undermine democracy and the peace process alike. Radical Islamist terror helps fuel their ranks while undercutting moderate forces in Israel. Their ascendance could lead to a reversal of Labor–Meretz achievements in the areas of civil rights (women, Arab minorities, and reformist strands of Judaism) and to measures that curtail democratic freedoms in the name of "national security."

It is unclear in the immediate aftermath of the May 1996 elections whether Prime Minister Netanyahu will embark upon substantive negotiations with Palestinian leaders over Occupied Territories' final status. Avoiding serious negotiations would almost certainly harm Israel's budding cooperative relations with the rest of the Arab world. This prospect could tip the scales in favor of radical Islamist movements while weakening moderate Arab regimes that have done the most on the road to democratization and peace.

2 First above, then below, and then peace?

"Top-down" democratization, wherever it has taken place in the region, has also influenced the peace process. Moved by a concern for their own political survival, leaders have sought peace partly to shift resources toward socio-economic reconstruction. "Peace from above" has not been restricted to the Arab world. Israel's Labor–Meretz coalition presented its public with a *fait accompli* in the 1993 Declaration of Principles. The gamble yielded an approval rating soaring overnight to 65 percent. Support for the Oslo agreement among Palestinians was similarly high. "Peace from above" need not be undemocratic if daring incumbents eventually face the electoral consequences of their foreign-policy decisions. The PA did so and prevailed politically while Israel's Labor Party paid a heavy political price following radical Islamist terrorist responses to Oslo.

The slow and carefully controlled pace of democratization in the Arab Middle East is less than ideal but offers, perhaps, one redeeming advantage. As Mansfield and Snyder point out, sudden leaps from authoritarianism to democracy increase the likelihood of war. Gradualism may not only guard against this unwanted effect but also helps create more stable democratic outcomes. As the literature on democratic transitions suggests, piecemeal democratization through political pacts helps advance strong and irreversible democracy. Stable democracies, in turn, are important building blocks in zones of peace. Threats to peace remain during the transitional phase but transitional regimes have been at the vanguard of peace-making in the Arab Middle East. Jordan, Egypt, and the Palestinians have gone the farthest toward normalizing relations with Israel, with support from Morocco and Tunisia. Unchanged autocracies have remained most belligerent. Experts rate the chances of full autocracies (Syria, Iraq, Iran, or Sudan) rapidly turning democratic too remote to inspire fear of a "sudden transition-increased bellicosity" problem. Nonetheless, few experts are optimistic that today's autocracies, however stable, can be viable partners in the creation of a peaceful regional order. Ongoing academic and policy debates over Hafiz al-Assad's regime indicate growing concern with his worth and credibility as a peace partner.

A more immediate threat than overly swift transition is the prospect that democratization from above will bog down and restore authoritarianism. Mansfield and Snyder found that movement toward autocracy (including autocratic reversion after failed experimentation with democracy) boosts the likelihood of war. Aspiring or resurgent authoritarians may use democratic political openings to launch nationalist-religious appeals to enhance their populist legitimacy while dismantling the democratic process itself. This pattern is sometimes evident in the political use of Islam. However, none of this is to say that regimes currently undergoing democratization are destined to regress toward authoritarian populism, Islamist or nationalist. The prospects of such regression increase when market-based reforms fail to transform the economies of the region. Economic restructuring is central to the connection between peace and democratization in the Middle East.

If democratization from above succeeds in maintaining genuine democratic openings among partners to the peace process, their leaders are unlikely to find themselves discredited for having embraced regional accommodation (although Israel's 1996 Israeli election results make the standing of moderates far more precarious). King Hussein and the PA are the models here. Growing democratization could continue hand in hand with efforts to construct a regional order compatible with socio-economic and political reconstruction. This should not be conceived as a rosy scenario; leaders of democratizing, accountable polities could well be forced to drive harder bargains. Should democratization stall, however, and should these leaders fail to deliver greater prosperity and more freedom, their other achievements could be undermined. Political challengers – secular and Islamist alike – might then succeed in dressing up their opposition to peace negotiations in pro-democracy rhetoric. It is doubtful, however, that a return to the "remote" (pre-1993) past would be feasible for any Middle East leader seeking survival in the face of popular demands for an improved present and a brighter future. This underscores, once again, the centrality of economic performance to both democratization and peace.

The road ahead

Understanding the dynamics of political change in the Middle East compels a proper understanding of the links between democratization and peace. The former influences both the political will and ability to pursue peaceful regional arrangements. The latter are important requirements for effective implementation of political reform at home. The fit between efforts to democratize the polity and embrace the peace process has been rather good thus far for the cases of Jordan and Palestine. Moreover, controlled democratization obviates Mansfield and Snyder's "sudden transition-increased bellicosity" problem and improves prospects for democratic stability, even if dangers of stalling and backsliding remain. The ideal sequence of relatively smooth and linear transitions to fully democratic and peaceful polities in the near future is far from guaranteed. Radicalizing political trends in Israel have no marginal impact on these double transitions.

Whether democratization will lead to democracy or theocracy remains an open question. Prediction is risky in regions where state and societal coercion discourage citizens from expressing their true preferences, a process that can conceal "bandwagons in formation" (Kuran 1995). Some analysts see Islamist bandwagons forming and expect them to emasculate democracy and shelve peace overtures. Others, pointing to unimpressive Islamist electoral results such as the 1996 Palestinian elections, warn against assuming sweeping Islamist revolutions ahead. If the "balloon theory" is correct, democratization and political inclusion may help moderate opposition to the peace process and place violent strands beyond the pale. In the end, the affinity between democracy and peaceful overtures on the one hand, and Islamic principles on the other, will become more empirically relevant if – and when – Muslim leaders speaking for that affinity prevail over rival claimants to Islam's heritage.

Both democratization and peace feed on a third transition affecting the region: economic reform. As noted elsewhere, the incipient foundations of peace in this region can be traced to the imperatives of economic liberalization. Leaders advancing economic openness have incentives to embrace the peace process (Solingen 1994a, 1994b and earlier chapters in this volume). Conversely, statist-nationalist, confessional, and populist coalitions resistant to economic openness have also rejected bilateral and multilateral peace negotiations. The political-economy strategy of ruling coalitions steering democratization – status quo vs. reform-oriented – is a crucial scope condition for assessing whether democratization favors peace. When economic reforms lag and distributive issues receive scant attention, democracy, prosperity, and peace will be collateral casualties. The consolidation of a genuine democratic opening sensitive to distributional effects of economic liberalization may be a necessary condition for sustaining a peace negotiated from above. The actual arrival of lasting peace in the Middle East may have to await a faraway tomorrow, but that should not discourage today's efforts to understand how the region's peoples may get from here to there.

Notes

1 As'ad AbuKhalil (1994: 677) defines "Islamic fundamentalism" as "all those movements and groups that aspire to the complete application of Islamic laws, as interpreted by leaders of the movements, in society and the body politic." Not all Islamist political movements are fundamentalist. See also Sivan (1995).
2 Norton (1995: 2). On the "balloon effect," see "Eric Rouleau Talks About the Peace Process and Political Islam," (Rouleau 1993).
3 *Journal of Palestine Studies* (Rouleau 1993: 125). The word "jihad" here has an unequivocal violent racial/religious/ethnic meaning, with citations such as "The Last Hour would not come until the Muslims fight against the *Jews* [my italics] and the Muslims would kill them" (p. 24).

7
ECONOMIC AND POLITICAL LIBERALIZATION IN CHINA

Implications for US–China relations

Introduction

Two approaches in international relations assess the rise of China in starkly different ways. The first stems from a general theory that great powers are bound to challenge each other, often by force. There are many variants of this approach but they all share a view of a world in which there is no recognized ultimate authority and where states strive for survival in zero-sum fashion. This competitive approach predicts that great powers will take advantage of each other's vulnerabilities and abstain from making more concessions than needed (Waltz 1979; Organski and Kugler 1980; Jervis 1982). Applied to China, this view predicts its rise will lead to a "power transition;" an aggressive, vastly militarized, hegemonic China espousing a version of a Monroe Doctrine and seeking to eject the US from the region. In this view, a US policy of engagement only whets China's appetite for power (Mearsheimer 2001: 400).

Yet empirical research has dealt a significant blow to theories focusing purely on relative capabilities and expansionist tendencies of great powers (Vasquez 1998; Legro and Moravcsik 1999; Shambaugh 2004/05). Indeed, as applied to China, the most aggressive era (under Mao) coincided with China's weakest relative power position. A far more powerful contemporary China shows greater restraint and pragmatic accommodation, thus far. Skeptics can, of course, argue that there is no anomaly here: China today is behaving strategically to avoid counter-balancing by regional states. But this raises the question of open-ended predictions often raised by balance-of-power theories: is China asserting its hegemony on the region or avoiding doing so to blunt counter-balancing? Which is it? Too many conceptual deficiencies and empirical anomalies should warn against predictions stemming from mechanistic power-based theories, yet those theories are likely to linger. The danger is that such theories have a way of *creating* realities on the ground, making sure the worst happens by perennially preparing for it. Security dilemmas find fertile ground in mutual mistrust and lack of transparency (Jervis 1978). More sophisticated variants of those theories have come to replace the more aggressive, zero-sum, capabilities-based versions.

A second approach builds on elements of the liberal tradition adapted to the conditions of an emerging global economy. Rosecrance's (1986, 1999) seminal study of "trading states" portrays an interdependent world where incentives to avoid war overwhelm incentives to fight. The search for absolute gains – in which everybody can benefit from cooperation – thus helps states transcend atavistic territorial ambitions. Rejecting rigid structural power theories, Rosecrance sees globalization as replacing the old foundations of state power – territorial size and stockpiles of classical factors of production – with new ones, embedded in the flows of goods, capital and labor; and managerial, financial and creative capabilities. Where territorial states aimed at conquest, the vocation of trading and virtual states resides in international commerce and the mastery of ideas, knowledge, creativity, capital, and information. Clearly there are many differences between this view emphasizing productive and trading energies and the previous one focused purely on military capabilities. Crucially, instead of inescapable systemic processes leading inexorably to wholesome competition, the trading state approach offers the important insight that, in the real world, the *choice* between presumed atavistic tendencies and interdependent alternatives *does* exist. But who makes that choice?

For starters, domestic groups with different preferences regarding a globalizing trading system make different choices. Ruling coalitions and constituencies favoring further "internationalization" create conditions for cooperation, whereas their "backlash" counterparts thrive under military competition and economic autarchy (Solingen 1998, 2007b).[1] On the ashes of earlier autarchic models, Deng Xiaoping and his internationalizing successors have made that choice, moving China away from the widespread hunger and turmoil of a previous era into a budding modernized state. As expected from a trading state standpoint, the post-1979 model required a peaceful rise or "peaceful development," a new matrix of regional relations, a "charm offensive" vis-à-vis ASEAN, a set of more mature economic and political relations with North East Asian neighbors (including Japan), and a new openness to multilateral cooperation and regional institutional arrangements. From the perspective of the architects of this new model, regional and global instability are anathema to efforts to lure foreign investment, natural resources, and broad international acceptability, without which continued economic growth and domestic political stability would be threatened. An internationalizing China and a stable regional environment pave the road to *xiaokang shehui*, a "well-off" society endowed with a majoritarian middle class (Shirk 2007).

The grand strategy of integration into the global economy has served China well, helping it attract an estimated $450 billion in foreign direct investment by 2003; capturing about 20 percent of all FDI going to the industrializing world today; and rendering China the world's third largest exporter. China's foreign trade increased from 10 percent of GDP in 1978 to about 44 percent in 2001 (Wang 2004). Foreign reserves are over 1.4 trillion dollars. And yet one should not minimize the serious political challenges to the model, including rural reform and urbanization, tensions between central and local interests, rising unemployment, an aging population, corruption, high dependence on foreign investment for continued growth, and various other potential bottlenecks on the road to sustainable development.

Relations between China and the US as of 2008, as any set of relations, include areas that can be categorized as benign, difficult, and potentially intolerable. The "benign" entails a lot of common ground, the ability to converge on focal points with minimal or moderate effort (increased cultural exchange, counter-terrorism, health, avoiding/minimizing global economic downturns). The "difficult" requires far more work than the benign, and entails potentially higher costs of adjustment on all sides (exchange rates, trade balances, energy resources, climate change, nuclear policies on North Korea and Iran, and relations with leaders involved in gross violations of human rights or destabilizing policies in Sudan, Myanmar, Venezuela, North Korea and Iran and others, are in this category). Yet on the whole, the difficult issues may not be as bad as they appear. By contrast, the "potentially intolerable" ones could derail US–China cooperation in the previous two categories (Taiwan, military modernization, democracy, human rights, and China's territorial integrity). This chapter concentrates on one issue in this third category that remains the focus of much academic and policy debate: does democratization matter for sustained cooperation? Is economic liberalization sufficient in itself for sustaining good relations?

Internationalization and the democratic peace

Internationalizing ruling coalitions beget regional cooperation that is both intensive (in depth) and extensive (in scope), creating robust conditions for the emergence of zones of stable peace.[2] How are these conditions affected by the presence or absence of democracy? The proposition that mature democracies do not fight wars *against each other* has become the closest claim to a law of international politics, the so-called democratic peace theory. There is an understandable intellectual and policy excitement offered by the possibility that the global reach of democratization might not only solve the internal security dilemma of citizens, but also security dilemmas among states. However, findings on the connections between internationalization, democracy, and international behavior offer a more nuanced picture.

First, democracy is a sufficient – but not a necessary – condition for the absence of war. States with different regime-types can avoid war and develop cooperative frameworks. Mixed democratic and autocratic dyads and clusters in East and Southeast Asia, for instance, developed patterns of cooperation on the ashes of brutal earlier conflicts. Eventual transition to democracy in some of these states may have improved the quality of cooperation among democratic dyads but was arguably not necessary for the emergence of cooperation. Elsewhere, the absence of war in South America for nearly a century – with few exceptions – coexisted with decades of authoritarianism, preceding the diffusion of democracy throughout the continent in the 1990s. Furthermore, deeper cooperation (denuclearization of the Southern Cone, the establishment of Mercosur) ensued only after a broader shift toward integration in the global economy, as a way of reinforcing internationalizing strategies. Even in the realm of nuclear policy, the Nonproliferation Treaty (NPT) – the most widely subscribed international security agreement – aggregates a wide range of regime types. Furthermore, Nuclear Weapons Free-

Zones emerged in regions where democracies were sometimes a minority (Latin America, South Pacific, Africa, and Southeast Asia). Autocratic regimes made commitments to denuclearize in Argentina, Brazil, Egypt, Kazakhstan, Belarus, Ukraine, South Korea, Taiwan, and many other cases. The vast majority of both democracies and autocracies have abided by their NPT commitments (although most *known* NPT violators have been autocratic, including Iraq, North Korea, Libya, and arguably Iran). Both democracies and autocracies have acquired nuclear weapons and both have failed to fully abide by the NPT's Article VI.

Second, in theory the confluence of democracy and internationalization makes the relationship between internationalizing coalitions and cooperative behavior more robust, particularly where internationalizing coalitions are strong domestically and throughout a region (as in East Asia). Strong internationalizing coalitions with wide support for their economic outlook can afford to reinvent themselves through the democratic process, as various East Asian cases suggest.

Third, even if democracies may not go to war against each other, inward-looking democratic dyads and regional clusters arguably lead to more shallow cooperation than internationalizing ones.

Finally, the conjuncture of inward-looking *and* autocratic dyads and clusters are likely to yield the most conflictive regional orders of all, combining the pernicious effects of both.

Transitions to markets and democracy

What do we know about temporal sequences regarding the onset of democracy and economic liberalization (internationalization) respectively? Figure 7.1 summarizes some general trends in recent decades. The vertical axis depicts regime type (democracy/autocracy) and the horizontal axis the nature of ruling coalitions (internationalizing/inward-looking), yielding four possible ideal-types:

Cell A denotes a democratic state ruled by an inward-looking coalition (India for many years, until the 1990s). Cell B points to an autocratic state ruled by an inward-looking coalition (many industrializing states in the post-1945 era; some contemporary Middle East states, among others). Cell C indicates an internationalizing ruling coalition steering a democratic state (Costa Rica, many European states). Cell D represents an autocratic state ruled by an internationalizing coalition (Singapore, China). Cells A and C (democratic) were rather unpopulated throughout much of the Cold War whereas cell B was crowded. Cell D became populated by Asian tigers in the 1960s, fueling the theory of "authoritarian advantage" (Díaz Alejandro 1983). This theory suggested that autocratic regimes were better equipped to carry out painful reforms. However, as Przeworski *et al.* (1996) concluded, the theory built on success cases (best practices) only, rather than average ones. Many authoritarians may have tried to internationalize but only a minority succeeded.

There were massive transitions from cells A, B, and D into cell C in the post-Cold war era as democratic and transitional regimes replaced many autocracies.[3] Some transitions entailed moves along one axis only (A to C, for instance, with formerly inward-looking democracies embracing internationalization, as in India; or D to C, with internationalizers moving from autocratic to democratic systems, as in

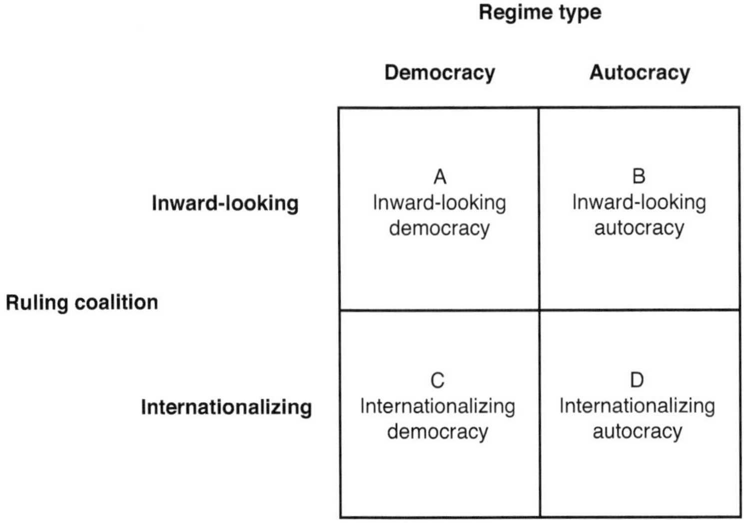

166 Regional effects of democratic institutions

Regime type

	Democracy	Autocracy
Inward-looking	A Inward-looking democracy	B Inward-looking autocracy
Internationalizing	C Internationalizing democracy	D Internationalizing autocracy

Ruling coalition (row label)

Figure 7.1 Regime type and domestic coalitions

Chile). Other cases entailed twin transitions (from B to C), following either of two stylized paths away from inward-looking authoritarianism. In the first path, democracy took hold before a turn to internationalization, in a two-step sequence (from cell B to A, then to C), as in various South American countries (but not Chile). This path conformed to the "democratic efficiency" theory, suggesting that democratization – even at a slow rate – makes internationalization more palatable because of its greater legitimacy and informational advantages.[4] From this standpoint, democracy makes internationalization more sustainable. In the second path, internationalizing coalitions first steered states into the global economy (cell D) and only later into the democratic/internationalizing cell C. Many Asian tigers fit this model.

Scholars have focused on economic crisis as the prelude to democratization (Lipset 1959). Others view rising expectations during rapid economic growth – not crisis – as triggering democratic transitions.[5] Gallagher (2002) found that China exceptionally defies both of these models for two reasons. First, Chinese FDI liberalization preceded the privatization of state industry and the development of a national private sector, unlike transitions in other socialist countries. Second, FDI has been the dominant source of external capital in China, unlike most other East Asian states. Hence "reform and openness" (*gaige kaifang*) weakened civil society (particularly labor) and strengthened the state, accounting for regime stability and delayed democratization. Others trace this stability to gradualism in economic reform (no shock therapy and no losers from reform), and to the clothing of reform in nationalist rhetoric. However, the assumption that there have been no losers, no demands for political change, and that nationalism can always deflate domestic criticism is questionable.[6] Further, democratization can lead to aggressive foreign policy behavior, as I discuss next.

Domestic transitions and external behavior

While acknowledging that mature democracies do not go to war with each other, Mansfield and Snyder (2005) found *transitions* to democracy far more problematic. Quantitative and qualitative evidence from the French revolution onwards suggest that leaders in transitional societies are prone to use nationalism instrumentally. The links between democratic transitions, intense nationalism, and war are found to be particularly strong for democratizing great powers. Mansfield and Snyder submit that their study validates the following hypotheses:

- Countries undergoing incomplete democratization with weak institutions are more likely than others to *become involved* in war.
- Countries undergoing incomplete democratization are more likely than others to *initiate* war.
- Incomplete democratization with weak institutions is especially likely to lead to war when powerful elites feel threatened by the prospect of a democratic transition.
- Countries undergoing complete democratization have a moderately higher risk of involvement in war shortly after the transition, but no elevated risk once democracy is consolidated. The increased risk of war for countries undergoing complete democratization applies mainly to states already involved in enduring rivalries whose nationalist and militarist institutions and ideologies were forged in earlier phases of democratization.

Mansfield and Snyder argue that China is still far away from the kind of sustained and balanced economic development that can lead smoothly to democratic consolidation. To be sure, they consider the diffusion of democracy not only inexorable but also a positive development for global peace and stability in the long term. At the same time, they warn of the need to get the sequence right, namely to consolidate central legal and economic institutions before proceeding to fully fledged political parties and electoral competition.[7] This is consistent with promoting the rule of law and independent courts; guaranteeing property rights; developing a rational, impartial and efficient administration, and allowing a professional and balanced mass media. The consolidation of these democratic institutions, in their view, can act as a barrier against leaders that may be tempted to secure their domestic political survival through parochial nationalism. Without prior consolidation of institutions leaders have incentives to use nationalism and violence to draw attention away from domestic cleavages and shore up their own legitimacy. War then becomes the by-product of nationalist provocations. Mobilizing nationalist support as a rallying theme is invariably a double-edged sword in democracies and autocracies alike. In emerging democracies the overlap between pro-democracy, nationalist, and economic protectionist forces is a source of concern for the sustainability of an internationalizing strategy.

How does this apply to China? China's internationalizing coalition has thus far prevailed over domestic forces favoring a return to closure. Yet some argue that democratization could empower farmers, the hinterland, the unemployed, and those segments of the military, state enterprises and the Communist party that have been adversely affected by economic openness to express themselves against internationalization (Zweig 2002; Shirk 2007). An economic downturn could magnify the power of inward-looking forces, as could economic inequality, local corruption, environmental threats, and inadequate social safety nets. In the 1990s internationalizing coalitions faced a dramatically different global economic, political, institutional, and strategic context than they do today. Uncertainties regarding the long-term effects of globalization render their political future more opaque, particularly if internationalization becomes reversible.

Notwithstanding the dangers of democratic transitions and illiberal democratization, one should consider the significant advantages of mature democracy for yielding a democratic peace. Democracies are found to be more prone to join international institutions, particularly democratic "clubs" such as the OECD and others; to prevail in wars they do fight; to abide by their international commitments; to enter more preferential trading arrangements than their counterparts; to reduce civil war tensions; and to be more likely to choose their wars wisely and win them at lower costs (although one could not have guessed that from the US war in Iraq). Democracies may not be the most reliable allies but their publics think they are.[8] Perceptions matter. The advantages of a democratic peace are not necessarily shared by mixed (democratic/autocratic) dyads and partners. Autocracies are less compliant with international agreements and liberal democracies are strikingly mistrustful of non-liberal states (Doyle 1983). Autocratic leaders are also more prone to "gamble for resurrection" by going to war; to lengthen wars; and to tolerate higher war costs. Transitional (mixed) regimes are deemed of particular concern because they are far more susceptible than either full democracies or full autocracies to political instability, armed conflict, terrorist attacks, and international crises (Peace and Conflict 2008).

Conclusions

The bulk of this chapter discussed recent findings relevant to the debate whether democratization affects the possibility of cooperation. The introduction also pointed to the perils of pure balance-of-power thinking. The US and China seem to have avoided this trap thus far (Christensen 2007). However, closure, isolationism, and nationalism – on both ends – can revive these dangerous, self-fulfilling modes of thinking. Democratization could arguably heighten nationalism but full joint consolidation of internationalization and democracy can offset proclivities toward war.

Along the range of issues stretching from benign to difficult to potentially intolerable in US–China relations, the question of a nuclear North Korea fell under the intolerable category as China strongly objected to insinuations of "regime change" and the US deplored China's unperturbed position on North Korea's nuclearization. These perceptions are changing, particularly after China's support for UN Security Council resolutions on North Korea following its nuclear test. The February 2007 breakthrough in the Six Party talks was a major step in the direction of implementing the September 2005 Joint Statement, even if problems and hard negotiations remain.

China's leverage over North Korea and its commitment to enforce the latter's compliance in phased implementation will test the possibilities for further cooperation. This issue-area has great potential to move into the "difficult" category but crucial steps remain to be taken. The February 2007 agreement established a working group on a Northeast Asia Peace and Security Mechanism which could provide the foundations for a stable, cooperative Northeast Asia.

There are important precedents for China's commitment to multilateral frameworks. Its "charm offensive" led to an understanding that a peaceful and prosperous Southeast Asia could guarantee continued overseas and regional investments, sustained flow of natural resources for China's growth and political stability, and smooth operation of crucial sea lanes in the Straits of Malacca that enable 80 percent of oil shipments to China. China signed the Southeast Asia Nuclear Weapons Free Zone Treaty in 1999; the Declaration on the Conduct of Parties in the South China Sea in 2002; the China–ASEAN Declaration on Strategic Partnership for Peace and Prosperity to coordinate foreign and security policy and China's accession to ASEAN's Treaty of Amity and Cooperation in 2003, ahead of any other superpower. China and ASEAN agreed to resolve quarrels concerning disputes in the South China Sea without the threat or use of force in 2004 and approved a Plan of Action to Implement the Declaration on the Strategic Partnership for Peace and Prosperity designed to deepen cooperation in economics and security. China has supported ASEAN's institution-building efforts in East Asia, including the ASEAN Regional Forum and ASEAN+3 processes (Johnston 1999, 2008; Solingen 2007c). Despite a different array of partners in Northeast Asia and strong historical rivals, China has entered the Six Party Talks which could help sustain a shared internationalizing strategy among the six. Yet differences between China, the US, and other regional partners regarding the nature of East Asian regional institutions remain.

Nobody can be certain of the tenor of US–China relations 20 years down the road. Decisions in international relations are largely based on imperfect information yet leaders can avoid mistakes others have made. One may quarrel about what issues are most important or most dangerous in US–China relations. An important task for the future will be to think through appropriate sequences and tradeoffs across these issues. Some Chinese experts perceive we exist in a "period of strategic opportunity" and many US experts agree. Those who share such convictions must make sure the opportunity is not wasted.

Notes

1. Although autarchy is a more extreme version, I use "autarchic" and "inward-looking" interchangeably here to convey a counter-internationalizing strategy.
2. The arguments in the second and third sections (titled "Internationalization and the democratic peace" and "Transitions to markets and democracy") are discussed more extensively in Solingen (1998, 2004, 2005a, 2007a, 2007b and Chapters 1 and 2 of this volume).
3. *Peace and Conflict* (2008) identifies as "anocracies" regimes that share an incoherent mix of democratic and autocratic features. By 2006 there were 77 democracies, 49 anocracies, and only 34 autocracies worldwide.

4   Democratization initially increases economic growth but may retard growth once moderate levels of democracy have been attained (Remmer 1989; Maravall 1994; Barro 1997). However, these findings do not speak to the issue of democracy rendering economic reform more legitimate, and hence more stable and less reversible.
5   Economic development does not invariably lead to democracy but the survival of democracy is more likely when the country is wealthier (Przeworski et al. 1996, 2000). Democracy is deemed least reversible where annual per-capita income rises above $6,000. At lower income levels, economic growth with low/moderate inflation heightens democracy's probability of survival. Very high levels of economic development arguably make democracy immune to anti-democratic coups.
6   The Chinese government reported some 87,000 disturbances of public order in 2005 (Christensen 2007). See also Shirk (2007), citing the Social Blue Book produced annually by the Chinese Academy of Social Sciences.
7   Berman (2007) is skeptical that the "right" sequence can reduce violence during democratic transitions. Carothers (2007) advises gradualism, not sequencing. Mansfield and Snyder (2007) suggest that the most likely implementers of well-sequenced reforms toward democracy are not dictators but moderate groups that seek to curtail the power of the old authoritarian elite but fear rapid descent into chaos. Carothers disagrees, arguing that democracy is the result of vigorous democrats *in* civil society, as in Chile, South Korea and Taiwan, among others.
8   US Deputy Assistant Secretary for East Asian and Pacific Affairs Thomas J. Christensen argued that "without a more open and democratic domestic system, based on the rule of law, and, therefore, a predictable political environment, it will be more difficult for China to achieve and maintain the internal stability and the trust among its neighbors necessary to achieve a smooth transition to a leading role in the international community" (Christensen 2007).

PART III
Regional institutions
Sources, design and effects

8

THE GENESIS, DESIGN AND EFFECTS OF REGIONAL INSTITUTIONS

Lessons from East Asia and the Middle East

Why do regional institutions emerge, what accounts for their variation in design, and what are their effects? There is little agreement on these three questions. Rationalistic perspectives dwell on relative power, collective action, or domestic politics to understand the origins, design and effects of institutions. Social constructivism emphasizes culture, norms, and identity. Each approach not only relies on different analytical categories but also varies in its relative attention to explaining institutional genesis, design, or effects. I focus on regional organizations as productive arenas for developing contingent propositions on institutions more generally. They include the Association of Southeast Asian Nations (ASEAN), Asia-Pacific Economic Cooperation (APEC), ASEAN Regional Forum (ARF), and the Arab League (League henceforth). These cases suggest that the nature of dominant domestic coalitions is often crucial for explaining incentives to create, design, and fine-tune the effects of institutions. However, this is mainly the case when the consequences of creating or designing institutions for power distribution, transaction costs, and norms are negligible or hard to estimate; those consequences are often sizeable, and can dilute the influence of domestic coalitions. Such coalitions often provide no more than permissive conditions for the emergence, design, and effects of institutions. Their influence is most decisive in explaining institutional genesis but is often underdetermining in explaining their design.

Section I reviews four international relations approaches to institutions. Section II builds on but also moves beyond these conventional "battles of conceptual suitors," developing three propositions. The latter identify specific conditions under which the nature of domestic coalitions are best suited to explain the genesis,

---

* I would like to acknowledge a Social Science Research Council-Japan Foundation Abe Fellowship and the University of California's Pacific Rim Program for research support. For their very useful comments on earlier versions I thank the editors, three anonymous reviewers, TaiMing Cheung, Peter Haas, Stephan Haggard, N. Ganesan, Iain Johnston, Margaret Kerns, Jeff Legro, Cecelia Lynch, John Ravenhill, Jürgen Rüland, Susan Shirk, and Richard Stubbs. I thank Wilfred Wan and Maryam Komaie for excellent research assistance.

design, and effects of regional institutions, and conditions under which they are not. Section III applies those propositions to the East Asian cases and Section IV to the Middle East. Section V summarizes substantive findings for these cases and the conclusion places them in broader perspective.

Focusing on East Asian and Middle East cases has several substantive and methodological advantages. First, it allows scrutiny of conventional assertions that East Asian or Middle East institutions are exceptional. Second, East Asian regional institutions are all too often studied in reference to the EU – the anomaly – rather than other industrializing regions. Comparisons between East Asia and the EU face the potentially confounding effects of heterogeneity in industrialization stages, whereas East Asia and the Middle East largely shared comparable initial conditions in the post-World War II era. Third, the two regions shared similar initial developmental conditions in the early post-1945 era, but their subsequent divergence offers an opportunity to examine the broader context against which regional institutions evolved in each region. Some have survived and developed; others have atrophied. Fourth, the chosen cases allow us to explore the propositions' applicability to both economics and security, issue-areas often studied in isolation. Indeed ASEAN and the Arab League include an even wider range of issue-areas, providing additional observations. Fifth, the cases offer significant variation in longevity from the oldest (the League, 1945), to middle-aged (ASEAN, 1967), to younger ones (APEC and ARF, 1990s). Sixth, the cases also offer variation across institutions in dependent variables of interest: genesis, design, and effects.[1] Seventh, the League – the oldest – has rarely been subjected to systematic cross-regional analysis. Finally, the cases offer many observations involving these institutions' emergence, circumstances involving their design, and spatial and temporal opportunities to observe their effects.

Genesis, design, and effects of international institutions: Rationalism and constructivism

Rationalist accounts of international institutions vary in the extent to which they rely on power, state efficiency, or domestic politics as core analytical categories. For neorealism, the *genesis* of institutions can be traced to powerful states that occasionally find them convenient instruments of statecraft. Unsurprisingly, given these imputed origins, their *design* resembles flimsy, supple artifacts, arenas for exercising power, pliable superstructures coating the deeper foundations of power, and subject to changes in those foundations, which can render institutions ephemeral. As residual actors – intervening variables at best – institutions have limited *effects*. The most powerful states accrue disproportionately whatever benefits these institutions yield. In a world where conflict is the norm, institutions are neither necessary nor sufficient for cooperation. Given their epiphenomenal status, institutions were not central to neorealist approaches but this earlier bias gave way to greater interest in institutions. At least four neorealist arguments explain the genesis, design, and effects of regional institutions: hegemony, defensive regionalism, "binding," and "bandwagon institutionalism" (Grieco 1997; Gruber 2000; Keohane and Martin 1995; Rosecrance 2001; Waltz 2000). Hegemons may have strong incentives to organize regional institutions, but so may have others seeking to balance against hegemons or other institutions. Weaker states may bind themselves to institutions to enhance their power within them or for fear of being left behind. Empirical research on – and a tighter typology of – neorealist hypotheses in this area are works in progress. Table 8.1 summarizes basic assumptions and hypotheses stemming from this and other approaches to the genesis, design and effects of international institutions.

Neoliberal institutionalism evolved from the assumption that states advance their interests by creating institutions to manage growing interdependence and overcome collective action problems. Institutions reduce uncertainty, enhance information about preferences and behavior, lower transaction costs responsible for market failure, monitor compliance, detect defections, increase opportunities for cooperation, reduce the costs of retaliation, facilitate issue-linkages, and offer focal points or salient solutions (Keohane 1984; North 1981; Williamson 1985). Efficiency considerations thus drive the genesis of institutions when states' benefits from creating them are greater than the transaction costs entailed in

TABLE 8.1 Approaches to the study of institutions: Basic assumptions and hypotheses.

Hypotheses	*Approaches*			
	Neorealism	Neoliberal Institutionalism	Domestic Coalitions	Constructivism
On Institutional Genesis	Explained by underlying international power configurations	Explained by market failure, need to overcome collective action problems	Explained by the nature and strength of domestic ruling coalitions	Explained by converging norms, collective purpose or identity
On Institutional Design	★ Institutions as arenas, tools ★ No independent utility functions (agents of states) ★ Highly flexible, supple	★ Institutions as arenas, tools ★ Transaction costs-reducing mechanisms ★ No independent utility functions (agents of states) ★ Relatively rigid (focused on detection and compliance)	★ Institutions as arenas, tools ★ No independent utility functions (agents of dominant domestic coalitions) ★ Moderately flexible (responsive to domestic coalitional changes)	★ Institutions as independent, purposeful agents ★ Symbolic representations ★ Flexible (focused on socialization and persuasion)
On Institutional Effects	Institutional output serves hegemonic designs, powerful states	Institutional output is pareto-optimal, enhances information constrains behavior, changes preferences over outcomes	Institutional output benefits dominant domestic coalitions, constrains behavior, changes preferences over outcomes	Institutional output constitutes actors and interests, defines purpose and meanings, specifies authority patterns

negotiation and enforcement (Powell and Di Maggio 1991). The theory has proven less apt in explaining why certain points become "focal" but not others (Johnston 2001) or why some solutions along the Pareto frontier – that leave everybody better off – are adopted over others (Krasner 1991). Haggard (1997) found "little evidence for the theory that higher levels of interdependence generate the demand for deeper integration," or that trade generates prisoners' dilemmas that only institutions (or hegemons) can resolve. Regarding *design*, as in neorealism, neoliberal institutionalist approaches view institutions as arenas or tools of states; not purposive actors but transaction-cost-reducing mechanisms. Institutional formality and autonomy are contingent on states' willingness to invest them with such features so as to extract substantial benefits (Gourevitch 1999). Institutions take different forms contingent on the type of collective action problem to be solved (Koremenos, Lipson, and Snidal 2001). Investments are not always crucially about material resources, talk is not always cheap, and formalization can undermine cooperation (Lipson 1991).

Regarding *effects*, institutions constrain and can change the context, preferences and beliefs over outcomes (Goldstein and Keohane 1993). Comparative empirical research measuring systematically the scope and distributional properties of such effects is rather recent. Measuring reductions in transaction-costs *a priori* (or even *a posteriori*) is difficult – particularly since reductions must be weighed relative to hypothetical environments without institutions (Kahler 1995) – but essential for validating neoliberal assumptions. Furthermore, the information-enhancing, problem-solving, hazard-mitigating, conflict-substituting, order-inducing, and cooperation-promoting qualities of institutions may not have Pareto-improving distributional effects. These ubiquitous, putative, public-good effects can be challenged by findings that most powerful states invariably accrue most benefits. Distributional effects consistent with sub-national preferences – not necessarily state-level efficiency – bolster domestic explanations. This compels information on how state interests are constituted independently of (and prior to) the state's observed behavior vis-à-vis the institution. Neglecting the sources of utility functions hinders the ability to predict which institutional design might prevail over several efficient institutional options, and hence, on whose behalf the benefits of efficiency will be skewed.

Whereas neorealism and neoliberalism are theories ontologically pivoted on states as unified actors, domestic-politics arguments focus on how domestic constituencies advance their interests by creating institutions. As Thelen (1999: 400) argues, functionalist theories "skirt the issue of the origins of institutions and the all-important matter of the material and ideological coalitions on which institutions are founded." Similarly, Haggard (1997) urges a proper understanding of preferences and capabilities of relevant domestic actors and of distributional effects within states, as a more productive path to understanding institutional *genesis*. Descriptive studies explaining a single state's approach to institutions through its domestic politics are more common than unified frameworks applied to several states.[2] Domestic-politics arguments apply different theories of preference formation and, in their rationalist form, reduce institutions to arenas for reaching political compromises that reflect changing domestic configurations and transnational coalitions (Krauss 2000). Such arguments can provide a credible account of institutional genesis but cannot always predict which institutional *design* will be favored (Solingen 2005a).

Kahler (2000) suggests that the nature of domestic coalitions may explain varying positions toward legalization, or the extent to which institutions display heightened obligation, greater precision in rules, and delegation of rule interpretation and enforcement to third parties. Thus, internationalizing coalitions – chiefly business – may be more prone to use legalization to enforce liberalization and ensure regional stability. By contrast, coalitions resisting internationalization – such as military and security bureaucracies – are arguably more likely to counter legalization due to high sovereignty costs or autonomy loss. There is little systematic comparative research testing linkages between coalitional configurations and institutional design, particularly beyond the EU. While cooperative regional arrangements might be predicted for internationalizing regions like East Asia, the multiple equilibria regarding design remains. It is not always self-evident which points on the institutional Pareto frontier are favored by domestic coalitions. Norms and identity can help map connections between coalitions and institutional features. Finally, the degree, nature, and scope of institutional *effects* can be gauged empirically, calibrated against the strength and preferences of primary domestic beneficiaries.

Constructivist approaches trace institutional genesis to converging norms, legitimacy, and identity (Klotz and Lynch 2007). "Logics of appropriateness" (March and Olsen 1998), not interests or rational expectations, determine institutional purpose. An institution's *design* embodies symbolic representations (Barnett and Finnemore 1999), the norms that engendered them, and internal socialization (Johnston 2008). Institutions reflecting democratic identities of member states exhibit norms of transparency, consultation, and compromise (Risse-Kappen 1995; Slaughter 1995). Experience with shared rules facilitates the development of rule-based institutions, making collective identity more viable. Socio-cultural theories are thus well equipped to identify focal points in institutional purpose and design (Elster 1989). Institutional *effects* can be far reaching, changing actors' beliefs and identities, and hence, their definition of interests. As handmaidens of new actors, tasks, and objectives, institutions are purposive agents specifying authority patterns and allocating responsibilities. Institutions "constitute and construct the social world" (Barnett and Finnemore 1999). Their independent authority stems from the legitimacy of the rational-legal authority they embody and/or from technical expertise and information. Output and practices enhance their legitimacy (Hall and Taylor 1998), sometimes at the expense of efficiency. Gauging the scope of legitimacy is problematic. Empirically, constructivism has gravitated more toward systemic than domestic sources of institutional origins and effects. Table 8.1 summarizes the four main approaches reviewed.

Propositions on the genesis, design, and effects of institutions

The perspectives outlined thus far provide a foundation for cross-paradigm studies of institutions, but how should these be pursued? Each approach dwells on a particular institutional dimension privileged by its ontology and epistemology.

Thus, for neorealism it is more efficient to understand power configurations underlying institutional genesis, whereas design and effects are mere derivatives. The emphasis in neoliberal institutionalism has been more on conceptualizing institutional persistence and design than empirical analysis of genesis and effects. Empirical studies attempting to measure transaction costs and distributional impact are more recent and have not invariably dispelled concerns with deducing origins from consequences (Hall and Taylor 1998). Constructivist studies have been largely oriented to analyzing institutional design, culture, and process; explaining change resulting from institutional identity and templates; and understanding normative diffusion. However, the puzzle of whether and when normative convergence requires the creation of formal institutions as organizations remains. Both neoliberal institutionalism and constructivism suggest that institutions can shape preferences and ideas, but Legro and Moravcsik (1999) found "no theory of this phenomenon" at the time. The work of Pevehouse (2002) and Johnston (2008), among others, have since contributed to that agenda.

Cross-paradigmatic understandings of institutions – though often only implicit – are ubiquitous. According to Gourevitch (1999), Edmund Burke was a culturalist in explaining institutional genesis and an instrumentalist in understanding their function. For Hurrell (1995) external threats and hegemony explain origins best, whereas functionalism and constructivism clarify their design. March and Olsen (1998: 952–954) identified four main ways of combining instrumental and normative logics in understanding institutions: 1) One logic dominates the other when its implications are precise whereas the other logic's implications are ambiguous[3]; 2) One logic establishes the fundamental constraints of major decisions whereas the other explains minor refinements; 3) One logic may explain institutional genesis whereas the other logic assumes primacy subsequently (the first logic is self-limiting, the second self-reinforcing); 4) One logic dominates axiomatically (according to one's views of the foundations of social life as instrumental or rule-based) whereas the other is a special case or derivative of the other.

This schema can be adapted in several ways. First, rather than collapsing all consequential logic under one rubric, I rely on Section I's more specific identification of preferences: those of power-maximizing states, interests-maximizing states, and sub-national coalitions. Norms-promoting agents constitute the fourth logic. Second, I explore the role of instrumental and normative preferences in three domains of institutional life: genesis, design, and effects. Conditions leading to the birth of an institution may not necessarily explain its design, which can reflect subsequent internal evolution or new contextual preferences or circumstances. Institutional effects can also vary accordingly and must be examined in isolation from the conditions and expectations that might have led to the institution's creation. This procedure both helps identify unexpected and unintended effects of institutions and minimizes *post-hoc* reasoning that imputes intentions on the basis of effects. Disaggregating these three – often conflated – dimensions enables more precise propositions, advancing cross-paradigmatic dialogue on specific aspects of institutional analysis.

These adaptations allow a more fine-tuned exploration of (four) explanatory and (three) dependent variables in institutional analysis while introducing greater complexity. Complexity can be reduced by establishing an analytical point of departure that enables us to weight the status of one particular explanation in the presence of others. Thus, the propositions that follow begin with the assumption that dominant domestic political coalitions create regional institutions that strengthen their own position in power (or thwart their decline). This point of departure specifies where states' preferences come from, and is arguably more tractable than measuring international relative power, state-level transaction costs, or normative convergence.[4] Despite these advantages, as will be clear soon, these propositions do not assume that domestic coalitions self-evidently "dominate" other explanations, as in March and Olsen's third example of cross-paradigmatic analysis. Rather, they are stated in ways that facilitate the identification of scope conditions under which dominant domestic coalitions may explain institutional genesis, design, or effects. Yet one could formulate similar propositions with alternative points of departure – relative power or norms, for instance – on the basis of specifications of power differentials or normative convergence. Those points of departure would not necessarily or axiomatically make relative power or norms the "dominant" explanation but rather a foundation for exploring their limitations.

Explaining institutional genesis

Proposition 1: *The nature and strength of dominant domestic coalitions best explain the origins of regional institutions when: (a) The domestic distributional implications of these institutions are clear to most actors; (b) The consequences for regional power distribution are negligible or unclear; (c) State-level transaction costs are unclear or not easily measurable; and (d) There is little normative convergence around the demand for an institution.*

Under those conditions there is clear *a priori* specification of the preferences of dominant domestic coalitions (state officials and societal allies) driving institutional creation. Uncertainty about how an emerging institution may affect power distribution across states renders relative power much less relevant (such situations are more common than neorealism makes allowance for). Similarly, uncertainty about whether a new institution will reduce states' transaction costs renders the latter less pertinent. Low normative convergence can make norms less central but can also lead to normative competition. Conditions where the implications for power, norms, and transaction costs are all uncertain may not be that frequent in reality. The fortuitous circumstances when domestic coalitions straightforwardly explain institutional creation could thus be rather limited. Clear normative convergence can make norms more prominent in creating institutions. When implications for state power, transaction costs, and domestic politics are sizeable or unambiguous it is harder to establish their relative weight in institutional creation, foretelling high contestation over what drives institutional genesis.

Explaining institutional design

Proposition 2: *The nature and strength of domestic political coalitions best explain regional institutional design when (a) The domestic distributional implications of institutional design are clear to most actors; (b) The consequences of design for power distribution across* states are negligible or unclear; (c) Variations in institutional design have little effect on transaction costs or such costs are not easily measurable; and (d) There is little normative convergence around a favored design.

Under these restrictive conditions, design would reflect dominant preferences of domestic coalitions. Yet reality is often more complex. The relative weight of each variable will be harder to assess when there are more clear and weighty implications of design for states' power or transaction costs, and when there is clear normative convergence for a given institutional form.

Explaining institutional effects

Proposition 3: *Regional institutions are more likely to benefit the dominant domestic coalitions that created them when: (a) The domestic distributional effects of institutions are both sizeable and clear to dominant domestic actors; (b) The institution's effects on power distribution across states are negligible or unclear; (c) The institution has modest effects on reducing states' transaction costs, or reductions are not easily measurable; and (d) The institution has little effect on an already weak normative convergence.*

Yet conditions where institutional effects on power, norms, and transaction costs are all uncertain or negligible may or may not be common. Institutions may have relatively unimportant distributional effects on domestic coalitions but significant effects on normative, power, or transaction costs considerations. They may upset existing normative convergence or forge such convergence where there was none. It is harder to explain which variable best accounts for institutional effects when those effects are salient and unambiguous for most candidate variables.[5]

East Asian (EA) institutions: Goldilocks and flexible regionalism

The empirical study gauges the heuristic value of these propositions. Stylized accounts of cases are based on extensive primary research.[6] The analytical point of departure stipulated that dominant domestic coalitions create regional institutions that strengthen those coalitions at home or prevent their decline. A prior characterization of those coalitions is in order. Most dominant coalitions in EA over the relevant period shared fundamental preferences for growth-oriented strategies as sources of domestic political legitimacy, dictating heavy reliance on the global economy and institutions (Solingen 2007b). Export-oriented growth was often guided by considerable state intervention and incepted by politicians allied with – or seeking to coopt – private interests. Beyond shared preference for export-led growth there was wide variability in institutional arrangements (democratic or authoritarian, statist or market-based) and in forms and levels of integration into the global economy. Such differences explain EA's regional institutional design: informal, process-driven, reliant on consensual decision-making, and largely oriented toward "open regionalism."[7] These institutional forms were compatible both with dominant coalitions' shared embrace of the global economy and their diverse developmental stages and domestic institutions. Resulting regional institutions were not rigid and legalistic but, in Goldilocks fashion, "just right" for accommodating diverse variants of export-led coalitions. The discussion below examines the extent to which power distribution, norms, and transaction costs make this analytical point of departure relatively unproblematic or contestable.

ASEAN

Genesis

ASEAN is the oldest surviving regional institution in EA.[8] Ravenhill (1998) does not find transaction costs and overcoming dilemmas of interdependence to be persuasive interpretations of its origin. Proposals for preferential trade agreements – ASEAN Industrial Project, ASEAN Industrial Complementation, and ASEAN Industrial Joint Venture – had all failed (Stubbs 2000). Reducing barriers to trade was only seriously considered in 1992 (AFTA), largely following domestic shifts in the 1980s. Dominant coalitions in ASEAN's Five launched models of growth through engagement in the global economy. Their converging interest in collaborating regionally was geared to protect their model from interrelated domestic insurgencies and regional threats.[9] Theirs was a very different conception of regional order than the one advanced by Indonesia's Sukarno, who rejected the global economy and institutions while inciting conflict with neighbors (*konfrontasi*). Differences across the Sukarno and Suharto models were more crucial in shaping cooperative regional policies than abstract conceptions of relative power and state survival. Military confrontation against Malaysia, increases in military expenditures, massive budget deficits, and economic isolationism characterized Sukarno's policies. Economic growth was at the heart of Suharto's strategy, embedded in the concept of "national resilience" (*ketahanan nasional*). Regional stability was a natural cornerstone, allowing ASEAN rulers to wield national and collective resilience to mutual benefit (Emmerson 1996). This model relied initially on state-directed lending and crony conglomerates variously favoring FDI, manufacturing, and natural resource exports while compensating import-substituting and rural interests (Solingen 1999; MacIntyre 1991). An embedded social bargain provided high per-capita growth, employment, investments in health and education, and increasing returns to small business and farmers. The bargain was pivoted on gradual and selective internationalization, with inward-looking groups retaining influence and resisting greater intrusiveness. Intra-regional trade was rather limited and regional integration not a priority. Following the 1985 Plaza Accord a stronger coalition of state officials and private entrepreneurs advocated FDI and capital liberalization. Two decades later ASEAN had become a market of 500 million people and a $600 billion combined GDP. AFTA acquired greater centrality only after more robust state/private internationalizing coalitions were in place (Kahler 1995).

This account supports Proposition 1 insofar as the nature and strength of dominant domestic coalitions explain ASEAN's origins well. Others have traced ASEAN's creation to Communist threats; yet these are hard to disentangle from internal considerations. Leaders created ASEAN to allay both regional conflict and internal subversion that might upset domestic stability, foreign investment, growth, and exports. ASEAN's ruling coalitions, not states, were threatened. Communist takeovers in Cambodia, Laos, and Vietnam (1970s) may have helped institutionalize ASEAN's first summit in 1976 (Ravenhill 1998). External threats may have made closer coordination more compelling but did not alter – indeed only strengthened – the domestic incentives that underpinned ASEAN's creation: protecting its ruling coalitions' favored model. Leaders feared internal subversion and insurgency but there was no agreement about what the prime source of external threat was (Foot 1995). The implications for ruling coalitions were clear; the implications for states' relative power much less so. ASEAN's expansion (late 1990s) to include former communist states might also be construed as a response to relative-power considerations: China's ascendancy. However, ASEAN's progressive inclusion of new states was also a natural corollary of maturing internationalizing coalitions inducing neighbors to discard old inward-looking models and maintain regional stability, FDI, and common growth. Furthermore, why "defensive regionalism" against China would have dominated over other potential responses (such as bandwagoning) in earlier decades but not later is unclear. Indeed, many consider ASEAN's policies toward China to resemble bandwagoning in the 1990s. These competing views give substance to the claim that implications for states' power distribution seemed unclear.

Finally, claims that collective identity and cultural similarities were the key drivers (Acharya 1999) remain unconvincing. Isolating the effect of common identity would, in any case, be far more effective if evidence could be marshaled that ruling coalitions designed their strategies independently of their immediate material incentives described above. Whether or not a common identity emerged decades later is also contested. In sum, negligible or unclear implications for relative power, transaction costs, or norms, and more clear implications for domestic ruling coalitions privilege the latter in explaining ASEAN's genesis, in line with Proposition 1's baseline conditions.

Design

ASEAN's informal design is geared toward "conflict-avoidance" rather than "conflict-resolution" or "dispute settlement."[10] It is not a collective security arrangement, and there is considerable disagreement over whether it is a security community (Leifer 1989; Kahler 1995). The 1976 Declaration of ASEAN Concord emphasized exclusive reliance on peaceful means for settling intra-regional differences. The Treaty of Amity and Cooperation promoted "perpetual peace, everlasting amity, and cooperation, establishing three basic principles: respect for state sovereignty, nonintervention, and renouncing the threat or use of force." An informal "ASEAN way" developed, emphasizing consultation, accommodation, reciprocity, informality, incrementalism, process over substance, personalistic networks, and avoiding provocative issues (Mahbubani 1995; Harris 2000). These were advanced through yearly summits, foreign ministers meetings, and meetings involving "senior officials" and others. Post Ministerial Conferences (PMC, ASEAN 10+10 dialogue partners) expanded since 1992 to discuss conflict resolution, transparency, and confidence-building.[11] A small ASEAN secretariat coordinates with national secretariats in foreign ministries.

Various approaches can explain this informal design but none determines it *a priori*. First, limited initial interdependence did not compel the legalistic framework anticipated by efficiency approaches, although there were subsequent moderate efforts at more formalized commitments such as AFTA. Second, informality was only natural in a neorealist world of sovereignty-sensitive considerations. However, presumed external threats could have generated a more formal alliance as well. Hence, informality does not appear to be a *sine-qua-non,* derivative of relative-power considerations. Third, ASEAN-style consensus supported a rapidly changing environment requiring regional and domestic stability for members at different stages of internationalization. Informal arrangements bolstering stability and collective appeal to international investors were thus quite suitable to internationalizing (export-led growth) models; yet other arrangements might have been compatible too. Finally, cultural forms – *musjawarah* and *mufakat* (Malay-style consultation and consensus) – advanced as explanations for ASEAN's design assume normative convergence; yet this explanation for ASEAN's design remains problematic. First, norms were overlaid on extant realities to explain ASEAN's *modus operandi*. During the 1980s, Singapore's Lee Kuan Yew and Malaysia's Mahathir advanced the 'ASEAN way" as a cultural construct to add a veneer of legitimacy to their autocracies, suggesting pure instrumentality. By 2000, Surapong Jayanama (Director General of Thailand's Foreign Ministry's EA Department) still pointed to ASEAN states' diverse political cultures and values as a continuing challenge.[12] Second, steps toward ASEAN's growing intrusiveness challenges the assumption that normative convergence favored only informality. The 1995 Southeast Asian Nuclear Weapon Free Zone Treaty acknowledged the right to refer disputes to the ICJ. ASEAN's AFTA adopted a dispute-settlement mechanism requiring majority vote in 1996. An ASEAN Troika was designed as an *ad hoc* body of foreign ministers to address urgent concerns in 1999. The 2005 Kuala Lumpur Declaration declared a commitment to establish an ASEAN Charter as a legal and institutional framework codifying all norms, rules, principles, goals, and ideals embedded in adopted agreements and instruments. The Charter establishing ASEAN as a legal entity and an economic community (but not a customs union) was approved in 2007, on ASEAN's 40th anniversary. The Charter's "Asean Minus X" provision allows members to opt out of economic commitments consensually approved by other members. Changes toward greater formality question the role of long-standing norms in generating informality.

ASEAN thus supports baseline Proposition 2 only to a limited extent. Its design was indeed compatible with the preferences of ruling coalitions but so were alternative designs. The implications of informality for power distribution across states were negligible. There is no firm evidence that the preference for informality stemmed from normative convergence or that formal institutions would have lowered transaction costs. If informality could have been anticipated by all perspectives, as this overview suggests, one must wonder why the literature has considered ASEAN's informality puzzling at all. Studying ASEAN through EU lenses seems the source of this ersatz puzzle. Relative power, transaction costs, norms, and domestic coalitions are all underdetermining, and did not necessarily compel ASEAN's informality.

Effects

Measuring the effects of 500-plus yearly ASEAN-sponsored meetings on transaction-costs reduction is difficult but some allowance can be made for such effects. Cooperation on a given issue sometimes opens paths to cooperation on others. The aftermath of the 1997 Asian crisis led to the 1997 Manila Framework Agreement; the 1997 Kuala Lumpur Summit and the Vision 2020 Plan calling for "a concert of Southeast Asian nations, outward-looking, living in peace, stability and prosperity";[13] the 1998 Hanoi Plan of Action to strengthen economic fundamentals, restore confidence and FDI, and regenerate economic growth; surveillance mechanisms to anticipate future crises; and the 2003 Bali Concord II's goals of an ASEAN Security Community, Economic Community, and Socio-cultural Community. The Concord's reaffirmation of converging internationalizing strategies is evident in its statement that: "For the sustainability of our region's economic development we affirmed the need for a secure political environment based on a strong foundation of mutual interests generated by economic cooperation," and commitment to enhance "economic linkages with the world economy."[14] China and ASEAN signed a landmark Framework Agreement on Comprehensive Economic Co-operation, including a Dispute Settlement Mechanism in 2004 (Solingen 2007a).

The claim that the "ASEAN way" altered members' identity is questionable and circular, since norms of *musjawarah* and *mufakat* have a domestic origin to begin with. Yet frequent meetings may have facilitated socialization and the creation of newer institutions (ARF). Above all, ASEAN enabled internationalizing coalitions to sustain themselves over decades of relative domestic and regional stability, and steady access to FDI and export markets. This favored model may have contributed to the expansion of middle classes and democratic institutions, but not universally. The aura of regional stability benefited internationalizing coalitions and their export-led models, supporting Proposition 3. Consequences for transaction costs or relative power were negligible; ASEAN reinforced rough equality among members, with Indonesia considered no more than "primus inter pares." Whether ASEAN also consolidated members' normative convergence remains contested. Economic openness, particularly to FDI, became widely shared, easily traceable to the objectives of dominant coalitions. Finally, ASEAN itself had little impact on progressive democratization in Southeast Asia. There were restrained responses to Myanmar junta's repression of domestic dissent. Article 14 of the 2007 ASEAN Charter established a consultative human rights body without provisions for enforcing compliance.

APEC

Genesis

Efforts to liberalize trade and investment, facilitate trade, and increase economic and technical cooperation led to APEC's creation (1989).[15] "Defensive regionalism" against other trading blocs played an important role in some accounts. Neither common security threats nor an enhanced US position can explain its emergence. Indeed, given initial US reluctance, APEC's origins are sometimes traced to East

Asian efforts to extract deeper US commitments to the region and stem future US trade pressures. Australia and Japan played catalytic roles while relying on existing regional NGO activities (Higgott and Stubbs 1995). ASEAN resisted APEC initially but domestic realignments (1980s-1990s), with an eye on improved access to US markets, weakened that opposition. The US preferred bilateralism and global institutions – where it played major roles – to regional institutions that might detract from both (Krauss 2000). This evolution questions a hegemonic logic for APEC's creation and reveals unclear implications for power distribution. US reluctance decreased in the mid-1980s when a new institutional context for managing trade tensions became more favorably and the Clinton administration hosted the first summit (1993).

Expansion of intra-regional trade from 30 percent (1970s) to nearly 70 percent (1990s) of total trade makes room for efficiency accounts of APEC's origins as a tool to manage growing interdependence. Enhancing information on members' preferences, policies, and performances was a key priority (Higgott 1995). Working groups gathered data on technology transfer, investment, fisheries, tariffs, and sectoral capacities. However, expectations of reduced transaction costs cannot explain the occurrence and timing of shifts in perception that interests might be better served by regionalism rather than by global multilateralism (Ravenhill 1998). State-level accounts obscure the role of the true agents of APEC's creation: ruling coalitions sharing significantly converging orientations to the global economy despite heterogeneous state size, power, regimes, norms, culture, and histories. Underpinning the significant expansion of regional trade and investment (1980s) were private corporations backed by state officials and informal networks of business representatives, economists, and public officials in private capacities – notably PECC – pressing governments to liberalize.[16] As Ravenhill (2006) argued, "if successfully managed… enhanced economic integration ultimately would *change the balance of interests in the political systems of member states*" [my emphasis]. Regional stability and cooperation would foster economic growth and defuse internal threats to ruling coalitions.

The rise of stronger internationalizing coalitions and concerns with a deadlocked Uruguay Round catalyzed action in the late 1980s (MacIntyre 1991). Australia, steered by its Treasury Department and backed by internationalizing firms, valued APEC as a means to "lock in" market mechanisms advancing liberalization at home and preventing exclusion from an Asian and North American bloc (Aggarwal 1995). APEC provided an opportunity for the Clinton administration to support internationalizing constituencies over protectionist ones (Pempel 2005). Manufacturing exports and dramatic FDI expansion had pushed ASEAN's domestic political economies toward further liberalization. The Kuching Consensus (1990) reassured them that a flexible, "outward-oriented" APEC would accommodate different paces, developmental stages, and political systems. Krauss (2001) detects differing and fluid cross-national coalitions along different issues. Growth triangles and free trade areas straddling borders progressively transformed regions with pre-market economies. By the mid-1990s provincial officials were actively fostering this process, particularly in China's coastal areas (Naughton 1999). These informal Japanese and Chinese networks and Korean firms, more than APEC, were lowering transaction costs.

APEC's origins must be considered against Mahathir's competing idea (1990) of an East Asian Economic Grouping (EAEG: ASEAN + Japan, China, and South Korea) excluding Pacific Anglo-Saxon states. This had elements of defensive regionalism against European and North American blocs but was also driven by Mahathir's domestic affirmative action policy to redistribute power and wealth from Chinese to Malays (Pempel 2005). This program was controversial and the EAEG offered Malaysia's Chinese enhanced opportunities to expand regionally while attracting Japanese FDI and aid. However, internationalizing constituencies throughout the region were highly dependent on US and Canadian markets. Furthermore, some ASEAN states were wary of Mahathir's designs. The US, Australia, New Zealand, Singapore, and Indonesia opposed EAEG. Some Japanese business and state officials looked at it more favorably (Saxonhouse 1995) as Japanese corporations expanded into ASEAN after the Plaza Accord. However, since the EAEG could not substitute for US markets, Japan remained lukewarm toward it (Pempel 1999; Solingen 2005a). Thus, most ruling coalitions did not regard EAEG as advancing their interests and turned it into a caucus (EAEC) within APEC. The idea did not completely fade away and by 1999 ASEAN, Japan, China, and South Korea kicked off ASEAN+3, a revised EAEG (Stubbs 2005).

In sum, APEC renders significant support for Proposition 1 tracing its genesis to the nature of domestic coalitions and their regional networks, such as PECC. The expected consequences of APEC for states' relative power were unclear. The case for normative convergence around an internationalizing economic project, though plausible, is hard to separate from the interests of ruling coalitions and associated economic networks. Although hard to validate empirically on the basis of existing information, the assumption that would-be member states might have considered APEC as a mechanism capable of reducing transaction costs is tenable. Associating those expectations to ruling coalitions and their networks makes them more tractable.

Design

APEC's design too can be traced to the nature of domestic coalitions that envisaged it as an informal mechanism of economic growth oriented to the global economy without coercing more trade liberalization than was politically feasible domestically. Both "open regionalism" and "concerted unilateralism" reflected APEC's minimum common denominator toward internationalization, a focal point that did not require dense institutionalization (Garnaut 2000). The consensus rule defined APEC as a horizontal, minimally hierarchical organization, enabling coalitions at different stages of openness to pursue their own timetable. ASEAN, China, and Japan resisted binding codes, prevailing over the US, Canada, Australia, and New Zealand who advocated formal targets and enforcement. APEC retained only voluntaristic commitments ("individual action plans") and weak evaluation procedures. Subsequent proposals for dispute-settlement mechanisms by an Eminent Persons Group (EPG) were bumped to the WTO. APEC's thin Secretariat provides advisory and logistical/technical services. Annual summits since 1993 are the most important events, progressively including political and security issues

(North Korea, terrorism). Maintaining regional stability and cooperation – crucial for ruling coalitions – is APEC's core latent objective (Ravenhill 2006).

APEC's design is thus compatible with Proposition 2: given clear domestic distributional effects, dominant coalitions coalesced around an informal APEC capable of accommodating diverse stages of economic openness. The implications of this format for states' relative power were marginal; US preferences failed to materialize, questioning APEC's depiction as a hegemonic US instrument. Although the US and Japan played critical roles, neither was able to impose their designs. ASEAN firmly opposed a more legalized APEC that might have constrained large powers but also themselves, given who might have set the rules (Krauss 2000). Some powerful states expected a more formal APEC to reduce transaction costs and enhance information, suggesting that variations in institutional design were expected to have clear implications for reducing transaction costs. Yet vast expansions of intra-regional trade and investment did not yield more formal structures, and efficiency assumptions of prisoners' dilemmas, common efforts to enforce compliance, or fears of cheating did not prevail. APEC's first (1993) EPG report recognized this, as well as the need for flexibility given different domestic conditions (Kahler 1995). Finally, although APEC's design was partially derivative of ASEAN's, the 'ASEAN way" was not a shared norm across APEC members (or, possibly, across ASEAN itself).

Effects

The Bogor Declaration and Osaka Summit Implementation committed industrialized members to reduce trade barriers by 2010, and industrializing ones by 2020. A subsequent agreement liberalized trade in information technology equipment. The Early Voluntary Sector Liberalization program was established to liberalize trade in nine sectors but stalled in 1998 and was transferred to the WTO. The focus since turned toward trade facilitation and economic/technical cooperation. APEC's effects hardly reflect anyone's hegemonic preferences but rather the lowest common denominator. Unilateral liberalization preceded APEC's arrival; stronger market forces in individual states deepened liberalization (Garnaut 2000). Ravenhill (2000) doubts APEC's influence on states' actions and finds "peer pressure" hard to document. Empirical studies measuring APEC's role in reducing transaction costs are hard to find. Neither has APEC led to value change but perhaps to tactical learning, revealing "a response to domestically generated needs and interests in the political economies of member states" (Higgott 1995, 74). Evidence for APEC's constraining effects on national policies is "insignificant" (Aggarwal and Lin 2001, 180) but Garnaut (2000) finds those effects to be under-recognized. EPG's Chair Fred Bergsten (1997), acknowledging limited evidence for APEC's effects, also notes that leaders used APEC's commitments to advance liberalization at home.

These findings are compatible with Proposition 3, tracing APEC's moderate institutional effects to the preferences of domestic coalitions that created APEC in the first place. Groups favoring internationalization were APEC's main beneficiaries. Only large corporations were systematically involved in its activities (particularly through PECC); labor, smaller enterprises, and others were marginalized. As a government official acknowledged, "APEC is not for governments. It is for business. Through APEC we aim to get governments out of the way" (cited in Ravenhill 2006). Yet not all conditions of Proposition 3, which assumes weak normative convergence, are met. APEC's output, if limited, reflects some consensus around norms of open regionalism and market-driven liberalization, even if not all domestic constituencies embraced this consensus. PAFTAD, PBEC, PECC and ABAC played important roles in promoting those consensual norms in the absence of material sanctions. However, disentangling ideological commitments from interests of domestic ruling coalitions is difficult (Aggarwal 1995; Kahler 1995). It is also feasible that, counter to baseline Proposition 3, APEC reduced transaction costs; yet there appear to be no systematic studies to confirm such reductions.

The ASEAN Regional Forum (ARF)

Genesis

Created in 1994, the ARF is the only inclusive multilateral institution promoting security cooperation in the Asia-Pacific.[17] Some have traced its emergence to the post-Cold War regional power vacuum and fears of intra-regional competition or hegemonic designs, particularly China's ascendancy and assertiveness over the Spratly Islands. Constituent states are highly heterogeneous in military and power capabilities. Middle powers like Japan, Canada, and Australia played critical roles in its genesis although some ASEAN members also claim paternity.[18] ASEAN included security matters in its 1992 Post-Ministerial Conference, which evolved into the ARF, and established the ARF Unit at the ASEAN Secretariat in 2004. Keeping the US engaged in the region, China and Japan down, and ASEAN relevant were said to be key objectives (Khong 1997). Fearing US hegemony and favoring bilateralism, China was initially lukewarm although ASEAN's control over the ARF provided China with some reassurance. Likewise, the first Bush administration was unenthusiastic and bilateralist. The Clinton administration later endorsed it. Insofar as the ARF is an inclusive forum advancing cooperative security, not a balancing mechanism like NATO, the ARF's emergence seems anomalous for neorealism. Furthermore, small states (ASEAN) are not expected to spearhead security institutions, nor are big powers assumed to acquiesce to them. However, the ARF's extreme informality and the fact that its implications for power distribution were unclear at its genesis, may account for the agreement to create it. Neither China nor the US, given a veil of ignorance regarding potential implications for power distribution, wanted to be excluded.

Shirk (1994) and Johnston (1999) acknowledge that facilitating communication and transparency, providing information and minimizing uncertainty (particularly vis-à-vis China) were important considerations in the ARF's creation, as were shared interests in economic prosperity and avoiding costly arms races. These priorities compel deeper probing into the domestic configurations underlying them. Maintaining macroeconomic stability, FDI, global access to markets and technology, and rapid growth, had become the reigning political strategies of EA's ruling coalitions by the 1990s including shifts toward economic openness by China and Russia. These coalitions favored regional cooperation and stability to reduce uncertainty, encourage savings and investment, and minimize unproductive and inflationary military expenditures. Conflict-prone environments had the potential for overriding economic growth by imposing unrestrained military budgets, government deficits, high interest rates, stymied savings and investments, and distorted exchange rates. Institutions that helped maintain underlying conditions for economic growth and sustained political control while containing military investments advanced these coalitions' collective interests. This internationalizing agenda, and the ARF itself, were anathema to groups adversely affected by reduced military-industrial complexes and ancillary industries sustained by "national security imperatives" such as China's People's Liberation Army (PLA).[19] The latter advocated balance of power and bilateralism, and regarded the ARF as a threat to its interests in the Spratly Islands (Shirk 1994). China's internationalizers resisted domestic opponents of the ARF (Johnston 2008).

Tracing the ARF's genesis to domestic coalitions provides some support for Proposition 1, but not for the baseline fortuitous conditions when the implications for power, norms, and transaction costs are unclear or negligible. Instrumental incentives of ruling coalitions (enhancing growth through regional stability and FDI) may overlap with normative convergence around war avoidance and common security as preferable to deterrence. Mutually reinforcing interests and norms thus may have underpinned the ARF's creation. The possible existence of such normative convergence is intriguing given the ARF's heterogeneity in cultural and legal traditions. There is no systematic evidence that state officials expected the ARF to reduce transaction costs but its potential to help deepen export-led growth was there. The implications for regional power distribution seemed unclear or negligible at the time of inception; furthermore, the ARF's design would help dissipate any such concerns.

Design

As another ASEAN derivative, the ARF is even less formal than ASEAN or APEC, lacking even a secretariat. ASEAN hosts all ARF's annual foreign minister and Senior Official meetings but not inter-sessional workshops. The ARF's chairmanship follows the annual rotation of ASEAN Chairs; its main document is the Chairman's Statement. The Third Statement emphasized consultation and consensus on future membership and gradual expansion, and commitment to key ARF goals and "geographical footprint" (Northeast Asia, Southeast Asia, and Oceania). The ARF commits studies to the Council for Security Cooperation in the Asia Pacific (CSCAP), established in 1993 as a non-official network linking security-related NGOs. CSCAP mandate to enhance information and increase military transparency typifies functions anticipated by neoliberal institutionalism. However, understanding why certain preferences for informality prevailed over others requires a turn to domestic politics. An informal, consensus-based design accommodated variation in domestic arrangements while buttressing synergies between domestic and regional stability so central to internationalizing coalitions. The ARF provided these coalitions with regional conditions necessary for making their domestic policies "resilient," a term favored by ASEAN leaders that resonated with others in the region. The ARF's 1998 communique noted the adverse repercussions of the Asian financial crisis for peace and security. The 2000 meeting reaffirmed the links between globalization and regional peace and stability, revealing a common understanding that the ARF is inextricably linked to the domestic coalitional foundation underpinning the region's evolution.

The ARF thus provides evidence for Proposition 2 insofar as its design was compatible with the interests of dominant ruling coalitions. Yet other – including more formal – institutional arrangements might have been compatible too. Other conditions of Proposition 2 seem to hold, including the expected negligible (or hard to estimate) implications of design for power distribution across states. Surely when extreme informality is equated with a "talking shop," institutional design is consistent with neorealism. Nevertheless the consensus rule precluding major powers from advancing their agenda at the expense of smaller participants seems at odds with neorealist expectations. Despite shared interests in economic prosperity and avoiding costly arms races, China's suspicions of multilateralism compelled a weak institution bound by consensus (Johnston 1999). Informal multilateralism (that might arguably tame the US and Japan) was favored over China's perceived worst outcome: US bilateralism with ASEAN, Japan, and Korea (Christensen 1999). The view that transparency is not an Asian tradition but a Western construct stressing clearly and legally defined property rules and regulatory mechanisms precluded convergence on a formal institution (Dibb, Hale, and Prince 1998). Norms, domestic coalitions, and expectations for lowering transaction costs, all of which were compatible with other institutional forms, underdetermined the ARF's design.

Effects

The ARF has no enforcement powers and is not a security community, collective defense, or collective security mechanism. Yet it has promoted dialogue on the Spratlys and Korean denuclearization through the Six-Party Talks, advanced confidence-building (including "White Papers" on defense policy and exchanges between military academies), encouraged participation in the UN Register of Conventional Weapons, enhanced maritime information exchanges, and approved a "Concept paper" identifying a three-step approach from confidence-building to preventive diplomacy and conflict-resolution, reaffirming ASEAN as the ARF's driving force. Agreement on preventive diplomacy has proven elusive largely due to China's resistance. The 2001 meeting launched an enhanced ARF chairman's role. The 2007 statement urged Myanmar to encourage peaceful transition to democracy and Iran to comply with UN Security Council resolutions. Taiwan Straits' issues are explicitly off the agenda; no effective ARF steps materialized on North Korea; and only limited coordination on terrorism, piracy, and other issues was achieved. These circumscribed effects are compatible with neorealist assumptions that only powerful states can enforce more than token institutional outputs. ARF meetings could thus hardly reduce transaction costs beyond facilitating bilateral and sub-regional discussions.

The ARF validates Proposition 3 insofar as: it supports basic objectives of ruling coalitions to preserve peace and stability, a prerequisite for EA's emergence as the engine of the 21st century global economy; and its effects on power distribution and transaction costs have been modest or hard to measure. Neither have its domestic effects been sizeable, adding only marginally to existing incentives of dominant coalitions to maintain peace and stability. Yet the ARF's cooperative security ideology and consensus principles have played a role in developing "habits of cooperation" even without material threats, socializing China to accept the legitimacy of multilateralism, transparency, and reassurance (Johnston 2008). The growing community of Chinese officials advancing confidence-building and arms control largely overlaps with foreign ministry internationalizers, WTO advocates, and other supporters of multilateralism (Shirk 1994). A compelling test of the power of socialization involves tracing changes in a multilateralist direction among PLA and nationalists opposing internationalization. The PLA resisted calls for China's disclosure of order of battle, arms acquisition plans, or full participation in the UN or Regional Arms Registers (Simon 2001). Yet China began endorsing military cooperation on piracy and a forum gathering high-level defense officials; in 2007 it restored participation in the arms register. Socialization effects thus align with those described in baseline Proposition 3.

Middle East institutions

The UN Arab Human Development Report (AHDR 2002) by leading Arab scholars suggests that "perhaps no other group of states in the world has been endowed with the same potential for cooperation, even integration, as have the Arab countries. Nevertheless...Arab countries continue to face the outside world and the challenges posed by the region itself, individually and alone." The Arab League's establishment in 1945 as the first postwar regional institution adds to the paradox of stunted institutional development. A proper understanding of ruling coalitions throughout the region reduces this sense of paradox. These coalitions shared fundamental preferences for a weak regional institution that could not limit their freedom of action. The League's design and effects guaranteed that outcome (Barnett and Solingen 2007).

The League of Arab States: Goldilocks between Arab unity and regime survival

Origins

The League began with efforts by Egypt, Iraq, Jordan, Lebanon, Saudi Arabia, Syria, and Yemen following British Foreign Minister Anthony Eden's 1942 initiative.[20] Ironically, ruling coalitions seeking to guarantee their own sovereignty and independence against advocates of Arab unity were the most important forces underlying the League's creation.[21] Saudi Arabia and Egypt opposed pre-1945 Jordanian and Iraqi Hashemites' unification schemes ("Greater Syria," "Fertile Crescent"). So essential was the penchant for independence during the League's creation that activities were restricted initially to economic, cultural, and social – but not political – cooperation. The 1944 Alexandria Protocol preceding its founding specifically eliminated joint defense and foreign policy from proposed committees. The 1945 Pact made no mention of common defense against external attack, common foreign policy, or coordinating military resources (Macdonald 1965). Concerns with security emerged only after rejecting the UN's 1947 partition of Palestine and a joint Arab military attack on Israel in 1948. The 1950 Joint Defense and Economic Cooperation Treaty (known as the Arab Collective Security Pact) addressed external threats (Israel), not inter-Arab ones.

Broader implications for regional power distribution were unclear at the League's inception. The League's formal rejection of unification and emphasis on sovereignty alleviated concerns, particularly Saudi, with Iraqi and Jordanian hegemonic designs. Egypt and Iraq subsequently vied for hegemony. The Secretary General was always Egyptian (except under Sadat) and Egyptians dominated the bureaucracy. Egypt could not invariably impose its will but came close to that under Nasser (Hasou 1985). Saudi Arabia sought hegemonic status in the 1970s, underwriting the League economically. Egypt resumed its influence when the League returned to Cairo, "forgiving" Egypt's "treacherous" Camp David commitments to Israel. The League was expected to enhance collective Arab power vis-à-vis the rest of the world, particularly the superpowers, "acting as a group will empower the Arabs and allow them to secure rights and legal claims in international agreements" (Arab Human Development Report 2002: 122). This was never realized; individual leaders' ambitions dominated the hierarchy of objectives throughout the League's history.

Interpretations of its genesis as an effort to manage interdependence do not apply. Interdependence was very low in the 1940s; inter-Arab trade remained rather stable at 7-10 percent of total trade since the 1950s and capital movements were small (Arab Human Development Report 2002). As Fischer (1995: 440) argued: "The potential economic benefits of ... [FTAs] in the context of the Middle East arise more from political than direct economic benefits, given a predicted trade pattern which is mainly with the outside world." The Arab Human Development Report (2002) identified the failure to consider either inadequate production capacity or similar production patterns – which undermine benefits from complementarity – as the first major obstacle to Arab cooperation. Economic models stressing factor endowments discount the benefits of Arab economic integration. Nor has transparency of intentions (enhancing information) been high in the hierarchy of objectives. Indeed, high public *ambiguity* vis-à-vis Arab unity, the West, and Israel helped leaders survive politically at home. Pan-Arab rhetoric, useful domestically, was never matched by clear, substantive steps in that direction.

Common language, nationality, history, and culture make normative convergence a plausible motive for the League's creation *prima facie*. Paradoxically, however, efforts to define clear collective Arab norms (Arabism) regarding unity, the West, and Israel threatened ruling coalitions (Barnett 1998). Clear norms (such as proscribing alliances with the West) would restrict leaders' freedom of action and create pressures for compliance from domestic and neighboring constituencies. The push-pull quality of Arabism forced leaders to attempt normative convergence while clashing over its essence. Pressures to develop focal points fueled competitive outbidding among leaders seeking to impose their own normative vision. Efforts to outdo other leaders yielded more extreme normative versions than any of them could bear, given domestic constraints. Arabism had more powerful (unintended) centrifugal effects than the intended centripetal ones it was assumed to encourage.

The League was created as a substitute for, not a conduit to, Arab unification. It thus mobilized two competing domestic camps: those who balked at any regional entity limiting independence and those who balked at one that did *not* advance Arab unity. The latter camp was particularly strong among pan-Arabists in Syria and Iraq. Following the 1944 Alexandria Protocol, Egypt's King and League critics ousted Prime Minister Nahhas Pasha – a League supporter – as a traitor.[22] Jordanian and Syrian prime ministers followed suit. Lebanese Christian Maronite leaders denounced the protocol as violating sovereignty. King Sa'ud worked to derail the meetings. This early domestic mobilization against the Protocol, however, could not reverse support for the League's concept once popular constituencies awakened to prospects of Arab unity. Rulers prevailed in the Pact's final version, ratified in 1945, which precluded intrusion in domestic affairs and sheltered individual regimes through Article 8, stipulating that members should "abstain from any action calculated to change established systems of government" in member states (Gomaa 1977). Leaders were thus primarily protecting their domestic political arrangements more than their states' "hard shells." Such protection reassured Lebanese Christians among others but not necessarily Muslim proponents of pan-Arab unity.

This account provides significant support for Proposition 1: ruling coalitions created the League to protect themselves from competing pan-Arab nationalist agendas. The Alexandria Protocol made potential domestic implications of unity clearer to domestic actors, inducing leaders' opposition. Efforts to reduce transaction costs were not central; implications for power distribution were unclear; and normative convergence over the proper interpretation of Arabism absent. Tensions between *kawmiyah* (pan-Arab) and *watanyia* (state nationalism) would also influence the League's design.

Design

Membership was restricted on the basis of Arab identity. Both the nature of domestic coalitions and the absence of normative convergence explain the League's design, informal and sovereignty-oriented. The Council was the key organ overseeing a permanent secretariat and six functional committees. All authoritative council decisions required unanimity and were binding *only* on states that accepted them (Macdonald 1965). Article 5 prohibited the use of force to resolve disputes and proposed mediation. However, even unanimous decisions against aggressors would not be binding on disputes over states' "independence, sovereignty or territorial integrity." The Pact thus foreclosed even the mildest intervention in a crucial conflict category. Article 8 codified nonintervention in domestic systems of government. The General Secretary represented pan-Arab aspirations. Although designed to execute Council policies, the Secretariat (235 employees in 1970) expanded and initiated copious activities through 15 specialized organizations, 14 committees, four defense bodies, five economic and monetary funds, and other agencies employing thousands. This was not a lightly bureaucratized institution. Nor were expectations that its design would reduce transaction costs very high. Meetings often led to high contestation.

Evolving pressures for an elusive normative convergence reinforced the original choice favoring informality. Shared language and culture might have obviated more formal arrangements but intense competition for the mantle of Arabism undermined development of focal points. Increasingly diverging interests among ruling coalitions sharpened tensions further. Competing political-economy models obstructed changes toward greater formality (Solingen 2007b). Lebanon's model based on extensive extra-regional trade and commercial and banking interests was threatened there and everywhere else. Protectionist inward-looking, statist, import-substituting and highly militarized models – advanced by Nasser and the Ba'ath in Syria and Iraq – diffused to other countries. These models, oriented toward self-sufficiency and statist entrepreneurship, led to further declines in intra-regional trade. Notably, the League's treaties on trade and capital movements specified that "the provisions of this convention shall not be applicable to articles subject to government monopoly" (Macdonald 1965: 194–198). The external expression of Nasser's import-substitution was akin to what Hirschman (1945) described as imperial commercial strategies, serving Nasser's domestic and regional goals at once. He used trade to induce maximum dependence by neighbors, turning them into raw materials suppliers, diverting Egypt's trade to weaker partners for whom trade utility was higher, and de-industrializing weaker competitors in export markets. Nasser and his bureaucratic and military allies maximized economic profit, military power, and regional influence, all of which sustained and reproduced their power at home.[23] Under the United Arab Republic (UAR) scheme, Egypt required Syria to import industrial goods exclusively from Egypt, paralyzing Syrian-Lebanese trade and restricting Lebanese exports to Egypt. As an open trading *entrepôt* connecting Europe and the Arab world, large segments of Lebanon's commercial class – and some Syrian businessmen – suffered (Hasou 1985). Syrian opposition to Nasser brewed among nationalized private interests and inward-looking, protectionist civil and military factions who proclaimed Syria's secession from the UAR in 1961 (Macdonald 1965). Threatened military industrial complexes, crucial pillars of inward-looking coalitions, resisted the 1963 proposed Syria-Iraq-Egypt unification scheme.

Following Egypt's 1973 war with Israel, Sadat replaced Nasser's model with economic liberalization (*infitah*) and growth, a policy requiring synergies across domestic reform, international aid, and regional stability, including downsizing military expenditures and avoiding war with Israel (military expenditures declined from 52 to 13 percent of GNP between 1975 and 1979). This policy led to the Camp David agreements, a huge chasm within the Arab world, and Egypt's exclusion from the League. Sadat's "Egypt-first" approach required new domestic bases of support. A new relationship with the US and the IMF fostered business interests in tourism, commercial-agriculture, and *munfatihun* ("openers" to the global economy) while threatening the bloated bureaucracy and military-industrial complex. Reforms proceeded in a faltering pattern under Mubarak, whose coalition remained besieged by protectionists, the military complex, Islamists, and Nasserites. Some ruling coalitions throughout the region endorsed incipient economic liberalization and privatization, particularly in Jordan, enhancing cleavages at home and abroad (particularly with Syria and Iraq), further weakening normative convergence within the League.

In sum, the League's experience is compatible with Proposition 2. Design had clear domestic distributional implications, and ruling coalitions favored informality. Beyond that, however, most other conditions suggested by the baseline proposition were not met. First, there were significant concerns that a more formal institution would strengthen hegemonic aspirations. Second, since leaders had little incentive to enhance information and transparency, more formal mechanisms were shunned. Third, normative convergence favoring informality developed over time; Nasserites sought to replace it with more formal unity but convergence on informality was restored by the 1970s. The League's informality thus seemed over-determined, overpowering competing pan-Arab norms favoring formal unity.

Effects

Given its origins and design, the League's limited effects are hardly surprising. There is little evidence that it constrained state behavior, reduced transaction costs, enhanced information, or redefined states' identities. It succeeded in only six of 77 inter-Arab conflicts between 1945 and 1981 (Awad 1994: 153; Hassouna 1975). Comparative studies by Zacher (1979) and Nye (1987) rank the League's success in abating conflict considerably lower than the OAU and the OAS. Although cited as uncommonly successful, the Lebanon-UAR 1958 crisis allowed Nasser to paralyze the League. Only after Lebanon's appeal to the UNSC, and US and British forces intervention to protect Lebanese and Jordanian "territorial integrity," was the League's secretary rushed to draft a resolution agreeable to all (Hasou 1985). League activities regarding Syria's complaints against Nasser were particularly hostile and unsuccessful. Nasser never hid his blueprint for the League, differentiating between "Egypt as a state" and "Egypt as a revolution." The first could seat at League events and conclude agreements, according to Nasser's spokesman Hassanein Heikal. But as a revolution, his regime dealt with Arabs as a single nation, never hesitating to "halt at frontiers…If the Arab League were to be used to paralyze our movement, we must be prepared to freeze [its] operations" (Hasou 1985: 115-116). And so Nasser did, threatening to withdraw from the League when cornered by Syria's complaint.

The League's origins and design all but guaranteed that its implications for power distribution across states would be insignificant and that it would yield little reduction in transaction costs or strengthen normative convergence. These limited effects benefited ruling coalitions in each state, allowing them to entrench themselves in power rather than abrogate sovereign rights on behalf of pan-Arabism. All these suggest significant support for Proposition 3: dominant coalitions could protect inward-looking self-sufficiency, state and military entrepreneurship, import-substitution, and nationalism. These models were hardly suitable blueprints for a regional institution capable of coordinating economic or security affairs.

Nasser and Sadat undermined the League in different ways, rendering it even less effective. Focal points failed to emerge in major crises, including the Baghdad Pact, the 1991 Gulf War, Saddam Hussein's 1990s brinkmanship, the 2003 Iraq War and ensuing debacle, or Iran's nuclear program, among others. The Arab Human Development Report (2002: 121) articulates the relevance of domestic politics best, tracing the fragility and ineffectiveness of Arab regional institutions to "too many regimes [that] cater to powerful entrenched interest groups." Plans for an Arab Common Market (1950s–1970s) never yielded results. A 1981 agreement proposed full exemption from tariffs and non-tariff barriers for manufactures and semi-manufactured goods, with little effect. The 1997 call for a Greater Arab Free Trade Area by 2008 introduced unprecedented schedules for across-the-board elimination of tariffs, tariff-like charges, and non-tariff barriers on industrial goods, but these remained high. The League's share of global exports is 3 percent. This paltry record contrasts with highly coordinated UN voting and anti-Israel activities. As Awad (1994: 150) argued, the League "lived by and for the Arab-Israeli conflict." This preoccupation, according to Gomaa (1977: 267) "accentuated the negative aspect of Arab nationalism and sapped much of its strength." The Israel factor was conducive to unity only intermittently; disagreements also led to fierce encounters on this issue. Against this long history of contestation that depleted the League's potential, the 2002 Saudi peace proposal represented an anomaly, an effective focal point that handed Israel a most difficult diplomatic dilemma largely fueled by its own deep domestic divisions.

Institutions in East Asia and the Middle East: Some comparative findings

Findings for these cases suggest that the nature of dominant domestic coalitions often explains incentives to create institutions, mold them according to their interests, and fine-tune their effects, in line with propositions suggested above. However, baseline forms of these propositions assume that institutional consequences for power, transaction costs, and norms are negligible or hard to estimate. Those conditions were not met half of the time, as consequences became sizeable. Furthermore, the nature of dominant coalitions was sometimes underdetermining, compatible with different institutional outcomes, and often provided no more than permissive conditions for the emergence, design, and effect of institutions.

On origins of institutions

Findings suggest that the role of domestic coalitions is essential for explaining the genesis of all four institutions. ASEAN, APEC, and the League match the circumstances outlined by baseline Proposition 1: domestic coalitions as privileged explanations, given low normative convergence and negligible consequences (of creating institutions) for relative power or transaction costs. The ARF's creation, while compatible with a domestic coalitional perspective, is also congruent with normative convergence around war avoidance and common security. Expectations for reducing transaction costs were arguably more significant for APEC. Overall, however, domestic politics provide an essential supplement to functionalist (efficiency) explanations (Kahler 1995). Higgott (1995) faults functionalist understandings for ignoring linkages between domestic politics and regional cooperation. Indeed, the general complementarity of national policies, argues Haggard (1997: 46) produced greater economic interdependence "without substantial coordination at the regional level." These findings hint that it would be impossible to understand the nature of East Asia's proliferating free trade agreements without proper attention to domestic politics.

Neorealist accounts of institutional origins hinging on hegemony face difficulties in EA. Hegemons may have incentives to build institutions that extend their power but the US did not particularly exhibit such tendencies during APEC and ARF's creation (the only two cases involving US participation here). Neither were ASEAN or the ARF driven by hegemons; middle powers and smaller states provided initial momentum for their creation. Hegemonic arguments do not explain progression from pre to post-institutional environments. More refined neorealist perspectives may explain why weaker states join existing institutions but not why they succeed in creating them or retaining pivotal roles. Weaker states were not mere regime takers here. The ARF also suggests that even great powers – China and the US – may acquiesce to institutions as *faits accomplis* even when they might have preferred the *status-quo ante*, at least initially. Institutions were expected to tame potential supremacy by Japan, China, and the US, or Indonesia's in ASEAN. The basic process of founding contemporary regional institutions seems less about balancing (Rosecrance 2001). Interpreting APEC's emergence as "defensive regionalism" may have merit but the ARF is an inclusive rather than a balancing mechanism. The consequences for power distribution of the Arab League's inception were unclear at the time. Leaders created the League to protect themselves from competing pan-Arab nationalist agendas, regional or home-grown.

Presumed convergence on pan-Arab nationalism may have provided momentum for initial negotiations to create the Arab League. Ironically, however, the League was created to *counter* this pan-Arab design. Tensions between *kawmiyah* and *watanyia* confirmed little convergence over the proper interpretation of Arab norms (Barnett 1998). The Alexandria Protocol made the potential domestic implications of unity clear to domestic actors, pushing Arab leaders to create an institution that would reduce pressures for unification. Normative convergence appears even less relevant for explaining the origin of East Asian institutions.

On design of institutions

Evidence suggests that domestic coalitions are under-determining explanations for institutional design in ASEAN, the ARF, and the League. Their design was compatible with the interests of dominant coalitions to be sure, but those interests were also compatible with other designs. Furthermore, Proposition 2's baseline conditions privileging domestic coalitions in explaining design are absent in these cases. The implications of design for relative power, transaction costs, and norms were not negligible. Yet these three variables too were under-determining, compatible with alternative designs. Only APEC's blueprint matches the conditions of baseline Proposition 2, where domestic coalitions do most of the explanatory work, compromising over an informal APEC that accommodates diverse stages and forms of economic liberalization and export-led growth. The informal design of ASEAN and the ARF was compatible with the nature of domestic coalitions, low normative convergence, and relative-power considerations. The informal design of the League was over-determined by the interests of ruling coalitions, efforts to stem hegemonic aspirations, and the defeat of pan-Arab norms of formal unity.

All East Asian cases suggest compatibility between internationalizing coalitions and informal institutional design. Yet Kahler (2000) notes the compatibility between internationalizing coalitions and legalized institutional forms.[24] Such coalitions can indeed emphasize formality to lock preferences in, but they can also cooperate in the absence of institutions or via alternate institutional options. Informality allowed coalitions with comparable – but not identical – platforms of engagement with the global economy to advance regional cooperation and stability, transcend disparate domestic institutions (democratic or not) and inward-looking political opponents, and logroll supportive constituencies (ABAC and CEO in APEC). Ravenhill (1998) does not find formalization compelling, emphasizing that both APEC and the ARF reflect reliance on economic growth to soften tensions. This synergistic view of economics and security can be traced to these coalitions' incentives to promote economic growth, domestic and regional stability, FDI, and global access. Gruber (2000) similarly traces EA's flexible arrangements to elites that enjoy political stability and little domestic opposition. Domestic coalitions thus offer only a baseline for understanding institutional design, albeit an important one at that. Ruling coalitions differed significantly across the two regions: military and associated industrial complexes had far more political clout in the Middle East, where export-oriented manufacturing was much weaker politically (Solingen 2007b). ASEAN and APEC commitments, by contrast, "reflect an innate trust in the virtues of free markets fostered by a homogeneous merchant class" (Inoguchi 1997). That was never the case for the League, which adopted unanimity over consensus and – unlike APEC and the ARF – shunned "open regionalism." The League and ASEAN retained exclusivist regional memberships instead.

Notwithstanding the compatibility between dominant coalitions and institutional design in all four organizations, such designs reflect more than the enabling conditions that gave them life; their forms may differ from their creators' intention. The informal and consensual nature of East Asian institutions provides a useful natural experiment for exploring their discourses, communicative logics, persuasion and socialization patterns (Johnston 1999). Constructivism has forced attention to blueprints of normative convergence around specific institutional forms. However, the task of identifying convergence *a priori*, or tracing intricate normative effects (as in the League's case), raises other methodological and conceptual challenges. Normative convergence around informality among ASEAN members may have been higher than in APEC or the ARF. Yet there was significant normative contestation in ASEAN as well, particularly over democracy and non-interference. Furthermore, steps toward progressive intrusiveness (arguably on Myanmar) and greater formality may question ASEAN's presumed long-standing norm-convergence. Above all, similarities in design across the two regions suggest that regional institutions may not be as peculiar or idiosyncratic as many region-specific (frequently norm-based) interpretations would have it.

Finally, the informal and sovereignty-sensitive nature of these institutions is consistent with neorealist premises that only powerful states can endow institutions with more binding procedures. Informality is compatible with "talking shops." For Grieco (1997), EA's flexible institutions reflect sensitivity to relative gains. Ravenhill (1998) finds changes in US relative power, particularly after the Cold War, to potentially explain the *timing* of APEC's (and the ARF's) emergence but not their design. The ARF, he argues, is not about balancing power but about collective security, transparency, and economic and trans-boundary issues. Overall, relative-power considerations do not capture well the important role played by smaller powers in designing these institutions. The consensus rule precluded major powers from advancing their agenda at the expense of the rest. The League's design – codified in Article 8 – reflected efforts to avoid hegemony no less than the preferences of dominant ruling coalitions.

On effects of institutions

All four cases validate expectations that institutions benefit their creators. Yet only ASEAN and the League meet Proposition 3's baseline conditions, privileging domestic coalitions in explaining institutional effects. The effects of APEC and the ARF were compatible with the preferences of those coalitions. However, APEC also diffused normative consensus around open regionalism and market-driven liberalization – hard to extricate from coalitional preferences – and arguably reduced transaction costs. Similarly, ARF statements matched the preferences of ruling coalitions for regional peace and stability, but institutional effects were marginal. Furthermore, the ARF's cooperative security ideology and consensus principles are found to have developed "habits of cooperation" (Johnston 2008). East Asian institutions had minimal effects on the whole, and various approaches provide plausible accounts for this outcome. Internationalizing coalitions and their informal networks – more than regional institutions – provided the foundation of EA's cooperative regional order. Nonetheless institutions offered venues for advancing shared objectives of economic growth via engagement with the global economy, and regional stability. These institutions may have benefited ruling coalitions at earlier stages of internationalization the most, by providing regional cover for domestic policies that they favored in any case.

One may also conceive of East Asian institutions as shaping an identity pivoted on global markets and institutions. However, standard constructivist studies of these institutions have not revolved around such identity thus far. Most have focused on "Asian values," sovereignty and non-intervention. Why such values have persisted and whether they will endure is a matter of contention. Discontinuities will require explanations for sudden departures. Neorealist accounts may be partially vindicated by this penchant for state sovereignty and the small magnitude of institutional effects. And yet, despite skepticism over these effects, it may no longer be possible to assume that an EA free of institutions would have completely resembled the one we observe today. Even hegemonic preferences – of the US – changed from the pre- to the post-institutional setting for APEC and the ARF (Krauss and Pempel 2003). Furthermore, these institutions helped pave the way for ASEAN + 3, the East Asian Summit, and the Six Party Talks, among others. The first developed financial arrangements following the Chiang Mai Initiative that compel further exploration along the lines suggested here. A presumably emerging cultural "Asianness" seems less the product of regional institutions than of three decades of exchange, primarily but not only economic, within and beyond the region. "Asianness" could thus be an unanticipated by-product of internationalizing coalitions oriented to the global economy as much as the region's.

Conclusions

In an effort to transcend conceptual debates in the analysis of regional institutions, this article outlines a research strategy sensitive to scope conditions, joint methodological shortcomings, and the institutional puzzle at hand (Kahler 1999), in this case: what explains the genesis, design, and effects of regional institutions? I introduce three main contingent propositions. First, domestic coalitions (internationalizing, inward-looking) are best positioned to explain the *genesis* of regional institutions when the consequences of their creation for regional power distribution or transaction costs are negligible or unclear, and where there is little normative convergence around the institution's creation. Second, domestic coalitions are likely to explain the *design* of regional institutions best when the consequences of design for relative power or transaction costs are negligible or not easily measurable, and when there is little normative convergence around a favored design. Third, regional institutions are more likely to benefit the domestic coalitions that created them when institutional effects on power and transaction costs are negligible or not easily measurable, and there is little normative convergence. The baseline forms of these propositions assume that the institution's consequences for power, transaction costs, and norms are negligible or hard to estimate. However, those baseline conditions were not met at least half of the time for the cases examined here; implications for relative power, norms, and transaction costs were sometimes sizeable.

Findings from these cases also suggest that the domestic argument was less challenged by other accounts in explaining institutional genesis but more so in explaining their design. The nature of domestic coalitions quite often explains incentives to create institutions but do not singlehandedly determine their design; power, ideas, and efficiency considerations can be relevant sources of institutional variation. While generally benefiting the domestic coalitions that gave them life, institutions also have intended, unintended, and unanticipated effects on relative power, norms, and transaction costs. Furthermore, the nature of domestic coalitions can be underdetermining, compatible with different institutional designs, often providing no more than permissive conditions for the institution's emergence and effects. Although fruitful as an analytical point of departure, the propositions also outline scope conditions which delimit their utility for explaining institutional genesis, design, and effects. Similar propositions can be crafted around alternative points of departure, including norms, international power distribution, or transaction costs.

Looking at EA from an EU perspective, a common but often unproductive comparison, has led many to consider the absence of formal multilateral institutions in EA puzzling. Yet formal institutions may be less compelling when members' time-horizons are long, gains from cooperation are repetitive, and peer pressure is important (Harris 2000). As Lipson (1991) suggests, informal agreements are less subject to public scrutiny and competing bureaucratic pressures, and hence are well-suited for changing conditions. They are also useful under uncertainty about future benefits or concerns with asymmetric future benefits, conditions encountered repeatedly in the cases examined here. Furthermore, problems of imperfect information and incentives to defect plague both verbal declarations and more formal agreements. The cases indeed cast doubt on blanket functionalist premises that formal institutions arise to manage interdependence. No such institutions emerged in a rapidly growing interdependent EA; the Arab League materialized in the midst of very low interdependence. Enhancing transparency and overcoming uncertainty may have played a role in the creation of the ARF and perhaps APEC but less so ASEAN or the League. Whatever the case may be, these objectives must be examined on the basis of *a priori* determination of actors' motives, often traceable to dominant domestic coalitions of state and private actors.

Findings also suggest extensive gaps in each perspective's ability to explain institutional effects singlehandedly. Neorealist approaches are not equipped to address constraining or constitutive (intended or unintended) effects of institutions on states, unless they stem from hegemonic assertion. Neorealist accounts emphasize the end of the Cold War, regional changes in power distribution, and changes in US relative power as the most likely variables explaining the genesis, design, and effects of regional organizations in these two regions. However, US power hardly explains their emergence and evolution, or why they were able to "anchor," "tame," or coopt would-be hegemons (China in the ARF, Egypt in the League). Functionalist accounts reveal difficulties in measuring transaction-cost reductions *a priori* and even *a posteriori*. Ample information (pivotal to efficiency accounts) and robust trust (pivotal to norm-based accounts) are said to obviate the need for institutions or amplify their effects. Yet there is little empirical work specifically gauging shifting levels of trust and transparency in these cases.[25] Such probes are difficult to design methodologically but remain important challenges. Changes in identity and norms are also hard to weigh and often take longer to germinate. Although neoliberal institutionalist studies have advanced our theoretical understanding of institutional origins, domestic politics provide more complete accounts of why institutions emerge, in whose interest they operate, when they are allowed to play a significant role, and why they may not be vital to – or a *sine qua non* for – cooperation. The preferences of domestic coalitions may be important in explaining genesis, but institutions do not subsequently evolve merely in perfunctory response to those preferences. Institutions can change the nature of coalitional competition at home, alter the preferences of coalitions in power and in the opposition, create new and competing constituencies, and socialize erstwhile adversaries (Haas 1964). Further probes on the utility of this approach may come from counterfactual consideration of *different* domestic coalitions that would have led to *similar* institutional arrangements as the ones observed.

Clearly, the applicability of these propositions to the cases analyzed here does not imply that they necessarily explain all regional institutions; this remains a matter of empirical investigation. The main purpose here was to advance a research agenda that puts extant literature to work in more productive and inclusive ways than has been the case for conventional studies of regional institutions. The propositions offer a foundation for a comparative research program that takes each approach seriously while delimiting scope conditions. Some complementarities between functionalist and domestic coalitional analysis are apparent; norm-based and coalition-based accounts are not inimical either. To begin with, coalitions are an outcome of leaders' efforts to coalesce both material and ideal interests. Furthermore, institutions can arguably transform the identity and interests of leaders and constituencies, both in power and in the opposition. Although some impute ASEAN leaders with developing a regional identity where none existed, a prior question should be what led leaders to converge on that objective in the first place.[26] Both domestic threats to ruling coalitions and reliance on growth and prosperity as legitimating governing tools are critical parts of the answer, yet they have been mere analytical sideshows in constructivist accounts.

Given EA's unparalleled integration in the global economy, it is particularly baffling that norm-based institutional accounts have largely overlooked systematic explanations of domestic changes related to internationalization (an important exception is Berger 2003). The prominence of *musjawarah* and *mufakat* is often mentioned in virtual detachment from this reality. Yet more institutionalization is taking place in EA along the lines of preferential trade agreements and growth triangles than perhaps any other institutional form. The analytical neglect of internationalization, and of the domestic coalitions that sanctioned it, obscures the most fundamental feature differentiating EA from other industrializing regions. Taking internationalization for granted is out of character with norm-based approaches. Would the ascribed normative sources of East Asian institutions have had the same effects absent the underlying coalitional landscape throughout the region? Would ruling coalitions antagonistic to the global economy have yielded the same institutional outcomes that are now traced to "common" culture? Counterfactual analysis and comparisons between most recent and earlier coalitional backdrops (Sukarno and *Konfrontasi*, for instance) provide some answers to these questions. Longitudinal comparisons require a cultural understanding of pre-ASEAN relations – when the region was known as the "Balkans of the East" – able to explain the *absence* of institutions at the time, independently of the domestic coalitional backdrop against which such relations unfolded.

In sum, institutionalist scholarship is now open to more nuanced, subtle, and contingent formulations than those suggested by rigid standard approaches. Finnemore and Sikkink (1998) urge a proper specification of the logic applicable to given actors under specific circumstances. Johnston (1999, 2008) provides a sophisticated blend of rationalist and constructivist insights, as do Hemmer and Katzenstein (2002). Gruber's (2000: 259) power-based theory looks beyond state preferences, arguing that it "makes more sense to talk about the preferences of the particular parties, groups, and individuals who govern them." Keohane (2001: 4) suggests that functionalist understandings are incomplete without the presence of "political entrepreneurs with both the capacity and the incentives to invest in the creation of institutions and the monitoring and enforcement of rules." Checkel (2001) points to domestic arrangements as delimiting the causal role of persuasion and social learning. Rosecrance (2001: 154) suggests that far more research is required for institutionalist theory to calibrate the relationship between incentives of institutional precursors – states, leaders, coalitions – and institutional results down the road. Institutions created by such precursors may, down the road, benefit them less than they benefit newcomers. These analytical directions bode well for the effort to place conceptual perspectives at the service of understanding institutions rather than the other way round, namely, turning the analysis of institutions primarily into an arena for broader, ultimately sterile debates.

Notes

1. *Genesis* here refers to events, social forces, and processes leading to institutional creation. *Design* refers to attributes including degree of formality, autonomy, and membership rules. *Effects* address the size and nature of the institution's impact (constraining state behavior, enhancing information, re-defining actors' identity) and their primary beneficiaries.
2. For important exceptions, see Moravcsik (1998) and Acharya and Johnston (2007).
3. A "logic of appropriateness" dominates when identities and their implications are clear (presumably to the actors) but not so the implications for preferences or relative capabilities. On focal points as more important when there is uncertainty about power and distributional impacts, see Garrett and Weingast (1993). On focal points as dominant under crisis or uncertainty, see Campbell and Pedersen (2001).
4. As with international power and transaction costs, measuring normative convergence is no easy feat. Yet there are situations where a given norm seems evidently salient or reflect low normative polarization (Finnemore and Sikkink 1998).
5. On equifinality and multiple interaction effects, see George and Bennett (2005).
6. Solingen (1999, 2000, 2005a, 2005b, 2007a, 2007b); Barnett and Solingen (2007). Extensive interviews were conducted in Singapore (December 1999, March 2000, September 2000, June 2003, May 2004, August 2005, September 2007); Bangkok (June 2003), Hanoi (1999); Tokyo (March 2001, February-March 2003, June 2003, September 2003, November 2004, March 2005, July 2005, July 2006); Shanghai (October 2001, August 2005), Beijing (December 2003, July 2004), Seoul (June 2000), New York (March 2000), and Washington DC (June 2004, October 2005).
7. "Open regionalism" enhances regional economic exchange without violating WTO requirements (most-favored-nation rule) or discriminating against extra-regional partners (Ravenhill 2000). East Asian regional institutions support rather than substitute global institutions. Open regionalism in security involves efforts to signal geographical openness and inclusiveness (Solingen 2005a).
8. ASEAN included Thailand, Singapore, Indonesia, Malaysia, and the Philippines as 1967 founding members; Brunei, Vietnam, Laos, Myanmar, and Cambodia joined subsequently.
9. The model was imprinted in ASEAN's Bangkok Declaration: "to accelerate… economic growth, social progress, and cultural development in the region…in the spirit of equality and partnership in order to strengthen the foundation for a prosperous and peaceful community of Southeast Asian Nations" (www.aseansec.org/1212.htm).
10. Members have not resorted to dispute settlement under the TAC, favoring bilateral management of conflicts and the International Court of Justice (ICJ) (www.asean.or.id).
11. The 10 dialogue partners are Australia, Canada, China, the EU, India, Japan, Russia, New Zealand, South Korea, and the US.

204 Sources, design and effects

12 "Asean urged to become more open to change," *The Nation (Bangkok)*, June 22, 2000.
13 www.aseansec.org/summit/vision9//htm
14 www.aseansec.org/15259.htm; Solingen (2004).
15 Australia, Brunei, Canada, Indonesia, Japan, South Korea, Malaysia, New Zealand, Philippines, Singapore, Thailand, and the US were founding members. The inclusion of China, Hong Kong, Taiwan, Mexico, Papua New-Guinea, Chile, Peru, Russia, and Vietnam brought it up to 21 members.
16 Pacific Economic Cooperation Conference; Pacific Trade and Development Conference (PAFTAD), a transnational group of market-oriented economists; and Pacific Basin Economic Committee (PBEC), a business initiative established in 1968 (Ravenhill 1998). APEC's Business Advisory Board (ABAC) included three business representatives appointed by each government (Ravenhill 2006).
17 The ARF includes Australia, Bangladesh, Brunei, Cambodia, Canada, China, European Union, India, Indonesia, Japan, North and South Korea, Laos, Malaysia, Myanmar, Mongolia, New Zealand, Pakistan, Papua New Guinea, Philippines, Russia, Singapore, Thailand, Timor Leste, United States, and Vietnam.
18 Personal interviews (Bangkok, Singapore, Tokyo, June–July 2003).
19 State enterprises, agriculture, and local governments resisting openness were also part of China's coalition opposing internationalization (Christensen 2001).
20 With Libya, Algeria, Kuwait, Morocco, Tunisia, Sudan, Bahrain, Palestine, South Yemen, Oman, Qatar, the U.A.E., Somalia, Mauritania, and Djibouti the League grew to 22 members by the 1970s.
21 They also demanded French withdrawal from Syria/Lebanon and rejected a Jewish state in Palestine (Tripp 1995).
22 Egyptian supporters of a pan-Arab agenda were few but important at the time (Macdonald 1965; Barnett and Solingen 2007).
23 Hitler's Germany was the imperial strategy's textbook. Arab nationalists considered European fascism "a virile politico-economic system superior to other Western models" (Macdonald 1965: 106).
24 Legalization does not necessarily contribute to higher compliance (Lutz and Sikkink 2000). Furthermore, Inoguchi (1997) finds greater institutional formality to be potentially detrimental to regional cooperation in East Asia.
25 Roberts (2007) found majorities in most ASEAN member states who mistrust their neighbors.
26 Katzenstein and Shiraishi (1997) trace informal regional institutions to common domestic norms favoring informality, a feature that would apply only to East Asian members of APEC and the ARF.

9

THE TRIPLE LOGIC OF THE EUROPEAN–MEDITERRANEAN PARTNERSHIP

Hindsight and foresight

The Mediterranean Basin joins industrialized and industrializing countries that are often identified with at least two important cleavages: the rich/poor or North/South division, and the alleged civilizational tensions between Islam and the West, particularly following September 11, 2001. The Barcelona process or European Mediterranean Partnership (EMP) emerged to bridge across those cleavages. This project was part of a broader scheme of European Union (EU) evolution in the post-Cold War era, one involving spatial and functional expansion, including efforts to design a common EU foreign policy. Both classical security issues (the availability of non-conventional weapons in the Middle East, terrorism, heavy dependence on oil and natural gas) and "new" security issues (migration, drugs, human rights violations, environmental degradation) influenced EU concerns with the political fate of the Mediterranean basin. These concerns led the Spanish presidency of the EU to organize a conference in Barcelona in November 1995, gathering the EU-15 and 12 South Mediterranean (SM henceforth) states. The outcome was the Barcelona Declaration or Euro-Mediterranean Partnership (EMP) designed to promote peace and prosperity in the Mediterranean region.

The EMP process brings to relief three institutional pillars of crucial relevance for enhancing cooperation across this mix cluster of internationalizing and inward-looking states: market reforms, democratization, and the role of regional institutions. These three institutions provided the "triple logic" or foundational rationale for the EMP. Yet the inherent wisdom, desirability, and motivations behind these logics was heavily contested by actors in North and South alike, given the different domestic distributional effects they entailed. The three pillars were rather incipient when the EMP was launched and remain so a decade and a half later.

---

* I would like to acknowledge support from the United States Institute of Peace and the Institute on Global Conflict and Cooperation, and excellent comments from Daniel Nelson, Andrea Goldstein, Wolf-Dieter Eberwein, and anonymous reviewers. The opinions, findings, and conclusions expressed in this publication do not necessarily reflect the views of the USIP.

The logic of economic reform

Economic proposals in the Barcelona Declaration included the establishment of a Free Trade Area between the EU and SM countries by 2010 and the removal of tariff and non-tariff barriers by SM partners. Economic aid and loans (European Investment Bank) were to benefit the SM's private sector, to encourage structural reform and privatization, and to attract foreign investment, a central priority of EU policy-makers. MEDA II (2000) expected the "structural adjustment facility" financed under MEDA I to target more specifically those reforms necessary for free trade with the EU on the one hand, and to streamline EU decision-making on the other.[1] The underlying objective was an effort to bring SM states into an increasingly freer and globalized economy to help them overcome their many socio-economic and political difficulties. The Commission proposed that MEDA allocations be closely tied to implementation of economic reforms and privatization.

Comparisons with other regions highlight the lagging progress of entrenched SM political-economy models. By the early 1990s, the Middle East had become the least self-sufficient area in the world in food, with among the highest rates of infant mortality and illiteracy (particularly female), high rates of unemployment and underemployment, enormous income disparities, high inflation, overvalued real exchange rates, and uncompetitive goods, much of it the legacy of statism and protectionism (Richards and Waterbury 1990; Bill and Springborg 1990; Owen 1992). Egypt's budget deficit quintupled from 1975 to 1989 and its external debt increased from 2 billion (1972) to 40 billion (1990). The UN Development Program's (1998) human development index combining life expectancy, education, and income ranked Egypt and Morocco 112th and 125th, respectively by the mid-1990s (Tunisia was 83rd). Pakistan and India ranked lower (138th and 139th) whereas South Korea ranked 30th, Thailand 59th, and Malaysia 60th. Average adult literacy was 56 percent in the Arab world but 98 percent in East Asia (excluding China) and much worse for women (36 percent in Egypt). Radical Islamist movements have shown little proclivity to support female education, known to be a critical factor in reversing birth rates and improving economic conditions.

Such statistics have been frequently cited in efforts to induce economic reform in MENA countries. But what is the underlying logic presumably connecting economic reform with regional cooperation? On this, there is far less agreement than meets the eye. The relationship between interdependence and conflict/cooperation is not a simple one (Solingen 2003). One effort to link the process of economic reform to the nature of regional relations focuses on the nature of political coalitions that emerge as a consequence of internationalization and economic reform (Solingen 1998, 2001a). Politicians worldwide rely on material and ideal aspects of internationalization to broker political coalitions across constituencies that respond differently to the opportunities and constraints of internationalization. Three ideal-typical coalitions tend to form: internationalizing, inward-looking and hybrid. Driven by their varying composition and incentives, these coalitions embrace different grand strategies regarding domestic and international political economy and institutions.

Both qualitative and quantitative studies found internationalizing ruling coalitions to be more prone to intensify their country's trade openness, expand exports, attract foreign investment, curb wasteful military-industrial complexes, shun WMDs, defer to international economic and security regimes, and advance regional cooperative orders that reinforce all those objectives. Inward-looking coalitions were found to restrict and reduce trade openness, exports, and foreign investment while building expansive military-industrial complexes and WMDs, challenging international security and economic regimes and exacerbating civic, religious, and ethnic-nationalist differentiation by emphasizing territoriality, sovereignty, and self-reliance. Coherent coalitional grand strategies are hard to find in the real world but the links between a commitment to internationalization and regional cooperation and stability have gained empirical confirmation.

Different coalitional combinations in different regions create different regional orders, "identities," and shared expectations about conflict and cooperation and, conversely, are affected by them. Inter-regional comparisons suggest that where internationalizing coalitions became dominant in a region there were better positioned to establish zones of stable peace, avoiding aggressive steps and mutually adjusting to resolve outstanding disputes. Dominant ruling coalitions in ASEAN states, for instance, produced relatively peaceful stability on the ashes of earlier wars. Internationalizing coalitions in Latin America's Southern Cone made MERCOSUR and denuclearization a reality in the 1990s. Even in the Middle East, proto-internationalizers made cooperative strides in the early 1990s with the Oslo and Multilateral Middle East Peace Process, blocked by recalcitrant region-wide inward-looking forces. The emergence of internationalizing "zones of peace" challenge inward-looking coalitions, undermining all pillars of their grand strategy from the merits of economic closure to the advantages of militarization. The evolution of ASEAN states had that effect on Vietnam, Kampuchea, Laos, and Myanmar. In time an internationalizing critical mass can overturn the domestic coalitional competition within inward-looking states easing their eventual transformation and inclusion. There is much skepticism, however, on the odds of the Middle East achieving that critical mass anytime soon.

War zones are more likely to emerge in dominant inward-looking contexts where the logic of their grand strategy – militarization, nationalist brinkmanship – tends to reproduce itself regionally. Kim-Il Sung's attack on South Korea (both ruled by inward-looking coalitions at the time), Perón's intimidations of neighbors with a fusion bomb, Nasser's encroachment in Yemen and blockade of Israel in 1967, Sadat's 1973 October War, Begin's invasion of Lebanon, Assad's threats to Israel and invasion of Lebanon, Arafat's threats to Jordan and Lebanon, Galtieri's attack on the Malvinas, Indo–Pakistani military encounters and nuclear swaggering, Saddam's invasions of Iran and Kuwait and Iran's threats to Saddam Hussein and others are all instances of this pattern.

The EU has evolved as a zone of stable peace and sought to transform inward-looking and hybrid coalitions to extend that zone southward. Cyprus, Malta, Israel (particularly under Labor-led coalitions), and Turkey, and possibly Morocco, Tunisia, and Jordan, were viewed as most promising from the standpoint of internationalizing shifts. Some had preferential trade agreements with the EU and the US, reduced tariffs, and stimulated private sector employment and foreign investment. Under Sadat's *infitah* ("opening up") initiative in the mid-1970s, Egypt began a slow process of liberalizing economic sectors, often providing a paradigm for lagging structural adjustment, regulatory reform, privatization, and trade liberalization (Cassandra, 1995).

Unsurprisingly from the perspective of the coalitional argument outlined above, Jordan, Morocco, Turkey, Egypt, and Tunisia strongly supported the Oslo and multilateral peace processes, regarded as a *sine qua non* for regional stability and economic development. Riad Al-Khouri (1994) made those connections clear, pointing to Jordan's economic hopes as riding on the peace process, which would allow for a reduced defense budget (over 30 percent of government spending) and enhanced attractiveness to foreign investors, with Jordan assuming its rightful economic role. Vociferous fundamentalism, he argued, was belligerent, xenophobic and anathema to peace and foreign investment. Al-Khouri's logic was shared among internationalizing quarters elsewhere in the region.

However, Islamist movements opposed to internationalization are not the only inward-looking political forces in the region. No less resistant to internationalization and its domestic political and economic implications is Syria's secular ruling coalition. Repression of the Islamist opposition has been harshest in Syria. The Assad's vast national security apparatus is a prime example of vested interests that would lose their *raison d'être* with regional peace and economic liberalization. This entrenched, oversized, Ba'athist state has largely resisted economic reform despite incipient steps in the 1980s that all but preserved the privileged position of statist sectors. State managers, military and security bureaus countered nascent private commercial and industrial groups, many of whom favored peace settlements. Syria's inward-looking regime kept Syria (and Lebanon) apart from most regional peace initiatives including the 1990s multilateral process. The "outer ring" of the Southern and Eastern Mediterranean arch, including Iraq, Iran, Sudan and others have similarly resisted meaningful economic reforms. No critical mass of internationalizers has prevailed over that SM arch. Progress has arguably been slower than virtually any other region and political resistance to economic openness remains strong. This outcome has largely frustrated MEDA's expectations regarding foreign investment.

The logic of democracy

The Barcelona process also aimed at encouraging "good governance," democracy and human rights. In the European experience, stable and mature democracies are considered to be better suited to deal with ethnic and religious fragmentation than autocracies. Differences can be channeled through established political parties and legal institutions able to adjudicate along more or less neutral (civic) lines. Only democracy and accountability, in this view, can guarantee human rights and personal freedoms, and democratic clusters are more likely to safeguard peace. Despite contradictory logics of democratization in the Middle East discussed below, the commitment of European publics to these principles makes it hard to envisage an EU Mediterranean policy that does not advance those norms. Democracy is seen as a win-win expected to deliver human rights to the SM and peaceful interactions with the EU.

Yet democratization in the SM has been rather slow relative to Latin America, Eastern Europe, East Asia, and sub-Saharan Africa. There was incipient but piecemeal movement towards selected democratic procedures in the 1990s, marked by significant reversals.[2] Morocco, a pioneer in its tolerance for freedom of the press and association with a relatively strong civil society (in regional terms), has seen some barriers placed on the monarchy. By the late 1990s the government, although appointed by the late King Hassan, was led by the traditional opposition. King Mohammed introduced additional improvements in representation. Jordan experienced competitive parliamentary elections since 1989 and a lively press debate over domestic and foreign policy, with intermittent setbacks since. Egypt restricted political participation through electoral laws and procedures that favored the ruling National Democratic Party, and convicted Muslim Brotherhood, human rights and pro-democracy organizations including noted scholar Saad Eddin Ibrahim. In line with modal SM electoral results, Tunisia's President Ben Ali "won" elections with nearly 100 percent of the vote. Palestinians elected their president and Legislative Council in their first free, internationally supervised elections in January 1996 but President Arafat precluded genuine political participation. Syria's highly authoritarian state placed stiff boundaries on Lebanese efforts to democratize. Pushed by strong EU incentives Turkey advanced farthermost in the process of democratization with the electoral victory of the Justice and Development Party (AKP) in November 2002.

Democratization-from-above – launched by ruling coalitions with varying degrees of support from powerful societal actors – coopted influential elites while placing strict controls on the expansion of political rights. EMP initiatives, including the development of networks of human rights organizations, economic and defense institutes, private organizations and NGOs were expected to reinforce democratization, economic reform, and regional cooperation. Yet EU Foreign Ministers' meeting in Marseilles (November 2000) deferred the adoption of a proposed Charter for Peace and Stability promoting human rights, conflict prevention, and crisis management. Then External Relations Commissioner Christopher Patten (2001) declared that "this was clearly not the right moment" and "we cannot expect wholesale changes to cultural traditions overnight." Such statements and MEDA's minuscule budget for the promotion of democracy and the rule of law in the SM reveal inconsistencies in EU efforts. Ambiguous EU practices made initiatives in the third basket of the Barcelona Process (euphemistically labelled "society and culture" to avoid pushback by SM counterparts) hardly effective. Yet the deplorable state of democracy, accountability, and the rule of law throughout the region has deep roots within the region, largely in the entrenched models of political survival that have lasted for several decades.

The logic of regional institutions

The merits of regional institutions in the eyes of EU officials and publics have been guided by the notion that "if it worked in Europe, why not everywhere?" The EU experience has had a profound influence in international relations regarding the role of regional institutions in cooperation. However, cooperation can come about even where there is either little integration or institutions whereas conflict is possible in the presence of both. Coalitional analysis across various regions supports this generalization regarding drivers of regional conflict and cooperation. The Arab League's record in this regard has been rather dismal and economic barriers among Arab states never effectively receded despite a decades-old rhetoric of integration. The GCC may be an exception. Institutions such as the Korean Peninsula Energy Development Organization (KEDO) ultimately failed to transform inward-looking North Korea into a cooperative denuclearized partner. A dense institutional framework in Latin America failed to advance Argentine-Brazilian cooperation over decades marked by guarded regional relations, minimal economic exchange and hazardous nuclear competition. Only dramatic domestic coalitional reversals in the 1990s incepted novel institutions such as Mercosur, whose effectiveness could not outlast their creators. Internationalizing coalitions, not institutions, deepened Southern Cone cooperation.

Strong belief in the role of institutions in cooperation explains the EU's active role in the Multilateral Middle East Peace Process (1993–1995). MENA Economic Conferences became an instrumental venue for promoting regional reconciliation through economic development, openness, and foreign investment. World Economic Forum organizers sought to stimulate privatization, new stock exchanges and capital markets, protocols on trade and regional agreements in transportation, energy and tourism, GDP growth, and rapid industrialization. Yet progress was slow and piecemeal, and effective regional institutions had a hard time emerging among SM states either in the inter-Arab or Arab–Israeli arenas.

Some SM actors regarded the EMP process as a "hub and spoke" model that competed with MENA integration processes. Yet repeated integrative efforts within MENA never took off. MENA's intra-regional exports remained about 8 percent of total exports for decades. Furthermore, integration with the rest of the world does not necessarily detract from intra-regional integration, as evidenced by East Asia and Mercosur's early years. Integration with extra-regional countries can change domestic political economies and improve intra-regional economic relations. EMP initiatives could complement and catalyze MENA's regional integration. On the whole, however, the prospects of deep and broad cooperation across the SM members were weakened by dominant inward-looking models of political survival, which also undermined EU-SM cooperation.

Dilemmas and hurdles in the logic of Barcelona

In sum, the following mutually reinforcing dilemmas and difficulties plagued the Barcelona process from within the SM, within the EU, and across the two.

Liberalization sequences

Democracy, economic reform, and multilateral cooperation do not obtain automatically, linearly, or inevitably. Leaders of SM states have been haunted by the dilemma of phasing this multifaceted process of change in, or run the risk of being phased out by it. Which will take place is hard to foresee. This first option has a second-order dilemma folded into it: leaders seem deadlocked between "democratic efficiency" arguments (democratization facilitates economic reform, helps build new political coalitions to overcome opponents of reform) and "authoritarian advantage" models illustrated by China and other East Asian tigers. Predictions about which model might prevail are hindered by what Kuran (1991) labeled "the predictability of unpredictability" or the imperfect observability of real private preferences under authoritarian rule in most of the Middle East, a phenomenon that foiled predictions of Eastern European democratization and marketization pre-1989.

The theocracy trap

Uncertainty about popular values and preferences underlies another quandary: the evolution of Islamist tendencies in the SM. Ruling coalitions and secular segments of society throughout the region confront a dilemma fueled by the fear that democratization may not lead to democracy but to Islamist theocracies. Political inclusion of Islamist movements (in Jordan, for instance) appeared to have led to diminishing political returns, perhaps overstating the threat from Islamist forces. Iran may also be posed for a favorable transition to more democratic institutions but these are forcefully resisted by powerful inward-looking forces including the Revolutionary Guards, clerics, state enterprises, and the judiciary. The challenge of protecting the integrity of democratizing institutions so that even a small plurality of votes cannot undermine the process remains.

Regional, sub-regional, or global multilateralism?

SM states expressed disappointment with EU economic proposals that fell short of any significant lowering of barriers to SM agricultural exports, which powerful national EU interests opposed. EU agricultural policies have adverse distributional effects on some constituencies, with self-defeating implications for the very reforms the Euro-Med Partnership seeks to achieve. Yet making economic reform in the SM countries contingent on EU policies seems wrongheaded as well. Integration into a *global* trading and investment regime has inherent advantages particularly if accompanied by sensible and equitable privatization and safety-nets. FTAs are not always compatible with full commitment to global multilateralism but can provide useful stepping stones for broader liberalization efforts.

What about the outer ring?

Whatever difficulties the EU faces with the pace of transformation of SM partners, they pale in comparison with the prospects for the "outer ring" (Iraq, Sudan, Iran, and Libya, not part of the EMP) to make meaningful inroads on the EMP's three institutional pillars. The outer ring adds new complexities and uncertainties including dilemmas regarding WMDs and terrorism. Progress made through the Barcelona process could help fend off destabilizing effects of outer-ring actors on

SM partners. Inducing peaceful economic transformations in the SM, however, can hardly be done without addressing outer ring spoilers.

EU baroqueness vs. crisis responsiveness

Challenges emanating from SM partners and outer ring spoilers prove too elusive for the EU's baroque design. There were difficulties implementing even minimal consensus arrived at the Barcelona process (on human rights, for instance) and little progress on crucial issues in the CFSP agenda. The debacle over Iraq brought this issue to the fore. More broadly, many continue to question the ability of the EU's complex institutional framework to respond to a rapidly changing SM. Considering the potential magnitude of the threats to EU stability and prosperity, no dramatic effort to advance effective change in the SM seems apparent.

Nesting Israel/Palestine into the triple logic

The Israeli-Palestinian conflict has been an important variable, although clearly not the main barrier to advancing the Barcelona process. Virtually all the dilemmas and hurdles identified above – slow economic reform and democratization, the outer ring, the theocracy trap – affect this conflict. Despite significant initial strides, the 1993 Oslo breakthrough collapsed under the weight of Islamist terror, Israel's intransigence, shattered negotiations, and faltering economic and political reform within the Palestinian Authority and its Arab neighbors. The "outer ring" exacerbated the difficulties by funding terrorism and undermining reform that might weaken inward-looking models throughout the region. Israel's military operations in the West Bank and Gaza – responsive to suicide bombings and other attacks on civilians – complicated Palestinian reforms. As of 2003 the puzzle of whether or not the micro Israel/Palestine situation can ever be nested in the triple logic that underlies the macro Mediterranean framework remains. Conversely, the viability of the EMP may partially hang on this balance.

Notes

1 The MEDA (MEsures D'Accompagnement) Regulation was adopted in 1996. Its beneficiaries were Algeria, Cyprus, Egypt, Israel, Jordan, Malta, Morocco, Lebanon, Syria, Tunisia, Turkey, and the West Bank and Gaza Strip. Up to 1998, MEDA committed €2.3 billion and disbursed 600 million for economic reform, social cohesion and regional cooperation. MEDA allocations for 2005–2006 were €5.3 billion.
2 For an overview, see Chapter 6 in this volume.

PART IV
Regional security trajectories

10

NUCLEAR LOGICS

Contrasting Paths in East Asia and the Middle East

The objective of this book (*Nuclear Logics*) has been primarily analytical, aiming at a better understanding of why states acquire or renounce nuclear weapons and revisiting how we study this subject. A prolific literature has been largely devoted to supply-side concerns related to international control of sensitive nuclear technologies.[1] The demand side – why nuclear aspirants contemplate or acquire nuclear weapons – has received less systematic attention, neglecting the thirty-year-old warning by Nobel Economics Laureate Thomas Schelling (1976: 80) that "the emphasis has to shift from physical denial and technology secrecy to the things that determine incentives and expectations." Three decades later, former chief UN weapons inspector Hans Blix acknowledged that removing states' incentives to acquire nuclear weapons remains the most important issue on the nonproliferation agenda: "No incentives, no weapons, no use."[2] IAEA Director-General and Nobel Peace Laureate Mohammad El-Baradei admitted that "technology has come out of the box…we need to have a different approach to handling issues of non-proliferation. This should not consist only of controlling the source of the water, but we must look at the reasons why countries are trying to acquire nuclear weapons."[3]

In an effort to shed light on this question, this book has reviewed both traditional and novel approaches to international relations while revisiting conventional wisdoms. As Lebow (2003: 388) argues, "The deeper we embed ourselves in a paradigm, the more difficult it becomes to abstract ourselves from it and look at the

---

* I owe an immense debt of gratitude to many scholars and practitioners willing to discuss their views with me during visits to the countries analyzed here, including current and former government officials. I am especially indebted to Nobuyasu Abe, Asher Arian, Amatzia Baram, Hans Blix, Michael Brecher, William Burr, Leszek Buszynski, T. J. Cheng, Alan Dowty, Lynn Eden, Nabil Fahmy, Sung Chull Kim, Ellis Krauss, Akira Kurosaki, Wen-cheng Lin, Chih-cheng Lo, Yossi Melman, Abbas Milani, Chung-in Moon, Young-Kyu Park, Daniel Pinkston, William C. Potter, Mitchell Reiss, Richard Samuels, Jeffrey Richelson, Arthur Stein, Robert Wampler, Ren Xiao, Andrew Yang, Herbert York, and the late Shalhevet Freier. As tempting as it is to blame them for any residual errors, these remain my own. For superb research assistance, I am grateful to Wilfred Wan, Colin Moore, Maria van Meter, Adam Martin, and Titus Chen.

world afresh." The effort here has been to avoid this conceptual trap and look at the problem kaleidoscopically in Rashomon fashion, from various angles, hoping to generate new insights. A focused comparison between East Asia and the Middle East provides fertile ground to explore old and newer paradigms regarding nuclear behavior. The two regions are at the forefront of the policy debate; they jointly account for a significant proportion of nuclear aspirants since the NPT's inception; despite comparable initial conditions in earlier decades – authoritarian rule, limited economic interdependence, regional security dilemmas, and state-building challenges – their nuclear trajectories have diverged significantly; each region exhibits anomalies that are useful methodologically for understanding regional effects; their disparate nuclear trajectories defy technological determinism since the best endowed in nuclear power and industrial technology (East Asia) were arguably less prone to acquire nuclear weapons; and there have been no systematic attempts to compare these two regions' nuclear behavior despite these and other research design considerations that make them an important analytical puzzle.

The empirical chapters (not included here) addressed this cross regional variation, examined different conceptual paths to explaining choices for or against nuclear weapons, transcended the limitations of mono-causal explanations, and pointed to advantages gained from integrating recent scholarship in international relations into the study of nuclear proliferation. In some cases, alternative causal paths were found to lead to the same outcome, making it difficult to assess their respective causal weight and estimate the necessity of a particular factor. As George and Bennett (2005: 25) suggest, "Case studies remain much stronger at assessing *whether* and *how* a variable mattered to the outcome than at assessing *how much* it mattered." Yet some cases have clearly revealed the tendency to overestimate particular variables and underestimate others. This chapter begins by recapitulating general findings and possible directions for future research, exploring the prospects for continuity and change through the lenses of theories reviewed, and discussing potential scenarios that might "test" assumptions regarding the effects of structural power, international institutions, norms, democracy, and models of political survival on nuclear choices. The final section begins the task of distilling policy implications for international and regional institutions, major powers, and NGOs in their common efforts to strengthen nonproliferation.

Overview of findings: Will the future resemble the past?

Neorealism

The cases that we reviewed point to the *perception* of existential security as a very important consideration in some cases. Yet understanding nuclear outcomes as the sole perfunctory reflection of international structure, balance of power, and self-help can come at a high analytical cost. Such perspectives are underdetermining, compete with alternative explanations in what should be their best arena of argumentation, fail to explain some of the outcomes observed, and are incomplete in explaining others. All cases raised the problem of underdetermination, where the theory conjures up multiple possible outcomes. States facing difficult structural conditions had multiple choices compatible with securing their survival, ranging from overt to ambiguous nuclearization and several non-nuclear alternatives. States opted for different solutions – nuclear and non-nuclear – to comparable security predicaments. Thus, self help as an analytic category did not provide clear markers for likely behavior, was unable to forecast whether nuclear weapons enhanced or undermined security, led to indeterminate predictions about regional outcomes, and invariably required additional information unrelated to power balances.

These shortcomings demand special attention because they relate to the theory's performance in its home court – high national security – where structural realist theory should perform best. Nuclear behavior provides easy grounds for testing theories of relative power, balance of power, and *state* security in an anarchic world. Since nuclear weapons are presumably the heart, or the inner sanctum, of states' security dilemmas, the study of why states acquire or renounce them loads the dice in favor of neorealism, constituting the most auspicious domain for corroborating its tenets. An additional consideration tilts explanations toward neorealism when analyzing security outcomes. Leaders, politicians, and bureaucrats are more likely to portray decisions for or against nuclear weapons as dictated by "reasons of state" rather than as domestic political expediency. Thus, much of the public record (and even the private one) often points to more "legitimate" considerations of balance of power and state survival as underlying nuclear decisions. Several consequences stem from this doubly privileged analytical position. First, the very fact that nuclear behavior as a subject matter favors neorealism in principle ironically does not make nuclear decisions an optimal arena for validating its canons from a methodological standpoint. A good or crucial test of any theory is one that forces the theory to survive *un*favorable conditions (Eckstein 1975). A theory that can be confirmed despite adverse circumstances gains significant analytical traction. A theory that cannot be easily confirmed even under the best circumstances suggests potentially serious problems. Second, because of its assumed status as "favored theory" in the analysis of nuclear choices, even partial deviations from unalloyed neorealist predictions constitute significant challenges to the theory. In its home turf, a theory must be able to explain the overwhelming majority of cases *with ease and at high levels of confidence* and parsimony, and without problems of underdetermination. Third, as the "most likely" explanation for this subject matter, neorealism should effortlessly crowd out other theories, voiding them of much explanatory value. One should not need to go any further than structural power to understand nuclear outcomes.

The empirical chapters suggest that structural power can be a useful category in some cases but, in its crude form, does not explain the overwhelming majority of cases easily or at high levels of confidence and parsimony, and it certainly does not avoid underdetermination nor obviate the need for exploring other hypotheses. If structural power told the story, then Egypt, adjacent to Israel, would have been far more likely to acquire nuclear weapons in a pattern of "reactive proliferation" than other Middle East states such as Libya. Israel was Egypt's main adversary in several wars and was suspected of developing nuclear weapons by the early 1960s. Furthermore, states with lower external existential threats (Libya and arguably early 1970s Iraq) forcefully pursued nuclear weapons whereas states with much higher threats (Taiwan, South Korea, Egypt, Vietnam, Japan, Syria, or Jordan for that matter) did not. As Betts (2000) argues, insecurity is not a sufficient condition for acquiring nuclear weapons; many insecure states have not. The reverse is also true; the absence of particularly severe external threats has not precluded states from considering or pursuing nuclear weapons. Disagreements over what constitutes a structural threat or a genuine deterioration in the balance of power, and how to measure their dynamics over time and across cases, is precisely one conceptual Achilles heel of structural realism. Do threats derive from changes in relative capabilities, from "rival" states as abstract entities trapped in international anarchy, or from the way particular leaders, regimes, or ruling coalitions interpret and define them? and what explains the latter? The dynamics of security dilemmas differ when particular *regimes* are perceived as proximate sources of threat rather than when threats are perceived to emanate from *states* as fixtures of strategic landscapes. Hence, an important frontier in the study of nuclear behavior entails a proper understanding of analytical distinctions and interplays between *regime* and *state* security, or internal and external political survival, which are often interrelated. External threats to states have been quite real for Taiwan, Israel, South Korea, and Japan, and harder to construe solely in terms of domestic regime survival considerations, although the latter provide important information in those cases as well. Leaders in Iraq, Iran, Libya, and North Korea construed state security as co-terminal with their respective regimes' survival. However, it is those regimes' models and policies, not merely their states' locations or relative power endowments, that have created threats where there were none, or enhanced them where they existed.

The cases of denuclearization in Japan, Taiwan, and South Korea are often considered to be among the most closely conforming to neorealism among post-1968 nuclear aspirants identified in chapter 1 (in *Nuclear Logics*). Yet problems of underdetermination, incompleteness, lack of parsimony, and powerful competing hypotheses emerge even there. First, unalloyed power-balancing perspectives would have expected at least two of these cases to engage in "reactive proliferation" following China's nuclear test in 1964. Relinquishing nuclear weapons in the face of such threats is counterintuitive for such arguments, particularly in the case of Japan. Second, competing structural arguments lead to disparate predictions about what states in the same situation as these three might do – from renouncing to acquiring nuclear weapons – leaving ample a priori ambiguity about which outcome best reduces vulnerability. Third, these states' choices are often traced to US alliances and commitments, which undeniably played significant roles yet beg the question of why technologically endowed states choose alliances over self-help, considering serious episodes of "abandonment" and "entrapment." Indeed, in all three cases, alliance was chosen over self-reliant deterrence at a historical moment *least* conducive to such decisions. During the 1970s, the hegemon at the other end of the alliance was dramatically weakened by the debacle in Southeast Asia, and Nixon's Guam doctrine spelled less than robust commitments to East Asian allies. Fourth, the United States could still coercively deny indigenous deterrents, as it did in Taiwan and South Korea. Yet US and Soviet efforts to compel nuclear aspirants (allies and foes) failed repeatedly, succeeded with some targets at some points but not others, or played secondary roles in their denuclearization. Superpowers' commitments to North

Korea, Iraq, Israel (or Pakistan, France, and Britain) did not lead them to renounce nuclear weapons. Nor did the absence of security guarantees play any role in Egypt, Libya (2003), South Africa, Argentina, or Brazil's decisions to reverse nuclear ambitions. Too many cases of denuclearization were not the result of successful hegemonic coercion. Superpowers' coercion on Iraq (until 2003), Argentina, Brazil, India, Pakistan, South Africa, North Korea, Israel, Iran, and Libya for several decades – provide numerous instances of the limits of hegemony (Dunn 1982). As Waltz (2003: 38) persuasively argues, "In the past half-century, no country has been able to prevent other countries from going nuclear if they were determined to do so." One logical inference from this statement would be that Japan, Taiwan, and South Korea were not as determined to acquire nuclear weapons as some believe. The empirical chapters provide some support for this proposition, suggesting that domestic models can explain from whence such resolve, or lack thereof, comes.

Positive and negative hegemonic inducements seem clearly insufficient to explain outcomes for many nuclear aspirants, making Japan, Taiwan, and South Korea more anomalous than typical. Indeed, in some sense, these three arguably provide hegemonic arguments with "easy" cases most likely to confirm their expectations. Yet even here the mechanisms of hegemony can be understood only by probing into domestic conditions that created acquiescence in these cases where so many others stood firm. Understanding relative receptivity to both coercive and persuasive aspects of US influence requires us to consider reigning domestic models of political survival. In all three cases, indigenous nuclear weapons would have seriously undermined favored strategies of economic growth, international competitiveness, and global access. The choice for alliance *itself* was the product of domestic models that favored it over other options, trumping internal demands for nuclear weapons and generating openness to hegemonic inducements. The links between commitments to internationalized models and renunciation of expensive nuclear competitions – as the respective chapters reveal – are thick in these cases. As Premier Miki expressed to Secretary Schlesinger in the mid-1970s, "Asian countries are feeling the need to strengthen their internal system, stabilize their political situation, and improve the public welfare. Military security is important but cannot be considered in isolation."[4] Thus there was far from the strong demand for nuclear weapons in Japan that would have presumably compelled a strong US denial. South Korea bears the marks of stronger hegemonic coercion, but even without it, nuclear weapons would have endangered Park Chung Hee's domestic model of political survival, risking sharp economic decline, increasing political and economic instability, and isolating South Korea from the regional and international market as well as the political and institutional forces that underpinned Park's model. Taiwan's quintessential external vulnerability stemmed from much weaker US commitments than to Japan and South Korea. Despite signs of some military demand for nuclear weapons, there was no consensus among KMT leaders who pinned their regime's survival on export-led economic growth.

A closer look at Japan illustrates both the utility and limitations of the US alliance for explaining Japan's renunciation of an indigenous deterrent. First, ironically, extending a nuclear umbrella over an ally does not necessarily constitute a "strong case" for validating the claim that alliance explains (the ally's) abstention. As argued earlier, social scientific claims are best corroborated when submitted to "hard" tests, where conditions for the operation of the claim are less easily met. One can be more confident about a theory when its tenets are instantiated under conditions least likely to support the theory. Conversely, our confidence is undermined when the theory does not hold well under conditions that ought to have favored its corroboration. Accordingly, a hard (methodologically "fit") case would be one in which US inducements through alliance are shown to prevail *despite* the target ally's very strong demand for nuclear weapons. Cases where US inducements operate *in the absence* of such demand are much weaker tests of this theory. Chapter 3 suggests that Japan's domestic politics did not generate strong demand for nuclear weapons. Hence, Japan does not seem a robust test of the alliance hypothesis. There was neither demand for a Japanese deterrent nor a supply of US coercion.

Second, Japan's critical NPT decisions took place in the 1970s, at the alliance's lowest point, when dilemmas of commitment would have featured prominently in Japan's calculations. Yet neorealist theory has excelled in raising this inherent *problematique* of alliances – credibility, commitment, entrapment – that nuclear weapons can only compound, even within NATO. Third, such dilemmas reinforce competing unalloyed neorealist hypotheses that self-help precludes great powers like Japan from relying on others for their own security. That the world's second largest economy, with sophisticated industrial and nuclear infrastructures, chose to depend on its ally's nuclear umbrella suggests more an anomaly than a confirmation that structural power calculations rule the world. As Waltz (1993: 64) argues regarding Japan, "One may wonder how a state with the economic capability of a great power can refrain from arming itself with the weapons that have served so well as the great deterrent." Yet Japan's predicted imminent acquisition of nuclear weapons has not happened over the past four decades, thus far not even after North Korea's 2006 nuclear test.[5] Fourth, Japan's decisions are even more startling from a neorealist viewpoint considering the sometimes ambiguous US position regarding Japan's nuclear options. How the United States would have responded had there been strong Japanese demand for nuclear weapons remains unclear, entirely in the domain of counterfactuals. Nixon and others certainly signaled forbearance and perhaps encouragement of Japan's nuclearization even during crucial debates over the NPT and subsequently. Even if this position was not dominant in successive US administrations, it had the potential of turning the alliance argument on its head, making it a latent source rather than a barrier to Japan's nuclearization. Finally, if alliances alone (rather than prestige or other considerations) told the story, post-World War II Britain and France might not have acquired nuclear weapons (Rosecrance 1964). At most one could classify the alliance as necessary in this case but certainly not sufficient for explaining nuclear outcomes, and only when one considers the alliance's role in Japan's domestic politics.

The power of hegemons to persuade and coerce states to forgo nuclear weapons should not be underestimated but neither should it be overestimated. Hegemonic pressures or inducements do not single-handedly and invariably account for outcomes. North Korea enjoyed the war-tested protection of two superpowers, China and the Soviet Union, yet nurtured nuclear designs early on, well before experiencing severe fears of abandonment with the Soviet Union's collapse. One cannot understand why such dilemmas were so extreme in this case without dwelling on *juche*, the Kims' autarkic model of domestic political survival since the 1950s. North Korea's search for nuclear weapons, which began in the 1960s, bred changes in relative power that would have predicted reactive nuclearization among neighboring states. Yet neither Japan nor South Korea altered their non-nuclear status for over three decades. Immediate responses to North Korea's 2006 nuclear test were met with reaffirmations that neither would develop nuclear weapons. An unalloyed neorealist logic (skeptical of alliance explanations) could explain why North Korea developed and tested nuclear weapons, but would also need to demonstrate that North Korea faced the most dire structural predicament of all East Asian cases examined in Part 2 (of *Nuclear Logics*).

Part 3 suggests that of all Middle East cases, Libya and Egypt arguably provide least support for neorealism, as do perhaps Iraq in the early 1970s and Iran since the 1990s. Decisions taken in Iran and Iraq in the 1980s, and Israel in the 1950s and 1960s, provide stronger support. Yet neorealism is underdetermining for all five cases, is problematic and non-parsimonious in most of them, and cannot easily exclude alternative explanations in any of the five. First, structural power accounts of Libya's nuclear pursuits suffer from more serious failings than most other cases. Egypt, the neighboring state most likely to overpower Gaddafi's regime, renounced nuclear weapons prior to Gaddafi's most determined efforts to acquire them in the 1990s. Libya accelerated its search for centrifuges and weapons designs just as Algeria's facilities came under IAEA supervision in the 1990s. Ironically for neorealist perspectives, Libya renounced nuclear weapons in the 1990s, *after* Egypt's largest research reactor with potential plutonium-producing capabilities had been built, *after* Egypt began alluding to potential changes in its nuclear posture arguably related to Iran's nuclearization, and *after* Algeria opted for a second large research reactor as well.[6] Had the logic of self-help applied, these developments would have led Libya in the opposite direction than the one observed. As Gaddafi himself reportedly stated (Chapter 10 in *Nuclear Logics*), his nuclear weapons "*had no target.*" His initial search for nuclear weapons in the early 1970s preceded the 1986 US attack. Israel provided a useful political target, but the timings of both Libya's efforts to acquire and relinquish nuclear weapons question the relevance of the Israeli factor from a structural power-balancing standpoint. Gaddafi heightened the search for nuclear weapons when Israel was least menacing (1990s), but Israel was declared no security threat after its fighter jets flew over Libya's skies and during Ariel Sharon's premiership. No significant changes in relative power between Libya and Israel can explain such transformation. The gap between the two states – despite Libya's abundant oil resources – was and has remained wide. Threats were constructed and deconstructed according to Gaddafi's evolving domestic models and regional implications.

Second, changes in the balance of power do not provide coherent, parsimonious, accounts of Egypt's denuclearization. Despite the rise in the conventional military power of Israel and other regional rivals with nuclear ambitions (Iraq, Libya, Iran), Egypt has rejected "reactive proliferation" since the 1970s. Egypt (under Nasser) considered nuclear weapons when its conventional gap with Israel was the narrowest, and abandoned nuclear aspirations (under Sadat) when the gap widened.

Egypt considered nuclear weapons when it arguably enjoyed stronger external (Soviet) security guarantees but abandoned them in their absence (the United States never provided Egypt with equivalent guarantees).

Third, Iraq's early nuclear efforts during the 1970s – prior to the war with Iran and Israel's attack on Osiraq – are much less compatible with neorealism than its nuclear behavior in the late 1980s. Saddam asserted that WMD helped him reverse the fate of wars (that he had initiated), presumably halting Iranian ground troops and deterring allied forces from entering Baghdad in 1991. Yet other Iraqis, including Saddam's cousin and former Minister of Defense Adnan Khayr Allah, thought nuclear weapons made Iraq more vulnerable. Other Iraqi officials confirmed that Saddam wielded nuclear weapons as symbols of dominance designed to intimidate domestic rivals no less than foreign ones. Saddam himself acknowledged that the mere threat of chemical weapons helped him crush internal revolts.

Fourth, the war with Iraq provides some support for balance-of-power considerations as a source of Iran's nuclearization but less so after 1991 and UN containment of Saddam (Chubin 2006). The 2003 war in Iraq eliminated Saddam altogether, although concerns with Pakistan arguably remained. Following Pakistan's 1998 test, Rafsanjani stressed that Iran "must be concerned" (Taykeh 2006: 144). Yet Pakistan's president Pervez Musharaf met with Khamene'i and Ahmadinejad in Tehran in early 2007, and discussed an Indo–Iranian natural gas pipeline that would cross Pakistan. Whether the United States became a genuine motive for Iran's sustained nuclear efforts remains contested. US overextension (Afghanistan, Iraq, North Korea, and other challenges) and concerns with Iran's terrorist networks are arguably more powerful deterrents against US attack than are any budding Iranian nuclear capabilities. Israel provides another important ideological and political justification that Iranian leaders have used instrumentally for domestic purposes. In the end, however, as Chubin and Litwak (2003: 105) argue, Iran has no existential threats requiring it to compensate for military imbalances with nuclear weapons. While others may reject this premise, the variability of means consistent with coping with external threats – evident in Iran's public debates – calls into question nuclearization as the only outcome compatible with neorealism. Competing Iranian leaders have defined threats and appropriate responses to them differently.

Fifth, Israel's concerns with its survival as a state are widely accepted as a source of alleged nuclearization. Extreme conditions of vulnerability in the 1950s and 1960s – a UN conventional weapons boycott, no external security guarantees – make it an easier case for neorealism, but not strong ground for testing the theory. As with other cases, however, even in Israel, balance-of-power considerations led to various possible outcomes, from an acknowledged nuclear deterrent to ambiguity and non-nuclear alternatives. This defies the notion of a single neorealist understanding or coherent strategic prescription regarding its nuclear choices (Reiss 1988). Given this underdetermination, Israel's ambiguous nuclear policy – as any other outcome – can be recounted as the product of relative power considerations a posteriori. But could ambiguity have been anticipated a priori? As argued in chapter 2, the same concerns with US responses that might explain ambiguity in this case failed to deter myriad other cases of nuclear aspirants that did not respond with ambiguity but with nuclear tests, defiance, or nuclear renunciation. Israel's choice for ambiguity had sources not only in external constraints but also in domestic ones. Said differently, although continuous US support was undoubtedly of utmost concern to Israeli decision-makers, it is unclear whether or not Israeli leaders would have formulated a different policy in the absence of that consideration. Other sources of ambiguity existed, and are recounted later in this chapter. Finally, the search for an ultimate deterrent – ambiguous or explicit – is amenable to constructivist interpretations that are quite different conceptually from balance-of power arguments. Such interpretations emphasize Israel's search for security not merely as a result of shifts in relative power but more as the product of resolve to avoid another Holocaust. Similarly, Israel's precarious status at the UN – where it saw Arab- and Muslim-backed initiatives prevail via the power of arithmetic majority, if not always on the basis of merit – deepened Israel's sense of isolation in a way not captured by balance-of-power considerations.

Sixth, Arab–Arab and Arab–Iranian disputes have arguably been a more fundamental motivating force for nuclear capabilities – from a neorealist standpoint – than have changes in Arab–Israeli and Iranian–Israeli relative power. The historical analyses of Iraq, Iran, and Libya, as well as Egypt's more recent concerns with Iran, suggest that Israel has provided a secondary layer of incentives at best.[7] Neither Israel's nor China's nuclearization in the 1960s turned these countries into the *primary* targets of reactive nuclear programs respectively in Iraq, Iran, Libya, or North Korea. Egypt, Taiwan, and Japan would have arguably had Israel or China as primary targets, but all three refrained from acquiring them.

Cumulatively, these findings pose significant challenges to neorealism. Ironically, as Sigal (1998: 249) has argued, "Realism seems to be the secular religion of the foreign policy establishment. Those who want to play a part in policy-making believe in it, or at least pay lip service to it by acting as if they believe in it, even if they do not." Yet predictions of proliferation do not necessarily flow automatically from systemic incentives, to which different states respond differently (Bueno de Mesquita *et al.* 1993). Competing hypotheses examined in the remainder of this chapter suggest additional limitations and caveats to an overemphasis on international power distribution as a source of denuclearization. At issue is not to question this theory's applicability in some cases but rather its nearly universal acceptance as the driving force of all or most nuclear programs. It is as important to recognize enduring contributions as is, borrowing from Mahoney (2005: 20), to "break out of a reigning theoretical straightjacket." Neorealism's contributions can be enhanced by specifying a priori the precise underlying measures of relative power and thresholds that lead to nuclearization, so as to avoid circularity and ex post facto rationalizations (such as "state X went nuclear because of acute insecurity," whereby the acuteness threshold is detected by a nuclear test). Sharpening core concepts will help cast the argument in falsifiable terms and enable more clearly defined and testable propositions. These improvements should include a better specification of when, how, and why hegemony may or may not account for nuclear outcomes. The task for unalloyed neorealism also entails explaining variation in nuclear outcomes independently of domestic or international institutional and normative considerations. Alternatively, studies can follow neoclassical realist variants (Christensen 1996; Glaser 2000) more open to domestic politics as filters defining geo-strategic threats.

Without such amendments and improvements, the inherent difficulties of a crude neorealist logic encumber our ability to extend its use into the future. Unalloyed neorealism considers great powers like Japan to be structural anomalies difficult to sustain: "How long can Japan…live alongside other nuclear states while denying [itself] similar capabilities?" (Waltz 1993: 66). Many scenarios have held China first and North Korea subsequently as sources of chain reactions.[8] Yet the structural power thresholds that would trigger an East Asian nuclear domino are unclear, and constantly shifting. Different imputed thresholds in North Korea's ascendance as a nuclear weapons state have already been crossed, from its expulsion of IAEA inspectors in 1993 to its plutonium extraction, discovery of alleged enrichment activities, repeated verbal threats to Japan and South Korea, declaration of "nukes" possession, and missile tests. The 2006 nuclear test has renewed predictions of Japan's nuclearization, yet Premier Abe responded that he "would like to clearly state that there will be no change regarding the three nonnuclear principles," reaffirming Japan's non-nuclear status.[9] If this response is sustained, Japan would have renounced nuclear weapons even as it witnessed three of its neighbors acquire nuclear weapons: the Soviet Union, China, and North Korea. Furthermore, an unalloyed neorealist analysis of China's rise in the past two decades would have portended further pressures on Japan to nuclearize. Japan's continued resistance to such presumed temptations have provided and will continue to provide crucial tests of unalloyed structural neorealism's predictive power. Conversely, Japan's hypothetical turn toward an indigenous nuclear deterrent would deal a nearly fatal blow (a conceptual "friendly fire" of sorts) to competing neorealist theories that, for many decades, regarded the US alliance as obviating the need for a Japanese deterrent.[10] Explanations relying on alliance would have to elucidate why balance of power mattered more for Japan vis-à-vis North Korea than vis-à-vis other nuclear-armed neighbors (including the Soviet Union/Russia and China), why a rising (internationalizing) China might be more of a threat than a radical Maoist one (to which Japan did not respond with an indigenous deterrent), and why US guarantees might be considered weaker today than ever before (as during the US debacle in Indochina and Nixon's Guam doctrine). The last condition does not sit well with the reality of a very strong US–Japan alliance as of 2006. A nuclear umbrella constitutes a hegemon's ultimate inducement, and Secretary Rice was quick to reiterate the US-extended deterrence commitment following North Korea's test. If alliance does not work in as strong a context as the US–Japan relationship, one might doubt its relevance under much less optimal conditions.

Such conditions seem to increasingly apply to South Korea, where the alliance has weakened significantly, potentially freeing South Korea's hand to pursue nuclear weapons. Yet South Korea's official response to North Korea's nuclear test dismissed such a turn away from the alliance, for reasons related no less to South Korea's domestic considerations than to alliance robustness. South Korea's attitudes toward both the US alliance and North Korea appeared to shift more in tandem with the relative power of domestic ruling coalitions than with changes in structural (international) power. The latter would anticipate Japan's nuclearization to drive South Korea willy-nilly into nuclear status (and vice versa), eroding restraints imposed by alliances. This possible nuclear domino effect or "breakout" in East Asia would strengthen unalloyed neorealism at the expense of alliance-based arguments. US commitments to Taiwan are arguably weaker, much less codified, far more contingent, and frequent subjects of contention within both Taiwan and the United States.[11] Rising existential threats to Taiwan from China, and fluctuating, conditional US commitments to Taiwan in the context of a hypothetical attack by China, would arguably make Taiwan a strong candidate for nuclearization. It is doubtful, however, that Taiwan will opt for this path, given alternative readings of what drives Taiwan's behavior vis-à-vis China and the density of economic and political interests at stake. I return to this scenario later.

Iran's alleged nuclearization has triggered concerns with similar nuclear snowball effects in the Middle East. Saudi Arabia, Turkey, and Egypt, some have argued, may be tempted to respond in kind (Campbell *et al.* 2004). As Egyptian researcher Wahid Abd Al-Magid suggested, Iran's nuclear warheads "will represent a threat to the Arabs before it does to Israel" (Feldner 2003: 2). Nuclear programs in Iraq and Israel did not drive Turkey or Egypt down the reactive proliferation path in the past, but in 2006, a defiant Iranian nuclear program has allegedly led Turkey, Algeria, Egypt, Morocco, Saudi Arabia, Tunisia, and the UAE to embark on nuclear power programs, potential precursors of a nuclear weapons race.[12] A weakened US military presence in Iraq hardly creates strong conditions for hegemonic denial of further nuclearization in the Middle East. Furthermore, the record of hegemonic success in preventing proliferation within and beyond this region suggests only moderate expectations for such a scenario. The United States has maintained relatively stable bilateral alliances with Egypt, Israel, Jordan, Turkey, Saudi Arabia, and other Gulf Cooperation Council (GCC) countries, although none has been as formally encoded as the US–Japan alliance, except perhaps for Turkey as part of NATO.[13] Recent reports alleging a potential Turkish drive to acquire nuclear weapons could provide yet another challenge to alliance based and hegemony arguments.

Finally, *contra* neorealism, Egypt has avoided nuclearization for decades as Israel's relative power has increased dramatically. Signs of possible revisions in Egypt's policy have been strongest as the threat of Iran's nuclearization has grown higher. The likelihood of this turn is, once again, hard to estimate, given unclear thresholds for changes in relative power to yield expected effects. If indeed Egypt embarks on a weapons-related program in the future, unalloyed neorealist perspectives would need to establish that Iran has been a strategic threat to Egypt rather than a political one, that it has been a more serious threat to Egypt's security than Israel has been (since dramatic steps were taken only after the rise of Iran as a threat and not vis-à-vis Israel for decades), and that the causal mechanisms and consequences of changes in relative power are independent from domestic considerations, such as popular pressures for emulating Ahmadinejad's defiance, which are unrelated to changes in the balance of power between Iran and Egypt. A Middle East nuclear domino would put to rest the notion of a common search for a Muslim bomb, suggesting instead multiple bids for nuclear weapons in the Muslim world from Pakistan to Iran, Egypt, Saudi Arabia, and Turkey. Such prospects would be more connected to domestic circumstances and to Sunni versus Shi'a identity-based competition – or constructed understandings of religion – than to classical balance-of-power considerations. Finally, the dramatic deterioration of the Nonproliferation Regime (NPR) following the South Asian tests, North Korea's test, and Iran's defiance of the IAEA might also play important roles in Egypt's future nuclear behavior.

Rational Institutionalism

Rational-institutionalism forces attention to the NPR as an important dimension weighing on nuclear decisions. That most states have abrogated their right to acquire nuclear weapons by ratifying the NPT is certainly a potentially powerful indication that the international regime matters. It is also plausible, however, that normative, security, or domestic considerations might have driven states' decisions for or against nuclear weapons. Such prior concerns could thus explain both nuclear decisions and NPT compliance. Egypt's ambassador to the United States Nabil Fahmy pointed out that

> in the spirit of candid and clear sighted analysis, one must be obliged to acknowledge that very few non-nuclear weapons states – parties – actually joined the treaty because it responded to their immediate security concerns. Most of the parties that joined NPT did so for political or economic reasons or circumstances, or because they had no reason to pursue nuclear weapons or nuclear programs from the beginning. Some parties did join because they assumed the NPT would generate a wider nuclear nonproliferation regime and disarmament effort, ultimately dealing effectively with nuclear weapons concerns. This was particularly true of states that initially had peaceful nuclear programs and the potential to develop them.

More systematic research on nuclear aspirants that abstained or indulged, as well as on non-nuclear aspirants, are needed to validate premises that cost-benefit calculations associated with the NPR indeed influenced nuclear behavior. This broader agenda remains a matter of empirical investigation.

As for the cases reviewed here, few provided strong support tor the NPR as the *main* determinant for renouncing nuclear weapons. State-centric rational institutionalist perspectives proved compatible in a few cases but inadequate, incomplete, or unnecessary for explaining nuclear choices and outcomes in several others. Persuasive institutionalist accounts would have had to establish that – had the NPR not existed at the time – Japan's domestic politics would have likely yielded an alternative decision, that is, to develop nuclear weapons. The historical record does not provide strong evidence for such a counterfactual. The NPT itself had limited currency in Japan's domestic debate, according to important participants. The decision to remain non-nuclear was logically prior to, not a consequence of, the decision to ratify the NPT. Ratification itself and Japan's subsequent receptivity to NPT injunctions were corollaries of a domestic consensus around the "economy first" Yoshida doctrine, which blunted potential domestic demand for nuclear weapons. Similar considerations operated in South Korea, which went beyond its

NPT commitments by agreeing not to develop indigenous enrichment and reprocessing facilities despite strong economic incentives for an energy-starved economy and despite strong security demands from nationalist sectors. Park and his allies had their eyes on the prize, and the prize was not nuclear weapons but an economic miracle that would undercut both domestic and North Korean challengers. Chiang Kai-shek's decision to forgo nuclear weapons had even less to do with the NPT, which granted nuclear status to its archenemy (China) while denying Taiwan statehood itself. Domestic considerations of economic growth – which was highly dependent on international markets, technology, investments, and political support – greatly influenced the KMT's nuclear policies. Absent this domestic model of political survival, Taiwan might have gone the North Korean way. Other potential institutionalist considerations – regional regimes capable of constraining East Asian powers – did not exist in the 1960s and 1970s, and thus could not explain decisions to renounce nuclear weapons either. New security institutions – the ASEAN Regional Forum (ARF), KEDO, and Six-Party Talks – did not emerge until the 1990s and, as of mid-2006, had failed to denuclearize North Korea. None of these institutions has had any bearing on Taiwan, which has been effectively excluded even from the most inclusive institution in the region, the ARF (Solingen 2008).

The NPT clearly did not prevent Middle East nuclearization. The region's NPT-compliance record has been dismal. As chapters on Iraq, Libya, and Iran document, these NPT members violated commitments and deceived the IAEA, approaching international institutions and international law with contempt, and not just on nuclear matters. The NPR raised barriers to sensitive technology transfers but not high enough to prevent clandestine acquisitions on a grand scale. Furthermore, the IAEA was unable to detect defections in pre-1991 Iraq, pre-2002 Iran, and pre-2003 Libya, although UNSCOM dismantled Iraq's WMD, and UNMOVIC read Iraq's nonexistent nuclear capabilities in 2003 accurately. Israel never signed the NPT, and so its nuclear activities were not violations of formal commitments. Since Israel perceived the UN as biased toward automatic majorities mustered by Arab, Islamic, and non-aligned slates and by the Soviet bloc, its abstention from the NPT seemed consistent with a rational-institutionalist logic of states as unified entities weighing the costs and benefits of joining institutions. An institution that was unwilling or unable to monitor compliance and detect defections adequately, and that could enable withdrawals ("legal" defections through Article X) was considered ill suited to improve Israel's security, according to Israel's Atomic Energy Commission director-general (Freier 1985). Yet Israel supported regionally based, mutually verifiable, and fully inclusive NWFZ as an institutional alternative to the NPT, conditioned on prior peace agreements with all regional parties.

Egypt's behavior seems compatible with institutionalist expectations insofar as it signed, ratified, and largely complied with NPT injunctions. That it did so despite its status as the foremost Arab regional power and in the presence of nuclear-armed Israel (presumably to induce Israel to follow suit) certainly seems more consistent with institutionalism than with neorealism. Yet Egypt weighed ratification for nearly twelve years, and its timing suggested that domestic political instrumentalities were at play no less than aggregate state-level considerations. Sadat was receptive to US economic inducements for NPT ratification and needed those resources to compensate domestic constituencies in the midst of efforts to liberalize the economy (*infitah*). The prospects of obtaining assistance for its nuclear energy program, which required NPT ratification, were also deemed important for a sustainable *infitah*. Sadat could also wield NPT membership as an external constraint to counter domestic criticism over Egypt's unwillingness to match Israel's nuclear capabilities. Such criticism subsided but never disappeared, compelling Egyptian leaders to mount progressively more defiant condemnations of the NPT for unfulfilled promises of Article VI and for "double standards" allowing Israel, India, and Pakistan to remain non-members. Egypt also consistently demanded a Middle East NWFZ that would compel all parties to abide by the NPT and threatened to block indefinite extension in 1995 unless Israel signed it. Egypt's NPT compliance has generally been acknowledged by the IAEA, although some remained skeptical.[14] In 2004, the IAEA reprimanded Egypt for failing to declare nuclear sites and materials as "a matter of concern" but reported no evidence of nuclear weapons procurement.[15] Egypt never signed the IAEA Additional Protocol or ratified the Pelindaba NWFZ and the CTBT.

Regarding detection failures (notably of defections incurred by Iraq prior to 1991, by Iran for nearly two decades, and by North Korea and Libya for decades), they may stem more from flawed institutional design than poor implementation, as discussed in chapter 2. Former Iraqi scientist Hamza (1998: 3), however, argues a different perspective: "The understanding that gradually emerged from a closer relationship to the IAEA was how weak and easily manipulated the agency was. …Further, according to Al-Saji and Mahmoud, if an inspector gained a reputation as antagonistic or aggressive, few states would allow him to inspect their facilities. Overall, the IAEA proved extremely useful to the Iraqi weapons program in obtaining nuclear technology." In the end, Hamza added, "the IAEA accepted and promoted power reactor programs in both Iraq and Iran – two oil-rich countries with high military expenditures, centuries-old antagonisms, and many possibilities for conflict. Under cover of safeguarded civil nuclear programs, Iraq managed to purchase the basic components of plutonium production, with full training included, despite the risk that the technology could be replicated or misused."

As a tool to deny nuclear capabilities to potential aspirants, the NPR suffered from a classic problem identified by rational institutionalism: persistent difficulties in achieving collective action. As Feinstein and Slaughter (2004) argue, rifts and paralysis within the UNSC allowed states to pursue WMD under the cover of NPT membership, as with Iraq, North Korea, and arguably Iran. Former UN Under Secretary General for Disarmament Affairs Nobuyasu Abe has claimed that "many voices in recent years have questioned either the ability or the readiness of the members of the Security Council to perform its responsibility concerning a wide range of challenges related to WMD."[16] In his view, the UNSC's inability to force Iraqi compliance despite several resolutions, its reluctance to act on North Korean violations, and its failure to implement the 1998 unanimous resolution condemning Indian and Pakistani nuclear tests validated these concerns. Even when collective action yielded sanctions, problems of disparate interpretations and resolve remained. Whereas some considered sanctions on Iraq as a means to compel inspections, others regarded them in more restrictive terms, as merely designed to deny Iraq the ability to import items for military use (Blix 2005: 56). Russia and

France have had a tendency to "defect" in the application of effective sanctions, which cannot be understood through state-level considerations more typical of rational-institutionalist theory but rather through domestic pressures leading to uneven implementation of sanctions. French and Russian firms had agreements to develop oil fields in Iraq and pressed their governments for expanded activities. Iraq's neighbors promptly exploited sanctions "fatigue" to expand exchanges with Baghdad favored by their domestic constituencies adversely affected by sanctions. By 2001, Egypt, Syria, and the UAE had signed free trade-agreements with Iraq.

Collective-action problems have also been rampant regarding Iran and North Korea (Samore 2004) with occasional successes, which are reported in chapters 6 and 8 (*Nuclear Logics*). Russia, France and China were reluctant to refer the cases to the UNSC, acceding eventually, although conflicting approaches to sanctions due to members' internal constraints have remained. Additional concerns have included the ability of dictatorships to deflect the pain inflicted by sanctions onto vulnerable constituencies (Lebovic 2007). Saddam's war adventures against Iran and Kuwait, for example, had already created deplorable economic and social conditions, which sanctions only worsened. The Oil-for-Food program alleviated these conditions somewhat but also channeled vast proceeds to Saddam's military-industrial complex, missile development, palaces, and political allies. Many of the same considerations have applied to North Korea, Libya, and Iran, forcing greater attention to domestic distributional effects of sanctions (Solingen 1995; O'Sullivan 2003). Libya has provided a seemingly successful case, but sanctions there have been related to terrorism rather than denial of nuclear weapons. Indeed, Libya continued nuclear purchases from the A.Q. Khan network after UN sanctions regarding Lockerbie were suspended.

Notwithstanding some shortcomings of rational-institutionalism, the empirical chapters suggest that the NPR can be credited with some successes. Export controls raised the costs of acquiring sensitive technologies and equipment; inspection regimes were tightened following the IAEA's discovery of extensive prescribed activities by Iraq prior to 1991; the IAEA also stood firm during the North Korean 1993 crisis; NPT Review Conferences and UNSC resolutions arguably changed the context against which states formulated decisions regarding nuclear weapons; institutional processes increased opportunities for cooperation and offered new focal points such as the Additional Protocol, the NPT's indefinite extension, and the CTBT. Efforts to provide the IAEA with the authority to collect its own information, to revamp the entire safeguards system, and to create incentives to forgo the development of sensitive technologies are under consideration. These and other achievements could be significant given that the NPR operates in the thorniest domain of national security, where the emergence and functioning of international institutions command Sisyphean efforts. From this standpoint, rational institutionalism faces vast disadvantages – particularly relative to neorealism – as a theory explaining nuclear choices and outcomes. As argued, nuclear issues load the dice in favor of theories hinged on self-help and unilateral pursuit of security. Achieving institutional cooperation, enforcing rules, and punishing non-compliance are arguably far more difficult in this arena than in economic, environmental, or other functional issues (Lipson 1984). Nuclear behavior does not constitute a "most likely case" for overcoming prisoner's dilemma situations and problems of collective action. Hence, to the extent that a significant number of states may have rejected nuclearization at least partly due to NPT positive inducements (technology provision) and disincentives (export controls, denial, monitoring, and punishment for non-compliance), the theory achieves significant analytical scores. This recognition should not ignore that a sometimes unquestioned lore often assigns far more weight to the NPT as the chief motive for nuclear decisions and outcomes than is warranted by extant empirical findings.

Nuclear Logics examined nuclear decisions by nine states over forty years in light of five major theories of international relations, an effort that could not permit detailed examination of counterfactuals. Controlled studies of what might have happened in the absence of the NPR could improve our understanding of mechanisms linking institutional constraints to choice. How many of these cases might have decided differently absent the NPR?[17] The future is likely to provide additional tests of regime effects. Ambassador Fahmy argued in 2005 that "some states are bound to reassess their [NPT] commitments or hesitate to make new ones without a change of course by the international community and more rigorous disarmament and nonproliferation efforts."[18] A rational-institutionalist research agenda would hold future compliance to be contingent on states' calculations under unfolding rules and procedures. Were such calculations to override relative power or domestic tendencies toward defection, regime effects might be considered strong. Were balance-of-power or internal tendencies to defect to coincide with regime disincentives, our confidence in regime effects might be lower. Either way, institutional reasoning must be able to explain why we observe such significant variation in East Asian and Middle Eastern compliance patterns.

If the NPR's dramatic deterioration does not alter the number of nuclear aspirants, this could suggest that its impact is marginal. Alternatively, the NPR's significant deterioration, exacerbated by North Korea's 2006 nuclear test and Iran's defiance, could presage additional departures from NPT commitments. Either way, the task of separating institutional effects from responses to changes in relative power or increased domestic pressures could be challenging. Understanding the mechanisms through which the NPR operates requires a theory of domestic politics that remains largely absent from much of the institutional literature on the NPT. This book has proposed one such framework, linking compliance and defection to domestic models of political survival, but other domestic theories can be developed. States are not monolithic abstractions and identification of underlying domestic forces provides better a priori specifications of state interests to comply/defect from international regimes. Prospects that regional institutional arrangements may reaffirm East Asia's denuclearizing trend or induce similar trends in the Middle East hinge largely on the continuity (in East Asia) and emergence (in the Middle East) of compatible models of domestic political survival.[19]

Norms and constructivism

A different institutionalist argument traces nuclear weapons-abstention to states' socialization into NPR norms, where a "logic of appropriateness" rather than interests or rational expectations explains denuclearization (Finnemore and Sikkink 1998; March and Olson 1998). Part 2 (in *Nuclear Logics*) does not provide much evidence that anti-nuclear-weapons-acquisition norms played critical roles in most historic decisions. Japan's renunciation is often explained through the taboo engendered by Hiroshima and Nagasaki. Since this taboo was home grown and preceded the NPT, it could not be traced to international socialization but could well have nurtured anti-nuclear norms worldwide.[20] Japan's unique experience with nuclear Holocaust arguably makes it a "most likely case" to support normative accounts of denuclearization. Its important pacifist movement sensitized Japanese leaders to opposition to nuclear weapons. Yet the fateful decisions of the 1960s–1970s may not be so easily traced to the "nuclear allergy," which – perhaps counterintuitively – was much stronger subsequently than during the first two decades of the postwar era (Imai 1975; Calder 1996; Akiyama 2003). Japan signed the NPT eighteen months after its adoption and delayed ratification by nearly seven years. Furthermore, the conduct of various government studies on Japan's nuclear options since 1968 suggests that nuclear weapons acquisition – although unlikely – was less than a taboo, particularly given special sensitivity to secret contingency studies following the 1965 *Mitsuya Kenkyū Jiken* simulation exercise (Okimoto 1978). Most importantly, Japanese opponents of nuclear weapons regarded the US–Japan alliance as "embedded nuclearization," where Japan's defense rested on the US nuclear umbrella, as was reiterated after North Korea's nuclear test. Nor do the surveys and government studies analyzed in chapter 3 suggest that nuclear weapons were "unthinkable." Institutional restraints such as the Atomic Energy Law and the Three Non-Nuclear Principles had significant force. However, there was continuous contestation over interpretations of Article IX of the Constitution (renouncing the right of belligerency but not referring specifically to nuclear weapons), which may explain why the Principles never became law (Chai 1997). Furthermore, compromises over the US introduction of nuclear weapons into Japan were another expression of nuclear embeddedness. As Mochizuki (2006) argues, "Japan's pacifism has always been pragmatic." Further research on Japan's anti-nuclear norms must come to terms with the fact that Japan took nearly seven years to ratify the NPT; both forceful proponents and opponents of nuclear weapons invoked memories of Hiroshima and Nagasaki (Harrison 2002); Japan's acceptance of nuclear embeddedness in US nuclear deterrence; and difficulties in extricating normative from rationalistic sources of Japan's opposition to nuclear weapons, as examined in chapter 3 and summarized below.

Japan was not alone in substituting US nuclear weapons for its own. South Korea and Taiwan also relied on US commitments, suggesting additional pragmatic compromises rather than principled condemnations of nuclear weapons. Indeed, all three countries encouraged the alliance and extracted repeated US pledges by occasionally insinuating that without them they might be forced to acquire indigenous deterrents. There was some support for a national deterrent in South Korea in the 1970s, countered by public statements reiterating that the alliance – not normative considerations – obviated that need. Furthermore, US nuclear weapons remained the South's favored deterrent for decades despite kinship ties with North Korea, a factor that calls into question the operation of nuclear taboos related to common identity or ancestry. Nor were such concerns dominant when Taiwan weighed its nuclear options against China in the 1960s and 1970s while pressing for protection by the US umbrella. Even important opponents of an indigenous deterrent, who included scientist Wu Ta-you, made their case on other than normative grounds. The experience of China's civil war, the KMT's massacre of 10,000–20,000 Taiwanese, the demands for extended deterrence, and the nature of war plans against China also question the strength of kin-related taboos as barriers to warfare. A North Korean official's threat to turn Seoul into "a sea of fire," other such implacable warnings, and its consistent search for – and threats with – nuclear weapons belies any influence of anti-acquisition norms.

That anti-nuclear-weapons-acquisition norms were not central in East Asia is far from anomalous, since they were not fundamental considerations in other cases of abstention or reversal either, including Argentina, Brazil, Libya, and South Africa. It should thus not be surprising that Part 3 finds little evidence of such norms having taken deep roots in the Middle East, given this region's poor record of NPT compliance and the actual use of chemical weapons by Egypt, Iraq, Iran, and Libya. The evidence thus far might suggest that norms favoring nuclear acquisition are more common in some areas of the Middle East and South Asia. Derived from nationalist, religious, and other identities, such norms invested nuclear weapons with redemptive value as tools of modernization and defiance of the international order. As Part 3 suggests, statements by leaders and "norm entrepreneurs" from Iraq to Iran and Libya revealed far less reluctance to advocate nuclear weapons as politically and normatively valuable than in East Asia (except North Korea). Identity themes were malleable tools that could lead to contradictory prescriptions. WMD *use* was proclaimed contrary to Islam in Iran's early post-revolutionary period. Following the painful war with Iraq, Rafsanjani encouraged WMD development, declaring that "the moral teachings of the world are not very effective when war reaches a serious stage." Ahmadinejad's spiritual mentor, Ayatollah Yazdi, proclaimed that *shari'a* does not forbid nuclear use, let alone acquisition, contradicting other religious interpretations. Islam thus provided a flexible normative foundation that could be marshaled to justify competing arguments. This selective and opportunistic use of identity themes – not unique to the Middle East – compels the need to ground their role on nuclear decisions in a theory explaining the sources of domestic receptivity to such themes. Even for the important case of NPT compliance in this region, the record does not suggest that Egypt's denuclearization resulted from abhorrence of nuclear weapons. NPT ratification was justified in the People's Assembly in purely pragmatic terms, as part of efforts to secure international support for a nuclear industry. Furthermore, statements by Nasser, Sadat, Mubarak, and other officials asserted that Egypt would acquire nuclear weapons if its security demanded it; and "norm entrepreneurs" advocating nuclear weapons on identity grounds have certainly not been absent in Egypt, as chapter 11 documents.

Some identity-based perspectives have linked Israel's nuclearization to memories of the Holocaust and perceptions of international abandonment during those crucial years. Although quite plausible, this connection remains to be studied more systematically in light of competing normative corollaries from the Holocaust experience. Ben-Gurion and Bergman at one extreme, and members of the Committee for Denuclearization at the other, with various views in between, all shared a common desire to prevent another Holocaust but differed in means-ends prescriptions. Surveys showing apparent widespread support for a mutually verifiable, regionally based, and fully inclusive NWFZ based on prior peace agreements with all parties suggests that nuclear weapons are certainly not the only, or even the ranking, normative preference stemming from the Holocaust experience. To some extent this may be reflected in extensive support for nuclear non-acknowledgment rather than open deterrence, since the former could arguably be more amenable, symbolically, to be superseded by effective alternative arrangements that can assuage anxieties about physical survival. Such arrangements become more concrete in the context of a regional transformation of leading models of political survival along internationalizing lines, as I discuss below. The essentializing treatments of both Japan and Israel as facile derivatives of traumatic historical experiences must be eschewed in favor of further empirical research on identity and norms that is also sensitive to other variables, from formal alliances providing a nuclear umbrella (Japan) to UN isolation (Israel), to the democratic nature of institutions at home and across the border – much sparser in the Middle East than in East Asia – with different implications for Japan and Israel.

Where does constructivist analysis of denuclearization go from here? Developments over the past four decades compel norm-based studies to take stock of how, why, and to what extent have norms condemning the consideration, development, acquisition, or transfer of nuclear weapons (as distinct from use) diffused throughout the world; whether and why those norms may have declined or atrophied; how and when do we know that this has taken place (or what constitutes a critical mass of anomalies); what may explain sudden departures from such norms; and why have competing norms valuing nuclear weapons acquisition emerged. Norms emerge and evoke through reflection and analysis, through following established mores, through public discussion, and through evolutionary selection that favors certain norms because of their consequential role (Sen 1999: 273). These four mechanisms provide good foundations for exploring the dynamics of both anti-acquisition norms and their competitors. The NPR, NPT review conferences, ancillary NGO, and track-two processes offer valuable contexts for exploring norm diffusion through analysis, reflection, and public discussion. Detailed tracing of socialization experiences (Johnston 2001) may improve our understanding of nuclear choices and the relative effectiveness of different contexts in strengthening or weakening norms. Constructivist accounts would be particularly valuable if they could isolate the effects of socialization from those of hegemonic coercion or rational nuclear learning. They could explore clustered behavior toward or away from nuclearization in different regions and why such differences obtain under the shadow of presumably shared [global] anti-nuclear-weapons-acquisition norms. They could apply evolutionary selection to explain why anti-acquisition norms may or may not decline relative to competing norms favoring nuclear weapons on the basis of identity, modernity, or redemption. The cases in this book also suggest that a theory of domestic politics would help reveal whether, when, and how norms can play important and even decisive roles in nuclear decisions (Checkel 1997). Such theories may help clarify when and why agents promoting anti-acquisition norms may be more effective than those advocating competing norms, and would force greater attention to the interplay between international norms and the domestic conditions that reaffirm, modify, or weaken them.

Constructivist approaches rely on different epistemological and ontological tools than rationalist alternatives and are sometimes less concerned with strict causation and prediction. Furthermore, more constructivist work today seems concerned with human-security issues than with regional nuclear trajectories. Nonetheless, the preceding discussion suggests ways in which constructivist tools may help estimate future nuclear developments in East Asia and the Middle East in response to norms and identity shifts. For instance, many fear that rising nationalism in China, Japan, the Koreas, and Taiwan could lead to a more fragile regional order. The literature on the shadow cast by history and memory on relations among East Asian states might suggest that the sustainability of the region's evolution toward denuclearization could be tenuous. At an extreme, those shadows would arguably turn East Asia into a "most likely" case for nuclearization, a perception that might be stronger among some scholars attentive to memory, history, and changing power balances than among those focusing on East Asia as a nascent security community or as the economic dynamo of the early twenty-first century. Some constructivist accounts may be able to propose tipping points while others would not. Yet all would need to identify the mechanisms leading from nationalism, memory, or identity to nuclear weapons, particularly since many other states have sublimated such emotions onto alternative paths. Identifying the direction and strength of those effects might be helped by an improved understanding of the role of democratic or authoritarian contexts in amplifying or reducing the instrumentalities of – and cultural receptivity to – history, norms, and identity.

Democracy and nuclear choices

Chapter 2 extended democratic peace analysis to infer that, since nuclear weapons symbolize most violent and extreme solutions, democracies may arguably shy away from acquiring nuclear capabilities to resolve disputes with fellow democracies. This conjecture may be lie validated by this book's cases, given that no democracy developed nuclear weapons to deter another democracy in East Asia or the Middle East thus far. Beyond these cases, however, it is unclear whether India and Pakistan conform to this generalization, since both shared democratic regimes at some points but only India remained consistently democratic since independence. Furthermore, the first five nuclear-weapons states included three democracies (United States, France, and Britain). Some might explain their nuclearization as efforts to confront autocratic rivals (fascism first, communism later), but extant evidence supports prestige and power balancing as more crucial considerations during the first nuclear age (Rosecrance 1964; Dunn 1982; Husbands 1982). The Southern Cone also raises questions regarding the relationship between interactive democracies and nuclear weapons, since joint democracies in Argentina and Brazil overlapped with periods of ambiguous nuclear programs until the early 1990s, when leaders advocating internationalizing models signed mutual inspection agreements and ratified the NPT.

The proposition that democracies may be less prone to violate international agreements than non-democracies gains some validation. Few democracies were found to have violated the NPT in the way that Iraq, Libya, North Korea, and arguably Iran did, the small incident with South Korea notwithstanding. Yet several democracies (and autocracies) have not fully complied with Article VI of the NPT. Autocracies have conducted most flagrant deceptions of the IAEA, supporting expectations from Gaubatz (1996). This poor record of compliance also provides one – yet untested – hypothesis for why India and Israel might have been deterred from entering denuclearization agreements or signing the NPT with adversarial autocracies (Pakistan had democratic interludes), as democracies facing problems of uncertainty over ratification and implementation of agreements by autocratic adversaries. Israel within 1967 borders was the only continuous Middle East democracy since its creation, and it abstained from the NPT but favored a mutually verifiable and comprehensive regional NWFZ.[21] It is plausible, but unconfirmed by systematic research, that Israel's democratic nature played an important role in deepening its mistrust for neighboring autocracies, perhaps leading it to search for robust nuclear capabilities in the 1950s and 1960s.[22] Ironically, more recent threats to obliterate Israel by Ahmadinejad have emerged from one of the least autocratic regimes in the region, although certainly not a democracy. In Israel's early years, extreme secrecy precluded democratic politics from intruding into the nuclear debate at the popular level, with some exceptions.[23] Leading journalist Dan Margalit (1997: 7) argues that Israel's democracy in the 1990s would have jailed Ben-Gurion's group, and Dimona would have never been built, another potential subject for a good counterfactual analysis. The limited available evidence at the popular level suggests that only a small minority across the political spectrum endorsed explicit nuclear deterrence. Disagreements within ruling coalitions – resulting from an unwieldy electoral system – are discussed later.

Beyond that, regime type does not seem too germane a consideration for explaining nuclear behavior. Both regions had mixed clusters (democracies and autocracies), which might have led to similar outcomes regarding nuclear trajectories but didn't. Except for Japan, all other East Asian nuclear claimants were non-democratic at the time they decided to eschew (South Korea, Taiwan) or acquire nuclear weapons (North Korea). All three lacked democratic institutional restraints and might have gone either way without having to account to domestic publics for their nuclear decisions. Non-democratic Taiwan, South Korea, and several autocratic Southeast Asian states largely abided by NPT commitments. Since the late 1980s, democracies in Japan, South Korea, and Taiwan maintained their commitments despite North Korea's repeated threats to the first two and China's intermittent threats to attack Taiwan.

Even dictatorships must sustain supportive coalitions, and the military has been a key player in sustaining dictators and voicing positions on nuclear weapons. Yet in Taiwan and South Korea the military was cajoled into supporting denuclearization, while in North Korea and the Middle East cases some military agencies were at the heart of nuclear weapons programs. The key difference was in the model of political survival within which military institutions were embedded: export-led versus *juche* and Middle East equivalents. The advent of democracy in Taiwan and South Korea did not alter these fundamental differences, except for eroding even further the military's political role. Even prior to the inception of democracy, domestic groups in Taiwan – including the Atomic Energy Commission's highest echelons – foiled nuclear efforts such as the 1967 plan. While most Middle East nuclear aspirants were autocracies (Iraq, Libya, Iran, Nasser's Egypt), most autocracies also avoided nuclearization in both regions. Some even reversed course and abandoned nuclear weapons programs (Egypt, Libya). Autocracies have thus not exhibited uniform nuclear behavior. A possible testable hypothesis is the extent to which democracies in Japan, Taiwan, and South Korea may have posed higher barriers to nuclearization than did autocracies in Iraq, Libya, Iran, or North Korea.

In the end, many international regimes, including the NPR, are subscribed to by various regime types. NWFZ were concluded in temporal and spatial domains with few democracies (Latin America, the South-Pacific, Africa, and Southeast Asia). Autocratic leaders initiated unilateral denuclearization in Argentina, Brazil, Egypt, Kazakhstan, Belarus, Ukraine, South Korea, Taiwan, and other cases. The vast majority of democracies and autocracies have abided by their NPT commitments. Two out of three non-NPT states as of 2006 are long-standing democracies that face threats from autocracies, India and Israel (Pakistan has been an unstable, intermittent democracy). However, as non-members, India and Israel have not legally violated the NPT. Recent agreements with India despite its nuclear tests, and countenance of Israel's nuclear status, have raised allegations of "double standards," suggesting that democratic states may regard nuclear weapons in the hands of other democracies as arguably more legitimate than in the hands of autocracies. Shaker Al-Nabulsi explains this potential bias as follows: "The world is silent with regard to nuclear weapons in the hands of countries with constitutional institutions that do not make war-and-peace decisions in accordance with a leader's temper, a ruler's dream, or a cleric's fatwa, but by means of constitutional, rational, democratic, and modern institutions. This is why the world is silent in the face of Israel's nuclear weapons, for example, but goes berserk when North Korea and Iran possess these dangerous weapons, which could spark World War III, leading to the destruction [of the world] – all because of a fatwa by Ayatollah 'Ali Khamene'i, the supreme spiritual leader of the Iranian republic, or a decision based on the midsummer night's dream of the North Korean dictator."[24] Whether or not there is greater tolerance for democracies acquiring nuclear weapons remains subject to empirical investigation. Democracies and autocracies are also hypothesized to differ with respect to illegal transfers of WMD technology to other states or terrorist organizations (India and Israel, as opposed to Pakistan, China, North Korea, and arguably Iran). Yet private firms from democratic states have been quite involved in such transfers. Democracies and autocracies may respond differently to international sanctions and positive inducements regarding nuclear weapons. Democracies may approach nuclear issues under strong domestic identity and normative constraints (Japan and arguably Israel) or under widespread domestic support (India).

Future scenarios will test many of these hypotheses. The proposition that democracies would not be likely to develop nuclear weapons in disputes with other democracies could be falsified if, for instance, Japan were to develop nuclear weapons in response to a unified (democratic) nuclear Korea. Refutability requires clear a priori definitions of both democracy and nuclear status.[25] Regarding definitions of democracy, Iran is not South Korea. Regarding definitions of nuclear status, South Korea – without indigenous reprocessing and enrichment facilities – may not be Japan (some experts consider "hedging" to blur definitional clarity). Either way, the behavior of both regime types may be contingent on the nature of their ties to the global political economy, to which I turn now.

Domestic approaches to political survival

Given the limits of alternative understandings of nuclear behavior, the lack of rigorous examination of domestic sources of nuclear postures is particularly puzzling. Singh and Way (2004) have corroborated an empirical connection between involvement in the world economy and nuclear abstinence.[26] Whereas nuclear behavior provides neorealism with "most likely" conditions for supporting its tenets, it also offers "least likely" conditions for corroborating domestic political survival approaches. As discussed in Part I of *Nuclear Logics*, evidence for the weight of domestic political considerations in nuclear outcomes is much harder to garner; leaders are far more likely to cast decisions favoring or rejecting nuclear weapons as "reasons of state," invoking national security, international institutional incentives, and normative considerations (for or against such weapons) rather than ulterior domestic political motivations or expediency. Hence, available historical sources document "reasons of state" more frequently and thoroughly, loading the evidentiary dice against domestic political justifications. Precisely because nuclear issues are least likely to validate the role of domestic politics, they provide a tough, crucial arena for investigating such effects. Consequently, even partial substantiation for the importance of domestic considerations gains particular significance in this unfriendly terrain for this theory. One might argue that the threshold for gaining confidence in this argument should be lower than for theories advantaged by leaders' needs to justify nuclear decisions as national security imperatives. Yet as the empirical probes suggest, there is no need to lower the bar. Models of political survival and nuclear policies are not merely loosely associated but indeed joined at the hip. Their omission may have led to an overestimation of other causal variables and to potential spurious effects (Brady and Collier 2004). Their inclusion may improve our understanding of the actual effects of security dilemmas, international norms, and institutions when interacting with domestic models.

Leaders vary in their tolerance for domestic and international, political and economic (including opportunity) costs entailed by nuclear weapons. What specific aspects of models that emphasize economic growth and openness to the global economy as tools of political survival make certain leaders more receptive to denuclearization than others? The answer ranges from the need to appeal to foreign investors with an interest in domestic economic growth and stability; to the related need to reassure neighbors in order to preserve regional cooperation and stability; to the requirement of securing access to international markets for exports, capital, technology, and raw materials; to the related aversion to risking reputational losses at home and abroad for uncertain nuclear gains; to the costs of alienating domestic agents of internationalization – both within and outside state structures – which would be adversely affected by nuclear weapons development. Clearly, there are several causal pathways linking the renunciation of nuclear weapons to models that emphasize economic growth through global integration. Nuclearization burdens efforts to enhance exports, economic competitiveness, macroeconomic and political stability, and global access – all objectives of internationalizing models – while strengthening state bureaucracies, agencies, and industrial complexes opposed to economic transformation.[27] As Part 2 suggests, denuclearization has often been related to broader programs of internationalization designed to strengthen market-oriented forces, leaders, and institutions – state and private – favoring export-led growth. Beyond these cases, the profile of nearly all nuclear aspirants who steered their countries away from nuclearization matches these expectations.[28]

Conversely, leaders and ruling coalitions relying on or promoting inward-looking bases of support have had greater tolerance – and in some cases strong incentives – for developing nuclear weapons. Nuclearization has entailed considerable domestic advantages for foes of internationalizing models in inward-looking, import-substituting regimes that favor extreme nationalism, religious radicalism, or autarky. Nuclearization has also borne lower international costs for leaders advancing models less dependent on external markets, investment, capital, and technology. Such leaders and their political allies have often relied on extreme language to compel and threaten regional adversaries, wielding potential nuclear and other WMD as means to coerce and intimidate. Statements such as North Korea's repeated threats to Seoul and Tokyo, Saddam Hussein's threats to Iran and Saudi Arabia together with his vow to "incinerate half of Israel," and Iran's warning that "the use of even one nuclear bomb inside Israel will destroy everything" are certainly more rare in domestic political contexts driven by internationalizing objectives. Most inward-looking nuclear aspirants have been NPT members who have misled IAEA inspectors or have violated NPR commitments. As a region, the Middle East has gravitated toward the inward-looking end of the spectrum for many years, although there have also been efforts to transcend that path (Lebanon, Turkey, Jordan, and, more recently, some GCC countries). North Korea's dominant political survival strategy has more affinity with that of post-1979 Iran, Saddam's Iraq, and Libya than with most of its neighbors. For all of the presumed devotion to brotherly unification with kin states (pan-Arabism or pan-Islamism in the cases of Saddam, Gaddafi, and Nasser, *Koryo* for Kim Il-Sung), inward-looking leaders have promoted extreme nationalist platforms of political survival.

Restating the argument, nuclearization has been less attractive and much more costly for leaders and coalitions pursuing integration into the global economy in order to advance domestic, regional, and international objectives. From this point of view, Middle East leaders faced lower barriers to, and stronger incentives for, nuclearization than East Asian ones. Whereas inward-looking models might have regarded nuclear weapons as assets in the arsenal of building regime legitimacy, outward-oriented ones regarded them as liabilities. The heavy regional concentration of internationalizing models in East Asia reinforced domestic incentives across the border for rejecting nuclearization.[29] The heavy regional concentration of inward-looking models in much of the Middle East had opposite effects, exacerbating individual incentives to develop nuclear weapons. As gleaned from the experience of an overwhelming number of nuclear aspirants in the second nuclear age, domestic survival models should be treated as more fundamental considerations in explaining nuclear choices than has been the case, not merely as afterthoughts or residual factors. The nuclear choices of all pertinent cases in the Middle East and East Asia since the 1960s are compatible with domestic survival models, which provide crucial information about which leaders and ruling coalitions are more sensitive to certain pressures and inducements but not others. Such receptivity may change over time even for the same state, as a result of changes in leadership, coalitions, and survival models, as in Egypt and Libya. In both of these cases, *infitah* and steps toward denuclearization were introduced in tandem, sometimes the same year (Egypt) or the same month (Libya). Regime survival has been a crucial logic in North Korea, Libya, Iraq, and Iran's nuclear efforts, and it explains domestic receptivity to denuclearization – with or without alliances – in Egypt, South Korea, and Taiwan, and many other cases from South Africa to Argentina, Brazil, and Turkey.

In many ways East Asia and the Middle East provide the toughest tests for hypotheses related to domestic models of political survival, because both regions are ridden with security dilemmas and a history of militarized rivalries. The latter, as argued, should make these regions easy cases for hypotheses emphasizing balance of power. By contrast, cases from Latin America, South Africa, and Europe in the second nuclear age could arguably provide more favorable grounds for domestic survival hypotheses (Solingen 1996, 1998; Liberman 2001). The challenge, as always, is to scrutinize the viability of hypotheses precisely where they are least likely to be validated. On those grounds, how do domestic survival models fare across the individual cases examined in East Asia and the Middle East, which provide difficult cases indeed for this argument? Japan's nuclear status has frequently been traced to its US alliance or the nuclear allergy, but both require a model of domestic politics that explains their respective roles. The alliance was a critical component of the Yoshida model of political survival, not an end in itself but a means to enable concentration on economic growth through global access, while avoiding militarization. Such a model also provided special receptivity – at the societal and leadership level – to anti-nuclear-acquisition norms. In a specific rejection of the war-oriented autarkic and militarized model of the 1930s, Japan's postwar leaders sought domestic political legitimacy and electoral approval through export-led economic growth and recovery. As Berger (1998: 29) notes, Japan's population "was more concerned with the task of rebuilding the economy than dwelling on the past." This created significant space for Yoshida Shigeru's model hinging on Japan as "merchant nation" (*chōnin kokka*). Prominent advocates of a denuclearized Japan (Nagai, Kōsaka, Kishida, Momoi among many others) could rely heavily on the alliance and the NPT as disincentives to be emphasized in domestic debates.[30] Regardless of their deep personal preferences, nuclear weapons were a political liability for leaders advancing a model of national security that was "economic in nature" (Inoguchi 1993: 36).

A 1957 US NIE got it fundamentally right: "Japanese policy with respect to the production of nuclear weapons is likely to be determined primarily by domestic and regional considerations."[31] An expert on Japan's nuclear policy asserted that "for the Japanese people, nuclear issues were more or less subjects for domestic politics or domestic social movements, which seemed to be rather insulated from the reality of international security" (Akiyama 2003: 89). Another suggested that "Japan may have likely remained non-nuclear regardless of any external security developments" (Kase 2001: 56). The Yoshida model, the nuclear allergy, the 1955 system, and institutional restraints were all part of the domestic landscape that trumped nuclearization. An emphasis on the alliance and anti-nuclear norms has obscured the importance of the domestic political-economy model on Japan's nuclear decisions, deprived the account of the nuts and bolts of politics underlying early nuclear choices and their path-dependent consequences, and overlooked domestic receptivity to certain solutions but not others. The model embraced by Japan's postwar politicians and the requirements of a "trading state" at peace with its region provide a powerful account for the absence of demand for nuclear weapons in Japan, and explains why Japan embraced the alliance to begin with. The nuclear umbrella is thus endogenous to Japan's forgoing of a national nuclear deterrent, insofar as the alliance itself was a derivative of a domestic compromise. Some domestic opponents of nuclear weapons regarded this compromise as a form of "embedded nuclearization" that contradicted nuclear norms. In sum, the Yoshida model – its expectations, achievements, and its legacy – arguably constituted necessary conditions for Japan's non-nuclear status. The alliance and the nuclear allergy made the outcome even more likely, but it is plausible that domestic considerations might have been sufficient in and of themselves.

Both the alliance and coercion may have been necessary for South Korea's denuclearization, but one can fully understand their respective roles only in the context of domestic survival models, which explain why alliance was chosen over autarkic *juche* in the first place, with ensuing consequences for relative receptivity to external inducements, positive and negative. What would have been the fate of the alliance had Park relied on North Korea's brand of *juche*? Park's model was not the result of external imposition alone; earlier US pressures on Syngman Rhee for economic reform rarely yielded fruit. US pressures and Park's own model worked in the same direction. As Reiss (1988: 95) argues, Park's objectives were to ensure political stability and economic growth. The two were symbiotic and left little room for nuclear weapons, which would have endangered growth, stability, and access to global markets, capital, and technology; alienated domestic support; risked sharp economic decline; and isolated South Korea from the regional and international market and institutional forces that underpinned the model. The alliance enabled the model's core objectives in addition to providing protection. Park could skillfully wield domestic pressures for both an alternative model and an indigenous deterrent in the 1970s to extract concessions from the United States. Yet he was not ready to sacrifice a 10 percent average growth rate on the altar of nuclear weapons. Park even deployed the threat from the North to consolidate support for his model: "There is an even more important reason for seeking high economic growth, and that is the need for us to maintain a position superior to North Korea in our present state of confrontation. …Unless a policy of high economic growth is sustained, there will be no way to meet increased defense spending" (Park 1979: 94–96). Subsequent democratization strengthened the model and overwhelmed the few advocates of nuclear weapons. Roh Moo-Huyn, presiding over one of South Korea's least friendly administrations vis-à-vis the United States since the 1960s, reaffirmed his intention not to develop or possess nuclear weapons.

Meeting most definitions of existential insecurity, Taiwan did not resort to nuclear weapons either. US pressures were certainly important here as well but, as Yager (1985: 192) suggests, "The unanswered question is, Why did the ROC authorities yield so readily to US demands?" The KMT's favored model of political survival – which hinged on economic growth, prosperity, and domestic stability – explains widespread receptivity to US demands and inducements. Nuclear weapons would have introduced massive stress at home, among neighboring countries and worldwide, with negative consequences for domestic growth and stability. KMT leaders had strong incentives to avoid regional conflict and instability in order to sustain attractiveness to foreign investors, controlled military expenditures, and ample foreign reserves (thanks to successful exports), given Taiwan's international isolation. Access to preferential export markets, international capital, investments, and nuclear technology to fuel the economic miracle required nuclear restraint. Without it, the political prospects of the KMT and its successors were fragile. Opponents of nuclear weapons could thus overwhelm domestic adversaries, as economic growth propelled Taiwan from among the poorest to among the most dynamic economies worldwide. The model also explains severe anomalies for neorealism, such as Taiwan's impressive embrace of the mainland – its presumed archrival – as a vital trading partner. While unveiling Taiwan's first formal national security policy, the deputy secretary-general of Taiwan's National Security Council, Michael Tsai, provided further reassurance: "We're not pursuing preemptive capabilities, and we will not develop nuclear weapons or weapons of mass destruction."[32]

Part 3 provides significant support for links between inward-looking models and pursuit of nuclear weapons. Saddam's model was anchored in the entrenched combined power of militarized state bureaucracies and enterprises, import-substituting interests, and the military-industrial complex, as well as their respective beneficiaries in state-controlled professional and labor organizations. The state dominated infrastructure, manufacturing, trade and services, employing at least half of the workforce and, together with the military-industrial complex, absorbed progressively more resources. The prominence assigned to oil and the military-industrial complex trumped manufacturing, industrial diversification, and non-oil exports. Saddam was much less preoccupied with fiscal policy, macroeconomic stability, export-competitiveness in manufacturing, or servicing foreign debts. He derided the international economic order. His nuclear program cannot be understood in isolation from these priorities. It became a core symbol of his broader strategy of self-reliance and a major tool to enhance his personal power and boost his model of political control at home and throughout the region. As Saddam acknowledged and his lieutenants confirmed, WMD kept his domestic and external enemies at bay, portraying an aura of invincibility. Chapter 7's account on pre-delegation of authority corroborates that he regarded the potential passing of his regime as co-terminal with Iraq's integrity. The structure, function, budgets, and manning of Iraq's nuclear program – the roots of which preceded both the Iran–Iraq war and the 1981 Israeli attack on Osiraq – point to its central role in Saddam's model of regime survival against domestic and foreign threats.

Iran's alleged nuclear weapons program can be more readily justified as a response to Saddam's 1980 invasion and Iraq's use of chemical weapons and missiles on Iranian troops and cities. Even in Iran, however, the domestic underpinnings of the nuclear weapons program are brought to relief by statements from one of the program's alleged "fathers." Asgar-Khani acknowledged that the program was needed also "for Iran's social cohesion and prestige. ...Internally Iran is in a state of disarray. I would now argue that, only by becoming a nuclear weapons state, can Iran consolidate its social coherence. Iran needs both soft and hard power to regain its national identity and prestige."[33] The program was advanced by a coalition of radical inward-looking forces largely opposed to internationalization, from radical mullahs (including Khamene'i) to the Ministry of Defense, Pasdaran, and massive state enterprises (bonyads) controlled by top clerics and the military. The inability of reformist leaders to overpower the ancien régime and change Iran's approach to the global political economy had significant consequences for the program's acceleration. Ancien régime supporters regard nuclear weapons "as an insurance policy against a forced change in the government," in other words, as a guarantee of regime survival and continued protection of vast state corporations and military privileges.[34] As Milani (2005b: 48) argues, Iran's "regime has sought the bomb for the same reason that it does everything: its monomaniacal commitment to self-preservation," namely, "self-preservation at home" (Milani 2005: 9). In the 1990s, the revolution had lost its luster for supporters at home and abroad. According to Chubin (2006: 8), the nuclear option, initially an insurance against Iraq, was in search of a rationale and offered a way out for rallying nationalist opposition and providing legitimacy to a failing regime hinged on economic and military self-sufficiency. Once coalitions and constituencies favoring nuclear weapons have developed, "a state can cross the point of political no return [and] this phenomenon is becoming all too evident in the case of Iran" (Takeyh 2004).[35]

Immediately after assuming power Gaddafi pursued nuclear weapons as a central pillar of his inward-looking model, wielding nationalistic and xenophobic objectives. He nationalized the oil industry and used windfall revenues to secure popular support while virtually eliminating private economic activities. The military was his core constituency and he nurtured it with promises of sophisticated weapons technology. In time, declining oil prices deprived Gaddafi of revenues needed to maintain the very constituencies his revolution had mobilized. Eccentric terrorist activities leading to international sanctions diluted his resources further at a time when expenditures for exotic weapons ceased to attract the imagination of an impoverished population. Feeble initial efforts to reform the economy in the 1980s made way for a more forceful statement by 2000 that "now is the era of economy, consumption, markets, and investment" (chapter 10 in *Nuclear Logics*). Private and public statements provide significant evidence that Gaddafi's 2003 decision to surrender his nuclear weapons program was made under conditions of declining resources for compensating domestic political allies and amidst continued domestic challenges to his rule. Both Gaddafi's most forceful attempt at economic reform (*infitah*) and his boldest approach to Britain and the United States in negotiating the surrender of his WMD programs took place in March 2003. Negotiations for the terms of denuclearization began prior to the 2003 Iraq war, although personal safety concerns may have furthered Gaddafi's extant incentives to trade WMD programs for external support for implementing an internationalizing shift. In the end, both external economic incentives that would enable him to reconstitute supportive domestic coalitions and concerns with his own fate compelled Gaddafi to adopt a new model, which turned nuclear weapons into a major liability. A political survival approach can thus explain both Gaddafi's efforts to seek nuclear weapons since the 1970s and his 2003 reversal.

The origins of Israel's nuclear program in the 1950s is often discussed within the context of the Holocaust, the 1948 military attack by all its neighbors, its conventional weapons inferiority compounded by arms embargoes, extensive Soviet military and political support to Arab regimes committed to destroying Israel, and its adversaries' early search for missile and chemical weapons and their actual use in battle. Decision-makers faced genuine dilemmas of state survival but domestic politics provided an important background for how the program emerged and developed. Mapai-led ruling coalitions advanced their political survival on explicit socialist principles that kept markets and private enterprise at arm's length, favored extensive economic controls and import-substitution, but – in the absence of natural resources – also depended on foreign capital and agricultural exports. A small group around Ben-Gurion embodying *Mamlachtiut* (statism) and autonomy from "sectarian" social forces launched the nuclear program in the late 1950s. Their emphasis on self-reliance was compatible with the political and economic foundations of Ben-Gurion's model and the development of a military-industrial complex. International economic access and external guarantees were in scarce supply (Keiss 1988; Dunn 1998). Domestic political survival hinged on the ability to provide both fail-safe assurances against external threats and adequate welfare for remnants of concentration camps and refugees from Arab states. Yet that left room for significant differences across factions on guns-versus-butter, economic self-reliance versus dependence, conventional versus nuclear deterrence, and domestic versus external guarantees of survival. Ben-Gurion guarded the nuclear program even from partners in the coalition who were more skeptical of his program. A policy of nuclear ambiguity became an equilibrium solution that circumvented risky external responses and serious domestic conflicts in a highly divided polity and society. Furthermore, Israel was not merely the only democracy in the region in the 1950s in the midst of autocracies that threatened it with extinction, but also part of a region dominated by inward-looking models suspicious of the global political economy and heavily rooted in military-industrial complexes. In this last respect, Israel was no exception. Nuclear ambiguity eventually eroded with certain statements by Israeli leaders, but "non-acknowledgement" lingered (Dowty 2005).

Finally, both Nasser's early efforts to acquire nuclear weapons and Sadat's subsequent shift to renounce them were compatible with their respective models of political survival. Nasser and the Free Officers introduced import-substituting industrialization and massive nationalizations of banking, industry, and infrastructure (including the Suez Canal), a model emulated by Saddam, Gaddafi, and others in the region. State expansion and forceful suppression of private entrepreneurship eliminated economic and political competitors to the state. Trade openness declined from over 53 percent in the early 1950s – prior to the revolution – to 33 percent average under Nasser. The military-industrial complex was Nasser's crucial partner, allocating itself nearly 24 percent of GDP. Nasser's search for hegemony over the Arab world led him to pursue unification schemes and to intervene in Yemen's civil war, including use of chemical weapons. In tandem with aspirations for economic self-sufficiency, militarization of the economy, and belligerent pan-Arab nationalism, Nasser's ruling coalition also sought nuclear weapons and delivery systems as early as the 1950s, a step that was encouraged by supporters of Soviet-style models of political control among others. Economic policies and foreign adventurism led to balance-of-payments crises, food and consumer goods shortages, high inflation, and reduced foreign credit and foreign exchange, all in the midst of population explosion and rising expectations. Ironically, the very model of political survival that made nuclear weapons an attractive feature also shrank available resources to levels that all but precluded them. Nuclear weapons proponents advocated self-reliance over Soviet nuclear guarantees. Among them, Nasser's advisor Haykal rejected possible mutual inspections with Israel, because "naturally Egypt will refuse to become a party in any agreement with Israel."[36]

Whereas Nasser's model thrived in this aura of inward-looking self-reliance, hyper-nationalism, and military-technical prowess, Sadat's emphasis on economic growth, foreign investment, exports, military conversion, and a new relationship with international markets and institutions did not leave much room for an expensive nuclear program. The economic prerequisites of Sadat's model required regional stability (peace with Israel) and precluded nuclear arms races with regional competitors. Transparent nuclear policies were also expected to endear Egypt to the West. In 1974, Egypt supported the NWFZ proposed by Iran and committed to accept full-scope IAEA safeguards, all with an eye on receiving economic benefits and nuclear power reactors from the United States. Resolving chronic energy shortages through nuclear power was deemed important for sustaining a planned *infitah* (economic opening). Nixon's 1974 visit to Egypt delivered an agreement to provide the power plants and solidified US–Egyptian relations. *Infitah*, also launched in 1974, increased Egypt's trade openness from an average of 33 percent under Nasser to over 61 percent in 1975 and 78 percent in 1979. FDI inflows more than doubled between 1974 and 1976, and military expenditures declined from 52 to 13 percent of GNP between 1975 and 1979. *Infitah* also increased Egypt's dependence on foreign loans and aid. Egypt received about $2 billion average annual military and economic aid since 1979, reaching nearly $60 billion in cumulative aid by 2005. Sadat also requested a foreign aid package of $18 billion from the G7 in 1979. Abandoning a nuclear weapons program also meant challenging Sadat's domestic political foes, particularly Nasserites and Islamist groups with prominent nuclear advocates. Sadat cancelled the Atomic Energy Authority's autonomy, transferring it to the Ministry of Electricity. In 1981, he persuaded the People's Assembly that NPT ratification was needed to secure international support for nuclear energy. Sadat's model, particularly relations with Israel and the United States, cost him much capital regionally, including Egypt's ousting from the Arab league.

The shift from Nasser to Sadat and its implications for nuclear policies are well summarized by Egyptian analyst Mohamed Kadry Said (2002: 1):

> Sadat realized that reaching a settlement to the Arab–Israeli conflict is a precondition for Egyptian development. To achieve this goal, Sadat concentrated his energy towards enhancing US–Egyptian relations and to foster a peace process with Israel. He worked hard to change the Egyptian domestic, regional and international environment in a way conducive to peace. Changing Egyptian attitudes towards arms control arrangements was one of the ways of realizing his aims.

Yet *infitah* never led to the kind of positive cycle observed among East Asian cases that renounced nuclear weapons: high economic growth, high integration in the global political-economy, high legitimacy for the internationalizing model, and lower incentives to resort to nuclear weapons.[37] Furthermore, heavy regional concentration of inward-looking models in much of the Middle East has exacerbated incentives of individual leaders, parties, and ruling coalitions to develop nuclear weapons, creating additional barriers to foreign investment and economic reform throughout most of the region. The strains and barriers to internationalization within Egypt explain strong lingering revisionist currents advocating nuclearization. The continuity of Egypt's current nuclear policies depends, to a significant extent, on whether or not this revisionist current can overwhelm a struggling ruling coalition with stronger internationalizing orientations.

In sum, identifying domestic models that underlie nuclear shifts in these nine cases takes us several steps beyond structural power explanations in understanding how external and internal factors interact to produce changes in nuclear behavior. Furthermore, the relative incidence of different models in each region certainly magnifies domestic incentives of leaders in one direction or another. Regions more highly integrated in the global economy enhance the prospects of internationalizing models, whereas regions less integrated pose more serious difficulties for denuclearization. The argument may not be equally supported in all cases, but it consistently sheds light on how domestic models regarding integration in the global political-economy have created different constraints, incentives, receptivity, and compliance patterns, and have conditioned the role that international power, institutions, and democracy played in nuclear decisions. Understanding domestic survival models thus provides fuller explanations for why security dilemmas are sometimes seen as more (or less) intractable, why some states rank alliance higher than self-reliance but not others, when and how hegemonic coercion and inducements are effective and when they play a secondary or marginal role, why nuclear weapons programs surfaced where there was little need for them (Libya), why such programs were abandoned where unalloyed neorealist structural perspectives would have expected them (Egypt), and how leaders filter different concepts of security through their preferred approach to political survival.[38] As Meyer's (1984: 47) landmark study of nonproliferation put it, "*all* the motive conditions will be filtered through the domestic political system…Therefore all the motive conditions are in some way tied to domestic politics."

The existence of an association between domestic models and nuclear policies gains support from different regions, making it an analytically indispensable category that should be integral to explanations of denuclearization. However, a framework contingent on evolving political survival models implies, by its very nature, no linear or irreversible trajectories in either direction. Leaders and ruling coalitions may reverse courses in response to domestic pressures and external contingencies, including global or regional economic and security developments.[39] Thus, Gaddafi's incentives changed in response to well-coordinated international sanctions, lower oil prices, the inducements of a globalizing economy, and the war in Iraq, all of which undermined his old would-be autarkic model. Propositions derived from this framework are also bounded – as noted in chapter 1 – in three ways: with respect to conditions of necessity and sufficiency in developing nuclear weapons, by the incidence of compatible models in the region, and by temporal sequences in the acquisition of nuclear weapons. This last scope condition implies that eliminating existing weapons may be more costly politically than eradicating precursor programs, and that the incentives emanating from the global political economy may operate more forcefully at earlier stages in the inception of internationalizing models and early stages in the consideration of nuclear weapons. These, as many other hypotheses proposed in this book, remain subject to further investigation.

Furthermore, the political survival argument is only probabilistic, as are most arguments in the social sciences. Internationalizing leaders may embrace nuclear weapons.[40] Inward-oriented leaders may decide to abandon them. Both instances would prove the argument falsifiable (subject to empirical refutation), a healthy attribute provided that anomalies do not overwhelm corroborations. But even if one finds this approach reasonably persuasive in explaining the past, it does not necessarily follow that it will also apply in the future (Hirschman 1986). Different dynamics could be at work, triggering conditions under which internationalizing models may no longer provide sufficient conditions for continued denuclearization. As Campbell *et al.* (2004: 13) suggest, "There is widespread concern that the calculus of incentives and disincentives has shifted during the past decade, with incentives increasing and disincentives declining. New threats have arisen while the nuclear taboo has weakened. And it is not just a single factor in this new strategic landscape that gives pause. Rather, it is the accumulation of multiple factors and their interplay and mutual reinforcement that account for many of these new dangers."

The framework proposed here provides a roadmap for considering the conditions under which its expectations might be corroborated or refuted. Figure 10.1 suggests four possible scenarios. The vertical axis refers to the two basic models, internationalizing and inward-looking. The horizontal axis maps two basic trends: toward nuclearization and away from it. Scenario I suggests a situation where leaders and coalitions continue to steer internationalizing models in their respective countries and, at the same time, retain commitments to denuclearization. This joint outcome would be compatible with the framework's expectations. This scenario matches the reality of most of East Asia in the early twenty-first century and has a reasonable likelihood to persist, provided that most central features analyzed in Part 2 remain in place, including regional and global conditions propitious for these models' survival. This scenario is supported, among many other considerations, by the presence of some 28,000 Japanese companies employing over a million workers in China as of 2005, double the number merely a decade ago, and of over one million Taiwanese entrepreneurs in the mainland.[41] Former MOFA official Kaneko Kumao (1996: 46) draws attention to another requisite for the continuity of Japan's model:

> Japan maintains cooperative nuclear agreements with six countries, the United States, Britain, France, Canada, Australia, and China. I personally negotiated…most of these. …If Japan misuses its civilian nuclear program for military purposes, a set of stringent sanctions will be imposed on it, including the immediate return of all imported materials and equipment to the original exporting country. Should that ever happen, nuclear power plants in Japan [would] come to a grinding halt, crippling economic and industrial activities. It is simply unthinkable that the nation would be willing to make such a heavy sacrifice – unless it [was] really prepared to start a war. In this sense, the bilateral nuclear energy agreements provide a rather effective deterrent, certainly more effective than the NPT.[42]

Scenario 3 entails the continuity of internationalizing models accompanied by discontinuities in nuclear policies. In other words, internationalizers go nuclear, which would constitute an anomaly for political survival arguments. This may be less likely under the current circumstances of a strongly internationalizing East Asia (including China), considered to be the locomotive of an expanding global economy. Should others backtrack on internationalizing models, however, such prospects could be higher. For instance, a Chinese leadership that does not cope appropriately with domestic challenges of economic transformation could be weakened or replaced by inward-looking opponents, with attending regional

	Internationalizing	Inward-looking
Denuclearization	1 Compatible	2 Anomaly
Nuclearization	3 Anomaly	4 Compatible

Figure 10.1 Models of political survival and nuclear outcomes: Four scenarios

consequences. Furthermore, internationalizing leaders everywhere are not immune to miscalculating by overplaying nationalist cards or falling victim to "blowback" and entrapment by constituencies more favorable to nuclearization.[43] The 2005 Chinese legislation codifying a declaration of war against Taiwan if the latter claims independence could provide an example of unintended effects of such miscalculations. In the Middle East, recent reports suggested that Turkey could, under certain circumstances, reconsider its nuclear status (Fuerth 2004). In the past two decades, Turkish leaders appeared to have transcended the Middle East's modal inward-looking path, consolidating an internationalizing model and renouncing nuclear weapons. If this choice were reversed while Turkey sustains the current model, the domestic survival argument would be refuted. If, however, Turkey were to reverse its nuclear commitments in tandem with the rise of progressively more inward-looking domestic models – exacerbated by EU exclusion – the argument would be sustained. Such domestic changes could also involve deterioration in Turkey's relationship with NATO, highlighting the importance of domestic considerations in shaping security policies.

Scenario 2 points to conditions where inward-looking models dominate within a nuclear aspirant which nonetheless embraces denuclearization. The past record of nuclear aspirants shows that this joint occurrence has been rare if not nonexistent. This scenario would constitute another anomaly for the basic argument and could be illustrated by situations where inward-looking regimes in North Korea and the Middle East join and implement durable, transparent, mutually and unconditionally verifiable agreements renouncing nuclear capabilities as part of broader peace settlements.[44] The prospects for this outcome do not seem very likely under current circumstances. However, if, for instance, Iran's and North Korea's nuclear policies change in tandem with domestic survival models, as in Egypt and Libya, the argument would be corroborated.[45] In East Asia, Scenario 2 would similarly involve the rise of domestic inward-looking models in pivotal states that nonetheless retain NPT commitments and compliance. This situation might be explained by path dependency or increasing returns of a three-decade old legacy of shunning nuclear weapons (except for North Korea).

Scenario 4 suggests the presence of resilient inward-looking leaders resistant to internationalization, a defining characteristic of much of the Middle East for many decades, accompanied by intermittent efforts to acquire nuclear weapons. This scenario is compatible with the basic framework of regime survival, and its permanence does not bode well for denuclearizing shifts in that region. In East Asia, the widespread replacement of internationalizing models of political survival is certainly plausible but seems to be a low-probability event as of 2006. The Asian crisis signaled more resilience than anticipated and, despite some political turnovers, did not lead to significant departures from internationalizing strategies. Such turns remain nonetheless plausible in conjunction with global recessions or other regional and domestic downward economic or nationalist spirals. Significant domestic evolutions away from internationalizing trajectories – from China to South Korea, Indonesia, and Japan – might encourage nuclear dominos. This outcome, although unlikely under present conditions in the world's most economically dynamic region, would be compatible with predictions in Scenario 4.

These scenarios offer some guidance regarding continuity and change in nuclear trajectories on the basis of evolving domestic models of political survival. More complex scenarios can be developed by supplementing them with propositions derived from other approaches to nuclear behavior. As the independent, non-partisan Commission on the Intelligence Capabilities of the United States Regarding Weapons of Mass Destruction acknowledged, strengthening competitive analysis and competing hypotheses must be a *sine qua non* in the analysis of WMD programs of other countries (see http://whitehouse.gov/wmd/index.html). It would be misleading to conclude that policies of engagement in the global economy make states less secure because they arguably thwart nuclear capabilities. Japan, Taiwan, and South Korea, without natural resources or nuclear weapons, seem far less vulnerable or insecure than North Korea, Iran, or pre-2003 Iraq. Internationalizing models have turned them into engines of the twenty-first global economy, with much higher levels of domestic political stability, social equity, human rights, expected life spans, employment, and educational endowments than nuclear-equipped but unstable Middle East models, despite rich natural and human resources.

Policy implications

As George (1993) suggested, theoretical analysis may be more helpful in conceptualizing the formulation of policy strategies than in providing detailed policy plans, or detailed elements of particular policies. This section thus offers very preliminary steps in the direction of translating what we know into what can be done. Clearly, different understandings of nuclear incentives can lead to different policy implications. No single approach opens the gate to the holy grail of denuclearization. Every approach raises the problem of causal versus manipulative variables in policy formulation. Even if the leading causal variable driving or discouraging proliferation could be identified (relative power, norms and institutions, democracy, or domestic survival models), that variable may not be easily manipulable. Furthermore, as Lebow (2003: 384) argues, "Our ability to predict, explain, control or manipulate social phenomena has been consistently confounded by the complexity and openness of social systems, and the ability of human beings to plan around and undermine any temporarily valid generalization." The challenge involved in outlining gaps between causal variables at work, and assessing what might be done with them to steer policy in more efficient directions, remains. Since policy-relevant studies along neorealist and neoliberal-institutionalist lines have been the staple in nonproliferation, I survey them only briefly and concentrate on tentative propositions that disaggregate the domestic context of nuclear aspirants.

The strategic circumstances of states vary from very threatening and precarious to relatively benign, setting up some background conditions but also raising an array of operational limitations. As different chapters suggested, hegemons and other powerful states with many resources can find it very difficult to translate them into preferred outcomes. Hegemons have relied on both forceful coercion and attractive enticements to discourage nuclearization, but those efforts have failed in a non-trivial number of cases. The specific domestic receptivity of targets to selected negative and positive inducements is a critical intervening factor between hegemonic efforts and responses by nuclear aspirants. Policies that assume states as unified entities inexorably buffeted by changes in the balance of power, and that rely on coercion or inducements without considering domestic political landscapes, are less likely to succeed. Ironically, acting on the assumption that states are monolithic structures under threat tends to reproduce such assumptions in target states, enabling their regimes to widen domestic sympathy. Surgical attacks on Iran's nuclear facilities could bring about just such rallying-round-the-flag effects. Milani (2005a, 2005b) also cautions against granting "security assurances" to Iran's regime that would forestall its inevitable demise by Iran's own disgruntled citizens. Yet granting such assurances can also prevent such regimes from wielding external threats to unify their publics, provided the public can learn about the existence of such assurances. Construing nuclear aspirants as monolithic states can thus subvert the successful design of positive and negative inducements. Furthermore, as studies in this book suggest, single-handed emphasis on structural power does not necessarily lead to any particular policy equilibrium but to a cacophony of options. Whereas some advocate forceful, including military, prevention or preemption as tools of nuclear denial, others regard the diffusion of nuclear capabilities as potentially stabilizing, requiring only that those newcomers be helped to transition into nuclear balance (Intriligator and Brito 1981; Waltz 1981; Bueno de Mesquita and Riker 1982). Additional prescriptions compatible with relative-power considerations that emphasize the dangers of diffusion point to export controls and economic sanctions.

For the most part, international institutions enjoy greater international legitimacy as agents of nonproliferation than any single state or any group of states that has already acquired nuclear weapons. The Nobel Peace Prize award to the IAEA is perhaps a reflection of that recognition. Chapter 2 discussed NPR-related mechanisms designed to prevent diffusion of sensitive technologies for military uses. The Fissile Material Cut Off Treaty, for instance, was conceived to prohibit use of fissile materials in nuclear weapons while enabling civilian use. New forms of control of enrichment and reprocessing technologies are being considered.[46] Most institutional solutions are crafted from the perspective of technological denial and supply of coercion. A major deficiency of the NPR, however, even when it can overcome problems of collective action, has been its lack of effective means of enforcement. Beyond their multilateral essence, rational-institutionalist approaches to the NPT have shared with neorealism explicit or implicit assumptions about unified states, without providing a coherent account of the sources of state preferences. As the chapters on Iraq, Libya, and North Korea suggest, measures that could be considered rational for application on target states as a whole may be far less rational when domestic distributional consequences are considered, creating unintended victims and strengthening already powerful dictators. Many such lessons have been learned in the past two decades by states, multilateral institutions, and NGOs. Policy instruments have all too often neglected domestic factors in the crystallization of nuclear preferences until relatively recently. Widespread economic sanctions, indiscriminating blockades, and exclusion from membership in international institutions can sometimes help uncompromising leaders coalesce national opposition. Lessons from Iraq and North Korea suggest that sanctions have not been effective in producing popular uprisings.

In sum, approaches pivoted on the concept of balance of power ignored, by definition, the domestic nature of states, and those pivoted on the NPR have similarly been inattentive to systematic domestic sources of demand for nuclear weapons. In both cases the basic problem has been, as Feinstein and Slaughter (2004: 144) note, "to treat North Korea as if it were Norway." Even studies emphasizing normative persuasion have overlooked domestic political conditions as integral and constitutive, rather than residual. This task would involve calibrating dominant domestic receptivity to norms against nuclear weapons acquisition as opposed to norms advocating nuclear weapons on prestige, modernization, or identity-related grounds. Sometimes even well-meaning critiques of globalization and the NPR as "Western constructs" have the unintended effect of strengthening domestic forces and "moral entrepreneurs" with nuclear weapons agendas as redemptive symbols. Normative-legal perspectives such as Feinstein and Slaughter's (2004: 140) reveal greater sensitivity to domestic drivers of nuclear proliferation when, for example, they argue that "it is not states that are the danger, but their rulers." Indeed, they go as far as suggesting that the international community – through multilateral or regional frameworks – has a "duty to prevent" rulers of closed societies from acquiring and using nuclear weapons.

A domestic political-survival approach may provide a window into the internal currents that sustain demands for such weapons.[47] Efforts to untangle how domestic political-economy agents and structures overlap with, reinforce, or undermine nuclear policy can help craft more effective policies. This is different from ad hoc depictions of the domestic scene in one country or another, often drawn without reference to an overarching comparative framework. It is also different from simply modeling the domestic politics of target states cleaved between "moderates" and "hardliners" on the basis of inductive "who's who" approaches. Such efforts are very useful and indeed progressive moves in the direction of disaggregating the domestic context of target states, but they do not always provide an underlying logic for what makes some leaders, institutions, and coalitions "moderates" or "hardliners." The framework suggested here provides one way to endogenize the question of who is likely to be a moderate or a hardliner, or to make it an integral part of the explanation. Understanding the deep psychological, philosophical, political, and normative sources leading individuals toward "moderate" or "hardline" nuclear choices can be both interesting and helpful but also a potentially open-ended and protracted enterprise with unknown universal applicability. This should nonetheless be part of the research agenda ahead. However, the pressing policy relevance of nuclear proliferation highlights the value of more discrete markers, shortcuts, or rules-of-thumb for identifying the motivations of leaders and constituencies in states aspiring to acquire nuclear weapons. Models of political survival provide a systematic tool, with premises backed in considerable preliminary evidence that are potentially applicable worldwide.

These models may not capture all the correlates of nuclear preferences and are, after all, only ideal-types, conceptual constructs, and not historical or "true" realities. As such, they need not fit every case or indeed any particular case completely (Eckstein 1975), but instead provide a heuristic, a helpful shortcut, and a comparative framework capable of reducing complex reality – and different cases – down to some fundamentals. Models of political survival can explain why different actors within the same state vary in their approaches and preferences regarding nuclear policy; why nuclear policies within states may vary over time as a function of the relative power of particular domestic forces; and why different stares vary in their commitments to increase information, transparency, and compliance with the NPR. This heuristic provides a different foundation for the design of positive and negative inducements to encourage denuclearization than those conceiving of states as unified actors. At the broadest level, positive inducements would aim at strengthening models of political survival pivoted on economic growth and integration in the global economy, which also curb domestic demand for nuclear weapons. Negative inducements would be directed at domestic actors with stakes in nuclear-industrial complexes and ancillary political-economic structures that thrive under protection and state control. Iran's largest conglomerates (bonyads) – fiefdoms of radical clerics and Pasdaran – may be cases in point.

Translating models of political survival into a more detailed set of policies requires a dedicated effort that goes beyond the already packed agenda for this book. That effort should take account of unintended effects of policies, informed by expert knowledge of domestic landscapes of nuclear aspirants. Some unintended effects can be anticipated whereas others cannot. Unintended effects can be positive and negative (Sen 1999: 257). Some attempts to shore up private sectors, for instance, may alienate groups who, while favoring other dimensions of internationalization, transfer their support to prophets of economic self-sufficiency. Research along these lines must also craft policies suitable to different institutional environments within which models thrive or decline. Iran is certainly not North Korea, even though both are authoritarian. Different institutional contexts may require different mixes of aid, trade benefits, investments, debt-relief, food, and selective removal from export control lists. The financial community may be allied with internationalizing or inward-looking camps under different conditions; carrots and sticks must thus be fine-tuned according to the circumstances of particular models. Policies must also countenance the fact that the ascendancy, design, and fate of domestic models of political survival have powerful internal dynamics that do not always render themselves open to external intervention. Finally, disaggregating the roles of different senders of positive and negative inducements (international institutions, great powers, and NGOs) can help create complementarities among them and reduce the potential for cross-purpose or neutralizing tensions. With all these caveats in mind, we can outline preliminary considerations that might guide further policy-oriented research:

Rewarding natural constituencies of internationalizing models

International institutions may provide incentives – positive and negative – to influence the relative appeal of different models. For instance, international economic institutions provide credit and define terms of trade and investment that may in principle strengthen internationalizing models. Their effects are mediated by the extent to which such institutions and their domestic beneficiaries in target states are able to advance economic growth and reform, with an eye on broad redistribution, equity, and low tolerance for corruption (particularly regarding privatization). External intervention can encourage health, education, and welfare and discourage oversized military-industrial complexes. Myopic policies insensitive to these objectives decrease political support for internationalization, plant the seeds of inward-looking reversals, and weaken the prospects for developing open economies with lower incentives to acquire nuclear weapons.[48] Externally induced structural adjustment can strengthen state and private actors involved in economic reform, privatization, export promotion, finance ministries, and central banks, but can also weaken agents of reform if designed with indifference to distributional, including equity, effects. International pressures for human rights standards empower domestic groups responsible for monitoring compliance with international agreements at the expense of repressive agencies, even if they also can trigger cycles of reprisal, which have recrudesced in Iran under Ahmadinejad. Nonetheless, awarding the Nobel Peace Prize to Iranian lawyer Shirin Ebadi was undoubtedly intended to strengthen human rights groups under assault by the Iranian judiciary. International environmental regimes entrust local civil networks with legitimacy to challenge industrial activities that damage the environment, including those resulting from nuclear-industrial complexes.

These examples are only suggestive of how broad constituencies opposed to nuclear weapons for different reasons can aggregate (logroll) as a consequence of ostensibly unrelated international influences. The stronger these constituencies become, the less willing they will be to bear the economic, social, and political consequences of nuclear programs and the external instability that they often induce. Clearly, the ability to encourage the path toward internationalizing models is itself a function of existing relative openness and of the relative strength of its political carriers, particularly in the private sector. Although unrelated to the nuclear program, sanctions on South Africa were effective at least partly because they consolidated opposition against apartheid among important segments of the outward-oriented financial and industrial community (Liberman 2001). As on other issues, Iran is not North Korea with respect to existing constituencies potentially oriented to an international economy. Iran's WTO membership can benefit a private sector – small and medium size firms – that was once thriving but has been adversely affected or coopted by the massive statization that followed the Islamic Revolution. Under near-total closure and without a critical mass of current beneficiaries from internationalization, the path in North Korea may be more difficult but not impossible. After all, current beneficiaries of Kim Jong-Il's model are not legion either.[49] Furthermore, the dominance of internationalizing models throughout East Asia provides not only a blueprint but also regional incentives for North Korea's leadership to soft-land by emulating the historical experience of its neighbors. Policies supporting North Korea's economic reform and export-processing zones help strengthen domestic reformers vis-à-vis their opponents.

Stripping autarkic or inward-looking regimes of the means to concentrate power

Many policies cited in the previous paragraph have adverse effects on inward-looking domestic actors. The introduction of markets, openness, transparency, foreign investment, conditionality, structural adjustment, and export-led industrialization harms state and private institutions and monopolistic enterprises that thrive under closure. Thus Milani (2005b: 50) suggests that an end to Iran's embargo will reduce the power of protectionist rackets, vigilantes, and monopolies such as bonyads, Mo'talefe, and Pasdaran.[50] UNSC resolutions banning exports of luxury items to North Korea – imposed after its nuclear test – punish Kim Jong-Il's associates most directly. Conditionality arrangements by some international institutions often threaten military-industrial complexes insofar as economic rationalization deprives the latter of resources and rents. The military, however, is not invariably pro-nuclear, and selected segments develop interests that can become intertwined with internationalizing agendas, as in China, and to a much more limited extent, in North Korea. Furthermore, conventional military establishments may weigh the costs of nuclear defiance today against the viability of conventional modernization in the longer run, as well as the opportunity costs of nuclearization for maintaining conventional capabilities (Betts 1980: 136). Alleged tensions in Iran between the regular military and Pasdaran bear on some of these considerations.

Iraq's experience suggests that the Oil-for-Food program benefited Saddam's military-industrial complex and security services even if UN inspections prevented reconstitution of WMD programs. Monopoly agencies, corrupt officials, smugglers, and black-market profiteers (state and private) also thrived, strengthening their control of the economy and the means of coercion. North Korea provides another example of difficulties in preventing dictatorships from shifting the burden of sanctions to innocent victims, and of the need to maximize efforts to deny control of aid allocation and distribution to domestic actors poised to gain from economic closure. Foreign providers to protectionist rackets can themselves be rogue state agencies or private profiteers whose operations are sometimes tacitly sanctioned by government officials, from Russia to Pakistan and Europe. However, even some legitimate trade, including that between Japan and North Korea, arguably benefits the military and party elite.[51] Sanctions imposed on North Korean money laundering, counterfeiting and narcotics trade activities in Macao's Banco Delta Asia are said to have directly disrupted a secretive North Korean agency (Unit 39) that provided Kim Jong-Il with patronage funds.[52] Furthermore, over two dozen other banks have also severed ties with North Korea. Sanctions on Yog'aksan General Trading Company targeted North Korea's main producer and exporter of missiles and the Korea Ch'anggwang Credit Bank, which manages finances and payments for missile exports (Pinkston 2003). According to ICG (2005), most revenue from missiles and drugs is accrued by the military directly, not the government. Active targeting of individual and corporate architects of nuclearizing policies can involve freezing personal bank accounts, canceling travel visas, and depriving them of diplomatic immunity. The UNSC resolution following North Korea's nuclear test banned trade related to WMD and luxury items, and authorized cargo inspections.

The December 24, 2006, UNSC resolution following Iran's defiance of a previous UNSC resolution banned trade in materials and technology for uranium enrichment, reprocessing, heavy water, and ballistic missiles, and froze assets of twelve Iranians (including Pasdaran commander Yahya Rahim Safavi) and ten companies involved in those activities. Russia's and China's economic interests (including Russia's interests in the Bushehr reactor) precluded the inclusion of a mandatory travel ban on people involved in nuclear activities. In addition to these multilateral measures, the US Treasury Department has began barring American banks from transactions with Iranian banks with reputed ties to terrorism, such as Bank Saderat, triggering similar steps by some European banks, lest they too might suffer adverse consequences from their own ties to Iranian banks.[53] A second major Iranian bank (most major banks in Iran are state-owned or controlled) – Bank Sepah – became the second target of sanctions for activities related to missiles or WMD. These measures will hurt projects under the purview of Pasdaran, bonyads, and other government interests. Despite its heavy dependence on foreign oil, Japan has supported some of these measures and downgraded its stake in the Azadegan oil field.

Crafting packages of sanctions and inducements that are sensitive to differences between energy-rich and energy-poor targets

The cases analyzed here point to considerable differences in the way in which leaders and coalitions from oil-rich versus oil-poor countries sustain inward-looking models. Rentier states such as Iran, Iraq, and Libya were able to rely on both coercion and extensive oil revenues to develop wide clientelistic networks supporting the regime (to some extent the Iraqi insurgency showed determined resistance by some Sunni elements to relinquish these privileges). Such resources have been far more limited for Kim Jong-Il, presiding over an energy-poor economy in dire need of external support. This key difference suggests an important research agenda in the study of positive and negative inducements. Such an agenda must understand the influence of the oil industry's power structure and its clientelistic networks on economic liberalization, their respective position on the nuclear program, and the presumed barriers posed by the "oil curse" for export-led strategies (through "Dutch disease" effects), democratization, and denuclearization (Komaie and Solingen 2007). East Asia's limited natural resources are thought to have provided better conditions for adopting export-led models and democratic institutions. Although these assumptions are not unchallenged, North Korea's demise of *juche* could arguably render the country more fit for markets, democracy, and denuclearization. Evolving realities in Iraq, Libya, Iran, and the GCC will enable further research on connections between the oil sector, economic reform, and nuclear programs.

Using democracy – where available – as an ally of denuclearization

Democracies and autocracies respond differently to international sanctions and inducements. The responses of both, however, are often contingent on the nature of their ties to the global political economy. Chapter 2 hypothesized that democracies may have been less likely to acquire nuclear weapons to face democratic opponents. Yet democratic regimes appear neither necessary nor sufficient for denuclearization. Some democracies have been highly favorable to nuclear weapons (India), and many autocracies have not pursued them. Nonetheless, democratic contexts offer much better opportunities for the international community to reach domestic groups favoring denuclearization. Democratization challenges the conditions that allow nuclear programs to thrive beyond public scrutiny by media, political parties, and interest groups, and allows these groups to help verify compliance with international agreements. The more democratic the state, the greater the opportunities for *suasion*, perhaps with diminishing returns for democracies surrounded by autocratic adversaries, particularly neighbors with nuclear designs.[54] Promoting domestic allies of denuclearization is much harder under autocratic controls, yet new mass technologies have enabled greater external access to disenfranchised populations, more so in Iran than in North Korea. Milani (2005b: 4) proposes a tacit grand alliance between the West and the predominantly pro-American Iranian people. In his view, popular support for the nuclear program is ephemeral and contingent, whereas the crisis of leadership is structural and deepening. Without patronizing or coopting reformist leaders, external supporters of democracy can help raise the political, strategic, and economic costs of Iran's nuclear program, which Milani argues would be far more effective in mobilizing Iran's domestic opposition. In a country where a million new jobs are needed every year, some conclude that nuclear weapons may be of less vital importance to Iran's population than concrete economic benefits.[55] Highlighting these opportunity costs is as effective as pointing to the high actual costs of defiant nuclear programs. Limited access to domestic audiences in North Korea makes it much more difficult to advance similar objectives, but such efforts are becoming increasingly less impossible in an era of mobile phones and a porous China border. By contrast, Gaddafi's shift encountered mixed reception in a regional context that retains an emphasis on inward looking models and defiance of internationalization.[56]

These considerations offer a foundation upon which more detailed strategies can be crafted, not as substitutes for, but rather in conjunction with, other multilateral policies including denial of weapons technologies to NPT violators and a verifiable fissile material ban.[57] No single instrument can yield immediate results or guarantee absolute compliance. As Blix (2005: 81–82) noted prior to the 2003 war, "A clause signaling forceful action in case of non-compliance would be valuable. Iraq did not move without forceful, sustained pressure, and it simply shrugged off economic sanctions." But this is different from overemphasizing threats of force that have unintended, although easily foreseen, domestic effects in target states. Effective policies should convert nuclear programs from rallying points to lightning rods, not the other way round. Some positive inducements take longer to yield results. US reassurances at the Six-Party Talks that it had "no intention to attack or invade the DPRK [Democratic People's Republic of Korea]" and that it "respects [its] sovereignty" are a case in point.[58] North Korea's subsequent nuclear test can be traced to many factors but cannot be construed as "proof" that such statements are ineffective. Though not sufficient to produce immediate outcomes, such commitments deprive inward-looking leaders from opportunities to exploit external threats to strengthen internal unity. Even if positive commitments are precluded from immediately reaching the wider population, they could make elements of the ruling coalition more susceptible to compromise. The Libyan experience suggests that even inward-looking regimes with long histories of radical self-sufficiency and nuclear weapons aspirations can be brought back from isolation. As Jentleson and Whytock (2005/06: 81–82) argue, "The combination of internal pressures and the coercive diplomacy strategy helped bring Gaddafi to a point where his hold on power was better served by global engagement than global radicalism."

Libya's experience also suggests that multilateral cooperation is of the essence in bringing about positive outcomes, even if such cooperation crystallized as a consequence of Libya's terrorist rather than nuclear activities. The adverse effects of multilateral steps by the IAEA on Tehran's stock market, Iranian businesses, and consumers were tangible and sharpened domestic debates over Ahmadinejad's policies. Yet consistent multilateral cooperation on Iran and North Korea has been hard to obtain, in-spite of the fact that their nuclear programs are more advanced than Libya's was.[59] French and Russian military-industrial and energy complexes are undoubtedly strong political forces to contend with but have sometimes been defeated by their domestic opponents and by strong external – including EU – pressure for collective action. North Korea's nuclear test drove the point home to Chinese leaders that China too can be adversely affected by failures of collective action, launching a domestic reassessment of its own policies. Certain US policies have undermined collective action no less, including withholding CTBT ratification and discussions of new generations of nuclear weapons and bunker-busting devices. The failure of all nuclear weapons states to make progress on Article VI, a contractual obligation under the NPT, may not be the main driver of nuclearization. Yet it certainly provides inward-looking proponents of such weapons worldwide with additional pretexts while weakening domestic constituencies receptive to denuclearization and internationalization.[60] Carter (2005) summarized eight "Ds" that have become part of the toolkit to prevent nuclear proliferation: dissuasion, disarmament, diplomacy, denial, defusing, deterrence, defenses, and destruction.[61] A ninth "D" should be added for "domestic" (or "DD," for "disaggregating domestic" effects), reminding architects of nonproliferation policy that each tool should be evaluated in light of distributional consequences within target states. Designing appropriate mixes of Ds, as well as their sequence and timetable, must be inextricably linked to the careful analysis of "qui bono?" or how each mix could affect the relevant internal constituencies that – in the end – shape nuclear logics.

Notes

1   See, for instance, National Academy of Sciences, Committee on International Security and Arms Control, *Monitoring Nuclear Weapons and Nuclear Explosive Materials: An Assessment of Methods and Capabilities* (Washington, DC 2005).
2   Carnegie Endowment Conference, Washington, DC, June 21, 2004.
3   "Al-Arabiyah Interviews IAEA Chief on Libya's Cooperation, Iran, Proliferation," *Al-Arabiyah* TV, February 24, 2004.

4 NSA, September 17, 1975, 01946.
5 Such predictions include those by Kahn (1970), Mearsheimer (2001) and Kissinger, who argued, "We must have no illusion: Failure to resolve the Korean nuclear threat in a clear-cut way will sooner or later lead to the nuclear armament of Japan – regardless of assurances each side offers the other" (Henry Kissinger, "Why We Can't Withdraw from Asia," *Washington Post*, June 15, 2003). Others consider Japan a virtual nuclear state (Levite 2002/03: 71).
6 Henry Sokolski, "President Bush's Global Nonproliferation Policy: Seven More Proposals," *The Heritage Lectures*, no. 829, April 19, 2004.
7 Jones (1997a); Fahmy (2001); Chubin (2006); Takeyh (2006). Jones (1997b) outright repudiates the argument that all other regional WMD programs are related to Israel's nuclear status.
8 Among many others, Vice President Richard Cheney speculated that Pyongyang's ambitions could trigger regional arms races (Yuri Kageyama, "Japan Rethinks Nuclear Taboo," *Washington Times*, August 15, 2003). Inoguchi Takashi suggested that "a loss of US self-confidence in Iraq is a threat to Japan, because it would prompt isolationism in America and a US withdrawal from South Korea, and that would expose Japan to a threat very, very directly… Then public opinion in the United States and Japan might get more favourable to the option of Japan going nuclear. …Aggressive South Korean pursuit of unification with the North could have a similar result by prompting a U.S. withdrawal from the peninsula" (Sieg, "North Korea"). Notice that Inoguchi's scenarios are sensitive to domestic dynamics.
9 Eric Prideaux and Akemi Nakamura, "Japan May Not Want to Go Nuclear but It's No Technical Hurdle," *Japan Times*, October 11, 2006.
10 Some consider Japan to be only months or moments away from becoming a nuclear weapons state, but the fact remains that it has not done so for over three decades (even after three North Korean nuclear tests).
11 In an implicit critique of US commitment to Taiwan, Lee Teng-Hui invoked the threat of Munich and Yalta ("A Strategy of Freedom in Asia," lecture hosted by the Formosa Foundation, Los Angeles, October 21, 2005).
12 *The Times* (London), November 4, 2006: 2.
13 Private voices in the Gulf have raised demands for US extended deterrence if Iran acquires nuclear weapons (Alani 2005).
14 Fawaz Gerges expressed that "I know that the official Egyptian line is to deny. But common sense and history tell me that the Egyptians, the Syrians, the Iraqis have either acquired or experimented with acquiring nuclear weapons" and "when Libya, which had been one of Khan's clients, agreed in 2003 to dismantle its nuclear weapons program, some Arabs grumbled publicly that closing the program would only be to Israel's advantage – and perhaps they worried privately that Libya's revelations would focus attention on their own secrets" (Donna Bryson, "Arab Nuclear Ambitions Spurred by Israel, Yes, but Iran, Other Concerns, Too," *Associated Press*, January 10, 2005).
15 See www.iaea.org/NewsCenter/Statements/2005/ebsp2005n002.html.
16 Second Moscow International Nonproliferation Conference, Hotel Metropol, September 19, 2003 (CEW).
17 According to Timerbaev (2005), "If there had been no NPT, the total number of nuclear-weapon-states…might have reached 30 or 40 by now." For eight useful guides for conducting counterfactual analysis in international relations, see Lebow (2000).
18 See www.carnegieendowment.org.
19 On the relationship between domestic models and regional institutions, see Solingen (2008).
20 Japan submitted resolutions advocating total elimination of nuclear weapons to the UNGA since 1994, which the United States has opposed since 2001.
21 Although positions on WMD hardened after Iraq's missile attacks on Israel in 1991, 82 percent of the Israeli public in 1998 supported an NWFZ if it included all states in the

Nuclear logics 259

region; only 19 percent favored open nuclear deterrence despite continued tension with most neighbors (Arian 2003). A 1994 survey during the Oslo era found 72 percent supporting Israel's accession to the NPT if all states in the region abandoned WMD.
22 Economics Nobel laureate Robert J. Aumann argued that as a democracy Israel cannot violate its international commitments, although its neighbors are not equally bound ("Removal of Weapons of Mass Destruction from the Middle East," National Security Studies Center, Haifa University, available at http://video.haifa.ac.il).
23 Ben-Gurion countenanced US inspections when in power but used them publicly against Eshkol to encourage his ousting prior to elections.
24 See Al-Siyassa (Kuwait), May 3, 2006. Available from http://memri.org/bin/articles.cgi?Page=archives&Arca=ia&ID=IA27706.
25 Roberts (1993) and Mansfield and Snyder (2005) suggest that weak and unstable democracies may lead to outcomes that differ from those expected for full-fledged liberal democracies.
26 The connection might arguably be even stronger if one includes cases that abandoned nuclear programs, excluded in Singh and Way (2004).
27 Bloated nuclear-industrial complexes have come to symbolize the excesses of state expansion among virtually all nuclear aspirants who developed nuclear weapons.
28 Solingen (1994a, 2001b); Liberman (2001). Testing a hypothesis along these lines, Singh and Way (2004: 876, 878) find that "the process of economy liberalization is associated with a reduced likelihood of exploring nuclear weapons" and that economic openness "has a statistically significant negative effect" on exploring, pursuing, or acquiring nuclear weapons.
29 East Asian states' economic, political, and institutional structures varied widely but all shared commitments to export-led growth (more centralized in South Korea, decentralized in Taiwan, and oligopolostic in Japan). Japan's model was more reliant on domestic markets initially (Pempel 1999). State bureaucracies played important roles in steering integration in the global economy in most cases.
30 On how Japanese officials sometimes *encouraged* US pressure on Japan to ratify the NPT in order to counter domestic opponents (including Nakasone), see memorandum from Philip Habib and Winston Lord to Secretary Kissinger (DNSA, February 20, 1975, JU01921). This source also makes clear that Japanese officials sensed ambiguity in the US position, which entailed little pressure for ratification at that point, and acknowledges that US preferences would not be the determining factor in Japan's decisions; the interests of Japanese leaders would.
31 NIE, June 18,1957 (NSA, NSAEBB155).
32 Edward Cody, "Taiwan Sets Self-Defense Objectives," *Washington Post*, May 21, 2006: A19.
33 Asgarkhani, Abumohammad. Iran, Sept. 11 and the Repercussions of 'Regime Change.' *The Daily Star*, September 15, 2003. Available at http://yaleglobal.yale.edu/display.article?id=2459.
34 Neil MacFarquhar, "Across Iran, Nuclear Power Is a Matter of Pride," *New York Times*, May 29, 2005: A1.
35 The chancellor of Amir Kabir Industrial University, Ahmad Fahimifar, acknowledged that "huge human and financial resources have been invested in this program" and hence the government "should not retreat at all." Khamene'i reassured him that there would be no retreat ("Iranian Academics Support Nuclear Program at Meeting with Khamene'i," Network 1, December 19, 2004).
36 "Cairo Editor Says Israel Plans to Test Nuclear Device Soon," *New York Times*, August 21, 1965: 2.
37 Why internationalizing models had difficulties taking root in the Middle East is outside the scope of this book but is discussed in Solingen (2007a).
38 On domestic politics as filtering external considerations, see Solingen (1998). A recent study by Schweller (2006: 5) also resorts to the concept of *filter* or domestic politics as mediating between systemic considerations and actual decisions. Neoclassical realist

studies sensitive to domestic politics include Snyder (1991); Christensen (1996); and Glaser (2000).

39 On how international crises of capitalism lead to realignments of domestic political structures, see Gourevitch (1986).

40 Some consider India to fit this case, although India became a nuclear power in 1974 under Indira Ghandi's inward-looking era and long before India's economic reforms of the 1990s. If India were to be found an anomaly, it would prove the argument's refutability. Alternatively, it could also be explained by the third scope condition, pointing to the higher political costs incurred in renouncing actual weapons rather than precursor programs, as with China and Israel.

41 Mark Magnier, "China and Japan Try to Ease Strain," *Los Angeles Times*, April 24, 2005: A3. For a competing argument, see Kitamura (1996: 11). Bueno de Mesquita *et al.* (1993) predicted that pro-nuclear groups in Taiwan would face a strong coalition of internal and external actors opposed to indigenous nuclear weapons. Domestic opponents of nuclearization within and outside the government would be sensitive to its economic and political consequences.

42 As of 2005, few Japanese experts and politicians believed Japan would go nuclear but some think it should. Interviews (Tokyo, June 2003, July–August 2004, March 2005); Kamiya (2002–03); Keller (2003); Hughes (2004: 93–94); Oros (2003); Kurosawa (2004). For a pro-nuclear view, see Nakanishi Terumasa, "Goals for Japan in Its 'Second Postwar' Period," *Japan Echo* 30, no. 5 (October 2003). This book goes to press under the fog of North Korea's nuclear test, too early to evaluate its repercussions.

43 "Blowback" entails using symbols (such as visits to Yasukuni) or policies (reciting historical grievances) to mobilize nationalistic support. While this may be done instrumentally and tactically, it can create self-entrapment, heightening the costs of renouncing such practices and, even worse, ingraining them as valid strategic concepts (Snyder 1991; Van Evera 1994: 32–33).

44 For such a scenario, labeled a "bold switchover," see Eberstadt *et al.* (2006).

45 According to Takeyh (2004: 58), this may be unlikely because "The emergence of bureaucratic and nationalist pressures in Iran is generating its own proliferation momentum, empowering those seeking a nuclear breakout. As time passes, the pragmatic voices calling for hedging are likely to be marginalised and lose their influence within the regime. The notion that the United States has the luxury of time is belied by Iran's internal domestic alignments on the nuclear issue."

46 For updated accounts on an extensive literature on technology denial, see inter alia Levi and O'Hanlon (2005) and Goldschmidt (2003, 2007).

47 For a preliminary effort to derive policy guidelines akin to "smart sanctions" and positive inducements sensitive to domestic politics, see Solingen (1995). In the intervening decade, experiences in Iraq, North Korea, Iran, and Libya led to additional efforts to disaggregate the domestic context, including those by Drezner (1999); Haass and O'Sullivan (2000); Niblock (2002); O'Sullivan (2003); and Lopez and Cortright (2004).

48 Solingen (1998, chapter 8) provides further elaboration on these effects.

49 According to Carlin and Wit (2006), about three million people constitute a "court economy" of beneficiaries of special goods and services. It is unclear, however, how many among this selected tier perceive the status quo to be preferable to economic reforms, including the demise of the "second (military) economy." For a balanced view of the advantages and difficulties of various scenarios concerning evolutionary economic and political transformation in North Korea rather than "regime change," see Haggard and Noland (2007).

50 According to O'Sullivan (2003: 74), US sanctions added to domestic sources of weakness faced by Iran's reformers.

51 Richard Armitage, "Japan-US ties crucial in changing world," *Daily Yomiuri*, March 16, 2005: 20.

52 David E. Sanger, "US Said to Weight a New Approach on North Korea," *New York Times*, May 18, 2006: A10; Steven R. Weisman, "U.S. Pursues Tactic of Financial Isolation," *New York Times*, October 16, 2006: A10.
53 Weisman, "U.S. Pursues Tactics"; Steven R. Weisman, "U.S. Prohibits All Transactions With a Major Iranian Bank," *New York Times*, January 10, 2007: 3.
54 According to Cox and Cooper (2006), democracies are less likely to sanction each other although they employ sanctions more than other regime types, advancing human rights and democratization through economic sanctions.
55 Abbas Maleki, BCSIA News, Summer 2006, at www.belfercenter.org. By some estimates, only 15 percent of voters actively support Ahmadinejad's model and the extremist religious parties that promote it. His executive powers are limited by Iran's constitution and by the coalition of interests represented in the government (see Simon Tisdall, "This Is More about National Pride than Nuclear Weapons," *The Guardian*, September 8, 2006).
56 Gaddafi's 2003 moves were denounced by some not only in the Arab world. Iran's nuclear negotiator Rowhani stated that "Iran is Iran. It is neither South Korea nor Libya....Both of them submitted themselves to America" ("Iran's Nuclear Negotiator Rowhani Holds News Conference," *Islamic Republic of Iran News Network*, November 30, 2004, in FBIS December 1, 2004 IAP20041201000099).
57 As Kimball argues, "A close reading of the NPT makes it clear that peaceful nuclear endeavors are a benefit that accrues only to those non-weapons NPT states that credibly fulfill their obligation not to divert nuclear material and technology for weapons" (see Daryl G. Kimball, "Iran: Getting Back on Track," *Arms Control Today*, October 2004).
58 "Joint Statement from Nuclear Talks," *New York Times*, September 19, 2005.
59 Samore (2005) estimated that it would take Iran at least five years to produce enough fissile material for a single weapon. More recent estimates suggest Iran is closer to that goal (David E. Sanger, "Atomic Agency Confirms Advances by Iran's Nuclear Program," *New York Times*, April 19, 2007: A10). According to a Pentagon report, Iran could have enough nuclear material for a nuclear weapon by 2010 (David Martin, *CBS News*, April 26, 2007)
60 A new proposal by very high former U.S. officials suggests steps in the direction of a world free of nuclear weapons (George P. Shultz, William J. Perry, Henry A. Kissinger, and Sam Nunn, "A World Free of Nuclear Weapons," *Wall Street Journal*, January 4, 2007).
61 Carter (2005) and Testimony of Ashton B. Carter, House Armed Services Committee, United States House of Representatives, Regarding Seven Steps to Overhaul Counterproliferation, March 17, 2004. Available from www.house.gov.

APPENDICES

Appendix I. Internationalizing coalitions

Political Entrepreneurs	N+	Country	Mean TO	Change in TO	Mean Exp/GDP	Change in Exp/GDP	Mean FDI $US Millions	Change in FDI $US Millions	Mean Milex/GDP	Change in Milex/GDP	Mean Milex/CGE	Change in Milex/CGE
Park Chung Hee (1964–1979)	15	S. Korea	49.3	2.8	18.2	1.3 (14)	68 (7)	(–12.8) (6)	4.6	–0.01	26.5 (13)	.3 (12)
Chun Doo Hwan (1980–1988)	9	S. Korea	72.7	1.1	34.6	1.6	184	78.2	5.2	–0.12	27.1	–0.2
Rho Tae-Woo (1989–1992)	5	S. Korea	61.5	(–3.7) (3)	36.2	–0.8	–97.5	–304.3	3.8	–0.1	21.4	–1.4
Kim Young Sam (1993–1998)	5	S. Korea	67.4	5.9	34.2	1.8	–1351	273.8	3.2 (4)	(–0.1) (4)	15.5 (2)	(–3) (2)
Chiang Ching-kuo-Li Teng Hui (1978–1988)	11	Taiwan	99.4	0.5	*	*	*	*	6.2	–0.26	40.5 (10)	(–2.3) (9)
Suharto (1968–1998)	31	Indonesia	46.8 (28)	2.2	27.4	1	989 (26)	(–2.4) (30)	2.6 (30)	(–0.03) (30)	13.3 (26)	(–.3) (25)
Lee Kuan Yew-Goh Chok-Tong (1965–1998)	34	Singapore	314 (28)	3.9 (27)	147 (29)	3.9 (28)	1768 (26)	151 (25)	5 (31)	(0.08) (30)	22.1 (29)	.4 (28)
Augusto Pinochet (1973–1989)	16	Chile	49.9	2.3	26.7	1.3	299	78.9	5.5	–0.06	15.3	0.3
Patricio Aylwin-Eduardo Frei (1990–1996)	7	Chile	60.2	–0.9	33.5	–0.6	428 (4)	(–217) (4)	2.1	–0.09	15.2 (6)	0.5 (6)
Carlos S. Menem (1989–1998)	9	Argentina	18.5	0.6	10.3	–0.4	3690 (4)	1319 (4)	1.4 (8)	(–0.1) (8)	30.6 (5)	(–3.6) (5)
Fernando Collor de Mello (1990–1992)	2	Brazil	15.8	1.95	12.1	0.9	633	536	0.9	–0.1	4.2	–0.6
Fernando H, Cardoso (1995–1998)	3	Brazil	17.1	0.1	7.3	–0.1	*	*	1.6 (2)	0.15 (2)	*	*
Thanarat/Leekpai (1960–1997)	39	Thailand	54.1	1.7 (38)	29.2 (26)	1.5 (25)	1021 (26)	263 (25)	3.1 (38)	(–0.02) (37)	18.1 (28)	.08 (28)
Anwar el-Sadat (1974–1981)	8	Egypt	65.5	6.1	23.4	0	535	94.3 (7)	22.4	–3	34.6	–6.8
King Hussein (1991–1998)	7	Jordan	*	*	40.7 (2)	(–2.5) (2)	32.5 (2)	(–3) (2)	8.1 (6)	(–0.2) (6)	24 (4)	(–1.2) (4)
Habib Bourgiba-Zine Ben Ali (1971–1995)	25	Tunisia	74.6 (22)	1.5 (22)	34.7 (23)	0.74 (23)	134 (20)	10.1 (20)	2.7	0.01	7.2 (2)	0.4 (23)
King Hassan 11 (1983–1996)	16	Morocco	52.3 (10)	(–0.2) (10)	22.4 (11)	0.45 (11)	166 (11)	37.6 (11)	4.4 (14)	(–0.19) (4)	18.2 (9)	.2 (7)
Yitzhak Rabin-Shimon Peres (1992–1996)	5	Israel	64.4 (1)	.3 (1)	32.7 (2)	1.2 (2)	(–243) (2)	(–151) (2)	9.2	–0.46	22.2 (4)	(–.4) (4)
Aggregate Coalitional Means	246		88.6 (223)	1.9 (221)	44.1 (204)	1.3 (201)	712 (115)	110 (169)	4.6 (236)	(–0.15) (236)	19.8 (201)	(.4) (194)

Sources: Solingen, 2001b. All data for Trade Openness, Exports/GDP and FDI 1993–1998 from *United Nations Statistical Yearbook* (1999); all other data for Trade Openness (1960–1992) from *Penn World Table* (Web address: www.nber.org/pwt56, published by the National Bureau of Economic Research, Cambridge, MA: 1995); all other data for Exports/GDP calculated from World Bank, *World Tables* (1995, 1989, 1980); all other data for FDI from World Bank, *World Tables* (1995). FDI reported at current prices; Data for Milex/GDP from *SIPRI Yearbooks* (International Peace Research Institute, Stockholm, 1999, 1996, 1995, 1990, 1989, 1986, 1984, 1975); Data for Milex/CGE from U.S. Arms Control and Disarmament Agency, *World Military Expenditures* (1996, 1990, 1982, 1976).

+ Note: Values for N represent the life-span of the coalition. Where different, actual N used for calculation is in parentheses and superscript.

Appendix II. Inward-looking coalitions

Political Entrepreneurs	N+	Country	Mean TO	Change in TO	Mean Exp/GDP	Change in Exp/GDP	Mean FDI $US Millions	Change in FDI $US Millions	Mean Milex/GDP	Change in Milex/GDP	Mean Milex/CGE	Change in Milex/CGE
Syngman Rhee's (1960–1963)	4	S. Korea	19.8	1.7[3]	*	*	*	*	5.5	(–0.6)[3]	*	*
Achmad Sukarno (1960–1967)	8	Indonesia	21	0.26[7]	18.7[3]	(–0.45)[2]	*	*	3.4	(–0.39)[7]	24.7[1]	*
Amin al-Hafiz-Ahmad Khatib (1963–1971)	9	Syria	37.9	–0.88	20.7[7]	(–0.37)[6]	*	*	8.6	0.2[8]	34.5[8]	(–3.8)[2]
Hafez el-Asad (1972–1997)	27	Syria	47.9[20]	0.9[20]	14.3[20]	(–0.28)[20]	*	*	12[26]	(–0.07)[26]	40.4[19]	1.5[19]
A.S. Aref-Hassan al-Bakr (1964–1979)	16	Iraq	71.5	1.9	*	*	*	*	10.5[14]	(0.33)[13]	36.4[13]	(–6)[12]
Saddam Hussein (1980–1987)	8	Iraq	67.8[8]	(–5.1)[8]	*	*	*	*	30.8[6]	8.4[6]	38.4[6]	6.9[1]
Gamal A. Nasser (1960–1970)	11	Egypt	37	(–0.7)[10]	20.1[6]	(–0.4)[5]	*	*	8.7	(0.92)[10]	29.9[7]	5.2[1]
Anwar el-Sadat (1971–1973)	3	Egypt	32.8	0.07	19.4	0.73	*	*	24.5	6.1	48.9	13
A. Khomeini-Sayed Khameini (1979–1989)	10	Iran	20.6	–2.1	4	–0.22	*	*	4.2[8]	(–0.19)[7]	33.5[8]	(–2)[7]
Menahem Begin (1978–1983)	6	Israel	87.9	–1.7	29	–0.5	–10	–14.7	26.6	–0.08	31	–1.9
Yitzhak Shamir (1990–1991)	2	Israel	66.6	–3.7	30.9	–2.2	–69	–80	11.7	–0.65	23.7	–1.4
Isabel Peron (1974–1976)	3	Argentina	13.4	0.6	5.6	0.3	10[1]	1[1]	2.2[1]	.6[1]	10	0.8
Leopoldo Galtieri (1981–1982)	2	Argentina	15.4	2.5	8.3	0.8	464	–186	6.1	0.2	20.4	4.5
Juscelino Kubitcheck (1960–1961)	2	Brazil	12.2	0.8	*	*	*	*	1.9	–0.3	*	*
Salvador Allende (1971–1973)	3	Chile	25.1	0.17	11.5	–0.53	(–5)[1]	*	2.8	0.3	8.6	–0.5
Zulfiqar Ali Bhutto (1971–1977)	7	Pakistan	28.4	0.84	*	*	8.8[5]	(–0.7)[4]	5.9	0.29	31.8	–1.1
Jawaharal Nehru-Indira Gandhi (1960–77)	18	India	10.5	0.04[17]	*	*	0	0	3.1	0.09[17]	18.6[11]	7[10]
Indira Gandhi (1981–84)	4	India	15.4	–0.2	*	*	50	13.5	3.3	0.05	18.3	0.08
Aggregate Coalitional Means	144		38.3[138]	(–.23)[133]	(15.6)[66]	(–0.27)[63]	37.6[26]	(–24.6)[23]	9.5[136]	0.62[128]	31[91]	0.9[85]

Sources: Solingen, 2001b. All data for Trade Openness, Exports/GDP and FDI 1993–1998 from *United Nations Statistical Yearbook* (1999); all other data for Trade Openness (1960–1992) from *Penn World Table* (Web address; www.nber.org/pwt56, published by the National Bureau of Economic Research, Cambridge, MA: 1995); all other data for Exports/GDP calculated from World Bank, *World Tables* (1995, 1989, 1980); all other data for FDI from World Bank, *World Tables* (1995), with the exception of Israel 1990–1992, data from Central Bureau of Statistics, Israel (Web address: www.cbs.gov.il/lmse.cgi, 1998, FDI reported at current prices; Data for Milex/GDP from *Sipri Yearbooks* (International Peace Research Institute, Stockholm, 1999, 1996, 1995, 1990, 1989, 1986, 1984, 1975); Data for Milex/CGE from U.S. Arms Control and Disarmament Agency, *World Military Expenditures* (1996, 1990, 1982, 1976).

+ Note: Values for N represent the life-span of the coalition. Where different, actual N used for calculation is in parentheses and superscript.

Appendix III. Hybrid coalitions

Political Entrepreneurs	N+	Country	Mean TO	Change in TO	Mean Exp/GDP	Change in Exp/GDP	Mean FDI $US Millions	Change in FDI $US Millions	Mean Milex/ GDP	Change in Milex/ GDP	Mean Milex/ CGE	Change in Milex/ CGE
A Frondizi-Alejandro Lanusse (1960–1973)	14	Argentina	14.2	(−0.33)[13]	10.1[9]	(−0.64)[8]	9[1]	*	1.9	(−0.05)[13]	14.9[7]	(−1.5)[6]
Jorge R. Videla (1977–1980)	4	Argsentina	13.9	−0.9	7.9	0.15	271	142[5]	5.6[3]	(−0.1)[2]	15.5	1.3
Raul Alfonsin (1983–1988)	6	Argentina	15.2	−0.17	8.7	0.15	512	158	3.8	−0.58	17.1	−0.6
Castelo Branco-Jose Sarney (1964–1990)	26	Brazil	16	0.03	7.3	0.19[25]	1477[18]	(−65)[17]	1.4[25]	0.004[24]	9[24]	(−.6)[23]
Itamar Franco (1992–1995)	3	Brazil	18.5	0.2	10.1	−1.7	(−292)[1]	(−1600)[1]	1.3	0.13	3.5	0.13
Mahathir bin Mohamad (1980–1997)	18	Malaysia	140	4.6	71.2	2.1	2493	267	4.3	−0.18	11.6[16]	(−.13)[16]
King Hassan II (1961–1982)	22	Morocco	44	0.38	20.4[18]	(−0.44)[17]	38.8[10]	8.9[9]	3.9	0.19	14.8[16]	.6[15]
Zia ul-Haq (1978–1987)	10	Pakistan	34.1	0.68	*	*	104	10.5	6.3	0.11	25.6	0.2
Benazir Bhutto (1988–1990)	3	Pakistan	35.8	−0.03	14.2	.5[2]	194	44.7	6.6	−0.03	27.2	1.1
Natvaz Sharif (1991–1993)	3	Pakistan	37.2	1.2	16.9	0.5	319	35.7	6.8	0.0001	27.1	−1.1
Morarji Desai (1978–1980)	3	India	15.8	1.1	*	*	2.7	2.7	3.4	−0.07	16.9	0.1
Rajiv Gandhi (1985–1990)	6	India	16.4	0.5	7.6[2]	0	225	17.2	3.3	−0.13	14.8	−0.72
Narasimha Rao (1991–1994)	4	India	194	0.3	9.6	0.6	339[3]	90[3]	2.5	−0.1	13.1	0.13
Muahmmad Reza Pahlavi (1960–1979)	20	Iran	45.6	0.43[19]	10.7[6]	(−1.3)[5]	*	*	7.9	0.11[19]	28.4	−0.23
Housni Mubarak (1982–1997)	17	Egypt	59.8[11]	(−1.6)[11]	20.9[12]	0.220[12]	193[12]	(−24.5)[12]	5.7[16]	(−0.48)[16]	15.7[14]	(−.16)[14]
King Hussein, Jordan (1960–1991)	16	Jordan	86.5[31]	29[30]	41[19]	1.1[18]	26.3[20]	1.5[19]	15	(−0.32)[31]	44.1[25]	(−.37)[24]
Ben Gurion-Yitzhak Rabin (1960–1977)	18	Israel	62.3	2.6[17]	24.8[13]	0.96[12]	78.4[5]	(−18.5)[4]	20.1	1.1[17]	42.4[11]	0.0001
Shamir-Peres (NUG) (1984–1989)	6	Israel	76.1	−0.2	32.9	1.1	94.3	16.7	17.8	−2.3	25.6	0.32
Benjamin Netanyahu (1997)	1	Israel	*	*	*	*	*	*	8.6	−0.1	*	*
Aggregate Coalitional Means	216		52.4[209]	1.1[205]	25[153]	.45[145]	655[129]	32.9[123]	7.6[214]	(−0.07)[206]	22.1[175]	(−.15)[169]

Sources: Solingen, 2001b. All data for Trade Openness, Exports/GDP and FDI 1993–1998 from *United Nations Statistical Yearbook* (1999); all other data for Trade Openness (1960–1992) from *Penn World Table* [Web address: www.nber.org/pwt56, published by the National Bureau of Economic Research, Cambridge, MA: 1995]; all other data for Exports/GDP calculated from World Bank, *World Tables* (1995, 1989, 1980); all other data for FDI from World Bank, *World Tables* (1995). FDI reported at current prices; Data for Milex/GDP from *Sipri Yearbooks* (International Peace Research Institute, Stockholm, 1999, 1996, 1995, 1990, 1989, 1986, 1984, 1975); Data for Milex/CGE from U.S. Arms Control and Disarmament Agency, *World Military Expenditures* (1996, 1990, 1982, 1976).

+ Note: Values for N represent the life-span of the coalition. Where different, actual N used for calculation is in parentheses and superscript.

Appendix IV. Coalitions by Country

Political Entrepreneurs	N+	Country	C	Mean TO	Change in TO	Mean Exp/GDP	Change in Exp/GDP	Mean FDI $US Millions	Change in FDI $US Millions	Mean Milex/ GDP	Change in Milex/ CGE	Mean Milex/ CGE	Change in Milex/ CGE
A. Frondizi-Alejandro Lanusse (1960–1973)	14	Argentina	H	14.2	(−0.3)[13]	10.1[9]	(−0.64)[8]	9[1]	*	1.9	(−0.05)[13]	14.9[7]	(−1.5)[8]
Isabel Peron (1974–1976)	3	Argentina	B	13.4	0.6	5.6	0.3	10[1]	1[1]	2.2[1]	.6[1]	10	0.8
Jorge R. Videla (1977–1980)	4	Argentina	H	13.9	−0.9	7.9	0.15	271	142[3]	5.6[3]	(−0.1)[2]	15.5	1.3
Leopoldo Galtieri (1981–1982)	2	Argentina	B	15.1	2.5	8.3	0.8	464	−186	6.1	0.2	20.4	4.5
Raul Alfonsin (1983–1988)	6	Argentina	H	15.2	−0.17	8.7	0.15	512	158	3.8	−0.58	17.1	−0.6
Carlos S. Menem (1989–1998)	9	Argentina	I	18.5	0.6	10.3	−0.4	3690[4]	1319[4]	1.4[8]	(−0.1)[8]	30.6[5]	(−3.6)[5]
Juscelino Kubitcheck (1960–1961)	2	Brazil	B	12.2	0.8	*	*	*	*	1.9	−0.3	*	*
Castelo Branco-Jose Samey (1964–1990)	26	Brazil	H	16	0.03	7.3	0.19[25]	1477[18]	(−65)[17]	1.4[25]	0.004[24]	9[24]	(−.6)[23]
Fernando Collor de Mello (1990–1992)	2	Brazil	I	15.8	1.95	12.1	0.9	633	536	0.9	−0.1	4.2	−0.6
Itamar Franco (1992–1995)	3	Brazil	H	18.5	0.2	10.1	−1.7	(−292)[1]	(−1600)[1]	1.3	0.13	3.5	0.13
Fernando H. Cardoso (1995–1998)	3	Brazil	I	17.1	0.1	7.3	−0.1	*[2]	*	1.6[2]	0.15[2]	*	*
Salvador Allende (1971–1973)	3	Chile	B	25.1	0.17	11.5	−0.53	(−5)[1]	*	2.8	0.3	8.6	−0.5
Augusto Pinochet (1973–1989)	16	Chile	I	49.9	2.3	26.7	1.3	299	78.9	5.5	−0.06	15.3	0.3
Patricio Aylwin-Eduardo Frei (1990–1996)	7	Chile	I	60.2	−0.9	33.5	−0.6	428[4]	(−217)[4]	2.1	−0.09	15.2[6]	0.5[8]
Gamal A. Nasser (1960–1970)	11	Egypt	B	37	(−0.7)[10]	20.1[6]	(−0.4)[5]	*	*	8.7	(0.92)[10]	29.9[6]	5.2[1]
Anwar el-Sadat (1971–1973)	3	Egypt	B	32.8	0.07	19.4	0.73	*	*	24.5	6.1	48.9	13
Anwar el-Sadat (1974–1981)	8	Egypt	I	65.5[1]	6.1	23.4	0	535	94.3[7]	22.4	−3	34.6	−6.8
Housni Mubarak (1982–1997)	17	Egypt	H	59.8[1]	(−1.6)[11]	20.9[12]	0.22[12]	193[12]	(−24.5)[12]	5.7[16]	(−0.48)[14]	15.7[14]	(−.16)[14]
Jawaharal Nehru-Indira Gandhi (1960–77)	18	India	B	10.5	0.04[17]	*	*	0	0	3.1	0.09[17]	18.6[11]	.7[10]
Morarji Desai (1978–1980)	3	India	H	15.8	1.1	*	*	2.7	2.7	3.4	−0.07	16.9	0.1
Indira Gandhi (1981–84)	4	India	B	15.4	−0.2	*	*	50	13.5	3.3	0.05	18.3	0.08
Rajiv Gandhi (1985–1990)	6	India	H	16.4	0.5	7.6[2]	0	225	17.2	3.3	−0.13	14.8	−0.72
Narasimha Rao (1991–1994)	4	India	H	19.4	0.3	9.6	0.6	339[3]	90[3]	2.5	−0.1	13.1	0.13
Achmad Sukamo (1960–1967)	8	Indonesia	B	21	0.26[7]	18.7[3]	(−0.45)[2]	*	*	3.4	(−0.39)[7]	24.7[1]	*

Appendix IV. Continued.

Political Entrepreneurs	N+	Country	C	Mean TO	Change in TO	Mean Exp/GDP	Change in Exp/GDP	Mean FDI $US Millions	Change in FDI $US/GDP	Mean Milex/GDP	Change in Milex/CGE	Mean Milex/CGE	Change in Milex/Milex
Suharto (1968–1998)	31	Indonesia	I	46.8	2.2	27.4	1	989[26]	(–2.4)[25]	2.6[30]	(–0.03)[30]	13.3[26]	(–.3)[25]
Muahmmad Reza Pahlavi (1960–1979)	20	Iran	H	45.6	0.43[19]	10.7[6]	(–1.3)[5]	*	*	*	0.11[19]	28.4	–0.23
A. Khomeini-Sayed Khameini (1979–1989)	10	Iran	B	20.6	–2.1	4	–0.22	*	*	4.2[8]	(–0.19)[7]	33.5[8]	(–.2)[7]
A.S. Aref-Hassan al-Bakr (1964–1979)	16	Iraq	B	71.5	1.9	*	*	*	*	10.5[14]	(0.33)[13]	36.4[13]	(–.6)[12]
Saddam Hussein (1980–1987)	8	Iraq	B	67.8[8]	(–5.1)[8]	*	*	*	*	30.8[6]	8.4[8]	38.4[3]	6.9[3]
Ben Gurion-Yitzhak Rabin (1960–1977)	18	Israel	H	62.3	2.6[17]	24.8[13]	0.96[12]	78.4[5]	(–18.5)[4]	20.1	1.1[17]	42.4[11]	0.0001
Menahem Begin (1978–1983)	6	Israel	B	87.9	–1.7	29	–0.5	–10	–14.7	26.0	–0.08	31	–1.9
Shamir-Peres (NUG) (1984–1989)	6	Israel	H	76.1	–0.2	32.9	1.1	94.3	16.7	17.8	–2.3	25.6	0.32
Yitzhak Shamir (1990–1991)	2	Israel	B	66.6	–3.7	30.9	–2.2	–69	–80	11.7	–0.65	23.7	–1.4
Yitzhak Rabin-Shimon Peres (1992–1996)	5	Israel	I	64.4[1]	.3[1]	32.7[2]	1.2[2]	(–243)[2]	(–151)[2]	9.2	–0.46	22.2[4]	(–.4)[4]
Benjamin Netanyahu (1997)	1	Israel	H	*	*	*	*	*	*	8.6	–0.1	*	*
King Hussein, Jordan (1960–1991)	16	Jordan	H	86.5[31]	2.9[30]	41[19]	1.1	26.3[26]	1.5[9]	15	–0.32[31]	44.1[25]	(–.37)[24]
King Hussein (1991–1998)	7	Jordan	I	*	*	40.7[2]	(–2.5)[2]	32.5[2]	(–3)[2]	8.1[6]	(–.2)[6]	24[4]	(–1.2)[4]
Mahathir bin Mohamad (1980–1997)	18	Malaysia	H	140	4.6	71.2	2.1	2493	267	4.3	–0.18	11.6[16]	(–.13)[16]
King Hassan II (1961–1982)	22	Morocco	H	44	0.38	20.4[18]	(–0.44)[17]	38.8[10]	8.9[9]	3.9	0.19	14.8[16]	.6[15]
King Hassan II (1983–1996)	16	Morocco	I	52.3[10]	(–0.2)[10]	22.4[11]	0.45[11]	166[11]	37.6[11]	4.4[14]	(–0.19)[14]	18.2[9]	.2[7]
Zulfiqar Ali Bhutto (1971–1977)	7	Pakistan	B	28.4	0.84	*	*	8.8[5]	(–0.7)[4]	5.9	0.29	31.8	–1.1
Zia ul-Haq (1978–1987)	10	Pakistan	H	34.1	0.68	*	*	104	10.5	6.3	0.11	25.6	0.2
Benazir Bhutto (1988–1990)	3	Pakistan	H	35.8	–0.03	14.2	.5[2]	194	44.7	6.6	–0.03	27.2	1.1
Nawaz Sharif (1991–1993)	3	Pakistan	H	37.2	1.2	16.9	0.5	319	35.7	6.8	0.0001	27.1	–1.1
Syngman Rhee's (1960–1963)	4	S. Korea	B	19.8	1.7[3]	*	*	*	*,[6]	5.5	(–0.6)[3]	*	*
Park Chung Hee (1964–1979)	15	S. Korea	I	49.3	2.8	18.2	1.3[14]	68[7]	(–12.8)[6]	4.6	–0.01	26.5[13]	.3[12]
Chun Doo Hwan (1980–1988)	9	S. Korea	I	72.7	1.1	34.6	1.6	184	78.2	5.2	–0.12	27.1	–0.2
Rho Tae-Woo (1989–1992)	4	S. Korea	I	61.5	(–3.7)[3]	36.2	–0.8	–97.5	–304.3	3.8	–0.1	21.4	–1.4

Appendix IV. Continued.

Political Entrepreneurs	N+	Country	C	Mean TO	Change in TO	Mean Exp/GDP	Change in Exp/GDP	Mean FDI $US Millions Millions	Change in FDI $US GDP	Mean Milex/ GDP	Change in Milex/ CGE	Mean Milex/ CGE	Change in Milex/
Kim Young Sam (1993–1998)	5	S. Korea	I	67.4	5.9	34.2	1.8	−1351	273.8	3.2[4]	(−0.1)[4]	15.5[2]	(−3)[2]
Lee KuanYew-Goh Chok-Tong (1965–1998)	34	Singapore	I	314[28]	3.9[27]	147[29]	3.9[28]	1768[26]	151[25]	5[31]	(0.08)[30]	22.1[29]	.4[28]
Amin al-Halfiz-Ahmad Khatib (1963–1971)	9	Syria	B	37.9	−0.88	20.7[7]	(−0.37)[6]	*	*	8.6	0.2[8]	34.5[3]	(−3.8)[2]
Hafez el-Asad (1972–1997)	27	Syria	B	47.9[20]	0.9[20]	14.3[20]	(−0.28)[20]	*	*	12[26]	(−0.07)[26]	40.4[19]	1.5[19]
Chiang Ching-kuo-Li Teng Hui (1978–1988)	11	Taiwan	I	99.4	0.5	*	*	*	*	6.2	−0.26	40.5[10]	(−2.3)[9]
Thanarat/Leekpai (1960–1997)	39	Thailand	I	54.1	1.7[38]	29.2[26]	1.5[25]	1021[26]	263[25]	3.1[38]	(−0.02)[37]	18.1[29]	.08[28]
Habib Bourgiba-Zine Ben Ali (1971–1995)	25	Tunisia	I	74.6|[22]	1.5	34.7[23]	0.74[23]	134[20]	10.1[20]	2.7	0.01	7.2[23]	.04[23]

Sources same as Appendices I, II, and III.

Appendix V. Test of significance

	Descriptive Statistics					ANOVA					
Variables	Coalitions	N	Mean	Std. Deviation	Variables		Sum of Squares	df	Mean Square	F	Sig
Trade openness: imports + Exports as % of GDP	Internationalizing	225	88.29	90.27	Trade openness: imports + Exports as % of GDP	Between Groups	251712.08	2	125856.04	31.89	<0.001
	Inward-looking	138	38.29	24.78		Within Groups	2245331.77	569	3946.1		
	Hybrid	209	52.39	40.19		Total	2497043.85	571			
	Total	572	63.11	66.13							
Exports as % of GDP	Internationalizing	206	43.99	45.06	Exports as % of GDP	Between Groups	54724.35	2	27362.17	23.66	<0.001
	Inward-looking	66	15.61	7.76		Within Groups	488025.16	422	1156.46		
	Hybrid	153	24.94	21.12		Total	542749.51	424			
	Total	425	32.72	35.78							
Foreign Direct Investment ($US Millions)	Internationalizing	175	711.59	1314.77	Foreign Direct Investment ($US Millions)	Between Groups	10355470.4	2	5177735.2	3.592	0.029
	Inward-looking	26	37.61	152.32		Within Groups	471393906	327	144157.6		
	Hybrid	129	654.78	1152.56		Total	481749376	329			
	Total	330	636.28	1210.08							
Military Expenditures as % of GDP	Internationalizing	239	4.59	4.22	Military Expenditures as % of GDP	Between Groups	2308.83	2	1154.42	26.19	<0.001
	Inward-looking	136	9.53	8.76		Within Groups	25828.84	586	44.08		
	Hybrid	214	7.58	7.27		Total	28137.67	588			
	Total	589	6.82	6.92							
Military Expenditures as % of CGE	Internationalizing	201	19.78	9.99	Military Expenditures as % of CGE	Between Groups	7619.93	2	3809.97	25.08	<0.001
	Inward-looking	91	30.7	12.66		Within Groups	70478.35	464	151.89		
	Hybrid	175	22.01	14.41		Total	78098.28	466			
	Total	467	22.74	12.94							
Number of Crises Initiated During Coalition	Internationalizing	18	0.11	0.32	Number of Crises Initiated During Coalition	Between Groups	16.86	2	8.43	4.065	0.023
	Inward-looking	22	1.41	1.74		Within Groups	114.04	55	2.07		
	Hybrid	18	0.94	1.7		Total	130.9	57			
	Total	467	0.86	1.52							

Bonferroni

Dependent Variable	(I) Coalitions	(J) Coalitions	Mean Diff. (I – J)	Std. Error	Sig.	95% Confidence Interval	
						Lower	Upper
Trade openness: imports + Exports as % of GDP	Internationalizing	Inward-looking	50.0018*	6.7921	<.001	33.6930	66.3130
		Hybrid	35.9027*	6.0348	<.001	21.4126	50.3928
	Inward-looking	Internationalizing	-50.0018*	6.7921	<.001	-66.3103	-33.6933
		Hybrid	-14.0992	6.8903	0.124	-30.6432	2.4449
	Hybrid	Internationalizing	-35.9027*	6.0348	<.001	-50.3928	-21.4126
		Inward-looking	14.0992	6.8903	0.124	-2.4449	30.6432
Exports as % of GDP	Internationalizing	Inward-looking	28.3768*	4.8100	<.001	16.8157	39.9379
		Hybrid	19.0434*	3.6294	<.001	10.3200	27.7669
	Inward-looking	Internationalizing	-28.3768*	4.8100	<.001	-39.9379	-16.8157
		Hybrid	-9.3334	5.0081	0.189	-21.3706	2.7038
	Hybrid	Internationalizing	-19.0434*	3.6294	<.001	-27.7669	-10.3200
		Inward-looking	9.3334	5.0081	0.189	-2.7038	21.3706
Foreign Direct Investment ($US Millions)	Internationalizing	Inward-looking	673.9895*	252.3541	0.024	66.7345	1281.2444
		Hybrid	56.8212	139.3288	1.000	-278.4542	392.0965
	Inward-looking	Internationalizing	-673.9895*	252.3541	0.024	-1281.2444	-66.7345
		Hybrid	-617.1683	258.1086	0.052	-1238.2705	3.9339
	Hybrid	Internationalizing	-56.8212	139.3288	1.000	-392.0965	278.4542
		Inward-looking	617.1683	258.1086	0.052	-3.9339	1238.2705
Military Expenditures as % of GDP	Internationalizing	Inward-looking	-4.9377*	0.7131	<.001	-6.6497	-3.2256
		Hybrid	-2.9888*	0.6248	<.001	-4.4889	-1.4888
	Inward-looking	Internationalizing	4.9377*	0.7131	<.001	3.2256	6.6497
		Hybrid	1.9488*	0.7281	0.023	0.2009	3.6968
	Hybrid	Internationalizing	2.9888*	0.6248	<.001	1.4888	4.4889
		Inward-looking	-1.9488*	0.7281	0.023	-3.6968	-0.2009
Military Expenditures as % of CGE	Internationalizing	Inward-looking	-10.9193*	1.5572	<.001	-14.6607	-7.1779
		Hybrid	-2.2273	1.2742	0.243	-5.2888	0.8343
	Inward-looking	Internationalizing	10.9193*	1.5572	<.001	7.1779	14.6607
		Hybrid	8.6920*	1.5928	<.001	4.8650	12.5191

Bonferroni (continued).

Dependent Variable	(I) Coalitions	(J) Coalitions	Mean Diff. (I − J)	Std. Error	Sig.	95% Confidence Interval	
						Lower	Upper
Number of Crises Initiated During Coalition	Hybrid	Internationalizing	2.2273	1.2742	0.243	−0.8343	5.2888
		Inward-looking	−8.6920*	1.5928	<.001	−12.5191	−4.8650
	Internationalizing	Inward-looking	−1.2980*	0.4576	0.019	−2.4281	−0.1679
		Hybrid	−0.8333	0.4800	0.264	−2.0186	0.3519
	Inward-looking	Internationalizing	1.2980*	0.4576	0.019	0.1679	2.4281
		Hybrid	0.4646	0.4576	0.943	−0.6655	1.5948
	Hybrid	Internationalizing	0.8333	0.4800	0.264	−0.3519	2.0186
		Inward-looking	−0.4646	0.4576	0.943	−1.5948	0.6655

*The mean difference is significant at the .05 level.

REFERENCES

Abu-Amr, Z. (1993). "Hamas: A Historical and Political Background." *Journal of Palestine Studies*, 22(4): 5–19.
AbuKhalil, A. (1994). "The Incoherence of Islamic Fundamentalism: Arab Islamic Thought at the End of the 20th Century." *Middle East Journal*, 48: 677.
ACDA [U.S. Arms Control and Disarmament Agency]. (1990). *World Military Expenditures and Arms Transfers*. Washington, DC: ACDA.
Acharya, A. (1999). "Culture, Security, Multilateralism: The 'ASEAN Way' and Regional Order." In K. R. Krause (ed.), *Culture and Security: Multilateralism, Arms Control, and Security Building*. London: Frank Cass.
Acharya, A. and Johnston, A. I. (eds) (2007). *Crafting Cooperation: The Design and Effect of Regional Institutions in Comparative Perspective*. New York, NY: Cambridge University Press.
Adams, F. G. (ed.) (1992). *The Macroeconomic Dimensions of Arms Reduction*. Boulder, CO: Westview.
Aggarwal, V. K. (1995). "Comparing Regional Cooperation Efforts in the Asia-Pacific and North America." In A. Mack, and J. Ravenhill (eds), *Pacific Cooperation: Building Economic and Security Regimes in the Asia-Pacific Region*. Boulder, CO: Westview Press.
Aggarwal, V. W., with Lin. K-C. (2001). "APEC as an Institution." In R. E. Feinberg, and Y. Zhau (eds), *Assessing APEC's Progress: Trade, Ecotech, and Institutions*. Singapore: ISEAS.
Akiyama, N. (2003). "The socio-political roots of Japan's non-nuclear posture." In B. L. Self and J. W. Thompson (eds), *Japan's Nuclear Option: Security, Politics, and Policy in the 21st Century*. Washington, DC: The Henry L. Stimson Center: 64–91.
Alani, M. (2005). "The Case for a Gulf Weapons of Mass Destruction Free Zone." *Security and Terrorism Issue*, 1 (October).
Alesina, A. (1994). "Political Models of Macroeconomic Policy and Fiscal Reforms." In S. Haggard and S. B. Webb (eds), *Voting for Reform: Democracy, Political Liberalization, and Economic Adjustment*. New York, NY: Oxford University Press: 37–60.
Al-Khazen, J. (1995). "Interview: Editor of Al-Hayat." *Middle East Policy*, 3:71.
Al Khouri, R. (1994). "The Political Economy of Jordan: Democratization and the Gulf Crisis." In D. Tschirgi (ed.), *The Arab World Today*. Boulder, CO: Lynne Rienner: 101–122.
Almonte, J. T. (1997–1998). "Ensuring the "ASEAN way." *Survival*, 39(4): 80–92.
Amin, G. A. (1980). *The Modernization of Poverty: A Study in the Political Economy of Growth in Nine Arab Countries 1945–1970*. Leiden: Brill.
Amsden, A. H. (1989). *Asia's Next Giant: South Korea and Late Industrialization*. New York, NY: Oxford University Press.
Amsden, A. H. (1991). "Diffusion of Development: The Late-Industrializing Model and Greater East Asia." *American Economic Review*, 81(2): 282–286.
Amsden, A. H. (2001). *The Rise of the "The Rest": Challenges to the West from Late-Industrializing Economies*. New York, NY: Oxford University Press.
Anderson, L. (1987). "The State in the Middle East and North Africa." *Comparative Politics*, 20(1): 1–18.

Arab Human Development Report. [AHDR]. (2002). *Arab Human Development Report 2002*. New York, NY: United Nations Development Program.

Arian, A. (2003). "Israeli Public Opinion on National Security 1998." *Memorandum* No. 67. Tel Aviv: Jaffee Center for Strategic Studies.

Awad, I. (1994). "The Future of Regional and Subregional Organization in the Arab World." In D. Tschirgi (ed.), *The Arab World Today*. Boulder, CO: Lynne Rienner.

Axelrod, R. M. (1984). *The Evolution of Cooperation*. New York, NY: Basic Books.

Baldwin, R. E. (1988). *Trade Policy in a Changing World Economy*. Chicago, IL: University of Chicago Press.

Barkey, H. (ed.) (1992). *The Politics of Economic Reform in the Middle East*. New York, NY: St. Martin's Press.

Barnett, M. N. (1992). *Confronting the Costs of War – Military Power, State and Society in Egypt and Israel*. Princeton, NJ: Princeton University Press.

Barnett, M N. (1998). *Dialogues in Arab Politics: Negotiations in Regional Order*. New York, NY: Columbia University Press.

Barnett, M. and Solingen, E. (2007). "Designed to Fail or Failure of Design? The Sources and Institutional Effects of the Arab League." In A. I. Johnston and A. Acharya (eds), *Crafting Cooperation: Regional Institutions in Comparative Perspective*. New York, NY: Cambridge University Press.

Barnett, M., and Finnemore, M. (1999). "The Politics, Power, and Pathologies of International Organizations." *International Organization*, 53(4): 699–732.

Barro, R. J. (1997). *Determinants of Economic Growth: A Cross-Country Empirical Study*. Cambridge, MA: MIT Press.

Bates, R. H. and Krueger, A. O. (eds) (1993). *Political and Economic Interactions in Economic Policy Reform: Evidence From Eight Countries*. Oxford: Blackwell.

Beblawi, H., and G. Luciani (1987). *Nation, State and Integration in the Arab World. Vol II: The Rentier State*. London: Croom Helm.

Bellin, E. (2004). "The Robustness of Authoritarianism in the Middle East." *Comparative Politics*, 36(2): 139–158.

Berger, T. (1998). *Cultures of Antimilitarism: National Security in Germany and Japan*. Baltimore, MD: The Johns Hopkins University Press.

Berger, T. (2003). "Power and Purpose in the Asia-Pacific Region: A Constructivist Interpretation." In G. J. Ikenberry and M. Mastanduno (eds), *International Relations Theory and the Asia-Pacific*. New York, NY: Columbia University Press.

Bergsten, C. F. (1997). *Wither APEC? The Progress to Date and Agenda for the Future*. Washington, DC: Institute for International Economics.

Berman, S. (2007). "How Democracies Emerge: Lessons from Europe." *Journal of Democracy*, 18(1): 28–41.

Betts, R. K. (1980). "Incentives for Nuclear Weapons." In J. A. Yager (ed.), *Nonproliferation and U.S. Foreign Policy*. Washington. DC: The Brookings Institution.

Betts, R. K. (1993). "Systems of Peace as Causes of War? Collective Security, Arms Control, and the New Europe." In J. Snyder and R. Jervis (eds), *Coping with Complexity in the International System*. Boulder, CO: Westview: 265–302.

Betts, R. K. (2000). "Universal deterrence or conceptual collapse? Liberal pessimism and utopian realism." In V. A. Utgoff (ed.), *The coming crisis: Nuclear proliferation, U.S interests, and world order*. Cambridge, MA: MIT Press: 51–86.

Bhagwati, J. (1993). "Regionalism and Multilateralism: An Overview." In J. de Melo and A. Panagariya (eds), *New dimensions in regional integration*. New York, NY: Cambridge University Press.

Bill, J. A. and Springborg, R. (1990). *Politics in the Middle East* (3rd edn). New York, NY: HarperCollins.

Bill, J. A. and Springborg, R. (2000). *Politics in the Middle East* (5th edn). New York, NY: Addison-Wesley.

Binder, L. (1988). *Islamic Liberalism: A Critique of Development Ideologies*. Chicago, IL: University of Chicago Press.

Binder, Leonard. (1978). *In a Moment of Enthusiasm: Political Power and the Second Stratum in Egypt*. Chicago, IL: Chicago University Press.

Blix, H. (2005). *Disarming Iraq: The Search for Weapons of Mass Destruction*. London: Bloomsbury.

Brady, H. E., and Collier, D. (eds) (2004). *Rethinking Social Inquiry: Diverse Tools, Shared Standards*. Lanham, MD: Rowman & Littlefield.

Brecher, M. and Wilkenfeld, J. (2000). *A Study of Crisis* (2nd edn). Ann Arbor, MI: University of Michigan Press.

Breuning, M., Bredehoft, J. and Walton, E. (2005). "Promise and Performance: An Evaluation of Journals in International Relations." *International Studies Perspectives*, 6(4): 447–461.

Bruno, M. (1988). "Opening Up: Liberalization with Stabilization." In R. Dornbusch and F. L. C. H. Helmers (eds), *The Open Economy: Tools for Policymakers in Developing Countries*. New York, NY: Oxford University Press: 223–248.
Bueno de Mesquita, B. and Riker, W. H. (1982). "An Assessment of the Merits of Selective Nuclear Proliferation." *Journal of Conflict Resolution*, 26: 283–306.
Bueno de Mesquita, B., Morrow, J. D. and Wu, S. S. G. (1993). "Forecasting the Risk of Nuclear Proliferation: Taiwan as an Illustration of the Method." In Z. S. Davis and B. Frankel (eds), *The Proliferation Puzzle: Why Nuclear Weapons Spread (and What Results)*. London: Frank Cass: 311–331.
Bueno de Mesquita, B., Smith, A. and Siverson, R. M. (2003). *The Logic of Political Survival*. Cambridge, MA: MIT Press.
Cable, V. and Henderson, D. (ed.) (1994). *Trade Blocs? The Future of Regional Integration*. Washinton DC: Brookings Institution.
Calder, K. (1996). *Pacific Defense: Arms, Energy, and America's Future in Asia*. New York, NY: William Morrow and Co.
Campbell, J. L. (2004). *Institutional Change and Globalization*. Princeton, NJ: Princeton University Press.
Campbell, K. M., Einhorn, R. J. and Reiss, M. B. (eds) (2004). *The Nuclear Tipping Point: Why States Reconsider Their Nuclear Choices*. Washington DC: Brookings Institution Press.
Campbell, J. L., and Pedersen, O. K. (eds) (2001). *The Rise of Neoliberalism and Institutional Analysis*. Princeton, NJ: Princeton University Press.
Campos, J. E., and Root, H. L. (1996). *The Key to the Asian Miracle: Making Shared Growth Credible*. Washington, DC: Brookings Institution.
Carothers, T. (2007). "How Democracies Emerge: The Sequencing Fallacy." *Journal of Democracy* 18(1): 12–27.
Cardoso, F. H. (1995). "The Ethics of Conviction." *Hemisfile*, 6(6): 4–5.
Carlin, R. L., and J. S. Wit. (2006). "North Korean Reform: Politics, Economics and Security." *Adelphi Papers*, 46, 382 (July): 1–65.
Carter, A. B. (2005). "Panel: New Approaches for Addressing the Threat of WMD Proliferation." Remarks presented at Non-Proliferation of Weapons of Mass Destruction: Current Challenges and New Approaches, Tufts University, Fletcher School of Law & Diplomacy, October 21.
Cassandra (pseudonym) (1995). "The Impending Crisis in Egypt." *The Middle East Journal*, 49(1): 9–27.
Chai, S.-k. (1997). "Entrenching the Yoshida Defense Doctrine: Three Techniques for Institutionalization." *International Organization*, 51(3): 389–412.
Chan, S. (1988). "Defense Burden and Economic Growth: Unraveling the Taiwanese Enigma." *American Political Science Review*, 82(3): 913–920.
Chan S. (1990). *East Asian Dynamism: Managing Growth, Order, and Security in the Pacific Region*. Boulder, CO: Westview Press.
Chan, S. (1992a). "Defense, Welfare and Growth: Introduction." In S. Chan and A. Mintz (eds), *Defense, Welfare, and Growth*. New York, NY: Routledge: 163–178.
Chan, S. (1992b). "Military Burden, Economic Growth, and Income Inequality: The Taiwan Exception." In S. Chan and A. Mintz (eds), *Defense, Welfare, and Growth*. New York, NY: Routledge: 163–178.
Chan, S. and Clark, C. (1992). *Flexibility, Foresight, and Fortuna in Taiwan's Development*. New York, NY: Routledge.
Chatelus, M. (1987). "Policies for Development: Attitudes Toward Industry and Services." In Beblawi and Luciani (eds), *Nation, State and Integration in the Arab World. Vol II: The Rentier State*. London: Croom Helm: 108–137.
Checkel, J. T. (1997). "International Norms and Domestic Politics: Bridging The Rationalist-Constructivist Divide." *European Journal of International Relations*, 3(4): 473–495.
Checkel, J. T. (2001). "Why Comply? Social Learning and European Identity Change." *International Organization* 55(3): 553–588.
Cheng, T.-J. (1990). "Political Regimes and Development Strategies: South Korea and Taiwan." In G. Gereffi and D. L. Wyman (eds), *Manufacturing Miracles: Paths of Industrialization in Latin America and East Asia*. Princeton, NJ: Princeton University Press. 139–178.
Christensen, T. (1996). *Useful Adversaries: Grand Strategy, Domestic Mobilization, and Sino-American Conflict, 1947–1958*. Princeton, NJ: Princeton University Press.
Christensen, T. (1999). "China, the U.S.-Japan Alliance, and the Security Dilemma in East Asia." *International Security*, 23(4): 49–80.
Christensen, T. (2001). "Posing Problems Without Catching Up: China's Rise and Challenges for U.S. Security Policy." *International Security*, 25(4): 5–40.
Christensen, T. J. (2007). U.S. Deputy Assistant Secretary for East Asian and Pacific Affairs. Statement Before the House Committee on Foreign Affairs, Subcommittee on Asia, the Pacific, and the Global Environment, Washington, DC. Release Date: March 27, 2007.

Chubin, S. (2006). *Iran's Nuclear Ambitions*. Washington, DC: Carnegie Endowment for International Peace.

Chubin, S. and Litwak, R. S. (2003). "Debating Iran's Nuclear Aspirations." *The Washington Quarterly*, 26(4): 99–114.

Cox, D. G. and Cooper, D. A. (2006). "Democratic Sanctions: Connecting the Democratic Peace and Economic Sanctions." *Journal of Peace Research*, 43(6): 709–722.

Cox, R. W. (1986). "Social Forces, States, and World Orders: Beyond International Relations Theory." In R. O. Keohane (ed.), *Neorealism and Its Critics*. New York, NY: Columbia University Press.

Cumings, B. (1984). "The Origins and Development of the Northeast Asian Political Economy: Industrial Sectors, Product Cycles, and Political Consequences." *International Organization*, 38(1): 1–40.

Dahl, R. A. (1989). *Democracy and its Critics*. New Haven, CT: Yale University Press.

De Lombaerde, P. and Söderbaum, F. (eds). (2013). *Regionalism*. London: Sage.

Deutsch, K., Burrell, S. A., Kann, R. A., Lee, M., Lichterman, M., Lingren, R. E., Loewenheim, F. L., and Van Wagenen, R. W. (1957). *Political Community and the North Atlantic Area: International Organization in the Light of Historical Experience*. Princeton, NJ: Princeton University Press.

Díaz Alejandro, C. F. (1983). "Open Economy, Closed Polity?" In D. Tussie (ed.), *Latin America in the World Economy: New Perspectives*. Aldershot: Gower Publishing: 21–54.

Dibb, P., Hale, D. D. and Prince, P. (1998). "The Strategic Implications of Asia's Economic Crisis." *Survival*, 40(2): 5–26.

Dodge, T. (2002). "Bringing the Bourgeoisie back in: The Birth of Liberal Corporatism in the Middle East." In T. Dodge and R. Higgott (eds), *Globalization and the Middle East: Islam, Economy, Society and Politics*. London: Royal Institute of International Affairs: 169–187.

Dodge, T. and Higgott, R. (2002). "Globalisation and Its Discontents: The Theory and Practice of Change in the Middle East." In T. Dodge and R. Higgott (eds), *Globalization and the Middle East: Islam, Economy, Society and Politics*. London: Royal Institute of International Affairs: 13–35.

Domke, W. K. (1988). *War and the Changing Global System*. New Haven, CT: Yale University Press.

Doner, R. F., Ritchie, B. and Slater, D. (2005). "Systemic Vulnerability and the Origins of Developmental States: Northeast and Southeast Asia in Comparative Perspective." *International Organization*, 59(2): 327–361.

Dornbusch, R. and Edwards, S. (eds) (1991). *The Macroeconomics of Populism in Latin America*. Chicago, IL: University of Chicago Press.

Dowty, A. (2005). *Israel/Palestine*. Cambridge: Polity.

Doyle, M. W. (1983). "Kant, Liberal Legacies, and Foreign Affairs." *Philosophy and Public Affairs*, 12(3): 205–235.

Drake, P. W. (1991). "Comment." In R. Dornbusch and S. Edwards (eds), *The Macroeconomics of Populism in Latin America*. Chicago, IL: University of Chicago Press: 35–40.

Drezner, D. (1999). *The Sanctions Paradox: Economic Statecraft and International Relations*. Cambridge: Cambridge University Press.

Dunn, L. A. (1982). *Controlling the Bomb: Nuclear Proliferation in the 1980s*. New Haven, CT: Yale University Press.

Eberstadt, N. Ellings, R., Babson, B. and Noland, M. (2006). "Special Roundtable: What If? Economic Implications of a Fundamental Shift in North Korean Security Policy." *Asia Policy*, 2 (July 2006).

Eckstein, H. (1975). Case studies and theory in political science. In F. Greenstein and N. Polsby (eds), *Strategies of Inquiry* (Vol. 7). Reading, MA: Addison-Wesley; 79–138.

Edwards, S. (1997). "Openness, Productivity and Growth: What Do We Really Know?" National Bureau of Economic Research, Working Paper 5978, Washington, DC.

Elster, J. (1989). *The Cement of Society: A Study of Social Order*. New York, NY: Cambridge University Press.

Emmerson, D. K. (1996) "Indonesia, Malaysia, Singapore: A Regional Security Core?" In R. J. Ellings and S. W. Simon (eds), *Southeast Asian Security in the New Millennium*. Armonk, NY: M. E. Sharpe.

Esposito, J. L. (1992). *The Islamic Threat: Myth or Reality?* New York, NY: Oxford University Press.

Evans, P. B. (1995). *Embedded Autonomy: States and Industrial Transformation*. Princeton. NJ: Princeton University Press.

Fahmy, N. (2001). "Prospects for Arms Control and proliferation in the Middle East." *The Nonproliferation Review* (Summer): 1–6.

Fattah, H. M. (2006). "Letter from Dubai: Emirate Wakes Up Famous. Thank You America." *New York Times*, 3/2/06: A4.

Fawn, R. (2009). "Regions' and Their Study: Wherefrom, What for and Whereto?" *Review of International Studies*, 35: 5–34.

Feinstein, L. and Slaughter, A.-M. (2004). "A Duty to Prevent," *Foreign Affairs*, 83(1): 136–150.

Feldner, Y. (2003). "Egypt Rethinks its Nuclear Program – Part III: The Nuclear Lobby (Continued)." *The Middle East Media Research Institute, Inquiry and Analysis Series* 120 (January 22). Online. Available at http://memri.org/bin/articles.cgi?Page=archives&Area=ia&ID=IA12003.

Finnemore, M. (1996). *National Interests in International Society*. Ithaca, NY: Cornell University.

Finnemore, M. and Sikkink, K. (1998). "International Norm Dynamics and Political Change." *International Organization*, 52(4): 887–918.

Fischer, S. (1995). "Prospects for Regional Integration in the Middle East." In J. de Melo and A. Panagariya (eds), *New Dimensions in Regional Integration*. New York, NY: Cambridge University Press.

Foot, R. (1995). "Pacific Asia: The Development of Regional Dialogue." In L. Fawcett and A. Hurrell (eds), *Regionalism in World Politics*. New York, NY: Oxford University Press.

Freier, S. (1985) "Israel." In J. Goldblat (ed.), *Non-proliferation: The Why and the Wherefore*. London: Taylor and Francis.

Friedberg, A. L. (1993/94). "Ripe for Rivalry: Prospects for Peace in a Multipolar Asia." *International Security*, 18(3): 5–33.

Frieden, J. A. (1991). *Debt, Development, and Democracy: Modern Political Economy and Latin America*. Princeton, NJ: Princeton University Press.

Frieden, J. A. (1995). "Capital Politics: Creditors and the International Political Economy." In J. A. Frieden and D. A. Lake (eds), *International Political Economy: Perspectives on Global Power and Wealth*. New York, NY: St. Martin's Press: 282–298.

Frieden, J. A. and Rogowski, R. (1996). "The Impact of the International Economy on National Policies: An Analytical Overview." In R. O. Keohane and H. V. Milner (eds), *Internationalization and Domestic Politics*. New York, NY: Cambridge University Press: 25–47.

Fuerth, L. (2004). "Turkey: Nuclear Choices amongst Dangerous Neighbors." In K. M. Campbell, R. J. Einhorn, and M. B. Reiss (eds), *The Nuclear Tipping Point*. Washington, DC: Brookings Institution Press.

Funabashi, Y. (1993). "The Asianization of Asia." *Foreign Affairs*, 72(5): 75–85.

Gallagher, M. E. (2002). "'Reform and Openness': Why China's Economic Reforms Have Delayed Democracy." *World Politics*, 54(3): 338–372.

Garnaut, R. (2000). "Introduction-APEC Ideas and Reality: History and Prospects." In I. Yamazawa (ed.), *Asia Pacific Economic Cooperation (APEC)*. New York, NY: Routledge.

Garrett, G, and Lange, P. (1996). "Internationalization, Institutions, and Political Change." In R. O. Keohane and H. V. Milner (eds), *Internationalization and Domestic Politics*. New York, NY: Cambridge University Press: 48–78.

Garrett, G., and Weingast, B. (1993). "Ideas, Interests, and Institutions: Constructing the EC's Internal Market." In J. Goldstein, and R. Keohane (eds), *Ideas and Foreign Policy*. Ithaca, NY: Cornell University Press.

Gasiorowski, M. J. (1986). "Economic Interdependence and International Conflict: Some Cross-National Evidence." *International Studies Quarterly*, 30(1): 23–38.

Gaubatz, K. T. (1996). "Democratic States and Commitment in International Relations." *International Organization*, 50(1): 109–140.

Gause, F. Gregory, III. (1992). "Sovereignty, Statecraft and Stability in the Middle East." *Journal of International Affairs*, 45(2): 441–469.

Gellner, E. (1983). *Nations and Nationalism*. Ithaca, NY: Cornell University Press.

George, A. L. (1993). *Bridging the Gap: Theory and Practice in Foreign Policy*. Washington, DC: United States Institute of Peace.

George, A. L., and Bennett, A. (2005). *Case Studies and Theory Development*. Cambridge, MA: MIT Press.

Ghosn, F., Palmer, G. and Bremer, S. (2004). "The MID3 Data Set, 1993–2001: Procedures, Coding Rules, and Description." *Conflict Management and Peace Science*, 21: 133–154.

Gilpin, J. M. (1987). *The Political Economy of International Relations*. Princeton, NJ: Princeton University Press.

Glaser, C. L. (1994/95). "Realists as Optimists: Cooperation as Self-Help." *International Security*, 19(3): 50–90.

Glaser, C. L. (2000). "The Causes and Consequences of Arms Races." *Annual Review of Political Science*, 3: 251–276.

Goldschmidt, P. (2003). "The Increasing Risk of Nuclear Proliferation: Lessons Learned." *International Atomic Energy Agency Bulletin*, 45(2): 24–27.

Goldschmidt, P. (2007). "Priority Steps to Strengthen the Nonproliferation Regime." Carnegie Endowment for International Peace, Policy Outlook 33, January 30, 2007. Online. Available at http://carnegieendowment.org/2007/01/30/priority-steps-to-strengthen-nonproliferation-regime/3s9o

Goldstein, J. and Keohane, R. O. (eds) (1993). *Ideas and Foreign Policy: Beliefs, Institutions, and Political Change*. Ithaca, NY: Cornell University Press.

Gomaa, A. (1977). *The Foundation of the League of Arab States*. London: Longman.

Goodman, J. B. and Pauly, L. W. (1995). "The Obsolescence of Capital Controls? Economic Management in an Age of Global Markets." In J. A. Frieden and D. A. Lake (eds), *International Political Economy: Perspectives on Global Power and Wealth*. New York, NY: St Martin's Press: 299–317.

Gourevitch, P. (1986). *Politics in Hard Time: Comparative Responses to International Economic Crises*. Ithaca, NY: Cornell University Press.

Gourevitch, P. (1999). "The Governance Problem in Strategic Interaction." In D. Lake and R. Powell (eds), *Strategic Choice and International Relations*. Princeton, NJ: University Press.

Gowa, J. and Mansfield, E. D. (1993). "Power Politics and International Trade." *American Political Science Review*, 87(2): 408–420.

Gramsci, A. (1988). *A Gramsci Reader: Selected Writings 1916–1935*. In D. Forgacs, (ed.), London: Lawrence and Wishart.

Grieco, J. M. (1997). "Systemic Sources of Variation in Regional Institutionalism in Western Europe, East Asia, and the Americas." In E. D. Mansfield and H. V. Milner (eds), *The Political Economy of Regionalism*. New York, NY: Columbia University Press.

Gruber, L. (2000). *Ruling the World: Power Politics and the Rise of Supranational Institutions*. Princeton, NJ: Princeton University Press.

Haas, E. B. (1958). *The Uniting of Europe*. Stanford, CA: Stanford University Press.

Haas, E. B. (1961). "International Integration: The European and the Universal Process." *International Organization*, 15(3): 366–392.

Haas, E. (1964). *Beyond the Nation State: Functionalism and International Organization*. Palo Alto, CA: Stanford University Press.

Haas, R. and O'Sullivan, M. (2000). "Terms of Engagement: Alternatives to Punitive Policies." *Survival*, 42(2).

Haggard, S. (1990). *Pathways from the Periphery: The Politics of Growth in the Newly Industrializing Countries*. Ithaca, NY: Cornell University Press.

Haggard, S. (1995a). "Inflation and Stabilization." In J. A. Frieden and D. A. Lake (eds), *International Political Economy: Perspectives on Global Power and Wealth*. New York, NY: St. Martin's Press: 447–459.

Haggard, S. (1995b). *Developing Nations and the Politics of Global Integration*. Washington, DC: Brookings Institution.

Haggard, S. (1997). "Regionalism in Asia and the Americas." In E. D. Mansfield, and H. V. Milner (eds), *The Political Economy of Regionalism*. New York, NY: Columbia University Press.

Haggard, S. (2004). "Institutions and Growth in East Asia." *Studies in Comparative International Development*, 38(4): 53–81.

Haggard S. and Kaufman, R. R. (eds) (1992). *The Politics of Economic Adjustment*. Princeton, NJ: Princeton University Press.

Haggard, S. and Kaufman, R. R. (1995). *The Political Economy of Democratic Transitions*. Princeton, NJ: Princeton University Press.

Haggard, S. and Noland, M. (2007). *Famine in North Korea: Markets, Aid, and Reform*. New York, NY: Columbia University Press.

Hakimian, H. (2001). "From MENA to East Asia and Back: Lessons of Globalization, Crisis and Economic Reform." In H. Hakimian and Z. Moshaver (eds), *The State and Global Change*. Richmond, UK: Curzon: 80–108.

Hall, P. A. and Taylor, R. C. R. (1998). "Political Science and the Three New Institutionalisms." In K Soltan, E. M. Uslaner, and V. Haufler (eds), *Institutions and Social Order*. Ann Arbor, MI: University of Michigan Press.

Halliday, F. (2005). *The Middle East in International Relations: Power, Politics and Ideology*. New York, NY: Cambridge University Press.

Hamza, K. (1998). "Inside Saddam's secret nuclear program." *Bulletin of the Atomic Scientists*, 54(5): 26–33.

Harris, S. (2000). "Asian multilateral institutions and their response to the Asian economic crisis: The regional and global implications." *The Pacific Review*, 13(3): 495–516.

Harrison, S. S. (2002). *Korean Endgame: A Strategy for Reunification and U.S. Disengagement*. Princeton, NJ: Princeton University Press.

Hasou, T. Y. (1985). *Struggle for the Arab World: Egypt's Nasser and the Arab League*. New York, NY: Columbia University Press.

Hassouna, H. A. (1975). *The League of Arab States and Regional Disputes: A Study of Middle East Conflicts*. Dobbs Ferry, NY: Oceana.

Heikal, M. H. (1978). *Sphinx and Commissar: The Rise and Fall of Soviet Influence in the Arab World*. London: Collins.
Hemmer, C. and Katzenstein, P. J. (2002). "Why Is There No NATO in Asia? Collective Identity, Regionalism and the Origins of Multilateralism." *International Organization*, 56(3): 575–609.
Henry, C. M. and Springborg, R. (2001). *Globalization and the Politics of Development in the Middle East*. Cambridge: Cambridge University Press.
Heston, A. and Summers, R. (1991). "The Penn World Table (Mark 5): An Expanded Set of International Comparisons, 1950–1988." *Quarterly Journal of Economics*, 106(9): 327–368. [1995 update in National Bureau of Economic Research, Cambridge, MA. (January), www.nber.org/pwt56.html].
Higgott, R. (1995). "APEC: A Skeptical View." In A. Mack, and J. Ravenhill (eds), *Pacific Cooperation: Building Economic and Security Regimes in the Asia-Pacific Region*. Boulder, CO: Westview Press.
Higgott, R. (1997). "De facto and de jure Regionalism: The Double Discourse of Regionalism in the Asia Pacific." *Global Society*, 11(2): 166.
Higgott, R. and Stubbs, R. (1995). "Competing Conceptions of Economic Regionalism: APEC versus AEAC in the Asia Pacific." *Review of International Political Economy*, 2(3): 516–535.
Hinnebusch, R. (1993). "State and Civil Society in Syria." *Middle East Journal*, 47(2): 243–257.
Hirschman, A. O. (1945) *National Power and the Structure of Foreign Trade*. Berkeley, CA: University of California Press.
Hirschman, A. O. (1963). *Journeys Toward Progress*. New York, NY: The Twentieth Century Fund.
Hirschman, A. O. (1968). *Journeys Toward Progress: Studies of Economic Policy-making in Latin America*. New York, NY: Greenwood Press.
Hirschman, A. O. (1982). *Shifting Involvements: Private Interest and Public Action*. Princeton, NJ: Princeton University Press.
Hughes, C. W. (2004). "Japan's Re-emergence as a 'Normal' Military Power." *Adelphi Paper*, 368–9.
Hurrell, A. (1995). "Regionalism in Theoretical Perspective." In L. Fawcett and A. Hurrell (eds), *Regional Organization and International Order*. New York, NY: Oxford University Press.
Husbands, J. L. (1982). "The Prestige States." In W. H. Kincade and C. Bertram (eds), *Nuclear proliferation in the 1980s*. New York, NY: St. Martins Press: 112–138.
Ibrahim, S. E. (1995). "Liberalization and Democratization in the Arab World: An Overview." In R. Brynen, B. Korany and P. Noble (eds), *Political Liberalization and Democratization in the Arab World: Vol. 1. Theoretical Perspectives*. Boulder, CO: Lynne Rienner: 29–60.
(ICG) International Crisis Group. (2005). "Iran: What Does Ahmadi-Nejad's Victory Mean?" *Middle East Briefing*, No.18, Tehran/Brussels, 4 August 2005.
Imai, R. (1975). "The Outlook for Japan's Nuclear Future." Discussion Paper 63. Santa Monica, CA: California Seminar on Arms Control and Foreign Policy.
Inoguchi, T. (1993). *Japan's Foreign Policy in an Era of Global Change*. New York, NY: St. Martin's Press.
Inoguchi, T. (1997). "Conclusion: A Peace-and-Security Taxonomy." In T. Inoguchi, and G. B. Stillman (eds), *North-East Asian Regional Security: The Role of International Institutions*. Tokyo: United Nations University Press.
International Institute for Strategic Studies (1992). *The Military Balance*. London: Brassey's.
Intriligator, M. and Brito, D. (1981). "Nuclear Proliferation and the Probability of War." *Public Choice*, 37.
Jacoby, N. H. (1966). *U.S. Aid to Taiwan: A Study of Foreign Aid, Self-help, and Development*. New York, NY: Praeger.
Jentleson, B. and Whytock, C. A. (2005/06). "Who 'Won' Libya: The Force-Diplomacy Debate and Its Implications for Theory and Policy." *International Security*, 30(3): 47–86.
Jervis, R. (1978). "Cooperation Under the Security Dilemma." *World Politics*, 30(2): 167–214.
Jervis, R. (1982a). *Deterrence and Perception*. Los Angeles: Center for International and Strategic Affairs, University of California.
Jervis, R. (1982b). "Security Regimes." *International Organization*, 36: 357–378.
Jetschke, A. and Lenz, T. (2013). "Does regionalism diffuse? A New Research Agenda for the Study of Regional Organizations." *Journal of European Public Policy*, 20(4): 626–637.
Job, B. L. (1997). "Matters of Multilateralism: Implications for Regional Conflict Management." In D. Lake and P. Morgan (eds), *Regional Orders: Building Security in a New World*. University Park, PA: Pennsylvania State University Press: 165–194.
Johnson, C. (1982). *MITI and the Japanese Miracle: the Growth of Industrial Policy 1925–1975*. Stanford, CA: Stanford University Press.
Johnson, C. (1993). "The State and Japanese Grand Strategy." In R. N. Rosecrance and A. A. Stein (eds), *The Domestic Bases of Grand Strategy*. Ithaca, NY: Cornell University Press: 201–224.
Johnston, A. I. (1999). "The Myth of the ASEAN Way? Explaining the Evolution of the ASEAN Regional Forum." In H. Haftendorn, R. O. Keohane, and C. A. Wallander (eds), *Imperfect Unions: Security Institutions over Time and Space*. New York, NY: Oxford University Press.

Johnston, A. I. (2001). "Treating International Institutions as Social Environments." *International Studies Quarterly*, 45(4): 487–515.
Johnston, A. I. (2008). *Social States: China in International Institutions, 1980–2000*. Princeton, NJ: Princeton University Press.
Jones, P. (1997a). "New Directions in Middle East Deterrence: Implications for Arms Control." *Middle East Review of International Affairs* (MERIA) 4 (December 1997): article 4.
Jones, P. (1997b). "Arms Control in the Middle East: Some Reflections on ACRS." *Security Dialogue*, 28(1): 57–70.
Jones, L. P. and I. Sakong (1980). *Government, Business, and Entrepreneurship in Economic Development: The Korean Case*. Cambridge, MA: Harvard University Press.
Kahler, M. (1989). "International Financial Institutions and the Politics of Adjustment." In J. M. Nelson (ed.), *Fragile Coalitions: The Politics of Economic Adjustment*. New Brunswick, NJ: Transaction Books: 139–158.
Kahler, M. (1992). "External Influence, Conditionality, and the Politics of Adjustment." In S. Haggard and R. R. Kaufman (eds), *The Politics of Economic Adjustment*. Princeton, NJ: Princeton University Press: 89–136.
Kahler, M. (1995). *International Institutions and the Political Economy of Integration*. Washington, DC: The Brookings Institution.
Kahler, M. (ed.) (1998). *Capital Flows and Financial Crises*. Ithaca, NY: Cornell University Press.
Kahler, M. (1999). "Rationality in International Relations." In P. J. Katzenstein, R. O. Keohane and S. D. Krasner (eds), *Exploration and Contestation in the Study of World Politics*. Cambridge, MA: MIT Press.
Kahler, M. (2000). "Conclusion: The Causes and Consequences of Legalization." *International Organization*, 54(3): 661–684.
Kahn, H. (1970). *The Emerging Japanese Super-state: Challenge and Response*. Englewood Cliffs, NJ: Prentice-Hall.
Kamiya, M. (2002–03). "Nuclear Japan: Oxymoron or Coming Soon?" *The Washington Quarterly*, 26 (1): 63–75.
Karawan, I. A. (1993). "Foreign Policy Restructuring: Egypt's Disengagement from the Arab-Israeli Conflict Reconsidered." Unpublished paper. Department of Political Science, University of Utah, UT.
Karl, T. L. and Schmitter, P. (1991). "Modes of Transition in Latin America, Southern and Eastern Europe." *International Social Science Journal*, 53: 269–284.
Karp, A. (1995). "The Demise of the Middle East Arms Race." *The Washington Quarterly*, 18(4): 29–52.
Kase, Y. (2001). "The Costs and Benefits of Japan's Nuclearization: An Insight into the 1968/70 Internal Report." *The Nonproliferation Review* (Summer): 55–68.
Katzenstein, P. J. (ed.) (1996). *The Culture of National Security: Norms and Identity in World Politics*. New York, NY: Columbia University Press.
Katzenstein, P. J. (2005). *A World Of Regions: Asia And Europe In The American Imperium*. Ithaca, NY: Cornell University Press.
Katzenstein, P. J. and Shiraishi, T. (eds) (1997). *Network Power: Japan and Asia*. Ithaca, NY: Cornell University Press.
Kaufman, R. R. (1989). "Domestic Determinants of Stabilization and Adjustment Choices." In B. Russett, H. Starr, and R. Stoll (eds), *Choices in World Politics: Sovereignty and Interdependence*. New York, NY: W. H. Freeman.
Kehr, E. (1977). *Economic Interest, Militarism, and Foreign Policy: Essays on German History* (G. A. Craig, ed., and G. Heinz, trans.). Berkeley, CA: University of California Press.
Keller, B. (2003). "The Thinkable." *New York Times Magazine*, May 4.
Keohane, R. O. (1984). *After Hegemony: Cooperation and Discord in the World Political Economy*. Princeton, NJ: Princeton University Press.
Keohane, R. O. (1986). "Reciprocity in International Relations." *International Organization*, 40(1): 1–28.
Keohane, R. O. (2001). "Governance in a Partially Globalized World." *American Political Science Review*, 95(1): 1–13.
Keohane, R. O. and Martin, L. (1995). "The Promise of Institutionalist Theory." *International Security*, 20(1): 39–51.
Keohane, R. O. and Milner, H. V. (eds) (1996). *Internationalization and Domestic Politics*. New York, NY: Cambridge University Press.
Kerr, M. (1971). *The Arab Cold War 1958–1967*. Oxford: Oxford University Press.
Khong, Y. F. (1997). "Making Bricks without Straw in the Asia Pacific?" *Pacific Review*, 10(2): 289–300.
King, G., Keohane, R. O. and Verba, S. (1994). *Designing Social Inquiry: Scientific Inference in Qualitative Research*. Princeton, NJ: Princeton University Press.
Kitamura, M. (1996). "Japan's Plutonium Program: A Proliferation Threat," *The Nonproliferation Review*, 3 (Winter).

Klotz, A. (1995). *Norms in International Relations: The Struggle Against Apartheid*. Ithaca, NY: Cornell University Press.
Klotz, A. and Lynch, C. (2007). *Strategies for Research in Constructivist International Relations*. New York, NY: M. E. Sharpe.
Kohli, A. (1990). "The Politics of Economic Liberalization in India." In E. N. Suleiman and J. Waterbury (eds), *The Political Economy of Public Sector Reform and Privatization*. Boulder, CO: Westview.
Komaie, M. and Solingen, E. (2007). "Carrots, Sticks, and Nonproliferation: The Case of Iran." Paper prepared for the Meetings of the International Studies Association, Chicago, February 27 – March 3, 2007.
Korany, B. (1994). "National Security in the Arab World: The Persistence of Dualism." In D. Tschirgi (ed.), *The Arab World Today*. Boulder, CO: Lynne Rienner: 161–178.
Koremenos, B., Lipson, C. and Snidal, D. (2001). "The Rational Design of International Institutions." *International Organization* 55(4): 761–799.
Krasner, S. D. (1991). "Global Communications and National Power: Life on the Pareto Frontier." *World Politics*, 43(3): 336–356.
Krasner, S. D. (1999). *Sovereignty: Organized Hypocrisy*. Princeton, NJ: Princeton University Press.
Krasner, S. D. (1985). *Structural Conflict*. Berkeley, CA: University of California Press.
Krauss, E. S. (2000). "Japan, the US, and the Emergence of Multilateralism in Asia." *The Pacific Review*, 13(3): 473–494.
Krauss, E. S. (2001). "*Regionalism and Regionalization within APEC*" Paper presented at a conference on Remapping Asia (Shonan Village, Japan, February 2002).
Krauss, E. S. and Pempel, T. J. (eds) (2003). *Beyond Bilateralism: U.S-Japan Relations in the New Asia-Pacific*. Palo Alto, CA: Stanford University Press.
Kaneko, K. (1996). "Japan needs no umbrella." *Bulletin of the Atomic Scientists*, 53 (2): 46–51.
Krauss, E. S. and Pempel, T. J. (2004). *Beyond Bilateralism: U.S.–Japan Relations in the New Asia Pacific*. Stanford, CA: Stanford University Press.
Kupchan, C. and Kupchan, C. (1991). "Concerts, Collective Security, and the Future of Europe." *International Security*, 16(1): 114–161.
Kuran, T. (1991). "Now out of Never: The Element of Surprise in the East European Revolution of 1989." *World Politics*, 44(1): 7–48.
Kuran, T. (1993) "Fundamentalisms and the Economy." In M. E. Marty and R. S. Appleby (eds),, *Fundamentalisms and the State: Remaking Polities, Economies, and Militance*. Chicago, IL: University of Chicago Press.
Kuran, T. (1995). "Fundamentalist Economics and the Economic Roots of Fundamentalism: Policy Prescriptions for a Liberal Society." *Fundamentalism and Public Policy*. Chicago: University of Chicago Press: 185–197.
Kurosawa, M. (2004). "Moving Beyond the Debate on a Nuclear Japan." *The Nonproliferation Review*, 11(3): 110–137.
Lamborn, A. C. (1991). *The Price of Power: Risk and Foreign Policy in Britain, France and Germany*. Boston, MA: Unwin Hyman.
Lake, D. A. (1997). "Regional Security Complexes: A Systems Approach." In D. Lake and P. Morgan (eds), *Regional Orders: Building Security in a New World*. University Park, PA: Pennsylvania State University Press: 45–67.
Lawrence, R. Z. (1995). "Emerging Regional Arrangements: Building Blocks or Stumbling Blocks?" In J. A. Frieden and D. A. Lake (eds), *International Political Economy: Perspectives on Global Power and Wealth*. New York, NY: St. Martin's Press: 407–415.
Lebovic, J. (2007). *Deterring International Terrorism and Rogue States: U.S. National Security Policy after 9/11*. New York, NY: Routledge.
Lebow, R. (2000). "What's So Different about a Counterfactual?" *World Politics*, 52(4): 550–585.
Lebow, R. (2003). *The Tragic Vision of Politics: Ethics, Interests and Orders*. New York, NY: Cambridge University Press.
Leca, J. (1994). "Democratization in the Arab World: Uncertainty, Vulnerability, and Legitimacy: A Tentative Conceptualization and Some Hypotheses." In G. Salamé (ed.), *Democracy without Democrats? The Renewal of Politics in the Muslim World*. New York, NY: I.B. Tauris: 48–83.
Legro, J. W. and Moravcsik, A. (1999). "Is Anybody Still a Realist?" *International Security*, 24(2): 5–55.
Leifer, M. (1989). *ASEAN and the Security of South-East Asia*. London: Routledge.
Levi, M. A. and O'Hanlon, M. E. (2005). *The Future of Arms Control*. Washington, DC: Brookings Institution Press.
Levite, A. E. (2002/03). "Never Say Never Again: Nuclear Reversal Revisited." *International Security*, 27(3): 59–88.
Liberman, P. (2001). "The Rise and Fall of the South African Bomb." *International Security*, 26(2): 45–86.

Lipson, C. (1984). "International Cooperation in Economic and Security Affairs." *World Politics*, 37: 1–23.
Lipson, C. (1991). "Why Are Some International Agreements Informal?" *International Organization*, 45(4): 495–538.
Lopez, G. A. and Cortright, D. (2004). "Containing Iraq: Sanctions Worked." *Foreign Affairs*, 83(4): 90–103.
Luciani, G. (2007). "Linking Economic and Political Reform in the Middle East: The Role of the Bourgeoisie." In O. Schlumberger (ed.), *Debating Arab Authoritarianism*. Stanford, CA: Stanford University Press.
Lutz, E. L. and Sikkink, K. (2000). "International Human Rights Law and Practice in Latin America." *International Organization* 54(3): 633–660.
Macdonald, R. (1965). *The League of Arab States*. Princeton, NJ: Princeton University Press.
MacIntyre, A. (1991). *Business and Politics in Indonesia*. Sydney: Allen & Unwin.
MacIntyre, A. (ed.) (1994). *Business and Government in Industrialising Asia*. Ithaca, NY: Cornell University Press.
Mack, A. and Kerr, P. (1994). "The Evolving Security Discourse in the Asia-Pacific." *The Washington Quarterly*, 18(1): 123–140.
Mahbubani, K. (1995). "The Pacific Way." *Foreign Affairs*, 74(1): 100–111.
Mahoney, J. (2005). "Clarifying comparative historical methodology." *Qualitative Methods*, 3(1): 19–22.
Malnight, J. and Solingen, E. (2014). Turning Inward: Ruling Coalitions and Mercosur's Retrenchment. *Routledge Handbook of Latin America in the World*. New York, NY: Routledge: 131–140.
Mansfield, E. D. and Milner, H. V. (eds) (1997). *The Political Economy of Regionalism*. New York, NY: Columbia University Press.
Mansfield, E. D. and Snyder, J. (1995). "The Dangers of Democratization." *International Security*, 20: 1–33.
Mansfield, E. D. and Snyder, J. L. (2005). *Electing to Fight: Why Emerging Democracies Go to War*. Cambridge, MA: MIT Press.
Mansfield, E. D. and Snyder, J. L. (2007). "The Sequencing 'Fallacy.'" *Journal of Democracy*, 18(3): 5–10.
Mansfield, E. D. and Solingen, E. (2010). "Regionalism." *Annual Review of Political Science*, 13(1): 145–163.
Maravall, J. M. (1994). "The Myth of the Authoritarian Advantage." *Journal of Democracy*, 5(4): 17–31.
March, J. and Olsen, J. (1998). "The Institutional Dynamics of International Political Orders." *International Organization* 52(4): 943–969.
Mares, D. (1997). "Regional Conflict Management in Latin America: Power Complemented by Diplomacy." In D. Lake and P. Morgan (eds), *Regional Orders: Building Security in a New World*. University Park, PA: Pennsylvania State University Press: 195–218.
Mayer, A. E. (1993). "The Fundamentalist Impact on Law, Politics, and Constitutions in Iran, Pakistan, and the Sudan." In M. Marty and R. S. Appleby (eds), *Fundamentalisms and the State*. Chicago: University of Chicago Press: 110–151.
Mearsheimer, J. J. (2001). *The Tragedy of Great Power Politics*. New York, NY: Norton.
Meyer, S. M. (1984). *The Dynamics of Nuclear Proliferation*. Chicago, IL: The University of Chicago Press.
Migdal, J. S. (1988). *Strong Societies and Weak States: State-Society Relations and State Capabilities in the Third World*. Princeton, NJ: Princeton University Press.
Milani, A. (2005a). "Iran's New President." *Hoover Digest* 4: 1–5.
Milani, A. (2005b). "U.S. Policy and the Future of Democracy in Iran." *The Washington Quarterly*, 28 (3): 41–56.
Milner, H. V. (1988). *Resisting Protectionism: Global Industries and the Politics of International Trade*. Princeton, NJ: Princeton University Press.
Maoz, Z. and Russett, B. (1992). "Alliance, Contiguity, Wealth, and Political Stability: Is the Lack of Conflict Between Democracies a Statistical Artifact?" *International Interactions*, 17(3, February): 245–267.
Mochizuki, M. (2006). "Japan's Drift away from Pacifist Policy." *Los Angeles Times*, September 22, 2006.
Moravcsik, A. (1998). *The Choice for Europe*. Ithaca, NY: Cornell University Press.
Naughton, B. (1999). "China: Domestic Restructuring and a New Role in Asia." In T. J. Pempel (ed.), *The Politics of Asian Economic Crisis*. Ithaca, NY: Cornell University Press.
Nelson, J. M. (ed.) (1990). *Economic Crisis and Policy Choice: The Politics of Adjustment in the Third World*. Princeton, NJ: Princeton University Press.
Nelson, J. M. (1992). "Poverty, Equity, and the Politics of Adjustment." In S. Haggard and R. R. Kaufman (eds), *The Political Economy of Democratic Transitions*. Princeton, NJ: Princeton University Press: 221–269.

Niblock, T. (2002). *"Pariah States" and Sanctions in the Middle East: Iraq, Libya, Sudan*. Lynne Rienner Publishers.

Noble, P. C. (1991). "The Arab system: Pressures, constraints and opportunities." In B. Korany and A. E. Hillal Dessouki (eds), *The Foreign Policies of Arab States: The Challenge of Change*. Boulder, CO: Westview Press: 49–102.

Noland, M. and Pack, H. (2005). "The East Asian Industrial Policy Experience: Implications for the Middle East." [Peterson Institute Working Paper Series. WP05–14]. Peterson Institute for International Economics.

North, D. C. (1981). *Structure and Change in Economic History*. New York, NY: Norton.

Norton, A. R. (1995). "The Challenge of Inclusion in the Middle East." *Current History*, 94(588): 16.

Nye, J. S., Jr. (1987). "Nuclear Learning and U.S.–Soviet Security Regimes." *International Organization*, 41: 371–402.

O'Donnell, G., Schmitter, P. C. and Whitehead, L. (eds) (1986). *Transitions from Authoritarian Rule: Tentative Conclusions About Uncertain Democracies*. Baltimore, MD: Johns Hopkins University Press.

Ogle, G. E. (1990). *South Korea: Dissent within the Economic Miracle*. London: Zed Books.

Okimoto, D. I. (1978). *Ideas, Intellectuals, and Institutions: National Security and the Question of nuclear Armament in Japan*. PhD dissertation, Ann Arbor, MI: University of Michigan.

Oneal, J. R. and Russett, B. (1997). "The Classical Liberals Were Right: Democracy, Interdependence, and Conflict, 1950–1985." *International Studies Quarterly*, 41(2 June): 267–94.

Organski, A. F. K. and Kugler, J. (1980). *The War Ledger*. Chicago, IL: University of Chicago Press.

Oros, A. L. (2003). "Godzilla's Return: The New Nuclear Politics in an Insecure Japan." In B. L. Self and J. W. Thompson (eds), *Japan's Nuclear Option: Security, Politics, and Policy in the 21st Century*. Washington, DC: The Henry L. Stimson Center: 49–63.

O'Sullivan, M. L. (2003). *Shrewd Sanctions: Statecraft and State Sponsors of Terrorism*. Washington, DC: Brookings Institution.

Owen, R. (1992). *State, Power, and Politics in the Making of the Modern Middle East*, New York, NY: Routledge.

Owen, R. and S. Pamuk (1999). *A History of Middle East Economies in the Twentieth Century*. Cambridge, MA: Harvard University Press.

Oye, K. A. (1992). *Economic Discrimination and Political Exchange: World Political Economy in the 1930s and 1980s*. Princeton, NJ: Princeton University Press.

Park, C. H. (1971). *To Build a Nation*. Washington, DC: Acropolis.

Park, C. H. (1976). *Toward Peaceful Unification*. Seoul: Kwangmyong.

Park C. H. (1979). *Korea Reborn: A Model for Development*. Englewood Cliffs, NJ: Prentice Hall.

Patten, C. (2001). Joint Debate on Common Strategy for the Mediterranean and Reinvigorating the Barcelona Process. *European Parliament*, 1.

Peace and Conflict. (2008). Center for International Development and Conflict Management, College Park, University of Maryland. Online. Available at www.cidcm.umd.edu/pc/chapter04/graphs/figure_4_1.asp

Pempel, T. J. (1998). *Regime Shift: Comparative Dynamics of the Japanese Political Economy*. Ithaca, NY: Cornell University Press.

Pempel, T. J. (1999). "Unsteady Anticipation: Reflections on the Future of Japan's Changing Political Economy." In T. V. Paul, and J. A. Hall (eds), *International Order and the Future of World Politics*. Cambridge: Cambridge University Press.

Pempel, T. J. (ed.) (2005). *Remapping Asia: Competing Patterns of Regional Integration*. Ithaca, NY: Cornell University Press.

Petrovic, B. and Solingen, E. (2005). "Internationalization and Europeanization: The Case of the Czech Republic." *New Political Economy* (UK), 10(3).

Pevehouse, J. C. (2002). "With a Little Help from My Friends? Regional Organizations and the Consolidation of Democracy." *American Journal of Political Science*, 46(3): 611–626.

Picard, E. (1990). "Arab Military in Politics: From Revolutionary Plot to Authoritarian Regime." In G. Luciani (ed.), *The Arab State*. Berkeley, CA: University of California Press: 189–219

Pierson, P. (2000). "Increasing Returns, Path Dependence, and the Study of Politics." *American Political Science Review*, 94: 2 (June): 251–67.

Pinkston, D. A. (2003). "Domestic Politics and Stakeholders in the North Korean Missile Development Program." *The Nonproliferation Review*, 10(2): 1–15.

Polanyi, K. (1944). *The Great Transformation: The Political and Economic Origins of Our Time*. Boston, MA: Beacon Press.

Porter, B. D. (1994). *War and the Rise of the State: The Military Foundations of Modern Politics*. New York, NY: The Free Press.

Posen, B. R. (1984) *The Sources of Military Doctrine*. Ithaca, NY: Cornell University Press.
Posen, B. (1993). "The Security Dilemma and Ethnic Conflict." *Survival*, 35(1), 27–47.
Potter, W. C. and Mukhatzhanova, G. (2008). "Divining Nuclear Intentions: A Review Essay." *International Security*, 33(1): 139–169.
Powell, W. W., and P. J. Di Maggio (eds) (1991). *The New Institutionalism in Organizational Analysis*. Chicago, IL: University of Chicago Press.
Powers, K. and Goertz, G. (2011). "The Economic-Institutional Construction of Regions: Conceptualisation And Operationalisation." *Review of International Studies*, 37(5): 2387–2415.
Przeworski, A. (1991). *Democracy and the Market: Political and Economic Reforms in Eastern Europe and Latin America*. Cambridge: Cambridge University Press.
Przeworski A., Alvarez, M., Cheibub, J. A. and Limongi, F. (1996). "What Makes Democracies Endure?" *Journal of Democracy*, 7(1): 39–55.
Przeworski A., Alvarez, M., Cheibub, J. A. and Limongi, F. (2000). *Democracy and Development: Political Institutions and Well-Being in the World, 1950–1990*. Cambridge: Cambridge University Press.
Rasler, K. A. and Thompson, W. R. (1989). *War and State Making: the Shaping of the Global Powers*. Boston, MA: Unwin Hyman.
Ravenhill, J. (1998). "The Growth of Intergovernmental Collaboration in the Asia-Pacific Region." In A. McGrew, and C. Brook (eds), *Asia-Pacific in the New World Order*. London: Routledge.
Ravenhill, J. (2000). "APEC Adrift: Implications for Economic Regionalism in Asia and the Pacific." *The Pacific Review*, 13(2): 319–333.
Ravenhill, J. (2006). "Mission Creep or Mission Impossible: APEC and Security." In A. Acharya and E. Goh (eds), *Reassessing Security Cooperation in the Asia-Pacific: Competition, Congruence, and Transformation*. Cambridge, MA: MIT Press.
Razi, G. H. (1990). "Legitimacy, Religion, and Nationalism in the Middle East." *American Political Science Review*, 84(1): 69–92.
Reiss, M. B. (1988). *Without the Bomb*. New York, NY: Columbia University Press.
Remmer, K. (1989). *Military Rule in Latin America*. Boston, MA: Unwin Hyman.
Richards, A. and Waterbury, J. (1990). *A Political Economy of the Middle East: State, Class and Economic Development*. Boulder, CO: Westview Press.
Riker, W. H. and Brams, S. J. (1973). "The Paradox of Vote Trading." *The American Political Science Review*, 67(4): 1235–1247.
Risse-Kappen, T. (ed.) (1995). *Bringing Transnational Relations Back In*. New York, NY: Cambridge University Press.
Risse-Kappen, T. (1995). *Cooperation among Democracies: The European Influence on U.S. Foreign Policy*. Princeton, NJ: Princeton University Press.
Rivlin, P. (2001). *Economic Policy and Performance in the Arab World*. Boulder, CO: Lynne Rienner.
Roberts, B. (1993). "From Nonproliferation to Antiproliferation." *International Security*, 18(1): 139–173.
Roberts, C. B. (2007). *"The ASEAN Community: Trusting Thy Neighbour?"* Rajaratnam School of International Studies Commentaries.
Rodrik, D. (1994). "The Rush to Free Trade in the Developing World: Why So Late? Why Now? Will It Last?" In S. Haggard and S. B. Webb (eds), *Voting for Reform: Democracy, Political Liberalization, and Economic Adjustment*. New York, NY: Oxford University Press: 61–88.
Rodrik, D. (Director) (1997, December 11). Globalization, Social Conflict and Economic Growth. *Prebisch Lecture*. Lecture conducted from John F. Kennedy School of Government, Harvard University, Geneva.
Rosecrance, R. N. (ed.) (1964). *The Dispersion of Nuclear Weapons: Strategy and Politics*. New York, NY: Columbia University Press.
Rosecrance, R. N. (1986). *The Rise of the Trading State*. New York, NY: Basic Books.
Rosecrance, R. N. (1996). "The Rise of the Virtual State." *Foreign Affairs*, 75(4): 45–61.
Rosecrance, R. N. (1999). *The Rise of the Virtual State: Wealth and Power in the Coming Century*. New York, NY: Basic Books.
Rosecrance, R. N. (2001). "Has Realism Become Cost-Benefit Analysis? A Review Essay." *International Security*, 26(2): 132–154.
Rosecrance, R. N. and Schott, P. (1997). "Concerts and Regional Intervention." In D. A. Lake and P. M. Morgan (eds), *Regional Orders: Building Security in a New World*. State College: Pennsylvania State University Press: 140–164.
Rosecrance, R. N., Solingen, E., and Stein, A. A. (2006). "Globalization and Its Effects: Introduction and Overview." In R. N. Rosecrance and A. A. Stein (eds), *No More States? Globalization, National Self-determination, and Terrorism*. Lanham, MD: Rowman and Littlefield.
Rothstein, R. L. (1977). *The Weak in the World of the Strong: The Developing Countries in the International System*. New York, NY: Columbia University Press.

Rouleau, E. (1993). "Eric Rouleau Talks about the Peace Process and Political Islam." *Journal of Palestine Studies*, 22(4): 45–61.
Roy, P. M. (1995). "The Islamic Movement: The Case for Democratic Inclusion," *Contention*, 4 (Spring): 107–127.
Ruggie, J. G., Katzenstein, P. J., Keohane, R. O. and Schmitter, P. C. (2005). "Transformations in World Politics: The Intellectual Contributions Of Ernst B. Haas." *Annual Review of Political Science*, 8(1): 271–296.
Ruggie, J. G. (1993). "Multilateralism: The Anatomy of an Institution." In J. G. Ruggie (ed.), *Multilateralism Matters*. New York, NY: Columbia University Press: 3–49.
Ruggie, J. G. (1998a). *Constructing the World Polity: Essays on International Institutionalization*. New York, NY: Routledge.
Ruggie, J. G. (1998b). "What Makes the World Hang Together? Neo-Utilitarianism and the Social Constructivist Challenge." In P. J. Katzenstein, R. O. Keohane, and S. D. Krasner (eds), *Exploration and Contestation in the Study of World Politics*. Cambridge, MA: MIT Press: 215–246.
Ruggie, J. G. (1993). "Multilateralism: The Anatomy of an Institution." In J. G. Ruggie (ed.), *Multilateralism Matters*. New York, NY: Columbia University Press: 3–49.
Sahliyeh, E. (1990). *Religious Resurgence and Politics in the Contemporary World*. New York, NY: State University of New York Press.
Said, M. K. (2002). "Security and Defense Dilemmas in the Middle East: The Nuclear Dimension." Pugwash Meeting No. 279. *Pugwash OnLine* (November 15–17). Online. Available at www.pugwash.org/reports/nw/kadrysaid.htm#1
Sala-i-Martin, X. and E. V. Artadi. (2003). "Economic Growth and Investment in the Arab World." In *The Arab World Competitiveness Report 2002–2003*. New York, Oxford University Press: 22–33.
Salamé, G. (1993). "Islam and the West." *Foreign Policy*, 90 (Spring): 22–37.
Salamé, G. (ed.) (1994). *Democracy without Democrats? The Renewal of Politics in the Muslim World*. New York, NY: I.B. Tauris.
Samore, G. (2004). "Meeting Iran's nuclear challenge." Stockholm: Weapons of Mass Destruction Commission, Report no. 21 (October).
Samore, G. (2005). "Diplomacy at a Loss over Iran's nuclear Program." The International Institute for Strategic Studies, March 24, 2005. Online. Available at www.iiss.org
Sample, S. G. (1997). "Arms Races and Dispute Escalation: Resolving the Debate." *Journal of Peace Research*, 34(1): 7–22.
Sanger, P. (1995). *The New York Times* (May 30).
Saxonhouse, G. R. (1995). "Trading blocs and East Asia." In J. de Melo and A. Panagariya (eds), *New Dimensions in Regional Integration*. New York, NY: Cambridge University Press.
Sayigh, Y. (1995). "The Multilateral Middle East Peace Talks: Reorganizing for Regional Security." In S. L. Spiegel and D. J. Pervin (eds), *Practical Peacemaking in the Middle East* (Vol. I). New York, NY: Garland Publishing: 207–230.
Schelling, T. C. (1976). "Who will Have the Bomb?" *International Security*, 1(1): 77–91.
Sen, A. (1999). *Development as Freedom*. New York, NY: Knopf.
Shambaugh, D. L. (2004/05). "China Engages Asia: Reshaping the Regional Order." *International Security*, 29(3): 64–99.
Shikaki, K. (1995). "Results of Public Opinion Poll #19." Survey Research Unit, Center for Palestine Research and Studies, 1
Shirk, S. L. (1994). "Chinese Views on Asia-Pacific Regional Security Cooperation." *NBR Analysis*, 5(5). Seattle, WA: The National Bureau of Asian Research.
Shirk, S. L. (2007). *China: Fragile Superpower*. Oxford: Oxford University Press.
Sigal, L. (1998). *Disarming Strangers: Nuclear Diplomacy with North Korea*. Princeton, NJ: Princeton University Press.
Sil, R. and Katzenstein, P. J. (2010). *Beyond Paradigms: Analytic Eclecticism in the Study of World Politics*. London: Palgrave Macmillan.
Simon, S. W. (ed.) (2001). *The Many Faces of Asian Security*. Lanham, MD: Rowman & Littlefield.
Singh, S. and Way, C. R. (2004). "The Correlates of Nuclear Proliferation: A Quantitative Test." *Journal of Conflict Resolution*, 48(6): 859–885.
Sivan, E. (1995). "Eavesdropping on Radical Islam." *Middle East Quarterly*, 2: 13–24.
Slaughter, A. (2004). *A New World Order*. Princeton NJ: Princeton University Press.
Snyder, J. (1991). *Myths of Empire: Domestic Politics and International Ambition*. Ithaca, NY: Cornell University Press.
Solingen, E. (1994a). "The Domestic Sources of International Regimes: The Evolution of Nuclear Ambiguity in the Middle East." *International Studies Quarterly*, 38(4): 305–337.
Solingen, E. (1994b). "The Political Economy of Nuclear Restraint." *International Security*, 19(2): 126–169.

Solingen, E. (1995). "Multilateral Arms Control in the Middle East: The Issue of Sequences." *Peace and Change*, 20(3 July): 364–378.
Solingen, E. (1996a). "Democracy, Economic Reform and Regional Cooperation." *Journal of Theoretical Politics*, 8(1): 79–114.
Solingen, E. (1996b). "Democratization in the Middle East: Quandaries of the Peace Process." *Journal of Democracy*, 7(3): 139–153.
Solingen, E. (1996c). *Industrial Policy, Technology and International Bargaining: Designing Nuclear Industries in Argentina and Brazil*. Stanford, CA: Stanford University Press.
Solingen, E. (1998). *Regional Orders at Century's Dawn: Global and Domestic Influences on Grand Strategy*. Princeton, NJ: Princeton University Press.
Solingen, E. (1999). "ASEAN, *quo vadis*? Domestic coalitions and regional cooperation," *Contemporary Southeast Asia*, 21(1): 30–53.
Solingen, E. (2000). "The Multilateral Arab-Israeli Negotiations: Genesis, Institutionalization, Pause, Future." *Journal of Peace Research*, 37(2): 167–187.
Solingen E. (2001a). "Domestic Coalitional Analysis and the Democratic Peace." *International History Review*, 23(4): 757–783.
Solingen, E. (2001b). "Mapping Internationalization: Domestic and Regional Impacts." *International Studies Quarterly*, 45(4): 517–556.
Solingen, E. (2001c). "Middle East Denuclearization? Lessons from Latin America's Southern Cone." *Review of International Studies*, 27: 375–394.
Solingen, E. (2003) "Internationalization, Coalitions, and Regional Conflict and Cooperation." In E. D. Mansfield and B. M. Pollins (eds), *Economic Interdependence and International Conflict: New Perspectives on an Enduring Debate*. Ann Arbor, MI: University of Michigan Press.
Solingen, E. (2004). "Southeast Asia in a New Era: Domestic Coalitions From Crisis to Recovery," *Asia Survey*, 44(2): 189–212.
Solingen, E. (2005a). "East Asian Regional Institutions: Characteristics, Sources, Distinctiveness." In T. J. Pempel (ed.), *Remapping Asia: Competing Patterns of Regional Integration*. Ithaca, NY: Cornell University Press.
Solingen, E. (2005b). "ASEAN Cooperation: The Legacy of the Economic Crisis." *International Relations of the Asia-Pacific*, 5(1): 1–29.
Solingen, E. (2006). "Domestic Politics and Regional Cooperation in Southeast and Northeast Asia." In S. C. Kim and E. Friedman (eds), *Regional Cooperation and Its Enemies in Northeast Asia*. London: Routledge.
Solingen, E. (2007a). "From Threat to Opportunity? ASEAN, China, and Triangulation." In E. Goh, and S. Simon (eds), *China, the United States, and South-East Asia: Contending Perspectives on Politics, Security, and Economics*. Oxford: Routledge.
Solingen, E. (2007b). "Pax Asiatica versus Bella Levantina: The Foundations of War and Peace in East Asia and the Middle East." *American Political Science Review*, 101(4): 757–780.
Solingen, E. (2007c). *Nuclear Logics: Contrasting Paths in East Asia and the Middle East*. Princeton, NJ: Princeton University Press.
Solingen, E. (2008). "The Genesis, Design and Effects of Regional Institutions: Lessons from East Asia and the Middle East," *International Studies Quarterly*, 52(1): 261–294.
Solingen, E. (2009). "The global context of comparative politics." In M. I. Lichbach and A. S. Zuckerman (eds), *Comparative Politics: Rationality, Culture, and Structure* (2nd edn). Cambridge: Cambridge University Press.
Solingen, E. (2010). "The Perils of Prediction: Japan's Once and Future Nuclear Status." In W. C. Potter and G. Mukhatzhanova (eds), *Forecasting Nuclear Proliferation in the 21st Century: A Comparative Perspective*. Stanford, CA: Stanford University Press.
Solingen, E. (2012a). "Ten dilemmas in Nonproliferation Statecraft." In E. Solingen (ed.), *Sanctions, Statecraft, and Nuclear Proliferation*. Cambridge: Cambridge University Press.
Solingen, E. (2012b). "Domestic Sources of Nuclear Behavior in the Middle East." In M. Kamrava (ed.), *The Nuclear Question in the Middle East*. New York, NY: Columbia University Press.
Solingen, E. (2012c). "Hindsight and Foresight in South American Non-proliferation Trends: Argentina, Brazil and Venezuela." In J. Wirtz and P. Lavoy (eds), *Over-the-Horizon Proliferation Threats*. Stanford, CA: Stanford University Press.
Solingen, E. (2012d). "Of Dominoes and Firewalls: The Domestic, Regional and Global Politics of International Diffusion" [Presidential Address]. *International Studies Quarterly*, 56(4): 631–644.
Solingen, E. (2013). "Three Scenes of Sovereignty and Power." In M. Finemore and J. Goldstein (eds), *Back to Basics: Rethinking Power in the Contemporary World*. New York, NY: Oxford University Press.
Solingen, E. (2014). "Internationalization, Coalitions, and War: Then and Now." International Security 39: 1 (Summer) forthcoming.

Solingen, E. and Ozyurt, S. S. (2006). "Mare Nostrum: The Sources, Logic, and Dilemmas of the Euro-Mediterranean Partnership," In E. Adler, B. Crawford, R. Del Sarto, and F. Bicchi (eds), *The Convergence of Civilizations: Constructing a Mediterranean Region*. Toronto: University of Toronto Press.

Solingen, E. and Wan, W. (2014). "Historical Institutionalism and International Security." In O. Fioretos, T. G. Falleti and A. Sheingate (eds), *The Oxford Handbook of Historical Institutionalism*. Oxford: Oxford University Press (forthcoming).

Stallings, B. (1992). "International Influence on Economic Policy: Debt, Stabilization, and Structural Reform." In S. Haggard and R. R. Kaufman (eds), *The Politics of Economic Adjustment*. Princeton, NJ: Princeton University Press: 41–88.

Stiglitz, J. E. (1996). "Some Lessons from the East Asian Miracle," *World Bank Research Observer,* 11(2): 151–77.

Stubbs, R. (2000). "Signing on to liberalisation: AFTA and the politics of regional economic cooperation." *Pacific Review*, 13(2): 297–318.

Stubbs, R. (1999). "War and Economic Development: Export-Oriented Industrialization in East and Southeast Asia." *Comparative Politics*, 31 (April): 337–356.

Stubbs, R. (2005). *Rethinking Asia's Economic Miracle*. New York, NY: Palgrave Macmillan.

Takeyh, R. (2004). "Iran Builds the Bomb." *Survival*, 46(4): 51–64.

Takeyh, R. (2006). "Prepared Testimony before the Subcommittee on Federal Financial Management, Government Information, and International Security" (July 20). Online. Available at www.cfr.org

Thelen, K. (1999). "Historical Institutionalism in Comparative Politics." *Annual Review of Political Science*, 2: 369–404.

Tilly, C. (1984). *Big Structures, Large Processes, Huge Comparisons*. New York, NY: Russell Sage Foundation.

Tilly, C. (1985). "War making and State Making as Organized Crime." In P. B. Evans, D. Rueschemeyer, and T. Skocpol (eds), *Bringing the State Back In*. Cambridge, UK. Cambridge University Press: 169–191.

Tilly, C. (1994). "States and Nationalism in Europe 1492–1992." *Theory and Society*, 23: 131–146.

Timerbaev, R. (2005). "What Next for the NPT? Facing the Moment of Truth." *IAEA Bulletin*, 46(2): 4–7.

Tripp, C. (1995). "Regional Organizations in the Arab Middle East." In L. Fawcett, and A. Hurrell (eds), *Regionalism in World Politics: Regional Organization and International Order*. New York, NY: Oxford University Press.

Tripp, C. (2001). "States, Elites and the Management of Change." In H. Hakimian and Z. Moshaver (eds), *The State and Global Change*. Richmond, Surrey: Curzon; 211–231.

Tussie, D. (2009). "Latin America: Contrasting Motivations for Regional Projects." *Review of International Studies*, 35 (Suppl. S1): 169–188.

United Nations (UN). Statistics Division. *National Accounts Statistics 1982–2004*.

United Nations Development Programme (1998). *Human Development Report 1994–1998*. New York, NY: UNDP.

Van Evera, S. (1984). "The Cult of the Offensive and the Origins of the First World War." *International Security*, 9(1), 58–107.

Van Evera, S. (1993). "Primed for Peace: Europe After the Cold War." In S. Lynn–Jones (ed.), *The Cold War and After: Prospects for Peace*. Cambridge, MA: MIT Press: 193–243.

Van Evera, S. (1994). "Hypotheses on nationalism and war." *International Security*, 18(4): 5–39.

Väyrynen, R. (2003). "Regionalism: Old and New." *International Studies Review*, 5(1): 25–51.

Vasquez, J. A. (1998). *The Power of Power Politics: From Classical Realism to Neotraditionalism*. Cambridge: Cambridge University Press.

Viner, J. (1950). *The Customs Union Issue*. New York, NY: Carnegie Endowment for International Peace.

Viorst, M. (1995). "Sudan's Islamic Experiment." *Foreign Affairs*, 74: 54–55.

Wade, R. (1990). *Governing the Market: Economic Theory and the Role of Government in East Asian Industrialization*. Princeton, NJ: Princeton University Press.

Walt, S. M. (1987). *The Origins of Alliances*. New York, NY: Cornell University Press.

Walt, S. M. (1996). *Revolution and War*. Ithaca, NY: Cornell University Press.

Waltz, K. (1979). *Theory of International Politics*. New York, NY: McGraw-Hill.

Waltz, K. (1981). "The Spread of Nuclear Weapons: More May Be Better." *Adelphi Papers 171*.

Waltz, K. (1993). "The Emerging Structure of International Politics." *International Security*, 18(2): 44–79.

Waltz, K. (2000). "Structural Realism after the Cold War." *International Security,* 25(1): 5–41.

Waltz, K. (2003). "More May Be Better." In S. D. Sagan and K. N. Waltz (eds), *The Spread of Nuclear Weapons*. New York, NY: W.W. Norton.

Wan, W. and Solingen, E. (forthcoming). "Why Do States Pursue Nuclear Weapons (or Not)." In R. Scott and S. Kosslyn (eds), *Emerging Trends in the Social and Behavioral Sciences*. Chichester: Wiley.

Wang, Z. (2004). "Conceptualizing Economic Security and Governance: China Confronts Globalization." *Pacific Review*, 17(4): 532–546.
Waterbury, J. (1983). *The Egypt of Nasser and Sadat: The Political Economy of Two Regimes*. Princeton, NJ: Princeton University Press.
Waterbury, J. (1994). "Democracy Without Democrats? The Potential for Political Liberalization in the Middle East." *Democracy Without Democrats?: The Renewal of Politics in the Muslim World*. London: I.B. Tauris: 23–47.
Waterbury, J. (1983). *The Egypt of Nasser and Sadat: The Political Economy of Two Regimes*. Princeton, NJ: Princeton University Press.
Waterbury, J. (1989). "The Political Management of Economic Adjustment and Reform." In J. M. Nelson (ed.), *Fragile Coalitions: The Politics of Economic Adjustment*. New Brunswick, NJ: Transaction Books: 39–55.
Weber, M. (1949). "Objectivity' in Social Science and Social Policy." In *The Methodology of the Social Sciences* (trans. and ed. E. A. Shils and H. A. Finch). Glencoe, IL: Free Press.
Weber, M. (1978). *Economy and Society: An Outline of Interpretive Sociology*. In G. Roth and C. Wittich (eds). Berkeley, CA: University of California Press.
West, R. L. (1992). "Determinants of Military Expenditure in Developing Countries: Review of Academic Research." In G. Lamb with V. Kallab (eds), *Military Expenditure and Economic Development: A Symposium on Research Issues* [World Bank Discussion Paper no. 185]. Washington, DC: World Bank: 19–34.
Wilkenfeld, J. and Brecher, M. (n.d.). "International Crisis Behavior Online". Online. Available at www.cidcm.umd.edu/icb.
Williamson, J. (ed.) (1994). *The Political Economy of Policy Reform*. Washington, DC: Institute for International Economics.
Williamson, O. E. (1985). *The Economic Institutions of Capital: Firms, Markets, Relational Contracting*. New York, NY: The Free Press.
Woo-Cumings, M. J.-E. (1998). "National Security and the Rise of the Developmental State in South Korea and Taiwan." In H. S. Rowen (ed.), *Behind East Asian Growth: The Political and Social Foundations of Prosperity*. New York, NY: Routledge: 319–340.
World Bank. (1991–1997). *World Development Report*. Oxford: Oxford University Press.
World Bank. (1991). *World Development Report 1991: The Challenge of Development*. New York, NY: Oxford University Press.
World Bank. (1993a). *The East Asian Miracle: Economic Growth and Public Policy*. New York, NY: Oxford University Press.
World Bank. (1993b). "Current Questions and Answers." (September). Unpublished paper. Washington, DC: The World Bank.
World Bank. (1994). *Social Indicators of Development*. Baltimore, MD: Johns Hopkins University Press.
World Bank. (1996). *World Development Report 1996: From Plan to Market*. New York, NY: Oxford University Press.
World Bank. (1998). *World Development Indicators*. Washington, DC: The World Bank.
Yager, J. A. (1985). "Nuclear Supplies and the Policies of South Korea and Taiwan toward Nuclear Weapons." In R. W. Jones (ed.), *The Nuclear Suppliers and Nonproliferation: International Policy Choices*. Lexington, MA.: Lexington Books: 187–195.
Zacher, M. W. (1979). *International Conflicts and Collective Security 1946–77: The United Nations, Organization of American States, Organization of African Unity, and Arab League*. New York, NY: Praeger.
Zweig, D. (2002). *Democratic Values, Political Structures, and Alternative Politics in Greater China*. Washington DC: US Institute of Peace. Online. Available at http://purl.access.gpo.gov/GPO/LPS22846.

INDEX

Numbers emboldened denote their appearance in a table, figure or chart.

Africa 25, 28, 45, 77, 121, 137, 165, 209, 236: North Africa 15, 21, 57–8; South Africa 23, 219, 232, 239, 253
Algeria 23, 47, 57, 58, 82, 85, 107, 120, **121**, 137, 140, 145–6, 154–6, 221, 225
APEC *see* Asia–Pacific Economic Cooperation
Arab League 124, 133, 135, 149, 174, 195, 197, 201, 244
Arab regimes 51, 73, 110, 159, 243
Arafat, Yasir 71, 109, 154, 158, 207, 209
Argentina 6, 7, 23, 25, 26, 41, 44, 51–3, 56–8, 63, 71–2, 75–6, 84, 103–8, 110–12, 165
ASEAN *see* Association of Southeast Asian Nations
Asia-Pacific Economic Cooperation (APEC) 18–19, 119, 135, 173, 184–8, 189, 196–201
Assad, Bashar 15
Assad, Hafiz 48, 73, 81, 108, 109, 110, 146, 154, 160, 207,
Association of Southeast Asian Nations (ASEAN) 6, 11, 18–20, 22, 69–70, 84, 86–7, 111, 113, 119, 124, 135, 147, 163, 169, 173–4, 181–7, 188–90, 196–202, 207, 227
authoritarianism 81, 100, 120, 122, 126, **138**, 139, 143, 146, 148, 159–60, 164, 166

Bella Levantina (Middle East Wars) 119, 122
Bharatiya Janata Party (BJP) 52, 78, 94, 98, 108
Bhutto, Benazir 48, 56, 78, 103, 105, 112, **265**, **267**
Bhutto, Zulfiqar 76, 103, 108–9, **264**, **267**
Brazil 6, 7, 23, 25, 29, 44, 52, 54, 56, 59, 71–2, 76, 83–4, 103–8, 110, 112, 165, 210, 219, 232, 234–6, 239, **263–6**

catalytic conditions 11, 122, 126, 131–5
causal logic **99**
Central American Common Market (CACM) 77
Chile 6, 10, 17, 44, 75, 83–4, 102, 104–8, 110, 112, 129, 166, **263–4**, 266
China 7, 10, 16–17, 20, 23, 25–6, 28, 41, 67, 81, 109, 111, **121**, 123, 134–5, 136, 140–3, 147, 150, 162–4, 166–9, 182, 184, 185–91, 197, 201, 206, 211, 218, 220–5, 227–9, 232, 234–6, 247–8, 254–5, 256–7
coalitions: confessional 37, 43–9; hybrid 8, 95–6, 103–5, 108–9, 112, 114, 207, **265**; internationalizing 3, 5–6, 8, 20, 28–9, 36–8, 40–9, 53, **55**, 56–7, 59–63, 66, 68–75, 79– 80, 83–5, 86–8, 102, 105, 115, 125, 165, 168, 177, 181–2, 184–5, 189, 198, 199, 207, 210, **263**; inward-looking, *see also* statist-nationalist 2, 4–6, 9, 22, 26, 50, 97, 102, 104–9, 113–5, 166, 194, 207, **264**; proto-internationalizing 105; statist-nationalist 52, **55**, *see also* inward-looking
Cold War 49, 122, 129, 141, 166
confessionalism 46, 48, **55**, 84
constructivism 174, **176**, 177, 178, 198, 231–4

democratization 9–10, 12–17, 21, 76, **138**, 139, 144, 148, 152–68, 205, 208–9, 211–2, 240, 255–6,
Dutch disease 128, 130, 133–**4**, 137, 255

economic closure 6, 79, 113–4, 207
Economic Commission for Latin America (ECLA) 76
economic openness 3, 16–17, 45, 94, 100–1, 113–4, 161, 168, 187–8, 208
economic reform 3–4, 13, 16, 18, 21, 29, 36, 39, 42, 49, 51, 53, **55**, 56,–7, 60, 62–3, 69, 78, 95, 96, 98–99, 103, 106–8, 110, 129, 133, 142, 144, 161, 206–12, 240, 242, 253, 255
Egypt 14, 16, 22–3, 25–6, 44, 47, 51, 53, 56–7, 61, 70–4, 76, 85, 102, 105, 107, 109, 112, 120, **121**, 123, 129–35, 137, 139–46, 152–8, 160, 165, 191–5, 201, 206, 208–9, 217–23, 225–9, 232, 236, 239, 244–5, 248, **263–6**
European Union 1, 46, 69, 71, 112, 205
European-Mediterranean Partnership (EMP) 21, 205

Foreign Direct Investment (FDI) 60, 104–5, 114, 130, 134–7, 163, 166, 181–2, 184–6, 188–9, 198, 244, **263–70**

Gaza 15, 48, 74, 153, 158, 212
Gaddafi, Muammar 51, 73, 76, 123, 154, 221, 238, 242–3, 246, 256–7
GCC *see* Global Cooperation Council
global market 5, 7, 20, 37–8, 53, 92–4, 199, 240
global political economy 5, 7, 36–8, 69, 86, 91, 96, 126, 237, 242, 246, 256
globalization 1–3, 27–9, 33, 60, 86, 105, 163, 168, 190, 251
Grand Strategy 4–6, 27, 36–8, 40, 49, 52–9, 63, 67, 72, 74, 79–83, 84, 87, 97–8, 100–1, 106, 111, 114, 163, 207
Gulf Cooperation Council (GCC) 69–70, 84, 146, 210, 225, 238, 255

Hamas 14–15, 47, 74, 155–8
hegemony/hegemonic 10, 16, 19–20, 23, 26, 47, 62, 77–9, 82, 99–100, 109, 123–4, 128, 130, 162, 174–6, 178, 185–8, 192, 195, 197–9, 201, 218–20, 223–5, 234, 244–5, 249–50
hyper-nationalism 28–9, 74, 135, 159, 244
Hussein, King of Jordan 69, 71, 108, 112, 133, 154, 160, **263, 265, 267**
Hussein, Saddam 51, 57–8, 63, 73, 75–6, 82, 103, 146, 154, 196, 207, 238, **264, 267**

IAEA *see* International Atomic Energy Agency
ideal-types 5, 8, 95, 97, 101, 113, 128, 166, 251
International Monetary Fund (IMF) 42, 45, 57, 59, 92, 97, 115, 128, 194
India 17, 25–6, 48, 52, 57, 63, 72, 76–9, 94, 98, 103–5, 108–12, 206, 219, 228, 234–6, **264, 266**
Infitah 72, 103–5, 135, 137,144, 146, 194, 208, 228, 239, 242–5
institutionalism 174: neoliberal 175, 178, 189; rational 226–9
International Atomic Energy Agency (IAEA) 215, 221, 224, 226–9, 235, 238, 244, 250, 257
international institutions 8, 24, 52, 57–9, 61–3, 92–3, 110, 115, 128, 168, 174–5, 229, 232, 250–2
international power 126, 128, **175**, 200, 245
internationalization 4–5, 8–9, 16, 26, 29, 35–47, 50, 61, 77, 81, 91–6, 106, 110–5, 163–6, 168, 177, 181, 186–7, 191, 202, 206–8, 237–8, 248, 253, 256–7
internationalizers *see* coalitions
inward-looking models 7, 26–7, 80, 126, 130, 134–6, 149, 182, 210, 212, 238, 241–3, 245, 248
inward-looking states 5, 6, 21, 207
inward-looking forces 17, 107, 168, 207, 211, 242, *see also* internationalizing
Iran 15, 24–6, 47, 50–1, 58, 73–5, 104, 108–10, 112, **121**, 142, 146, 154–5, 157–8, 190, 208, 211, 218, 221–3, 225, 238, 242, 250, 253–5, 255–7, 264–5, 267
Iraq 23, 48–9, 74, 77, 82, 84, 110, **121**, 134, 140, 142, 146, 150, 154, 192, 212, 221–2, 228–9, 243, 250, 256, **264, 267**
Islamist 14–16, 22, 47–8, 51, 57–8, 77, 103–4, 155–9, 161, 195, 206, 208, 211–2, 244
Islamization 64
Israel 6, 13–16, 25, 48, 51–3, 56, 62, 67, 69, 71–3, 77–8, 83, 98, 103–8, 109–10, 112–3, **121**, 133, 135, 137, 142, 145–6, 152 –3, 156–61, 192, 194, 196, 207, 210, 212, 217, 221–3, 225, 227–8, 232–3, 235–6, 238, 241, **243–5, 263–5, 267**

Japan 10–11, 24–6, 28, 111, 119, 123–4, 130, 132, 134, 137, 140, 143, 185–90, 218–20, 224–5, 231, 233–7, 239, 255
Jordan 14, 57, 69, 71–3, 78, 82–3, 107, 110, 112, **121**, 133–4, 142, 146, 152–8, 160, 193, 195, 208–9, **263, 265, 267**

Kim Il Sung 51, 75, 80, 109
Kuomintang (KMT) 129, 131, 132, 135, 140, 142, 219, 227, 232, 241,
Kuwait 82, 84, 109–10, **121**, 138, 146, 154, 207, 229

Latin America 6, 45, 149, 207, 210, 239,
Latin American Free Trade Association (LAFTA) 76
Lebanon 75, 85, 109–10, **121**, 126, 130, 133, 140, 153, 194, 207,
Liberalization 16, 20, 38–40, 45–6, 48, 50, 57, 60–1, 63, 70, 72, 78, 84, 95, 101, 104, 162, 166, 177, 186–7, 194–5, 199, 210
Libya 25, 51, 76, 120, **121**, 140, 154, 217, 219, 221, 229, 239, 255, 257,
linkages 3, 117, 184, 197
logrolling 8, 35, **37**, 38–9, 43, 47–9, 54, **55**, 58, 94, 96–8, 112–3

Madrid Conference 72
MERCOSUR 7, 69, 86, 112–3, 164, 207, 210
Mexico 60–1, 71
Middle East 6–7, 10–13, 43, 58, 69, 72, 79, 83, 87, 106–9, 113, 119–20, 122–4, 130, 133, 135, 137, 139, 141–4, 148–9, 152, 154, 160, 191, 206, 210, 221, 227, 230, 238–9, 245, 248
MILEX 40–2, 52–3, 61, 106–9, 114, 141–3, 146–7, **263–6, 268**
militarism 48, 108, 132
militarization 7, 9, 45, 49, 72, 75, 86, 109, 113–4, 148, 207, 239, 244
military budgets 5, 29, 40, 44–5, 60–1, 72, 142, 145–7, 189
military-industrial-complex 12, 44
models of political survival 5, 26, 219, 239, 241, 244
Mubarak, Hosni 14, 16, 103–5, 109, 112, 142, 154, 194, 232, **265–6**
multilateral 13, 17, 19, 62, 71–3, 75, 78, 83, 161, 163, 169, 185, 188, 190–1, 207–11, 250–1, 255, 257
Myanmar 84, **121**, 147, 164, 184, 190
mythmaking 49–50, 56, 79

290 Index

Nasser 26, 51, 54, 57, 72–3, 75–6, 82, 103–4, 107–9, 123, 129–33, 135, 140, 146, 192, 194–6, 207, 221, 232, 236, 238, 243–5
Nasserism 100, 110, 112, 128, 133, 136–7, 146
nationalism: nationalist *see* coalitions
NATO, *see* North Atlantic Treaty Organization
neoliberalism 176
neomercantilistic 62
neorealist 7, 10, 16, 18–19, 22–4, 115, 123, 174–5, 190, 197, 199, 201, 220–7
Netanyahu, Benjamin 15, 48, 52, 58, 70, 106, 108, 110, 158–9, **265, 267**
NGO 185, 189, 209, 216, 233, 250, 252
Nonproliferation Treaty (NPT) 22, 24–6, 71, 111, 164–5, 216, 220–1, 226–36, 238–9, 244, 247–8, 250, 256–7
North Atlantic Treaty Organization (NATO) 46, 111, 188, 220, 225, 248
North Korea 7, 10, 12, 13, 22–3, 25–6, 41, 44, 49–51, 75–6, 79–81, 84–5, 102, 108, 111, 123, 132, 135, 141–2, 148, 150, 164–5, 168–9, 187, 190, 210, 218–20, 222–4, 226–32, 235–6, 238–40, 248–57
nuclear proliferation 27, 216, 251, 257
nuclearization 7, 10, 22–3, 25, 109, 123, 168, 217, 220–25, 227, 230–34, 236, 238, 240, 245, 247–9, 254, 257

OSLO (process) 13–15, 69, 73, 105, 110, 112–3, 124, 158–9, 207–8, 212,

Pakistan 23, 47–8, 51, 56, 72, 76, 78, 103, 108, 112–3, 207, 222, 228–9, 234, 236, **264–7**
Palestinian Authority 72, 157, 212
Palestinian Liberation Organization (PLO) 58, 69, 72–3, 78, 83, 108, 110, 112, 152, 154
Pan-Arab 19, 109, 133, 137, 144–6, 148, 192–3, 195, 197–8
Park, Chung-Hee 40, 61, 63, 80, 101, 104, 106, 111, 129–30, 131, 142, 219, 227, 240, 243, **263, 267**
Pax Asiatica 10–11, 119, 123–4, 149
Perón, Juan 26, 52, 57, 75, 103, 198, 110, **264, 266**
personalism 49, 52, **55,** 75
populism 5, 16, 44–6, 48, 97, 110, 160
privatization 38, 71, 101, 129, 167, 195, 206, 208, 210–1, 253

rationalism 174
regional: dynamics 80, 83; orders 1–3, 6–7, 9, 17, 27, 40, 53, 62–3, 67, **68,** 70–1, 73, 83–4, 86, 91, 95–6, 98, 113, 160, 165, 181, 199, 234; outcomes 2, 7, 28, 125, 217; relations 2, 7, 28, 33, 110, 125, 163, 206, 210
regionalism 1–3, 10, 18–20, 27–9, 70, 98, 135, 149, 182, 184–6, 188, 197–9
rentier 11, 130, 134, 136–8, 140–1, 148, 150, 255
Rhee, Syngman 63, 80, 106, 109, 129, 141, 240
Russia 57, 61, 83, 189, 224, 228–9, 254–5, 257

Sadat, Anwar 72, 103–5, 107–10, 112, 135, 137, 139, 144–6, 154, 194, 196, 208, 227–8, 232, 243–5, **263–4, 266**
Saudi Arabia 47, 56, 72, 82, 84, 120, **121,** 138, 154, 191–2, 225
Somalia 58, 76
South Asia 7, 24, 43, 48, 51, 74, 78, 131, 226, 232
South Korea 7–8, 10, 17, 23, 26, 39–41, 43–44, 57, 61, 75, 80–1, 87, 102, 105–7, 111, **121,** 129–31, 133–5, 141, 143, 165, 206–7, 218–9, 221, 224, 226, 235–8, 240–1, 249
Southern Cone 7, 9, 43, 52, 67, 69–71, 83, 111, 113, 164, 207, 210, 234
statism 8, 45, 48, 82–3, 126, 137, 206, 243
strategic interaction 86
strategy *see* Grand Strategy
sub-regional 28, 190, 211
Sudan 15, 47, 51, 57, 73–5, 77, 79, **121,** 130, 140, 145, 154–5, 157–8, 208
Sukarno 26, 102–4, 106–9, 111, 149–50, 181, 202, **264**
Syria 15–16, 25, 41, 44, 48, 69, 72–4, 76, 81, 85, 103, 108–110, **121,** 133, 137, 140, 142–6, 153–4, 191, 194–5, 208, 218, 229, **264, 268**

Taiwan 10, 17, 23, 25–6, 39, 41, 43, 57, 67, 70, 75, 102–4, 106, 111, 119, **121,** 129, 132, 134–5, 142, 218–9, 225, 227, 231–6, 241, 247–9, **263, 268**
technology 3, 5, 36, 38, 40–3, 60, 68,72, 92, 94, 96, 134, 185, 187–8, 215–6, 227–30, 236–8, 240
territoriality 9, 74, 114, 145, 207
Trade openness 8–9, 40, 61, 84, 102, 114, 126, 207, 244, **263–5, 269–70**
trading states 124, 163, 240
Tunisia 14, 107, **121,** 126, 130, 137, 142, 145, 154, 156, 158, 208–9, **263, 268**
Turkey 17, 44, 46, 121, 129–30, 137–40, 147, 209, 225, 239, 248

United Nations (UN) 59, 63, 109, 135, 146, 168, 190–1, 206, 222–3, 227–9, 233, 254

Vietnam 124, 134, 140, 207

war zones 6, 74–5, 85
West Bank 159
WMD 99, 109, 114, 207, 211, 227, 232, 236, 243, 254
World Bank 59, 63, 113, **263–5**

Yemen 57, 75, 85, 109, **121,** 129, 131, 145, 154, 156, 191, 207, 244
Yew, Lee Kuan 101, 183, **263**

zones of stable peace 67–8, 98, 164, 207